G000255238

SURREY
COUNTY COUNCIL
WITHDRAWN FROM STOCK
AND OFFERED FOR SALE
WITH ALL FAULTS BY
SURREY COUNTY LIBRARY

SOLD

THE PRESERVING BOOK

THE PRESERVING BOOK

**Devised
and
edited by
Caroline
Mackinlay
and Mike
Ricketts**

SURREY
COUNTY LIBRARY

641.4

Editor	Caroline Mackinlay
Production Editor	Joan Durrant
Home Economist	Hilary Foster
Art Director	Mike Ricketts
Designer	Martin Atcherley
Design Assistant	Eric T. Budge
Photographer	Rod Shone

Devised, designed and edited at The Nassington Press,
73 Newman Street, London W.1.

Line illustrations by Vana Haggerty
Diagrams by Andrew Farmer and friends
Headline setting by Quick Brown Fox
Monochrome photographs printed by Grade One
Filmset by Keyspools Ltd, Golborne, Lancs.
Printed in Great Britain by Cox and Wyman Ltd,
London, Reading and Fakenham

Copyright © 1978 The Nassington Press Ltd.

All rights reserved. No part of this publication may be
reproduced, stored in a retrieval system, or transmitted in
any form or by any means – electronic, magnetic,
mechanical, photographic or otherwise – without
permission in writing from the copyright owner.

First published in Great Britain by
Macmillan London Limited
London and Basingstoke
in association with Pan Books Ltd
Associated companies in Delhi, Dublin,
Hong Kong, Johannesburg, Lagos, Melbourne,
New York, Singapore and Tokyo

British Library Cataloguing in Publication Data
Mackinlay, Caroline
Ricketts, Michael
    The Preserving Book
    1 Food – Preservation – Amateurs' Manuals
    I Title
641.4   TX601
ISBN 0 333 24620 9

We should like to thank Dr Susan Passmore and
her colleagues at Long Ashton Research Station
for the valuable advice and help we have had from
them throughout the production of every section
of this book.

With thanks to Ruth for reasons she will understand

Conditions of Sale
This book shall not, by way of trade or otherwise, be lent, re-sold, hired out or
otherwise circulated without the publisher's prior consent in any form of
binding or cover other than that in which it is published and without a similar
condition including this condition being imposed on the subsequent
purchaser. The book is published at a net price and is supplied subject to the
Publishers Association Standard Conditions of Sale registered under the
Restrictive Trade Practices Act, 1956.

Contents

Contributors

Victoria Proctor

'My appreciation of good food and cooking,' said Victoria Proctor, 'must have been inherited and absorbed from my father's mother who was French. On her annual visits a large hamper accompanied her filled with cheeses, butter, half a lamb in the piece, ducklings, globe artichokes, figs, oil, wine and so on. "It grew in the sun" was the explanation to convince us that many of the foods on her side of the Channel were superior, although we lived in the country and had an excellent kitchen garden.

'I longed to cook but, as children, we were never allowed in the kitchen. Later I married into the RAF and travelled widely. Then the war put a stop to all but meagre rations. Posted to Canada we were frequently on the move so I still had no opportunity to cook seriously. I read many cookery books, took a course in dietetics and bribed or coaxed my way into every type of kitchen, including a convent and a logging camp, but watching was not enough and theory only a shadow.

'After the war I went to the Cordon Bleu school in London and took a diploma course; at last I had my hands actually cooking. At the end of the year I was offered a post to teach there and at Winkfield Place. I discovered I loved teaching, and for me it was a wonderful combination. Often when people come for an interview, I sense in them the same need I had myself, to be taught about every food, and from that knowledge to produce simple or elaborate, but always good-looking dishes.'

Victoria Proctor, now the senior teacher at the Cordon Bleu school in London, has written the opening chapter on **Jams, Jellies and Marmalades**.

Olive Odell

'Cookery has been my hobby and relaxation since my days as a medical student,' said Olive Odell. 'After I married in 1950 and moved to the country to become a farmer's wife, I joined the Women's Institute and trained in my spare time as a cookery and preservation judge and demonstrator.' Mrs Odell is now Vice-Chairman of the National Federation of W.Is and Chairman of the Home Economics committee. She has written and edited several books and leaflets for the Women's Institutes, writes articles for various magazines and has contributed to the Reader's Digest book, *Food from your garden.*

The chapter on **Candied, Glacé and Crystallised Fruits**, is her contribution to this book.

Mary Norwak

Mary Norwak took up food writing when small children had to be coped with, as food fitted in so well with family life.

She has been cookery editor of *Farmers' Weekly* for 15 years and is currently editor of *Co-Op Freezer World* and also of *Freezer Family* to which she has contributed since its early days. She specialises in freezing and in farmhouse food – she lives with her family in a farmhouse in Norfolk – has 40 cookery books in print, and is still writing them. She has also, she added, written the only book covering the whole range of kitchen antiques.

Mary Norwak has written the chapters on **Home Freezing** and **Pickles, Chutneys and Sauces**.

Katie Stewart

'My parents were Scottish and I spent my childhood in Aberdeen,' said Katie Stewart. 'After a training in hotel management and catering I went to Paris to learn French and worked as a children's nanny to a wealthy and very kind family with whom I travelled all over France. When my French was passable I did a Cordon Bleu diploma in Paris and then came back to England to a job as home economist with a food company.'

She then decided to go to America 'because I knew that the USA were much ahead of us in that kind of work', and got herself a job with the Nestlé company in White Plains. 'This was a move that certainly laid the foundation for whatever success I may have achieved because it was in the States that I learned how to set material down on paper, how to develop new recipes and I worked closely with an advertising agency in New York as well as with many American magazines.'

On returning home Katie Stewart joined Fleetway Publications to work on a new magazine called *Woman's Mirror* and when it folded seven years later she turned freelance. She began to write for *The Times* 'the year they took the advertisements off the front page and started a woman's page'. She also became cookery editor of *Woman's Journal* and has worked for them both for 12 years. She has done four series of cookery programmes for Grampian television, numerous broadcasts for the BBC and has written many books including the well-known *Times Cookery Book*. Her latest is *The Young Cook's Calendar* (Piccolo, paperback) on which her son, then 12 years old, acted as adviser and chief taster.

Katie Stewart contributes the chapter on **Cooking for the Freezer**.

Susan Passmore

Dr Susan Passmore is a Senior Scientific Officer and Research Associate of Bristol University and all types of home food preservation are her special interest. The subject of her Ph.D. was cider spoilage microorganisms, on which she worked at the Agricultural Research Station at Long Ashton. She is a West Country lass, born in Exeter in 1948, and educated there and at Bristol University where she took her degrees.

She is now the Senior Microbiologist in the Home Food Storage and Preservation Section of Long Ashton Research Station and looks after publications and the scientific side of their liaison with home economists, and she advises on food safety and hygiene.

In spite of her weighty titles and degrees, Sue Passmore does not take life too seriously. She enjoys the country and the fresh air. 'My outside interests,' she said 'are participating in sport, especially hockey and tennis, and watching most others. My hobbies include handicrafts, particularly crochet, and home and car maintenance.'

Although the chapter on **Bottling** is a personal contribution she advised us throughout in her official capacity on metrication, safety and scientific accuracy.

Beryl Gould-Marks

'I have visited over 60 countries and followed my nose into many strange bazaars and bistros in order to find out about people and their eating habits,' says Beryl Gould-Marks. She tries out the more conventional dishes as well wherever she goes – and that spans the world from Java and Singapore to Martinique and Venezuela. She is the author of many books including *Eating the Russian Way, The Adventurous Cook, The Home Book of Italian Cooking, Eating in the Open.*

The daughter of a gastronome she has always loved food as an art rather than a métier and studied at the Cordon Bleu in Paris (she is bi-lingual in English and French).

Drying, Salting and Smoking are her favourite hobbies, and the sections she has written here reflect her enthusiasm. She has also written the chapter on **Fruit Cheeses, Butters and Curds** – because she loves making them.

Ben Turner

'I started making wine in 1945 just after the war,' said Ben Turner, 'and beer in 1949. I made all the mistakes possible as at that time very little information was available to the amateur.'

His first book, published in 1959, explained in simple terms the principles of fermentation, in the belief that this would make for a better understanding of the recipes.

He became the founder Secretary of both the National Association of Amateur Winemakers in 1961 and of the Amateur Winemakers' National Guild of Judges in 1963.

He has now written 30 books and countless articles on every aspect of the subject and enjoys an international reputation. In 1974, he turned his hobby into his career and is now a full time writer, lecturer and broadcaster. Ben still makes around 100 gallons of wine and 25 gallons of beer each year, but says that he has never been 'drunk'. He only sees pink elephants when the media make fun of homemade wine or beer.

He denies being an expert because he is always learning something new. He does, however, admit to being an oenophile and drinks wine every day. Ben Turner is married, has five grown up children, weaned on the bottle, and lives in Ruislip.

He wrote the chapters on **Wine and Beermaking** and **Cider and Perry** for this book.   7

Introduction

This book is a bumper guide to the simplest, safest and best ways of preserving food, storing it and using it. Here in one volume you have all the necessary information on the different methods of preservation. These cover bottling, freezing, pickling, drying, smoking, salting; making jams and jellies and other luxuries like candied fruits and fruit syrups. There is also a section on making wines and beer, with esoteric extras such as morello cherry 'brandy' and bilberry 'port'.

The photographs in colour and black and white have been specially taken and the illustrations drawn to give the reader as much help as possible.

The book gives full details of equipment (and where you can get it), preparation, safety measures and storage plus a wealth of enticing recipes in every section. The 'how to do it' techniques are carefully and clearly explained. Once absorbed they should help you to make your family more self-sufficient, to rely less on the shops and so enable you to stretch a tight budget further.

We have designed the book for beginners as well as for the experienced. Beginners will like it, we hope, because it is easy to follow and preserving is fun to do; while the 'old hands' will be interested in new techniques and recipes. The various tables are invaluable to all.

The people most involved in preserving food in the past were those with gardens or allotments but now that nearly everyone has a car, and country markets and 'pick-it-yourself' places are easily accessible, most people can get fruit and vegetables in bulk at reasonable prices, so everyone can have a go. This does not, of course, apply to the unusual fruits such as medlars, quinces, mulberries and boysenberries, but we have included these for the benefit of the lucky people who can get hold of them, as recipes are not easy to come by.

Just two important points to remember about preserving: once you have made your preserves, labelled and stored them, don't keep them too long. Nothing really improves with overlong storage. Plan to use your preserves steadily throughout the year – and this applies also to food in the freezer – so that by the time the next season arrives, your stores are used up and you are ready to start on another batch.

Secondly, for the benefit of all concerned, we have included metric as well as imperial measures. You can opt for pounds, ounces and pints, or alternatively, kilos, grams and litres – whichever you prefer. But it is essential that you don't mix them (you will see why in the note 'Metrication' on this page). Just decide which set of measures you will use and stick to it for each recipe.

The contributors to this book are all experts in their own subjects and each individual is an enthusiast, as you can tell from their writing. We hope that some of their enthusiasm will rub off on you and that you too will find the art of preserving absorbing and even amusing, and that you will get real satisfaction from contemplating the rows of well-stocked jars and bottles on your shelves.

Commonsense metrication

All quantities in the recipes in this book are given in both metric and imperial measures. Our form of metrication is recommended by the **Long Ashton Research Station**, who have approved all the metric versions of our recipes.

The metric measures are not usually conversions from the imperial ones. An exception is where a standard-sized piece of equipment is used, eg the demijohn or gallon jar used in winemaking – in this case $4\frac{1}{2}$ litres is taken as an approximate equivalent of a gallon.

In other cases, we have tried always to take a sensible metric amount rather than an approximate equivalent. For instance, where an imperial recipe asks for one pound of sugar, the metric version asks for 500 grams (or half a kilogram), which is the size of the pack in which sugar is now sold, and in which other foods of the same kind will eventually be sold. The other metric ingredients in the recipe have then, of course, to be put into the same proportions to 500 grams as are the imperial ones to one pound. This means that, because 500 grams is slightly more than one pound, the finished metric product will be slightly bigger than the imperial one.

In other recipes, eg those for jelly preserves, a liquid measure is necessary for the ruling ingredient. Here, where the imperial measure is one pint, the metric version becomes 500 millilitres, which is half a litre. And here, as half a litre is slightly less than one pint, the other metric ingredients also weigh or measure slightly less than the imperial ones. In fact, the imperial proportions of 1lb sugar to 1 pint juice metrically become 400g sugar to 500ml juice. And here the finished metric yield is slightly smaller than the imperial one.

This, we hope, explains why the metric figures may at first sight appear to be inconsistent – 1lb sometimes being put beside 500g, sometimes beside 400g, and so on.

What has to be realised is that we are not giving imperial quantities and metric equivalents, we are giving separate recipes, each designed to suit its own system.

From this you will see that it is very important to follow **either** the imperial **or** the metric weights and measures in any one recipe.

Catrine Mackinlay

9

Jams, jellies and marmalades

Making jams and jellies is almost entirely a pleasure, with few of the tiresome fiddles which go along with most household chores. It's a job that most housewives look forward to. The heady smell of fruit cooking, the frothy pink as raspberries and sugar melt together, the beautiful colour and texture and elegant form of the fruits; the pink and white of strawberries, the shiny purple-black corrugations of blackberries, the matt glow of apricots make the mere thought of jam and jelly-making something desirable. It even arouses the emotions – a feeling of elation when the jam sets just as expected, and dire frustration when the jelly doesn't. Finally the rows of jars of translucent colour neatly labelled and ready for eating are a source of real delight, and even righteous pride for the family cook. But these rich and beautiful raw materials call for delicate and precise handling when it comes to transforming them into the family's favourite luxury. Jam making is not difficult but the more time, attention and loving care you can spare for it the better the results will be, as Victoria Proctor explains so clearly and enthusiastically in the following pages.

Jams, jellies and marmalades

Jam making is a most rewarding and important branch of cookery. It is not only more economical to make jam than to buy it, it is also more satisfying to use your own creative ability. Preserving is a hobby you can enjoy at any time of the year and it will please that squirrel instinct, latent in most of us, to store away the results of your own efforts.

A shelf of jars neatly labelled and well arranged is a lovely sight, with the muted tapestry colours of the jams, the crystal brightness of jellies and the soft amber of marmalades. If you are an experienced jam maker this is easy to achieve, but it is not difficult even for a complete novice. Once you understand the principles of jam making and have a few small successful batches to your credit, you will feel confident to try your hand at many more. It is advisable to begin by making an easy jam such as plum or black currant.

There are several categories of jam making using fruit, or some kinds of vegetable, and sugar.

Jam itself is made from cooked fruit and sugar, boiled together until the cooled result will set to a soft spreading consistency.

Jellies are made from the strained juice of cooked fruit and sugar.

Breakfast marmalades are made by cooking citrus fruits until the peel is very soft and then adding sugar.

Extra flavourings may be added to jams and marmalades. As a luxury, a small glass of liqueur or fruit brandy can be stirred into jam just before putting it into jars. It is best to choose a fruit flavoured liqueur and, if you are experimenting, only add it to the last jar or two just in case you do not like it.

There are also confections known as conserves and preserves, and stiff sweetened purées of fruit and sugar.

Here arises a confusion of meaning between the words conserve and preserve. In the United States, some European countries and other parts of the world it is taken that a preserve is made from whole small fruits or cut up large fruit preserved in a heavy syrup, and it may be served in a small dish and eaten with a spoon. Conserves, becoming increasingly popular, are interesting combinations made from two or more fruits, one usually a citrus fruit, with additions of nuts, candied peels, preserved ginger or raisins, according to the recipe. They can be used as jam. We do not make preserves and conserves as much as they do abroad – hence the confusion of phraseology: they are worth making.

Basic principles of jam, jelly and marmalade making

You must understand certain principles before you can become a good jam maker. Lack of knowledge leads to hit-or-miss methods – perhaps good jam if you are lucky, otherwise a disaster and you cannot think where it has gone wrong. To follow a recipe slavishly, carefully watching the clock, will not always give good results. Your own judgement also counts. Good jam will have the fresh flavour of the fruit used and be a good colour; it will set so it is no longer runny, and it will keep well.

For jam, fruit needs pectin, a gum-like substance found in the fruit itself, and acid to draw the pectin into solution to help in setting. Sugar is also needed to set jam, to sweeten and improve the flavour and to ensure good keeping properties.

Problems can occur because different fruits vary in the amount of pectin and acid they contain. A general list can help here (see page 14), and a good recipe will allow for a lack of pectin or acid, and supply it from other sources.

Given a correct proportion of pectin and acid, the next consideration is whether a fruit needs a short or long cooking time to soften it and draw the juices – this must happen before the sugar is added. Some fruits, like raspberries, are soft and juicy, and only need short cooking, with little, if any, water to soften them further and extract the juice. Other fruits, such as plums, black currants and gooseberries, must have water added to soften them during the slow cooking needed to make them tender. The preliminary boiling is also necessary to extract the pectin from the fruit.

Sugar is only added after you are sure the fruit, and skins, have been thoroughly softened because it has a toughening effect if added too early. This is particularly evident with black currants and in marmalades.

Once the sugar has been added and has dissolved, then rapid boiling takes place until the setting point is reached.

Equipment for jam making

As with every craft, there is equipment designed to make it easier. If you want to make jam often, it is wise to invest in a good **preserving pan**. Copper or brass ones are beautiful to look at, and some jams, especially green gooseberry and greengage, made in a copper pan, keep their colour well during cooking. However, copper pans are very expensive, need frequent cleaning and destroy vitamin C. The majority of preserving pans sold today are made of aluminium or stainless steel, and of these aluminium is much the cheaper. A heavy-based pan will prevent sticking and burning. Choose one that is shallow in relation to its size, for good evaporation. An average size is 25cm (10in) across the base and 11cm (4$\frac{1}{2}$in) deep.

Small quantities of jam can be made successfully in a **heavy saucepan** large enough to enable fast boiling without the jam boiling over.

A **wooden spoon** is needed for stirring – this should be larger than usual, and comfortable to hold and handle. A **metal spoon** is better for skimming where this is necessary, or a special **skimming spoon** with perforations is ideal.

A **nylon sieve** should be used if sieved jams are made; metal sieves can give some jams an unpleasant flavour.

A **lemon squeezer**, a **good grater**, a piece of **butter muslin** for whole spices, and a sharp, **stainless steel knife** or two are also needed.

Scales are essential if you have to ascertain the

Making jam

1 Prepare the fruit. **2** Put fruit in preserving pan, adding water if required and simmer gently to

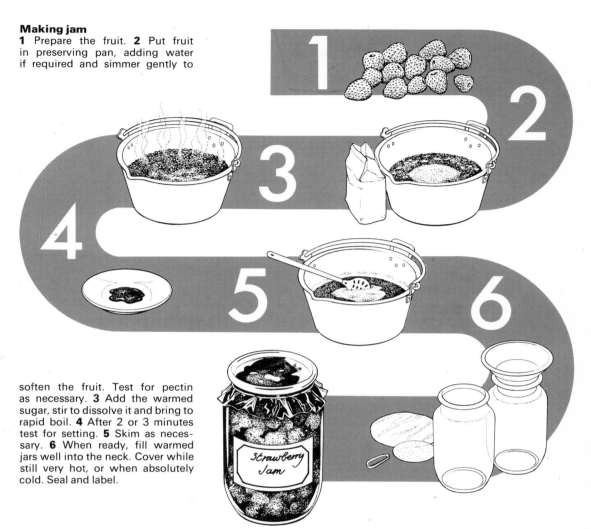

soften the fruit. Test for pectin as necessary. **3** Add the warmed sugar, stir to dissolve it and bring to rapid boil. **4** After 2 or 3 minutes test for setting. **5** Skim as necessary. **6** When ready, fill warmed jars well into the neck. Cover while still very hot, or when absolutely cold. Seal and label.

weight of the fruit, and you should have a **measuring jug** for the water – it is not wise to guess.

A **sugar thermometer** can be useful when testing for setting but is not essential. You will also need a **small plate** or **saucer**.

A **small jug** or **ladle** can be used for filling the jars, but a **jam funnel** is not an expensive item and it makes filling faster and cleaner.

If you can, collect and use standard 450g (1lb) and 225g ($\frac{1}{2}$lb) glass **jam jars** for filling. An odd assortment of coffee jars, pickle jars and so on lacks uniformity and looks untidy. The jars should be washed thoroughly, dried and well warmed in the oven before you begin jam-making. Warm jars do not crack when filled with hot jam. Make sure all previous labels have been removed, some stick obstinately and leave a deposit very difficult to wash off, but a little methylated spirit removes it easily.

Modern jam jars which have **twist-on lids** with integral gaskets are good, especially if you can procure new lids for them. Otherwise, existing lids can be used a second time, providing they are undamaged and unpierced, and are scalded to scrupulous cleanliness. No discs are needed.

Packets of **labels** are convenient as they also contain **covers** and **waxed discs** for the top of the jam. Rubber bands are also included, but as during long storage these can perish and cause the Cellophane covers to loosen, it is better to tie the covers firmly with **string** if storing them longer than a month or two.

Method for making jam

Choosing fruit

If you are able to grow your own fruit it is easy to pick it at the peak of condition for converting into jam.

Gather it on a dry day and choose it just slightly under-ripe; over-ripe fruit does not contain so

13

Jams

much pectin. A few perfectly ripe fruits may be included for colour but they must be firm and undamaged. Fruit that has over-ripened may need too long boiling to set into jam, and this spoils the colour and flavour. Damaged fruit can impair the keeping quality of the jam. Soft fruit, such as raspberries and loganberries, must be really firm, and if wild blackberries or raspberries are used, search carefully for the little white maggots that cannot always be easily seen. Spread the fruit on a plate for an hour and they will crawl out!

When buying fruit for jam, ask the co-operation of the greengrocer; if you are a good customer he will be ready to help. Sometimes local people with a garden sell the surplus through a shop. Buying fruit wholesale from local markets and sharing it with friends can be economical. And watch local advertisements for opportunities to pick fruit yourself. Do this in time so that you don't miss the first picking which will be the slightly under-ripe fruit that you want.

Preparing fruit
The fruit should be picked over to remove any stalks and leaves. Gooseberries need topping and tailing. Currants are easily stripped from their stalks by running a fork down the stem. Strawberries and raspberries are hulled. Larger fruits, such as plums and apricots, are cut in half with a stainless knife and twisted so the stone can be easily taken out. Kernels can give added flavour – a large hammer will crack the stones, which are surprisingly hard. Blanch the kernels to remove the skins and then chop or halve them, but only use a few as they can be bitter. Apples and quinces are peeled thinly, quartered and cored. As you work, remove any blemishes, and put the fruit into the measured water in the preserving pan with a little lemon juice to prevent browning.

Adding pectin or acid
The next thing is to decide whether the fruit you are using has a good setting quality or whether pectin or acid is needed during the initial cooking. Your recipe will usually tell you this, and suggest in what form to make the additions.

Some fruits, notably strawberries, black cherries and blackberries, are lacking in pectin. This is why recipes are often given which mix these fruits with others of a richer pectin content, for example blackberry and apple jam, strawberry and gooseberry jam. Red currant, gooseberry or apple juice can be used where pectin is deficient. Apple juice is the easiest to use, as apples are readily available. Cut up washed cooking apples or windfalls, removing any blemishes, keeping on the cores and skins, put into a preserving pan and add 1 litre (1¾ pints) water to each 1kg (2lb) apples – this should barely cover the apples. Simmer gently for 1 hour and strain. If to be kept, it must be sterilised, by the method used for bottling fruit juices (see bottling chapter). Red currant and gooseberry juice can be used in the same way.

Commercial pectin (one brand is called Certo) can be bought from the chemists – this is mostly made from apples and is useful for people who have no garden, or don't want to spend time making their own pectin.

The addition of pectin means less loss of yield, through long boiling, and a better colour and flavour with the 'difficult' jams such as marrow and ginger. But adding too much pectin can spoil colour and flavour.

Fruits high in pectin
Sour cooking Apples or sharp green dessert Apples. Crab Apples. Barberries. Cranberries. Black, red or white Currants. Damsons. Under-ripe Gooseberries. Grapefruit. Japonica fruits. Lemons. Limes. Loganberries. Oranges. Firm Plums. Quince. Rowan berries.

Fruits with medium pectin content
Barely ripe Apricots. Bilberries. Under-ripe Blackberries. Morello or May Duke Cherries. Greengages. Mulberries. Ripe Plums. Under-ripe Raspberries. Sloes.

Fruits low in pectin
Sweet Cherries. Elderberries. Medlars. Melons. Peaches. Pears. Pineapples. Rhubarb. Strawberries. Vegetable Marrow.

Fruits with good acid content
Sour cooking Apples or sharp green dessert Apples. Crab Apples. Barberries. Bilberries. Morello or May Duke Cherries. Cranberries. Black, red or white Currants. Damsons. Gooseberries. Grapefruit. Greengages. Japonica fruits. Lemons. Limes. Loganberries. Mulberries. Oranges. Pineapples. Firm Plums. Under-ripe Raspberries. Rowan berries. Sloes.

Fruits low in acid
Sweet Apples. Ripe Apricots. Late ripe Blackberries. Sweet Cherries. Elderberries. Medlars. Melons. Peaches. Pears. Quinces. Ripe Raspberries. Rhubarb. Ripe Strawberries. Vegetable Marrow.

If a fruit is lacking in acid it can be added in several forms, such as lemon juice or juice from gooseberries or red currants, tartaric acid (commercially made from under-ripe grapes) or citric acid. Both the latter can be bought in small quantities from a chemist – one or other may be mixed with a little cold water – 5ml (1 teaspoon) acid to 15ml (1 tablespoon) water – if there is no water in the recipe; or they can be put into the pan with the water.

Preliminary cooking
Before putting the fruit into the preserving pan rinse it quickly in a colander under a cold tap. If hard fruits are to be cut, rinse them first. Drain off excess water. Add extra pectin and acid if needed. A small nut of butter or 5ml (1 teaspoon) of glycerine rubbed on the bottom of the pan helps to prevent skins sticking, and also prevents scum formation.

If water is to be added, measure it in. Not all fruits need water – soft, juicy fruit yields its own juice as it is heated. Sometimes a spoonful of fruit is crushed to provide juice to start cooking the rest of the fruit. After a wet summer, the fruit can be extra plump and juicy so cut down the water a little. Conversely, after a dry season the fruit, especially berries, can be smaller and firmer so a little more water may be needed.

The fruit is now gently cooked to soften it; skins of black currants and gooseberries especially can be tough, and it cannot be too strongly stated that sugar must not be added until the fruit is really broken down or the skins will be hard; also the flavour and colour of the jam will not be so fresh if the sugar is put in too early. At this stage, too, the liquid is slowly reduced and this is where a fairly shallow wide pan helps the evaporation.

Stir the simmering fruit from time to time as skins can sometimes stick to the bottom of the pan and may burn. Soft pulpy fruits may only need about 15–20 minutes' simmering to soften them to pulp. Hard and tough skinned fruits can take over twice as long.

Testing for pectin

Should you wish to test for pectin, it can be done now after the boiling and softening process, before the sugar is added. Put 5ml (1 teaspoon) of the juice into a cup or small glass, cool and mix in 15ml (1 tablespoon) of methylated spirit; leave it for a minute or two and the juice should clot into one soft lump. If it breaks into several blobs then continue simmering until you get a more concentrated juice by evaporation, and repeat the test. If there is still not enough pectin, the jam will need added pectin in the form of Certo or apple juice or undiluted red currant juice. 100g (3oz) Certo, or 150ml ($\frac{1}{4}$ pint) of juice, to each 500g (1lb) of fruit used, should give a set.

The more pectin present the more sugar can be used, which explains why recipes for black currant jam, rich in pectin, seem to have a large proportion of sugar to fruit and a large yield as a result.

As you become experienced in making jams and jellies you increase your knowledge of the fruits which will set easily and testing for pectin will not be necessary, but it is interesting to do and makes you feel very efficient!

Warming the sugar

While the preliminary simmering is going on the sugar can be warmed. Cane or beet sugar can be used in the form of loaf or cube sugar, or granulated sugar. Preserving sugar can be bought and gives a clear finish (important if you are entering your jam at the local flower show!). Demerara sugar may be used for the dark, stronger flavoured jams, where its flavour will not be too intrusive. For jam-making, honey may replace a quarter of the amount of sugar, but this is not advised when making jellies. It saves time to heat the sugar before adding it, so that it dissolves more quickly and does not cool down the cooked fruit. It can be warmed through in the oven in a mixing bowl or on an enamel tray. Do not overheat and so bake sugar crystals into a crust or lump. Add the amount given in the recipe; too little sugar will mean a poor set and the jam may not keep well, too much will result in an over-sweetened jam and it will crystallise after keeping a short time.

Warming the jars

At the same time, the jars should be well washed and then rinsed and drained. They can be dried well by hand and put into a slow oven to warm, otherwise they can be drained well and then put into the oven where they will dry as they warm. There must be no trace of moisture inside when they are filled, so warm them thoroughly.

Adding the sugar

After the preliminary cooking, the warmed sugar is added. Stir to dissolve it; spoon out a little juice and examine it to make sure there are no crystals. Then increase the heat so that the jam reaches a rolling boil and stir just enough to avoid the jam sticking. At this point it may be necessary to skim, using a metal spoon, but frequent spooning is wasteful. If the fruit was quickly rinsed in a colander just before cooking, and if a small piece of butter was added during the first boiling, little skimming should be needed.

Testing for setting

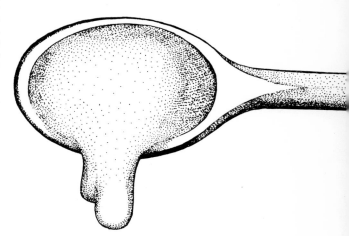

After two or three minutes of rapid boiling, begin testing the jam for setting point. Take up a little of the jam on the wooden spoon, hold it above the jam for a second or two. If the jam runs back freely, repeat the test every two or three minutes until it looks like a heavy syrup. As this syrup gets thicker the jam is nearing setting point. At this stage it is safer to lower the heat slightly under the pan to avoid over-boiling. When a blob of jelly forms and then breaks away slowly, setting point has been reached.

Jams

If testing with the wooden spoon seems difficult to master at first, have ready a cold plate or saucer and try testing, at the same time-intervals, by putting a small spoonful of the jam on to this; after a few seconds, run a finger through it, and if the pathway remains and the surface of the jam wrinkles slightly, the jam will set.

Should you have a sugar thermometer, have it ready in a measure of warm water and a reading should give 104°C, 220°F, when the jam is at setting point.

It is as well to try two of these tests to make sure. Towards the end of testing, turn the heat off, or draw the pan to one side, and work as quickly as possible or the jam may overcook.

Sometimes jam is seen with all the fruit in the top half of the jar and nothing much below. If making jam with whole strawberries, or large pieces of fruit, such as quince, cool it in the preserving pan until a skin shows it is thickening slightly and then stir it. If the fruit floats again, cool it a little longer and repeat. As it cools, the jam should thicken just enough to hold the fruit in suspension but do not wait too long or bubbles may form as you pour.

Potting and covering

Remove the jars from the oven where they have been warming and carefully pour in the jam – a small measuring jug is useful and use a funnel if you have it. A double sheet of newspaper keeps the table top clean. Fill the jars well up into the necks as the jam will shrink as it cools and a large space looks unsightly; also the waxed disc may not cover it. If a small amount of jam is left, too little even for a 225g ($\frac{1}{2}$lb) size jar, turn it into a very small jar or dish and use it at once. It is nice to have a sample to try.

Jam should be covered while still very hot (it **must** be hot if you are using twist-top jars) or left until absolutely cold – never cover it when warm or tepid. Fit a small waxed disc, waxed side down, to cover the surface of the jam completely, press down to seal, wipe the rim of the jar, cover it and tie down. Then label your jars and store them in a cool, dry and preferably dark place. They can be kept for up to two years.

Should you have misjudged the boiling time, and the jam is runny when cold, turn it all back into the preserving pan and re-boil until you have a confirmed set. Make sure the jars are clean and dry, and finish as before.

Potting the jam
As the jam approaches setting point, rows of matching jars, warm from the oven, are set out in neat rows. The jam is poured in very carefully, right to the neck of the jar and covered while still very hot.

Guidelines for making jam

1 Collect all equipment.
2 Choose and prepare your fruit.
3 Make or buy extra pectin and acid if needed.
4 Prepare the preserving pan with butter or glycerine, and place the fruit in it with extra pectin and acid, if needed, and the measured water.
5 Cook gently to soften the fruit and reduce the liquid.
6 Warm the sugar and the washed and dried jars.
7 Add the sugar to the pan, dissolve and boil rapidly.
8 Test for setting.
9 When setting point is reached, pour into the warmed jars, cover, label and store.

What can go wrong

Mould. There should be no real problem in keeping jam well if it was carefully made and stored, but mould can sometimes appear if the jam is kept in a warm or steamy place, or if the covers were not put on securely. Look at the jars occasionally and if a spot of mould has appeared, take away the mould and use that jar right away. There are two ways of helping to prevent mould if, after precaution, it still appears. A film of brandy, less than 5ml (1 teaspoon), can be run over the surface before covering, likewise a film of golden syrup from a warmed teaspoon will help.

Another preventive is paraffin wax, which can be bought from any good chemist. This is much used in America and Canada. It is gently melted and poured on to the hot jam to a depth of about 3mm ($\frac{1}{8}$in). Turn the jar so the wax touches the sides, let it set to make an airtight seal, and cover as usual when the jam is cold.

Fermentation. Jam can also ferment, and become uneatable, if insufficiently cooked, if damp or mushy fruit was included or if too little sugar was used for the amount of fruit. Less sugar can often be added than the amount given in a recipe, and will give better flavour and colour, but the jam will have to be sterilised unless it is to be used within a few weeks; it will also not set so firmly and will be more like a preserve than a jam.

To sterilise jam, use $\frac{1}{2}$ litre (1lb) spring clip or screw-band jars, immerse the jars in hot water, bring the water to the boil and boil for 7 minutes. Screw-bands should be put on slightly loose and tightened on removal from water.

Crystallisation. Crystallisation can be seen sometimes both on the surface and through the jam; this is due to too much sugar being used or, more likely, to over-boiling or under-boiling after the sugar has been added. This can also occur if the sugar has not dissolved properly before rapid boiling. This jam can be eaten, but will be oversweet, dry and crunchy.

Recipes for jams

Size of jars: 450g or 1lb.

Yields given in the following recipes are approximate

Apple and Ginger Jam

2kg (4lb) green cooking
   apples
1¾kg (3½lb) sugar
2 lemons
25g (1oz) piece of root ginger
175g (6oz) crystallised ginger,
   chopped
1 litre (1¾ pints) water

Yield: 6 jars

Peel and core the apples, simmer the skins and cores with the water in a covered pan for half an hour. Chop the apples and put into the preserving pan with the grated rind and juice of the lemons; add the root ginger tied in a piece of muslin.

Strain 700ml (1¼ pints) of the liquid from the skins and cores, add to the apples and simmer until they are very soft. Remove the root ginger, stir in the warmed sugar and dissolve. Add the crystallised ginger. Boil rapidly, stirring slowly, until a little jam will set on testing. Pot and cover as usual.

Apricot Jam

1½kg (3lb) firm ripe apricots
1¾kg (3½lb) sugar
2 lemons
25g (1oz) blanched, skinned
   and halved almonds
500ml (¾ pint) water

Yield: 6 jars

Halve the apricots, remove the stones and cut across again if large. Put the fruit into the preserving pan, pour in the water, and the juice squeezed from the lemons, and simmer gently until the fruit is soft. Stir in the warmed sugar and dissolve.

Bring to a brisk boil stirring slowly to prevent sticking. Put in the almonds and after 10 minutes test for setting and continue until setting point is reached. Skim if necessary. Pot and cover as usual.

Dried Apricot and Orange Jam

750g (1½lb) dried apricots
1½kg (3lb) sugar
2 medium-sized oranges
5ml (1 level teaspoon)
   tartaric acid
2 litres (3½ pints) water

Yield: 6 jars

Separate and rinse the apricots, then soak them for 24 hours in the water. Turn the fruit and water into the preserving pan, add the acid and the grated rind of the oranges (only the zest, not the bitter pith).

Simmer for about half an hour, until the apricots are soft and pulpy. Stir in the warmed sugar and dissolve, add the strained orange juice, boil fast until setting point is reached on testing. Pot and cover as usual.

Blackberry and Apple Jam

1kg (2lb) blackberries
1¼kg (2½lb) green cooking
   apples
1½kg (3lb) sugar
250ml (½ pint) water

Yield: 5 jars

Pick over the blackberries to remove stalks and pieces of leaf. Rinse them quickly and put into the preserving pan. Peel, core and cut up the apples, add to the pan with the water and simmer until the fruit is tender. Add the warmed sugar and stir over a low heat until dissolved, then boil fast until a little will set when tested. Pot and cover as usual.

Blackberries should be used as soon as possible after gathering as they spoil quickly.

Black Currant Jam

2kg (4lb) black currants
2¾kg (5½lb) sugar
1¾ litres (3 pints) water

Yield: 9 jars

Remove the stalks from the currants (running the stalk through a fork is a good way).

Discard any small green currants and put the fruit into a preserving pan with the water. Simmer until the skins are very soft and the liquid well reduced; the skins will toughen if this preliminary cooking is hurried and it can take 40–45 minutes. Add the warmed sugar, dissolve, then boil fast, stirring as necessary to prevent sticking. This jam sets easily so test frequently as over-boiling will spoil the flavour. Skim, pot and cover as usual.

Bilberry (or Blueberry) Jam

2kg (4lb) bilberries
1¾kg (3½lb) sugar
2 large lemons
Pinch of salt
250ml (½ pint) water

Yield: 6 jars

Rinse the bilberries quickly in a colander, put into the preserving pan and crush a little. Add the water, a good pinch of salt, and the grated rind and strained juice of the lemons. Simmer until soft and pulpy. Add the warmed sugar, dissolve and boil until the jam will set softly, stirring slowly. This jam does not set stiffly so do not over-boil it. The lemon and salt bring out the delicate flavour. Pot and cover as usual.

Morello Cherry and Red Currant Jam

1kg (2¼lb) morello cherries,
   weighed after stoning
750g (1½lb) red currants
1½kg (3lb) sugar
150ml (¼ pint) water

Yield: 5 jars

Stalk the cherries and stone them over the preserving pan to catch any juice (a cherry stoner, which can be bought from kitchen equipment shops, will make this easier). Pour in the water and add the stalked red currants. Cook gently to draw the juice from the currants, then simmer for about 25 minutes to soften the cherries. Stir in the warmed sugar to dissolve it,

then boil briskly until setting point is reached. Skim, turn off the heat and let the jam stand for 10 minutes or so to prevent the cherries floating. Pot and seal.

Cranberry and Apple Jam

1kg (2lb) fresh or frozen
  cranberries
1kg (2lb) sour cooking apples
2kg (4lb) sugar
250ml (½ pint) water

Yield: 7 jars

Rinse the cranberries in a colander, drain and put them into the preserving pan with the water. Peel, quarter, core and cut up the apples, add to the pan and simmer slowly. The cranberries break up quickly but continue simmering until the skins are soft. When pulpy and reduced, add the warmed sugar and dissolve. Bring to a fast boil.

Test for setting after a few minutes and repeat until setting point is reached. Skim, as necessary, pot and cover as usual.

This is delicious served with cream cheese on crackers, as a side dish for curries or with any rich meat.

Recipes for jams

Chestnut and Vanilla Jam

1½kg (3lb) large chestnuts
Weight of the sieved
    chestnuts in granulated
    sugar
15ml (1 tablespoon) brandy
5ml (1 teaspoon) vanilla
    essence
250ml (½ pint) water

Yield: about 6–8 small jars

Using the point of a small sharp knife, make a cut across the curved side of each chestnut and boil them until soft with some water, just to cover them – this may take 15–20 minutes. Draw the pan off the heat, remove a few chestnuts at a time, remove both skins and rub the nuts through a wire sieve, or strainer. If skins become difficult to remove, bring to the boil again. It is a tedious job, so it's worth bribing someone to help you, and the result certainly justifies the effort. Weigh the sieved nuts, take an equal amount of sugar, dissolve it in the 250ml (½ pint) water, then boil. Stir in the chestnuts and cook slowly, stirring all the time until the mixture darkens and thickens. Add the 5ml (1 teaspoon) of vanilla, or to taste, and stir in the brandy. Put into small jars and seal. Store in a refrigerator.

This jam does not keep well so it is better made in small quantity, and the brandy will help to prevent mould for a few weeks. The cooked, sieved chestnuts may be stored in a freezer for 1–2 months and the jam can be made as wanted. It is particularly good with ice-cream or used to top meringues and cream.

Damson Jam

2kg (4lb) damsons
2½kg (5lb) sugar
600ml (1 pint) water

Yield: 8 jars

Pick over the damsons and discard any that are damaged. Put them into the preserving pan with the water and simmer gently for about half an hour, until the fruit is soft and pulpy. As soon as the stones float free, begin taking them out. Add the warmed sugar and stir until dissolved, then boil rapidly, stirring occasionally to prevent burning, until a set is obtained. Skim, although not much skimming should be necessary if a small nut of butter was added at the beginning. Pot and cover as usual.

Dried Fruit Jam

200g (8oz) dried figs
200g (8oz) prunes
200g (8oz) raisins
200g (8oz) dates
2 lemons
300g (12oz) demerara sugar
50g (2oz) almonds, blanched,
    skinned and chopped
500ml (1 pint) water

Yield: 4 jars

Stone the prunes and dates then cut them up with the figs and raisins. Pour over the water and leave to soak overnight. Next day turn it all into a heavy pan, add the grated rind and juice from the lemons, the sugar and the almonds. Simmer until it thickens to a soft paste or purée – it will not set – stirring slowly as it can burn easily. Pour into heated jars and seal.

This is good with cream cheese for sandwiches and useful as a filling for a sponge sandwich cake. Try it on sliced bananas with yogurt or soured cream.

Gooseberry Jam

2kg (4lb) green gooseberries
2½kg (5lb) sugar
700ml (1¼ pints) water
6 sprays of just open
    elderflowers (if available)

Yield: 8 jars

Wash the gooseberries, top and tail them with a small knife. Put them into the preserving pan, pour in the water and cook gently until the skins are very soft.

If elderflowers are to be used, shake them well, rinse them and tie in a piece of butter muslin; push the bag well down into the water before simmering the fruit, and tie the bag to the handle of the pan.

Stir in the warmed sugar, dissolve slowly, then bring to a fast boil. As the jam begins to thicken, remove the bag of elderflowers, pressing it against the side of the pan with a spoon. Test for setting as usual, every few minutes, as gooseberry jam sets quickly. Pot and cover as usual.

Elderflowers and gooseberries are ready about the same time, and a few sprays of elderflower give a wonderful flavour to gooseberry jam.

Gooseberry varieties which turn red on ripening will turn the jam pink as it boils, after sugar is added.

Greengage Jam

2kg (4lb) greengages
2kg (4lb) sugar
400ml (¾ pint) water

Yield: 7 jars

Wash the greengages, cut round them and twist to separate the halves, remove the stones. Put them into the preserving pan with the water and simmer until the fruit and skins are soft. Meanwhile crack about six of the stones, remove the kernels and dip them into boiling water to skin them easily, halve or coarsely chop them. Add the warmed sugar to the softened fruit, dissolve, then boil fast until the jam begins to thicken, stir in the kernels and continue boiling until setting point is reached. Pot and cover as usual.

If you are lucky enough to find, or grow, an old variety of greengage, such as the Cambridge gage, they have a superb flavour.

Loganberry Jam

2kg (4lb) firm ripe
    loganberries
2kg (4lb) sugar
15ml (1 tablespoon) lemon
    juice
150ml (¼ pint) water

Yield: 7 jars

It is important to follow either the imperial or the metric weights and measures in any one recipe. Do not mix them.

Pick over and hull the berries. Put the water into the preserving pan, then add the loganberries and lemon juice. Cook very slowly until the juice flows, then simmer until the fruit is very soft. Give a stir occasionally as it may stick – it should take about 20 minutes. Add the warmed sugar, dissolve slowly, then boil quickly until the jam will set on testing. Pot and cover as usual.

Loganberries are easy to grow and make a delicious jam; if the seeds are disliked, sieve after the initial cooking to soften, add 400g (1lb) sugar to each 500ml (1 pint) of purée and finish as usual.

Both youngberries and boysenberries can be made into jam in the same way, but use the juice of a whole lemon in this recipe.

Marrow, Lemon and Ginger Jam

2kg (4lb) marrow, weighed after peeling and cubing
2kg (4lb) sugar
3 large lemons
250g (8oz) crystallised ginger, cut into small pieces
1 piece root ginger tied in muslin
30ml(2tablespoons) salt

Yield: 6 jars

Peel and quarter the marrow, remove seeds and any pithy centre, then cut into 1cm ($\frac{1}{2}$in) cubes or pieces. Put these into a large bowl sprinkling the salt between the layers; leave overnight, covered. The salt will draw liquid from the marrow and help to firm it. Strain off as much of the liquid as possible, sprinkle the sugar between and over the marrow cubes and leave for 3–4 hours.

Turn the marrow into the preserving pan, add the grated rind and the strained juice of the lemons, and the piece of root ginger tied in muslin.

Heat gently to dissolve the sugar, bring to the boil and add the crystallised ginger; boil until the pieces of marrow are clear in a really heavy syrup. The jam may not set to a 'wrinkle' but should be thick enough to spread without being runny. Leave to cool for a few minutes to suspend the pieces of marrow. Remove the root ginger, pot and seal.

Mulberry Jam

2kg (4lb) mulberries
2kg (4lb) sugar
1kg (2lb) sour cooking apples
1 litre (1½ pints) water

Yield: 7 jars

Choose very dark firm red mulberries; they are almost black when fully ripe, and a few of these riper ones may be included. Especially after a wet summer, mulberries need a lot of boiling to set into jam, which causes loss of flavour. If you have apples, strong apple juice helps the set; if not, it is advisable to use commercial pectin and follow the manufacturer's recipe.

Wash the apples, cut up roughly and put into a pan with the water, simmer to a soft pulp, taking about half an hour, then strain the juice to obtain 500ml ($\frac{3}{4}$ pint).

Put the apple juice into the preserving pan, add the mulberries, crush them a little then simmer gently until they are soft and broken down. Add the warmed sugar and stir to dissolve, then boil rapidly until a little will set on testing. Pot and cover as usual.

Mulberries are often left unpicked in the country, but they make a beautiful dark crimson jam with a distinctive flavour.

Elderflowers

Quinces

Elderberries

Boysenberries

Barberries

Medlars

Mulberries

Recipes for jams

Rhubarb and Ginger Jam

1½kg (3lb) rhubarb, young and tender
1½kg (3lb) sugar
3 lemons
25g (1oz) root ginger tied in muslin
125g (4oz) crystallised ginger, chopped

Yield: 5 jars

Trim both ends of the rhubarb stalks but do not peel. Cut up into short pieces and layer up with the sugar in a mixing bowl, cover and leave overnight to draw the juice. When ready put it into the preserving pan with the root ginger, and the grated rind and strained juice from the lemons. Simmer until pulpy, stirring occasionally to prevent burning. Stir in the crystallised ginger, remove the root ginger and then boil until the jam thickens to a soft set.

To obtain a stiffer set, add 250ml (½ pint) of thick apple or red currant juice, boil and finish as above.

Rose Petal Jam

250g (8oz) rose petals from fully open fragrant red roses
750g (1½lb) sugar
15ml (1 tablespoon) lemon juice
5ml (1 teaspoon) orange flower water
500ml (¾ pint) water

Yield: 7–8 125g (4oz) jars

Snip any hard white points from the petals, put them into a heavy pan with the water and simmer gently, covered, for half an hour. Strain the petals, pressing them gently, and set aside. Add the sugar and lemon juice to the water in which the petals were cooked, dissolve, and boil, uncovered, to a thick syrup. Add the orange flower water and stir in the petals just enough to mix them through the syrup, it should be very thick. Pour into small 125g (4oz) jars which are dry and warm. Cover and seal.

This jam forms a sugary crust on the surface which helps to keep it. If the petals from the old-fashioned shrub roses are used they will almost dissolve. It is a very sweet preserve and only a little is needed, used with cream to fill a sponge cake, over ice-cream, or with clotted cream on freshly baked scones.

It is important to follow either the imperial or the metric weights and measures in any one recipe. Do not mix them.

Plum Jam

2kg (4lb) plums
2kg (4lb) sugar
500ml (¾ pint) water

Yield: 7 jars

Wash, halve and stone the plums; crack a few stones, blanch, skin and halve the kernels. Cook the plums and water in a preserving pan for about half an hour until the skins are soft. Stir in and dissolve the warmed sugar then boil briskly adding the kernels towards setting point. When a set is obtained, skim if necessary, pot and seal.

This is one of the easier jams to make. The small myrobalan or cherry plums are excellent for jam; remove the stones during the first cooking. Jam made with Victoria plums has a beautiful colour.

Raspberry Jam

2kg (4lb) firm ripe raspberries
2kg (4lb) sugar
Juice of 1 lemon, or 150ml (¼ pint) red currant juice, undiluted

Yield: 7 jars

Put a small bowl of raspberries into the preserving pan and crush them; add the rest of the fruit and the red currant or lemon juice then simmer until soft and pulpy. Add the warmed sugar, stir to dissolve. Boil for three minutes then test. When a soft set is obtained, pot and cover as usual.

White raspberries also have excellent flavour and may be included.

Quince Jam (1)

2kg (4lb) quinces
2½kg (5lb) sugar
5ml (1 level teaspoon) citric acid
2 litres (3½ pints) water

Yield: 8–9 jars

Peel, quarter and core the quinces, cut them in small pieces using a sharp knife as they are very hard. Put them into a preserving pan with the acid and water. Simmer for about ¾–1 hour until the fruit is tender. Add the warmed sugar, dissolve and boil briskly until a set is obtained. Pot and cover as usual.

Quince Jam (2)

2kg (4lb) quinces
2 large lemons
1 orange
Sugar
2½ litres (4 pints) water

Yield: about 7 jars

Wipe and cut up the quinces including the peel and seeds. Simmer with the water in a preserving pan until the fruit is soft enough to sieve easily and the liquid is well reduced. Put through a nylon sieve, measure the pulp and return it to the clean pan; add 300g (12oz) sugar for each 500ml (1 pint) of pulp, and the grated rind and strained juice of the lemons and orange. Stir over a low heat to dissolve the sugar, then boil, stirring slowly until setting point is reached. Pot and cover as usual.

Recipes for jams

Raspberry Jam (uncooked)

1kg (2lb) raspberries
1kg (2lb) sugar

Yield: 4 jars

Put the hulled raspberries into a large mixing bowl, and put the sugar into another bowl. Put both into a warm oven (170°C, 325°F, Gas Mark 3), and leave until they are hot right through (20–25 minutes). Add the sugar to the raspberries and beat together thoroughly. The heat should dissolve the sugar. When well beaten, pot and seal in the usual way. This 'jam' will keep three months or longer but is best made in small quantities and stored in the refrigerator or a cold place.

Red Currant and Orange Jam

2kg (4lb) red currants
2kg (4lb) sugar
4 good oranges
A pinch of ground cinnamon

Yield: 6 jars

Stalk the currants, rinse them and put them wet into the preserving pan, add the finely grated rind of the oranges and the cinnamon. Halve the oranges, remove pulp and juice and put with the currants. Stir and cook gently until the juice runs from the red currants then simmer until the skins are soft. Add the warmed sugar, stir to dissolve, bring to a fast boil and test frequently as it sets quickly. Pot and cover as usual.

Strawberry Jam

2kg (4lb) small, firm and just ripe strawberries
1¾kg (3½lb) sugar
100ml (6 tablespoons) lemon juice *or* 250ml (½ pint) red currant juice

Yield: 6 jars

Hull the berries, put a few into the preserving pan and crush them, add the rest of the fruit and the lemon or red currant juice. Put in the warmed sugar, heat and stir slowly to draw the juice and dissolve the sugar. Then boil quickly until setting point is reached. Skim as necessary and let the jam cool until a skin forms on the surface; stir gently and fill into warmed jars. Cover and seal.

Freezer Jam

625g (1¼lb) ripe strawberries or raspberries
1kg (2lb) caster sugar
30ml (2 tablespoons) lemon juice
½ bottle of Certo

Yield: about 1¾kg (3½lb)

It is important to use fully ripe fruit. Remove the hulls and completely crush the strawberries or raspberries, one layer at a time, with a large wooden spoon. Stir in the sugar with the lemon juice and the Certo and mix well, stirring 2–3 minutes. Using a small glass measuring jug, fill into plastic containers, leaving $\frac{1}{10}$th headspace to allow for expansion in the freezer. Cover at once with the lids and leave at room temperature for 24 hours, or till the sugar is dissolved, before freezing and storing in the freezer. They can be kept from one season to the next. Thaw each container in the refrigerator before using. Keep any that is left unused in the refrigerator and use it within 1–2 weeks.

These jams have the taste of fresh fruit and make delicious fruit sauces. Do not make more than one batch at a time.

Conserves and preserves

Conserves are made from two or more fruits one usually citrus, with nuts or candied peel or raisins added (see recipes opposite). They can be used as jam. Preserves are generally made from only one kind of fruit, preserved in a heavy syrup, (see opposite).

Paraffin wax (from any good chemist) makes a good seal for the conserves; careful storage is needed if they are to keep well.

Rhubarb and Orange Conserve

2kg (4lb) tender rhubarb
1¾kg (3½lb) sugar
6 medium-sized oranges
2 lemons
350g (12oz) raisins
125g (4oz) almonds, blanched, skinned and roughly chopped

Yield: about 4kg (8lb)

Trim the rhubarb, wipe with a damp cloth and cut into small pieces, layer it in a mixing bowl with the sugar and leave overnight. Turn the rhubarb and sugar into a preserving pan, add the grated rind and strained juice of the oranges and lemons. Simmer, and stir gently until it thickens and sets, stir in the raisins and almonds, cook a minute longer. Pour into small warmed jars, cover and seal.

Golden Plum Conserve

750g (1½lb) good yellow plums
1kg (2lb) demerara sugar
1 large orange
1 lemon
50g (2oz) preserved ginger
250g (8oz) seeded raisins
50g (2oz) coarsely chopped walnuts
30ml (2 tablespoons) brandy
150ml (¼ pint) water

Yield: about 2kg (4lb)

Wash, halve and stone the plums, putting them into a small preserving pan with the water, and the grated rind and strained juice of the orange and lemon. Cook gently until the plums are very soft. Stir in the warmed sugar, dissolve and bring to a fast boil; put in the raisins, halved if large, and the cut up ginger. When nearly at setting point stir in the walnuts; when a set is obtained remove from the heat, cool slightly and stir in the brandy. Put into small warmed jars and when cold run a film of brandy on top of each one and cover and seal as usual.

Strawberry Preserve

2kg (4lb) small or Alpine strawberries
2kg (4lb) sugar
60ml (4 tablespoons) lemon juice or 5ml (1 level teaspoon) tartaric acid

Yield: 3–3½kg (6–7lb)

Hull the berries and layer them in a bowl with the sugar, cover and leave overnight to extract the juice and firm the berries. Put into the preserving pan with the lemon juice, or acid, bring to a slow boil and boil gently for 5–6 minutes. Return to the mixing bowl for 12 hours and then boil again gently until the syrup thickens. This process helps to keep the fruit plump. When stirring, do it gently to keep the fruit whole. Cool for 10–15 minutes, so that the strawberries

no longer float, before putting into warmed jars. Pot and make an airtight seal, especially carefully.

Raspberries and loganberries can be made into preserves in the same way.

Melon and Lemon Preserve

2kg (4lb) cubed cantaloup or honeydew melon
1¾kg (3½lb) sugar
2 large lemons

Yield: 6 jars

Prepare the melon, catching any juice, and cutting into 1cm (½in) cubes as nearly as possible. Layer these in a bowl with the sugar, cover and leave 24 hours.

Turn it all into a preserving pan, add the grated rind from the lemons, halve the lemons, remove the pieces of pulp with a grapefruit knife and put these and any juice with the melon and sugar. Heat gently to dissolve the sugar completely then boil until the syrup is thick and the melon cubes clear and tender.

Cool until the fruit will remain suspended in the syrup, pour into warmed jars, cover and seal well.

Jellies

Generations of housewives have held a jar of jelly to the light asking for a verdict on clarity and colour. Perfect jars of jelly used to be one of the hall-marks of a good still-room. Many people think of jelly making as the most difficult branch of preserving, but the basic principles for making jellies are the same as for making jam (see page 12), and given a little knowledge of these and some equipment, anybody can make good jelly. It takes a little longer than jam, and space is needed to keep it out of harm's way while it is being strained, but the various steps can be woven conveniently into the day's work and may be spread over two days.

Garden-produced fruit is useful, but not essential – blackberries, elderberries and sloes are hedgerow fruits; wild raspberries have a superb flavour for making jelly; mountain ash or rowan berries, and bilberries or blueberries, mixed with apples, make excellent jelly.

Herb jellies are lesser known, except for mint jelly. They are made by using good flavoured herbs in an apple jelly base, and these delicate tasting jellies are a lovely accompaniment to cold meats, poultry and game. A jar or two would make a very acceptable gift.

Equipment for jelly-making

A **good preserving pan**, and if possible, a smaller one as well for small batches of jelly – often less is made than with jam.

A **sharp stainless knife**.

A **lemon squeezer**.

A **good grater**.

A **measuring jug**.

A **wooden preserving spoon**.

A **skimming spoon**.

A **jam funnel**.

A **large mixing bowl** to catch the strained juice.

A **jelly bag** and **stand**, or siutable material to improvise.

String, if you use a cloth bag for straining.

A supply of 225g (8oz) and 450g (1lb) **glass jam jars**, also a few smaller jars for herb jellies.

A **nylon sieve** or **large strainer** for sieving the pulp if it is wanted for further use.

Covers and **labels**.

Method for making jelly

Choosing fruit

As for jam, the fruit for making jelly should be fresh, firm and barely ripe; some fruits are not suitable – sweet cherries, peaches, pears, strawberries or melon would need so much pectin and acid to set the juice that the delicate flavour would be spoiled.

The best fruits to use are those with pectin and acid in sufficient amounts particularly those with a definite flavour.

Preparing fruit

Pick over the fruit to remove large thick stalks and any small wild-life, and discard damaged or bruised fruit. It is not necessary to stalk or hull berries, or to peel and core hard fruits, as these parts will be strained out during the making. If you are satisfied the fruit is quite clean there is no need to wash it, but if washing is necessary, rinse quickly in a colander and then drain. The quince has a downy skin and is better wiped with a dry cloth.

Large hard fruits are cut into pieces, with bruises removed, before simmering; plums can be halved, a few stones cracked and a few kernels skinned and added for flavouring.

As for jam, pectin, acid and sugar, in correct proportions, are needed to set the fruit juice into a good jelly. If in doubt about the pectin or acid content of the fruit you are using, consult the list (see page 14). If there is only a small amount of one type of fruit available, some other fruit can be mixed with it, and here again the list will help; it is as well to test for pectin, using the method given for jams (see page 15), if a mixture of juices is being used for jelly. Extra pectin or acid can be added (see page 14), if needed.

Weigh the fruit and rinse quickly if necessary. Put the fruit into a preserving pan with a good surface area for evaporation. Add the recommended amount of water measured accurately. Juicy berries need little, if any, water, a few berries can be crushed to start the juice flowing; hard fruits are barely covered with water to allow for reduction during the longer simmering period. For soft berries needing no water, the preserving pan can be rinsed and left wet, this helps the juice to flow.

Preliminary cooking

Simmer slowly until the fruit is very soft, and never hurry this stage. Hard fruits generally need about 50 minutes, plums and damsons 25 to 30 minutes. Soft berries should be pulpy in 15 to 20 minutes.

Straining

The pulp and juice is strained through a suspended, scalded and still damp jelly bag, or through an improvised bag made of suitable material. A flannel jelly bag is worth buying if jelly is made often, but a bag can be made using calico or flannel or a close weave linen; for small amounts, a well scalded closely woven tea towel may be used, but be careful it does not smell of soap from previous laundering.

After use, a jelly bag is cleaned, scalded and dried thoroughly before putting away. Do not wash it in soap or detergent. Inevitably a jelly bag, although quite clean, will be stained after using a few times.

If you do not have a stand, a high stool turned upside down, or a kitchen chair up-ended on to the seat of another will provide four legs on which to tie the tapes on the corners of the bag, or the string if you are using an improvised bag. Alternatively, a piece of fine material may be placed over a large nylon (not metal) sieve and used as a strainer. Put a bowl underneath and leave the juice to drip undisturbed; it is tempting to squeeze or press the bag but this will cloud the jelly. It is suggested that the jelly should drip overnight, but if this is not convenient, leave it for several hours – and do not leave the juice long after straining, 24 hours is the limit, or it may ferment and will not set.

When using a fruit strong in pectin and flavour, such as black currants or damsons, a second extraction can be made, returning the pulp to the pan after 10 minutes' draining, adding 500ml (1 pint) of water just to cover the pulp and simmering for 30 minutes or so before straining again and leaving to drip into the first lot of juice.

Adding the sugar

It is necessary to measure the juice to calculate the amount of sugar needed; this is usually 400g (1lb) sugar to 500ml (1 pint) of juice, but can vary between 300g (12oz) for fruits low in pectin, such as medlars and bilberries, to 500g ($1\frac{1}{4}$lb) for a fruit with a very high pectin content. Measure the juice into the cleaned preserving pan and heat.

Warm the sugar in a wide bowl or baking tin,

but do not let it get too hot. While this is not absolutely necessary it does save time as the sugar then dissolves quickly in the reheated juice. Adding warm sugar also helps to prevent crystallisation of the finished jelly. Adding the sugar cold will give a deeper colour as longer heating will be needed, so if the juice looks pale in colour use your own judgement here. Add the warmed sugar to the heated juice and dissolve it.

Testing for setting

Once the sugar has dissolved, boil fast and begin testing for a set after five minutes – the spoon test is good for jelly (see page 15). If a sugar thermometer is available use it as well; jelly correctly made will usually register 104°C, 220°F, at setting point; it is as well to keep the thermometer in a jug of warm water before and during use.

Towards the end of testing, turn off the heat, and work as quickly as possible or the jelly may begin to set in the pan. Skim if necessary – a perforated skimmer is useful.

Making jelly
1 Prepare the fruit. **2** Cook fruit slowly in required amount of water until very soft, adding acid or pectin

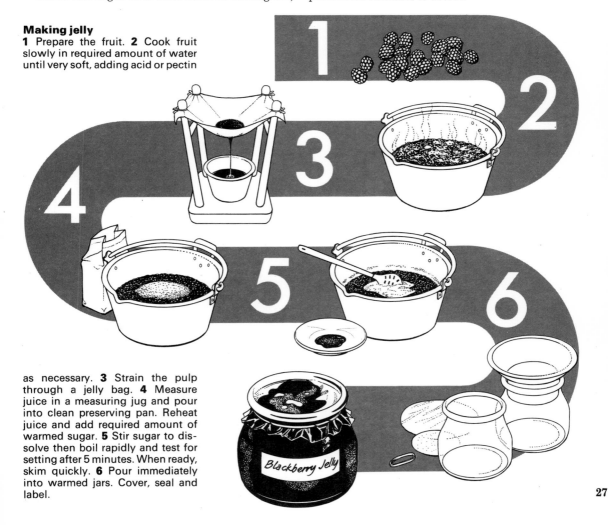

as necessary. **3** Strain the pulp through a jelly bag. **4** Measure juice in a measuring jug and pour into clean preserving pan. Reheat juice and add required amount of warmed sugar. **5** Stir sugar to dissolve then boil rapidly and test for setting after 5 minutes. When ready, skim quickly. **6** Pour immediately into warmed jars. Cover, seal and label.

27

Jellies

Potting and covering

Using a jug or measure, quickly fill the warmed jars almost to the top; any small pieces of scum will float and can be taken out. Sometimes jelly is strained through damp muslin before being put into jars – this is to strain out every particle of scum, for exhibition – but it has to be done very quickly and is not easy with a large amount.

Fit a waxed disc, wax down, on to the surface of the jelly at once, and either cover and tie down immediately or leave until it is quite cold. Wipe jars when jelly is set to avoid tilting the liquid jelly. Label, and store in a cool dry place, if possible away from strong light as the colour of jellies can fade. They can be kept for up to two years, but it is a good idea to eat up preserves before the new season.

Should you have misjudged the boiling time, and the jelly is runny when cold, turn it all back into the preserving pan and re-boil until you have a confirmed set. Make sure the jars are clean and dry, and finish as before.

Examine your stored jars occasionally to check for mould or fermentation.

Purée from pulp

For economy's sake, the pulp from the jelly bag can be put through a nylon sieve and used to make a puréed jam suitable for quick use for cooking purposes. Add 500g (1lb) sugar to same amount of weighed purée, boil together until setting point is reached. Pot and cover as usual. A Victorian cookery book adds: 'This is suitable for the kitchen and nursery.'

Some purées can be used for fruit fools, or as sauces, adding lemon or apple juice for extra flavour.

Guidelines for making jelly

1 Collect all equipment.
2 Choose and prepare your fruit.
3 Cook fruit with correct amount of water, and added pectin or acid if necessary, slowly until very soft.
4 Pour the pulp into a jelly bag; leave to drip.
5 Measure juice into the cleaned preserving pan and heat.
6 Warm the required amount of sugar and the washed and dried jars.
7 Add warmed sugar to the heated juice, dissolve, and then boil very fast.
8 Test for setting after five minutes.
9 Strain the jelly quickly (if necessary) and pour at once into the jars.
10 Cover, label and store.

What can go wrong

Mould. Jelly may go mouldy if the fruit is over-ripe, or picked wet, or if any slightly mouldy fruit escapes notice. This will also happen if the jars are not warm and perfectly dry, and if the jelly is not stored carefully.

If mould appears on jam or jelly after a short time, it is probably a fault in the making; if after a month or two, it is more likely to be a fault in storage (ie too damp/warm).

Mould can also appear if paraffin wax is used wrongly; it should be spooned on 3mm ($\frac{1}{8}$in) deep while the jelly is still hot, and covered when cold.

Consistency too runny. Jelly may be too runny if a good recipe is not followed and the quantities are not weighed and measured. Or if a pan is used which does not give sufficient area for evaporation – while cooking, the contents of the pan should only be 10–12cm (4–5in) deep.

Cloudiness. If the contents of the jelly-bag are disturbed or squeezed, the jelly will be cloudy.

Disappointing appearance and flavour. If the process of simmering the fruit before the sugar is added is hurried, the result will be a less good colour and a less good quality juice.

Jelly will also have a less good appearance if the jars are moved before it is set – if they have to be moved, be careful not to tilt them – or if smears of jelly are not wiped from the rims of the jars before covering.

Difficulty in handling. If you do not work quickly enough once the sugar and juice are boiling, the jelly will set in the pan and be hard to ladle out. Everything you need must be to hand.

Recipes for jellies

Yields are not given for jellies as the juiciness of fruit varies according to the season, but about five 450g (1lb) jars are usually obtained from 1½kg (3lb) sugar.

Apple Jelly

2kg (4lb) green cooking apples or crab apples
Sugar (see below)
1¼ litres (2¼ pints) water

Wash the apples, cut them into pieces and put into the preserving pan. If windfalls are used remove any bruises. Pour in the water barely to cover the apples and simmer gently for about 45 minutes until very soft. Strain through a jelly bag overnight. Measure the juice into the preserving pan, bring it to simmering point and add 400g (1lb) sugar for every 500ml (1 pint) juice. When the sugar has dissolved put in any chosen flavouring tied in muslin and boil fast for 5 minutes, then test for a set and repeat every minute or two until a set is obtained. Take the pan from the heat, remove the bag of flavouring and skim quickly. Pour at once into heated jars. Cover and seal.
Suggested flavouring
1 A few thin strips of lemon or orange peel.
2 4 or 5 cloves tied in muslin.
3 A 5cm (2in) piece of stick cinnamon.
4 A piece of dried root ginger.
5 8 or 9 rose geranium or lemon verbena leaves tied together.
6 1 or 2 sprays of pineapple or eau-de-cologne mint.
7 2 quinces cut up with the apples, but not with crab apples.

Barberry Jelly

1½kg (3lb) ripe barberries (fruit of the Common Berberis)
5ml (1 level teaspoon) tartaric or citric acid
Sugar (see below)
1¼ litres (2¼ pints) water

Pick the berries from any stalks and leaves and discard any spotted ones. Wash and simmer the berries in a pan with the water and acid for ¾ to 1 hour, or until soft and pulpy. Strain through a jelly bag, measure into a preserving pan and weigh 400g (1lb) sugar for each 500ml (1 pint) of juice. Warm the sugar, add to the simmering juice and stir in to dissolve. Then boil quickly. Test after 5 minutes and continue testing until a little will wrinkle when pushed with a finger on a cold saucer. Pot quickly, cover and seal.

This jelly is a deep claret colour with a sharp flavour; good to serve with cold poultry or ham, also good to eat with cream cheese.

Black Currant Jelly

1½kg (3lb) black currants
Sugar (see below)
900ml (1½ pints) water

Use fully ripe but firm currants. There is no need to remove all the stalks but take away any large ones or leaves; it is not necessary to be thorough as stalks will be strained out later. Rinse the fruit in a colander quickly, put into the preserving pan with the water, and simmer for 45–50 minutes until pulpy. Turn into a jelly bag to drip overnight. Measure the juice, reheat in the clean pan and add 400g (1lb) warmed sugar for each 500ml (1 pint) of juice. Dissolve slowly, then boil rapidly. Test for setting after 5 minutes and then every 2 or 3 minutes until a little will set on testing. Skim. Have warmed jars ready and fill them quickly. Cover and seal as usual.
Note: A second extract can be made, after the first straining, by putting the pulp back into the pan and adding 850ml (1¼ pints) water. Simmer for half an hour, strain it again through the bag and add it to the first lot of juice. Finish as above.

Blackberry or Bramble Jelly

2kg (4lb) blackberries, picked firm and just ripe, with a handful of red under-ripe berries
5ml (1 level teaspoon) citric or tartaric acid
Sugar (see below)
600ml (1 pint) water

Rinse the fruit quickly in a colander, put into the preserving pan with the acid, add the water and stir and crush the fruit with a wooden spoon as it heats to simmering point. Simmer it for half an hour, or until very soft, and strain it overnight through a jelly bag. Measure the juice and return it to the clean pan, reheat and add 400g (1lb) sugar to every 500ml (1 pint) of juice. Stir to dissolve, then boil rapidly until the jelly will set on testing. Pour it quickly into warmed jars. Cover and seal.
Note: If berries are plentiful, a good and unusual jelly can be made with the largest red ones. It needs patience and a small pair of scissors to gather them. Use 850ml (1¼ pints) water, otherwise the method and proportions are the same. This jelly is ruby coloured, it has a sharp delicious fruity flavour and may take the place of red currant jelly if currants are scarce.

Blackberry and apple jelly can be made by using equal quantities of fruit and omitting the acid.

Damson Jelly

2kg (4lb) damsons
Sugar (see below)
1¼ litres (2¼ pints) water

Wash the fruit and simmer it with the water in the preserving pan until it is a soft pulp. Simmer slowly and stir occasionally. Pour through the jelly bag to strain and drip well. Measure the juice into the preserving pan and add 400g (1lb) sugar for each 500ml (1 pint) of juice, dissolve the sugar and bring to a rapid boil. Begin to test for setting after 5 minutes. When a set is obtained, skim, pour quickly into warmed jars and seal.

Plum jelly can be made the same way, using the same proportions. Red or purple plums make excellent jelly.

It is important to follow either the imperial or the metric weights and measures in any one recipe.

Recipes for jellies

Mint jelly

For making mint jelly the round-leaved apple mint has a specially good flavour and is easy to grow.

Elderberry and Apple Jelly

1kg (2lb) elderberries
1kg (2lb) sour cooking apples
Sugar (see below)
1 lemon
900ml (1½ pints) water

Rinse the elderberries in a colander after removing the larger stalks. Put them into the preserving pan with a little of the water and crush to break them up a little with the back of a wooden spoon.

Wash and cut up the apples roughly, removing any bruises, add them to the pan with the strained juice from the lemon, thin strips of lemon peel, and the rest of the water. Simmer slowly for 30–40 minutes to pulp and reduce well. Turn into the jelly bag and leave to drip overnight.

Measure the juice into the preserving pan, heat to simmering point. Allow 400g (1lb) sugar to 500ml (1 pint) of juice, add to the pan, dissolve, then boil fast until a little lifted and turned on the spoon will form drops which run together and break or flake away. Be careful not to over-boil as this jells only to a soft set. Pour into hot jars and cover as usual.

Gooseberry Jelly

2kg (4lb) green gooseberries
Sugar (see below)
1 litre (1¾ pints) water
A few sprays elderflower, if available

Wash the gooseberries, but there is no need to top-and-tail them. Put into the preserving pan with the water and simmer until well pulped. Put the pulp into the jelly bag and leave to drip overnight. Measure the juice into the pan, reheat, then stir in 400g (1lb) warmed sugar to 500ml (1 pint) of the juice, stir to dissolve, then boil fast until a little will set on testing. Skim, pot quickly and tie down.

If available, a few sprays of elderflower tied in muslin can be added after the sugar. This changes the flavour of gooseberry to that of muscat grape and is a delicious variation, but remove the bag after a few minutes, when the flavour seems strong enough.

Mint Jelly

A good handful of fresh mint
1½kg (3lb) green cooking apples
Sugar (see below)
300ml (½ pint) cider
30ml (2 tablespoons) wine vinegar
Green food colouring
600ml (1 pint) water

Wash and cut up the apples, put into the preserving pan with the water, cider, vinegar and two or three sprays of mint. Simmer to a soft pulp and pour into a jelly bag. Strain and drip overnight. Measure the juice and weigh 400g (1lb) sugar for each 500ml (1 pint) of juice. Heat the juice, stir in the warmed sugar, and dissolve on a low heat. Finely chop 2–3 tablespoons of the youngest mint leaves. Boil the dissolved sugar and juice rapidly and just as setting point is reached, skim the jelly and stir in the chopped mint with a few drops of green colouring. Stir round once or twice, pour into small warmed jars. Cover as usual.

It is important to follow either the imperial or the metric weights and measures in any one recipe. Do not mix them.

Japonica Jelly

1½kg (3lb) japonica fruits
Sugar (see below)
7·5ml (1½ level teaspoons) citric acid
2–3 cloves
2½ litres (4½ pints) water

Wash and cut up the fruit, put into the preserving pan with the water, acid and cloves. Simmer until the fruit is well softened; it may take 50–60 minutes as this is a hard fruit. Turn the pulp into a jelly bag to drip all night.

Measure the juice into the preserving pan, warm a good 300g (12oz) sugar to each 500ml (1 pint) juice, add and stir gently to dissolve. Then boil rapidly until setting point is reached. Skim, pot quickly and cover.

Medlar Jelly

2kg (4lb) ripe medlars
Sugar (see below)
2 large lemons
1¾ litres (3 pints) water

Wipe the medlars with a dry cloth, put them into the preserving pan with the water and simmer long and slowly to a pulp; this can take over an hour to reduce well. Strain in the jelly bag overnight. Measure the juice into the preserving pan and for each 500ml (1 pint), warm 300g (12oz) sugar. Bring the juice to simmering point, add the warmed sugar and the strained juice from the lemons. Dissolve. Boil fast and begin testing for a set after 8 minutes. When a soft set is reached, pour into 225g (8oz) pots, and cover. This jelly stiffens during storage. It is good to serve with lamb or boiled ham, as well as for use as a table jelly.

Herb Jellies

1½kg (3lb) sour apples or windfalls
Sugar (see below)
150ml (¼ pint) white wine vinegar
A good bunch of young mint or tarragon or 2–3 sprigs of lemon thyme or sage
750ml (1¼ pints) water

Wash and cut up the apples, put them into the preserving pan with the water and vinegar. Strip the leaves from the herb stalks, put the stalks with the apples and simmer 30–40 minutes. Strain through a jelly bag and drip overnight.

Measure the liquid and return to the pan to reheat, then add 400g (1lb) warmed sugar to 500ml (1 pint) juice. Tie the herb leaves into a muslin bag, add to the dissolved sugar and boil rapidly until the jelly sets on testing. Squeeze and remove the bag of herbs, skim, pour into small warm jars and seal.

The taste of herbs should not be too strong. If during the boiling with the sugar the jelly is tasted occasionally, the bag of leaves can be removed when judged necessary. A few drops of green food colouring may be added after skimming.

Recipes for jellies

Quince Jelly

2kg (4lb) quinces
Sugar (see below)
2 lemons
3 litres (5 pints) water

Wipe the quinces in a dry cloth then cut them up and put into the preserving pan with the water which should barely cover them, add the peel cut thinly from one of the lemons and the strained juice of two lemons. Simmer long and slowly 1–1½ hours. Strain through a jelly bag and drip all night.

Measure the juice into the preserving pan, add 500g (1¼lb) warmed sugar to each 500ml (1 pint) of reheated juice; stir until the sugar has dissolved, then bring to a rapid boil until setting point is reached. Skim, pot and cover.

A quince tree is easy to grow in England (south of York) and the fruit makes a wonderfully fragrant jelly. A spoonful or two added to the fruit for an apple pie gives a lovely flavour.

Raspberry Jelly

2kg (4lb) firm ripe raspberries
Sugar (see below)
5ml (1 level teaspoon)
   tartaric acid

Rinse the preserving pan with cold water and leave it wet, put in the raspberries, crushing a few. Put on a very low heat to draw the juice; mix the acid with a little water, add to the pan. Increase the heat just enough to simmer the fruit until pulpy, about 10–15 minutes.

Pour into the jelly bag and leave to drip overnight. Measure the juice into the clean preserving pan, weigh 400g (1lb) sugar to 500ml (1 pint) juice and warm it. Reheat the juice, add the sugar, dissolve and then reboil rapidly. Test for setting after five minutes and then every minute or two until a set is reached. Skim quickly, pour into warmed jars. Pot and seal.

Red Currant Jelly

2kg (4lb) juicy red currants
Sugar (see below)

All red currants or a mixture of white and red currants may be used. Rinse them in a colander but do not remove the stalks. Put them into the preserving pan and heat gently until the juice is running, then simmer very gently for half an hour until pulpy, softly crushing the fruit occasionally. Pour into a jelly bag and leave to drip overnight.

Measure the juice and allow 500g (1¼lb) sugar to 500ml (1 pint) as this fruit is rich in pectin and acid and will take more sugar. Warm the sugar, stir it into the reheated juice, dissolve, boil fast for one minute then skim very quickly and pour it at once into hot jars. Setting will occur rapidly and speed is essential. Cover and seal as usual.

The yield from this jelly is small but it has a wonderful flavour as it is concentrated. If currants are not plentiful use 900ml (1½ pints) water to 1½kg (3lb) currants and make as for Black currant Jelly (page 29).

Red Currant and Raspberry Jelly

1kg (2lb) red currants
1kg (2lb) raspberries
Sugar (see below)
500ml (¾ pint) water

Rinse the red currants in a colander, put with the raspberries and the water in the preserving pan and set over a low heat to draw the juice, crushing occasionally. Simmer for about half an hour to soften the fruit and extract all the juice. Strain through a jelly bag and drip overnight. Measure the juice and allow 400g (1lb) warmed sugar to 500ml (1 pint) juice. Reheat the juice, stir in the sugar to dissolve, then boil rapidly until a set is reached. Skim, fill warmed jars, cover and seal.

Sloe and Apple Jelly

1½kg (3lb) sloes
750g (1½lb) cooking apples or
   crab apples
Sugar (see below)
Water

Rinse the sloes in a colander, wash and cut up the unpeeled, uncored apples. Just cover the fruit with water and simmer slowly until all the fruit is soft, it will take about an hour. Pour into a jelly bag and leave to drip overnight. Measure the juice, and weigh 400g (1lb) sugar for each 500ml (1 pint) juice. Warm the sugar, reheat the juice and stir in the sugar until dissolved. Bring to a fast boil until setting point is reached. Pot, cover and seal as usual.

This jelly has a lovely colour and fine flavour. It is good to serve with rich meats, rabbit or hare.

Rowan and Apple Jelly

1kg (2lb) rowan berries
1kg (2lb) apples, preferably
   crab apples
Sugar (see below)
1 lemon
1 litre (1½ pints) water

Take the berries from the stalks and rinse them in a colander, wash the apples and cut them up, or leave whole if using crabs. Put both into the preserving pan with the thin peel and juice of the lemon and the water which should barely cover the fruit. Simmer slowly until reduced to a pulp; it will take about 45 minutes. Pour into the jelly bag and leave to drip overnight. Measure the juice, reheat and add and dissolve 400g (1lb) warmed sugar for each 500ml (1 pint) of juice. Boil fast, test after 5–6 minutes and continue until a set is reached. Pour into heated jars, cover and seal.

This jelly is excellent eaten with game or rich meats. It is acid in flavour and the proportion of apples to berries may be altered as wished. Rowan jelly can be made without apples, but using 2 lemons to 2kg (4lb) berries.

Potting the jelly
Pouring the jelly into the jar is
done as quickly as possible to
prevent the jelly setting in the pan.
A waxed disc is at once put on the
jelly surface and the jar covered.

Marmalades

Wherever the British live in the world, there is marmalade on the breakfast table – an astonishing amount must be made every year. Much of this is bought from shops, but many households never making or eating much jam, make large batches of marmalade in January and February. It is almost a rite, a way of life.

The word marmalade is said to have originated from the Portuguese word for quince, 'marmelo', and earlier marmalades were sweet pastes of quince, peach or plum. In France the word marmalade is given to a compote, or to a thick sweetened purée of fruit, frequently made from apples or apricots. Here, in Britain, we generally think of marmalade as being made from citrus fruit with shredded peel suspended in jelly.

Nowadays there are quite a number of citrus fruits available and it is interesting to concoct different flavours and textures. Marmalades vary from delicate jellies to the dark, bitter kinds with soft chunky pieces of peel.

Seville oranges, and other varieties of bitter orange, make an aromatic marmalade much in demand for its fine, sharp taste, and as their season is very short – they are at their best only during January and February – the most should be made of them. If you have a freezer they may be frozen whole or ready sliced for making marmalade later. Note the amount. (If storing for more than a week or two, there may be a slight loss of pectin – add $\frac{1}{8}$th extra fruit to compensate.) There are also tins of sliced cooked oranges ready to have sugar added and be made into marmalade at any time.

Lemons, limes and grapefruit all make excellent marmalade, alone or in combination. The sweet oranges and tangerine varieties are better mixed with one or the other of the sharper citrus fruits. Tangerine peel gives delicious additional flavour to a delicate marmalade.

Apart from the breakfast table, marmalade is useful in the kitchen for making sweet sauces, adding to cooked apples, quinces or pears, making tarts, and a spoonful, with the peel chopped, is often added to a fruit cake or gingerbread mixture.

Equipment for marmalade-making

The equipment needed for marmalade is much the same as that for making jam. A shallow **preserving pan** is essential for the preliminary simmering. A **small stiff brush** is useful when washing the fruit.

A **chopping board,** a **vegetable peeler,** and a **really sharp stainless knife** make for efficient slicing of peel. A **mincer** or **shredder** is helpful, but not essential. **One or two large mixing bowls** are needed for soaking the fruit and peel, and a smaller bowl, with a **square of butter muslin** or **cheese-cloth** to drape over it, is needed to take the pips and oddments of pith.

A **good grater** and **lemon squeezer.**

A **large wooden preserving spoon** and **5ml spoon or teaspoon.**

A **skimming spoon.**

A **measure or two for the water** and filling the

jars. A **jam funnel** ensures cleaner jars when filling.

A **jelly bag** or other suitable material for straining, with string, and a **stand** are required for the jelly marmalades.

Plenty of clean **standard-sized jars. Waxed discs, covers, fine string or strong rubber bands, or twist-top lids, labels** and **scissors.**

A **pressure cooker** saves a lot of time when softening peel, and two or three batches can be finished together in the preserving pan. Small quantities, usually up to 5 jars, can be finished, using the pressure cooker without the lid. The instructions of the maker should be followed here.

Method for marmalade-making

While many of the jam-making principles apply to marmalade too, one or two extra points should be noted.

Preparing fruit

Fresh fruit should be used as soon as possible after it has been bought, or else frozen for later use.

The fruit needs washing well as dirt may have collected in the rough skins, and skins are waxed with a fungicide – a brush may be needed for the Seville oranges.

The peel may have thicker pith than usual and some can be removed, but do reserve it. A sharp knife is essential for slicing as tough peel and a blunt knife make cutting tiring work.

Cut through the peel in quarters, remove and divide again if large, then slice as you prefer or the recipe indicates. Cut up the fruit on a large flat dish to catch the juice.

Much of the pectin is contained in the pith and pips so these are kept for cooking with the pulp and peel. Lay a piece of muslin over a bowl and put the pips in this, adding any discarded pith. If the pith is in large pieces, chop it across so it takes up less room. Tie the bag loosely but neatly. Tie string firmly round the top so it can be tied to the handle of the pan later.

When the preparation is finished, it may be more convenient to leave the actual making of marmalade until the next day. Put the pulp, juice, sliced peel and muslin bag into a large bowl, pour over the measured water, cover and leave to soak overnight. But the marmalade may be made right away if you prefer to finish the process in one day. In this case, put it all into the preserving pan with the muslin bag tied to the handle, so that it hangs down into the pan. A nut of butter or 5ml (1 teaspoon) of glycerine rubbed on the bottom of the pan will help to reduce excessive scum later.

Preliminary cooking

An important stage is to simmer slowly for $1\frac{1}{2}$–2 hours, stirring occasionally, until well reduced and the peel is so tender that a piece of it can be disintegrated when rubbed between your thumb and fingertips. This process also extracts the pectin. The natural acid in the fruit may need supplementing with lemon juice, citric or tartaric acid and if so, this will be stated in the recipe. It is a common error to hurry this simmering stage, but that results in toughened peel and more boiling with the sugar will be necessary.

Another method is to boil (or pressure cook) the fruits whole before cutting them up (see Seville Orange Marmalade, whole fruit method, page 41). This makes cutting much easier.

Have the warmed sugar (see page 15) ready. Squeeze the muslin bag against the sides of the pan with the back of the preserving spoon and remove it.

Adding the sugar

Stir in the sugar to dissolve it thoroughly then bring to a fast rolling boil. Stir occasionally and begin to test for a set (see page 15) after 10 minutes.

Put the jars to warm (see page 15), they must be perfectly dry on removal from the oven.

Testing for setting

A set should be obtained after 15–20 minutes' boiling, the spoon test is useful here, turning a little on the spoon above the pan until the last few drops cling and cut away slowly in a flake.

Any scum should be skimmed off right away with a metal spoon as it sets quickly and will be difficult to remove once it clings round the peel.

Potting and covering

Turn off the heat. Put a wooden board on the table, with the measure, funnel, damp cloth and covers.

Cool the marmalade until a thin skin forms and the liquid has thickened just enough to hold the peel and prevent it from floating.

Remove the jars from the oven, place them on the board, near the pan to avoid drips, and fill them to within 5mm ($\frac{1}{4}$in) of the top. Wipe the rims free of any splashes.

Cover with twist-top lids if you have them, or fit a waxed disc, waxed side down, to fit closely on the top of each jar.

Marmalade is often sealed when cold, so cover it with a clean cloth and leave it overnight or as convenient, then put on the covers and seal them airtight. Wipe the jars if there are any drips. Label neatly and store them, as far as possible, in a dry, cool cupboard, away from strong light.

Should you have misjudged the boiling time, and the marmalade is runny when cold, turn it all back into the preserving pan and reboil until you have a confirmed set. Make sure the jars are clean and dry, and finish as before.

Making marmalade

1 Wash fruit well, cut it up, putting pips and pith in muslin bag. **2** Turn into preserving pan with required amount of water and simmer slowly till peel is soft and quantity is reduced to half. **3** Add the warmed sugar and stir to dissolve. **4** Boil rapidly for 10 minutes and test for setting. **5** When ready, skim at once and allow to cool slightly. **6** Stir round and pour into warmed jars. Cover with a cloth until cold. Then cover, seal and label.

Marmalades

Guidelines for making marmalade

1 Wash fruit well, using a stiff brush.
2 Cut up the fruit. Put pips and discarded pith into a muslin bag.
3 Soak pulp, juice, sliced peel and muslin bag in the water in a bowl.
4 Prepare the preserving pan with butter or glycerine.
5 Turn contents of bowl into the pan and tie muslin bag to handle, so that it hangs into the pan.
6 Simmer gently for 1½–2 hours to soften peel.
7 Warm sugar and jars.
8 Stir sugar into pan, dissolve thoroughly, then bring to a fast boil. Test for set after 10 minutes.
9 Fill jars to within 5mm (¼in) of brim.
10 Cover, seal, label and store.

Marmalade
The tools for the job — much the same as for jam but be sure the knife is really sharp as Seville oranges are tough-skinned. The muslin over the bowl is for pips and pith, and is tied into a bag and hung to the spoon to add extra pectin to the mixture.

What can go wrong

Discoloration. If the fruit is sliced with a carbon steel knife, discoloration can occur.

Burning. If insufficient water is used to the proportion of fruit, the peel cannot soften during the preliminary cooking and the contents of the pan could burn easily.

Tough peel. If long, slow simmering to soften the peel is not carried out, the peel will be tough in the finished marmalade. This slow, lengthy cooking also frees the pectin and ensures good reduction.

Failure to set. If extra lemon juice, or citric or tartaric acid is not added where indicated, a good set may not be obtained, since the total amount of acid present in citrus fruit is not always sufficient in proportion to the amount of finished marmalade. This applies especially if using sweet oranges, tangerines and grapefruit.

Poor flavour and colour. Failure to reduce the contents of the pan adequately before adding the sugar means prolonged boiling after adding it; this can spoil both flavour and colour. At this stage 15–20 minutes' rapid boiling should effect a set.

Crystallisation. If the sugar is not dissolved before bringing to the boil, crystallisation is made more likely. Too much sugar can also cause this.

Scum. If skimming is not done at once when the marmalade has reached setting point, scum will cling to pieces of peel, be distributed through the marmalade and so spoil the appearance.

Floating peel and bubbles. If the marmalade is not cooled until a skin begins to form and then gently stirred before potting, the peel will float and be unevenly distributed. On the other hand, if cooled too much, bubbles can form on pouring and will be trapped through the marmalade.

Mould. If the jars are not absolutely clean and dry, mould will probably occur during storage.

Cracked jars. If the jars are not warm when filled, condensation may occur, and the jars may crack.

Shrinkage. If the jars are not filled almost to the top, shrinkage while cooling results, and the growth of bacteria is encouraged.

Recipes for marmalades

Sweet Orange Marmalade

1kg (2lb) sweet oranges
2 Seville oranges
2kg (4lb) sugar
10ml (2 teaspoons) citric acid
2½ litres (4 pints) water

Yield: 7 jars

Wash the fruit, remove the peel in quarters, if the pith is rather thick some can be removed, but reserve it. Shred the peel to the desired thickness and put into a bowl with half the water, cover and leave overnight. Cut up the fruit, putting the pips into a muslin bag with any reserved pith, and put it all into another bowl with the acid and rest of the water; cover and also leave overnight.

Mix the contents of the two bowls and simmer, with the bag of pips, 1½–2 hours, until the liquid is well reduced and the peel is soft.

Remove the muslin bag, add the warmed sugar, dissolve slowly, then boil fast for 15 minutes. Test for a set and when obtained remove any scum quickly. If the peel floats, stand the marmalade to cool until a thin skin forms. Fill the warmed jars, lay on waxed discs and cover when cold.

Four Fruit Marmalade

2 grapefruit
4 sweet oranges
4 lemons
750g (1½lb) green cooking
　apples
3kg (6lb) sugar
4 litres (7 pints) water

Yield: 10 jars

Wash the fruit. Cut the grapefruit, oranges and lemons downwards into four or five sections and slice thinly, putting the pips and any thick pith into muslin. Peel, quarter and core the apples, adding the peel and cores to the muslin bag, then cut up the apples and put all together into a large bowl with the water. Cover and soak overnight.

Turn it all into the preserving pan and simmer until the water is reduced to about half and the peel is well softened. Squeeze the muslin bag and remove it. Add the warmed sugar, stir gently to dissolve it, then boil rapidly. Test after ten minutes and then every minute or two until a little will set on testing. Skim, cool a little, stir once or twice, pour into heated jars and finish as usual.

Seville and Sweet Orange Marmalade

6 Seville oranges
3 sweet oranges
1 lemon
2¾ kg (6lb) sugar
3½ litres (6 pints) water

Yield: 10 jars

Wash the fruit, cut in half and squeeze the juice putting it into the preserving pan. Slice the peel finely and add to the juice in the pan with the water. Tie the pips in muslin together with any stringy bits and hard ends of peel, put this also into the pan and simmer gently for 2 hours or until the peel is soft. Remove and squeeze the bag of pips, put in the warmed sugar, stir to dissolve, then boil fast and begin testing for a set after 10 minutes. Skim quickly, cool slightly to suspend peel, pot, cover and seal as usual.

Citrus fruits

As well as the bitter orange, other citrus fruits – lime, sweet orange, lemon, grapefruit also make well-flavoured marmalade.

It is important to follow either the imperial or the metric weights and measures in any one recipe. Do not mix them.

Lemon Marmalade

9 large lemons
Sugar (see below)
3½ litres (6 pints) water

Yield: 7 jars

Wash and dry the lemons. Remove the peel thinly with a peeler and cut it into fine strips, put it into the preserving pan with the water. Cut the pith from the lemons, put half of it into a muslin bag and discard the rest. Cut up the pulp, catching all the juice, and add the pips to the muslin bag.

Put the pulp and bag of pith and pips with the water and peel, bring to simmering point and cook gently 1½–2 hours until it is reduced to about half the original quantity and the peel is very soft. Remove the muslin bag squeezing it well. Measure the contents of the pan and for every 500ml (1 pint) weigh and add 400g (1lb) sugar. Dissolve, then boil rapidly. Test for setting after 15 minutes, then every few minutes until setting point is reached. Skim quickly, then leave to cool until a thin skin forms. Stir round once or twice and pot and seal as usual.

Seville Orange Marmalade

6 Seville oranges
2 lemons
2kg (4lb) sugar
2¾ litres (4½ pints) water

Yield: 7 jars

Wash the oranges and lemons, quarter and slice thinly across, catching all the juice, and discarding the pips and hard ends of the quarters. Put the sliced fruit into a large bowl with the water, cover and leave for 24 hours, then put into the preserving pan and simmer slowly until reduced to half and the peel is softened. This may take 2–2½ hours. If inexperienced, a chalk mark on the outside of the pan helps you to judge the level of reduction. Add the warmed sugar, stir to dissolve, then boil rapidly for 10 minutes and begin to test for setting. When setting point has been reached, skim at once, cool for about 15 minutes, stir round gently and pour into heated jars. Cover and seal as usual.

Three Fruit Marmalade

2 grapefruit
2 sweet oranges
4 lemons
3kg (6lb) sugar
3 litres (6 pints) water

Yield: 10 jars

Choose large, thin-skinned fruit and wash them. Quarter the oranges and lemons, cut the grapefruit into eighths and slice them all finely; save the pips and tie them in a muslin bag, with any hard ends or stringy bits. Put all together into a large bowl, cover with the water and soak for 24 hours.

Turn it all into the preserving pan and simmer for about 2 hours until the peel is very soft. Squeeze and remove the muslin bag. Add the warmed sugar, stir until dissolved, then boil rapidly for about 20–25 minutes or until setting point has been reached. Skim, cool about half an hour, stir to distribute the peel evenly, then pour into warmed jars. Cover and seal as usual.

Recipes for marmalades

Mincer Method Marmalade

6 Seville oranges
2 sweet oranges
2 lemons
3kg (6lb) sugar
4 litres (7 pints) water

Yield: 10 jars

Wash the fruit, halve, squeeze the juice and put it into a large bowl with the pips tied in a muslin bag. Put the orange and lemon rinds through a mincer, catching any juice, and add to the bowl with the water. Leave to soak for 24 hours. Turn it all into the preserving pan and simmer for about 2 hours to soften the peel and reduce the liquid by half.

Remove the bag of pips, squeezing well, and add the warmed sugar. Dissolve over gentle heat then boil fast 20–30 minutes or until a test shows the marmalade is setting. Skim, leave to cool a little then pour into warmed jars and seal.

Mincing the peel, instead of slicing it, saves a lot of time. The marmalade will not be quite as clear but it has a very good flavour.

Grapefruit and Ginger Marmalade

3 large thin-skinned grapefruit
3 lemons
2¼kg (5lb) sugar
5ml (1 teaspoon) tartaric acid
A piece of root ginger
175g (6oz) chopped crystallised ginger
3 litres (6 pints) water

Yield: 8 jars

Wash the fruit well and cut in half. Using a grapefruit knife, remove all the flesh and juice into a preserving pan. Tie the pips in a muslin bag with the lemon skins and root ginger; cut the grapefruit skins into short fairly fine strips and add these to the pan with the water and acid. Simmer for 1½ hours or until the peel is very soft and the contents of the pan reduced to about half.

Remove the muslin bag and squeeze it well, stir the warmed sugar into the pan until dissolved, put in the crystallised ginger and boil rapidly, stirring slowly until, on testing, setting point is reached. Leave to cool until a thin skin forms, stir to distribute the ginger and peel, then pot and seal as usual.

Dark Thick-cut Marmalade

1kg (2lb) Seville oranges
1kg (2lb) granulated or preserving sugar
1kg (2lb) demerara sugar
Juice of 2 large lemons
30ml (2 tablespoons) black treacle
2½ litres (4 pints) water

Yield: 7 jars

Wash the fruit and squeeze the juice, putting the pips into muslin. Cut the orange peel into short 5mm (¼in) wide strips and put them into the preserving pan with the lemon and orange juice and the water. Add any coarse pieces of pith to the pips, tie into a bag and put into the pan. Simmer gently for 2 hours or more, making sure the peel is really tender as it is cut larger than usual, and that the liquid is well reduced.

Squeeze and remove the muslin bag. Stir in all the warmed sugar, add the treacle, and when the sugar has dissolved, boil quickly. Test for setting after ten minutes and repeat every minute or two until a set is obtained. Skim quickly and cool the marmalade until a skin is forming. Stir to prevent the peel rising when poured into the warmed jars. Pot and cover as usual.

Pineapple and Lemon Marmalade

1 good-sized firm pineapple
4 lemons with thin skins
2kg (4lb) sugar
1¾ litres (3 pints) water

Yield: 6 jars

Peel the pineapple, cut in thin slices and remove the core (but keep it); cut again into small segments; put into a bowl, sprinkle with half the sugar and leave overnight. Wash and quarter the lemons, then cut into fine slices, removing the pips into a muslin bag with the pieces of core from the pineapple. Put the lemon slices and bag into the preserving pan with the water. Simmer gently until the peel is soft and the liquid reduced by about half. Squeeze and remove the bag, add the pineapple pieces and sugar from the bowl together with the rest of the sugar, dissolve, then boil fast until the marmalade thickens and will set on testing. Skim, pot and seal as usual.

Tangerine Jelly Marmalade

1kg (2lb) tangerines
1 medium-sized grapefruit
2 lemons
1½kg (3¼lb) sugar
5ml (1 level teaspoon) citric acid
3 litres (5¼ pints) water

Yield: 5 jars

Wash the fruit, peel the tangerines and cut the peel into fine strips to give about 125g (4oz), put these into a muslin bag.

Peel the grapefruit and lemons and chop the peel coarsely. Cut up all the fruit and put it with the peel into the preserving pan. Add the water, acid and muslin bag, and put to simmer gently. As tangerine peel disintegrates with long boiling, remove it after half an hour, draining it over the pan without squeezing, then rinse the peel in a strainer and leave it on a clean cloth.

Continue simmering the pulp and chopped peel for 1½ hours then strain through a jelly bag or scalded cloth overnight. Put the juice back into the rinsed preserving pan, reheat, add the warmed sugar and dissolve. Bring to a fast boil, add the tangerine peel and continue boiling rapidly until a little will set when tested. Skim, and cool about 15 minutes to prevent the peel floating. Pot and seal as usual.

Seville Orange Marmalade
(whole fruit method)

9 Seville oranges
Sugar

Yield: 7 jars

Wash the oranges and put into a large saucepan with enough water to cover them well. Simmer for one hour, change the water and simmer for a further hour until the oranges are so tender that a match or head of a pin will easily pierce the rind.

Take out the oranges, cool them and reserve the liquid, then take off the peel and slice it into fine shreds. Cut up the pulp, discarding the pips, weigh it and to every 400g (1lb) pulp allow 600g (1¼lb) sugar and 500ml (1 pint) of the liquid in which the oranges were last boiled, made up if necessary with water.

continued overleaf

Lemon and Lime Marmalade

500g (1½lb) lemons
500g (1½lb) limes
2kg (6lb) sugar
2½ litres (6 pints) water

Yield: 7–9 jars

Wash the fruit, remove the peel thinly, and cut off the pith, reserving some of it. Cut the peel into fine strips, then cut up the fruit, putting the pips and pith into a muslin bag. Put the fruit and water into the preserving pan with the peel and the muslin bag. Simmer slowly for 1½–2 hours until the peel has softened and the contents of the pan are reduced to half. Squeeze and remove the bag. Stir in the warmed sugar and when it has dissolved, boil fast until a little will set on testing, after about 15–20 minutes.

Remove any scum, cool 20 minutes or so, until the peel no longer floats, stir round once or twice and pour into warmed jars. Cover and tie down as usual.

Put the pulp, sugar and liquid into the preserving pan, stir over low heat to dissolve the sugar, then add the peel and bring to a fast boil for 10 minutes. Begin testing for a set and when this has been reached, skim, turn off the heat and leave the marmalade to cool until a skin begins to form. Stir to even out the peel then pour into warm jars, cover and seal as usual.

Pressure-cooker Marmalade

500g (1½lb) Seville oranges
Juice of 2 small lemons
1kg (3lb) sugar
625ml (1½ pints) water

Yield: 3–5 jars

Wash the oranges, halve, remove the pulp and cut it up, tying the pips in a muslin bag. Shred the peel to the thickness you prefer. Remove the trivet or rack from the pressure cooker and put in the pulp, lemon juice, half the water, the shredded peel and the bag of pips. Cook at 'medium' (10lb) pressure setting for 15 minutes.

Reduce pressure at room temperature; squeeze and remove the bag of pips, add the other half of the water and bring to boiling point in the open pan; add the warmed sugar, stirring to dissolve it, then boil rapidly and test for setting after 5 minutes, continue testing every minute or two until setting point is reached. Skim, cool until a thin skin forms, stir once or twice then fill into warmed jars. Cover and seal as usual. Only make one batch at a time – do not try to double the quantity.

Miss Tucker's Marmalade 1856

'Take 20 Seville oranges, take their weight in sugar, grate the rinds of ten into the sugar, pare the other ten rather thick. Put the parings into cold water, boil half an hour, repeat this three times in fresh water which will make them tender and extract the bitter. Drain them quite dry and cut them into thin strips about half an inch long. Cut the oranges, squeeze out all the pulp – from this take out the pips and stringy parts. To the remainder add sugar and let it boil three quarters of an hour on a very slow fire. No water is necessary.'

Half this quantity makes about 5 or 6 standard jars of excellent breakfast marmalade.
Note: Although not actually mentioned it is understood that the strips of peel would be added to the pulp, and the sugar gently dissolved before boiling.

Jelly Marmalade

4 Seville oranges
4 sweet oranges
2 lemons
Sugar
4 litres (7 pints) water

Yield: 5 jars

Wash the fruit. Remove the peel thinly from one Seville orange, one sweet orange and one lemon, shred this finely and simmer it in 1 litre (2 pints) water in a covered pan for an hour until tender. Reserve the drained peel and the liquid. Cut up all the fruit fairly small and simmer, in the liquid drained from the strips of peel and the remaining 3 litres (5 pints) of water, for about 2 hours, then turn it all into a scalded jelly bag or cloth and leave overnight to drip.

Dark and chunky
Marmalades vary from the pale transparent to the dark chunky. Above are the ingredients for dark thick-cut (page 40). Black treacle adds to the rich, dark look.

Measure the juice, allow 400g (1lb) sugar to 500ml (1 pint) of juice. Put the juice into the clean preserving pan, reheat and stir in the warmed sugar; when dissolved add the reserved shreds of peel and boil rapidly until the marmalade will set on testing. Skim, leave to cool about 15 minutes, stir to distribute the peel and fill into warmed jars. Cover as usual.

Fruit cheeses, butters & curds

The old-fashioned kissing-cousins of jams and jellies – the fruit cheeses, butters and curds – have been sadly neglected in these days of mass production. Once their glowing opaque colours were on pantry shelves in almost every country home. You have only to look in old cookery books to find recipes for them. Now, though you still sometimes see lemon curd on the supermarket shelves, fruit cheeses and butters have almost entirely disappeared from the market. Yet they are simple to make and very good to eat, and they are so different from the more usual preserves that they are well worth trying. And they are a way of using windfalls, hedgerow fruits and unusual garden crops.

Once you have learned the principles for making them, you can invent your own combinations of ingredients, using the same methods. Slivers of almonds, walnuts or candied fruits can be added to make a richer jar. There are interesting ways of presenting them. Try slabs of fruit cheese with clotted cream, to be eaten with a spoon. Or put a fruit butter in a Swiss roll, top curd tarts with a meringue. You can find unlimited new uses for these rediscovered tangs and textures. And they are certainly a delicious way of husbanding your resources.

Fruit cheeses

A fruit cheese is halfway between a jam and a jelly. The fruit is sieved, but it is cooked to a stiff purée with sugar, so testing for setting is not necessary. These preserves were originally called cheeses because they were often eaten instead of a cheese course. They were potted in special moulds, turned out when wanted and served cut in thick slices. Bread and butter was eaten with them and sometimes cream cheese. Now they are eaten with cold meats or curries and are an alternative to pickles or chutneys. Because of the amount of sugar used in them they keep well and improve with keeping – so keep them for two to three months before using them. They can be stored for up to 12 months. Fruit cheeses need a lot of fruit, so only make them when there is a glut.

Fruit butters

These are quite like fruit cheeses, but take less sugar. The texture is much softer and they are sometimes spiced. They are made in the same way, and are usually spread on bread and butter, but they can also be used in trifles, as fillings for sandwich cakes, or as sauces for ice-cream. As they contain less sugar they do not keep well, so should be used up fairly quickly.

Make them in small quantities, do not store for more than three to six months, and inspect your jars from time to time – if they are not kept in a dry place, they can go mouldy quickly.

Fruit curds

Fruit curds are made with the juice and grated rinds of citrus fruits or with fruit purées, sweetened, enriched and thickened with sugar, eggs and butter. Make in small quantities, store in a refrigerator, and keep only up to three months, inspecting your jars frequently. They can be used in many different ways – for instance, for curd tarts, curd puffs and as cake fillings, or sometimes as a sharp sauce for meats.

Equipment for making fruit cheeses, butters and curds

A **large heavy saucepan** or **preserving pan** – stainless steel, aluminium, or undamaged enamel – for cooking fruit.

A **smaller saucepan** for butters.

A **double saucepan,** or a **basin** standing over a pan of boiling water, for curds.

For fruit cheeses: small, shallow, old-fashioned china moulds, if you have them, or small jars – these could be cheap tumblers; the important point is that the neck must not be of less diameter than the base, because the cheese has to be turned out. If you want to use a deeper mould, warm it slightly and ease the cheese away from it with a knife. Le Parfait 'Terrine' jars are also suitable (see bottling chapter).

For butters and curds: glass jars. Twist-top jars are **not** suitable for curds, which are not brought to a high enough temperature to make a seal.

Wooden spoons with long handles.

A **ladle.**

Scales.

A **measuring jug.**

A **grater** and a **lemon squeezer** for citrus fruits.

A **nylon sieve,** and **liquidiser** (optional).

A **stainless steel knife.**

A **perforated metal spoon** with a long handle for removing pips, stones and scum (if any).

An **oven cloth** or **glove.**

Waxed discs and **plastic covers,** or **paraffin wax,** or **lids.**

Labels.

Method for making fruit cheeses, butters and curds

Suitable fruits

Apples, apricots, black currants, crab-apples, cranberries, damsons, lemons, medlars, oranges, pears, plums and quinces.

Preparation of fruit purée

Brush the pan with glycerine to prevent fruit sticking. Wash, pick over and if necessary cut up the fruit, but do not peel or core (stones can be removed when the fruit is boiling). Just cover with cold water and gently simmer in the covered pan until very soft and pulpy, then liquidise and/or sieve to remove pips and skin and to make a purée. Don't sieve too much at a time, as this may cause waste. This purée is the start for fruit cheeses, butters and some curds.

Fruit cheeses

Weigh the purée in a bowl, first weighing the bowl. Allow 500g (1lb) sugar to each 500g (1lb) pulp (do not try to cut down the amount of sugar).

Put the sugar in the pan with the fruit and cook very slowly until the sugar has dissolved, then cook, still very slowly, until the 'cheese' is thick. This may take from $\frac{3}{4}$–1 hour. Stir frequently, then continuously, as the mixture thickens, to prevent burning. The cheese is sufficiently thick when a wooden spoon drawn across it shows the bottom of the pan, and the mixture only slowly recovers it. Big flat bubbles will also appear. For a beginner, it may be difficult to judge when the consistency is right. Care should be taken not to overcook, and (for a beginner) it is best only to make small quantities, about 1kg (2lb), at a time.

Warm moulds or jars and brush inside with glycerine or oil to prevent sticking. Spoon in the hot cheese. Cover and store as jam (see page 16), or if using moulds, use paraffin wax – it should be spooned on to 3mm ($\frac{1}{8}$in) deep, while the cheese is still hot and covered when cold. The cheese can be turned out and cut in slices.

If the cheese is not set, it should be boiled again.

It is possible to use the pulp from jelly to make cheeses (see page 28), but only strong flavoured pulps, such as black currant or plum, should be considered.

Fruits to choose
Fruits with a tang or a texture or both – like plums, damsons, pears, quinces – are the kind to use.

Fruit butters
Weigh the fruit purée and allow 250–375g (8–12oz) sugar (according to sweetness of fruit) to each 500g (1lb) fruit purée. Put the purée back in the pan, add the sugar, and spices, too, if being used. Stir and heat until the sugar is dissolved. Continue to cook until smooth, creamy and thick and there is no free liquid. Stir frequently. Pour into warm pots, put waxed discs on top, or use paraffin wax (see cheeses), then cover and store in a cool, dry cupboard.

Fruit curds
The fruit purée or juice and rinds of citrus fruits should be cooked slowly in a double saucepan, or a large basin over a pan of boiling water, with sugar and butter (which is best unsalted), until the sugar has dissolved, and the butter has melted. Then lightly beaten new-laid eggs are strained into the mixture. Now is the moment when the skill comes in, for it must be cooked gently and stirred frequently until it just begins to thicken and will coat the back of a wooden spoon. It must not be allowed to boil or it will curdle. As it continues to thicken, remove from the heat and pour at once into small warmed pots. Put a waxed disc on each pot, to cover the surface completely, and smooth it over pressing down lightly with the finger to get rid of any air pockets. Cover, label, store in the refrigerator. Twist-top jars are **not** suitable for curds.

Fruit cheeses, butters & curds

Guidelines for making fruit cheeses and butters

1 Choose and prepare your fruit.
2 Rub the pan with glycerine and simmer the fruit slowly, then liquidise and/or sieve to make a purée.
3 Weigh the purée and calculate the amount of sugar needed. Add sugar to heated purée and dissolve slowly.
4 For fruit cheeses, stir till very thick. For fruit butters, stir till thick, smooth and creamy.
5 Pot, cover and store.

Fruit curds

1 Cook the juice and rind of citrus fruits, or a fruit purée, slowly in a double saucepan with sugar and unsalted butter, until the sugar has dissolved and the butter has melted.
2 Strain in lightly beaten new-laid eggs.

3 Cook gently, stirring frequently, until just beginning to thicken. Do **not** boil.
4 Remove from heat and pour at once into warmed pots.
5 Cover and store.

What can go wrong

Burning. Saucepan not heavy enough; sugar undissolved before boiling; not stirred frequently; saucepans not brushed with glycerine or butter.
Mould. Jars not filled to the top; jars not properly dried before filling; jars not properly sealed.
Fermentation. Insufficient cooking; not enough sugar; incorrect storing.
Air bubbles. Preserve poured into jars too slowly.
Too liquid – especially with fruit cheeses. Insufficient cooking; not enough sugar.
Deterioration – especially with fruit curd. Kept too long or stored in too warm a place.

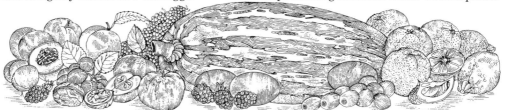

Damson Cheese

Damsons
Water
500g (1lb) sugar to each 500g (1lb) fruit purée

Wash damsons, remove stalks. Put in heavy pan, just cover with water, put on the lid. Simmer until tender. Remove stones, then liquidise fruit and/or sieve. Weigh the purée, put it back in the pan, warm through, add the required amount of sugar, stir until dissolved. Cook gently until really thick, stir frequently. Pot, cover and store.

Quince Cheese

Ripe quinces
Water to cover
500g (1lb) sugar to each 500g (1lb) fruit purée

Wipe the fuzz off the quinces, then cut them up small. There is no need to peel them or to remove cores. Put the fruit in a heavy pan, just cover with water, put on the lid and simmer until the fruit is quite soft. Then proceed as for Damson Cheese (above).

Medlar Cheese

Medlars are rarely seen now; some old gardens have a tree and they are on sale in Greek shops occasionally. They make excellent preserves.

Medlars, washed and cut up
Juice of 1 lemon
Water
To each 500g (1lb) fruit purée allow:
500g (1lb) sugar
Small pinch of ground cardamom (or to taste)

Squeeze the lemon. Put medlars and lemon juice in a pan, cover with water.
Cook slowly until mushy. Liquidise and/or sieve. Add the cardamom and sugar.
Now follow instructions in method for Fruit Cheeses (see page 44).

American Spicy Apple Butter

Apples
375g (12oz) sugar to each 500g (1lb) fruit pulp
Cider vinegar or water to cover
Spices such as cinnamon, cloves, allspice and

ginger to taste
Grated lemon rind (optional)

Wash the apples, cut them up small. Cover with the cider vinegar or water, add spices and lemon rind. Simmer until fruit has softened. Now follow instructions in method for Fruit Butters (see page 45).

Plum Gumbo

2kg (4lb) plums
1½kg (3lb) sugar
250g (8oz) sultanas, chopped finely
2 thin-skinned oranges
1 thin-skinned lemon
125g (4oz) small walnut pieces

Yield: 3kg (5–6lb)

Peel the orange and lemon rind finely, without any white pith. Chop the rinds finely, squeeze the juice. Put the rind, juice, plums, sugar and sultanas in a heavy pan. Simmer until thick and the plums are cooked and soft – at this stage you will be able to lift out the stones. Stir in the walnuts, continue simmering until it is very thick for another 10 minutes. Pot, cover and seal.

Cranberry Butter

Cranberries can often be bought deep frozen, or fresh in the autumn. They make unique preserves, which are even better than red currant jelly to serve with ham, mutton or lamb.

Cranberries
Water to cover
375g (12oz) sugar to each 500g (1lb) fruit purée

Wash the cranberries, if necessary, cover with water. Simmer till soft.

Liquidise and/or sieve. Now follow instructions in method for Fruit Butters (see page 45).

Dried Apricot or Peach Curd

350g (12oz) dried apricots, soaked overnight
Juice and rind of 1 lemon
350g (12oz) caster sugar
225g (8oz) unsalted butter
4 large eggs

Yield: 2kg (4lb)

Cook the fruit with the lemon juice and rind until soft in the water used for soaking. Liquidise or sieve. Now follow instructions in method for Fruit Curds (see page 45).

Lemon Curd

275ml (11floz) lemon juice from 5–6 juicy lemons
5–6 large new-laid eggs
200g (8oz) unsalted butter
500g (1¼lb) caster sugar

Yield: about 1½kg (3lb)

Wash the lemons, grate the rinds, squeeze and strain the juice.

Now follow instructions in method for Fruit Curds (see page 45).

Orange Curd

275ml (11floz) orange and lemon juice, from about 3 large thin-skinned oranges and 1 large lemon
200g (8oz) unsalted butter
300g (12oz) caster sugar
5–6 large new-laid eggs

Yield: about 1½kg (3lb)

Follow instructions in method for Fruit Curds (see page 45). Lemon juice is added in this recipe to sharpen the flavour which would otherwise taste rather bland.

Marrow and Ginger Curd

2kg (4lb) marrow, peeled and seeds removed
To every 500g (1lb) marrow purée allow:
500g (1lb) sugar
250g (8oz) butter
4–5 eggs
Rind and juice of 2 lemons
100g (4oz) stem ginger, chopped, or 5ml (1 teaspoon) ground ginger

Cook marrow without water in a covered pan until it is really soft, with the ginger and lemon juice and rind. Liquidise or sieve.

Now follow instructions for the preparation of Fruit Curds (see page 45).

Orange Curd and Apple Pie

675g (1½lb) sweetened apple purée flavoured with a little rum
Orange curd
8–10 finely crushed ginger biscuits
3 stiffly beaten egg whites
75g (3oz) caster sugar

Serves 4

Put layers of apple purée, biscuit crumbs and orange curd in a glass ovenproof dish, ending with a layer of crumbs. Fold the sugar into the egg whites, pile on top of the pie, dredge with caster sugar. Bake at 150°C, 300°F, Gas Mark 2, for ¾–1 hour, to set and lightly brown the meringue.

Seedless Raspberry Curd

500g (1lb) raspberries, hulled, washed and drained
500g (1lb) sharp apples, washed and roughly chopped, including peel, cores, etc

To each 500g (1lb) fruit purée, allow:
250g (8oz) unsalted butter
4 large new-laid eggs
500g (1lb) caster sugar
Water

Yield: about 1kg (2lb)

Put the fruit in a pan with very little water, and cook slowly until softened. Then put the fruit through a fine nylon sieve. Measure the purée and put it in a double saucepan, or a bowl over a pan of hot water. Add the required amount of butter and sugar. Heat gently until the sugar has dissolved and the butter has melted, stirring from time to time. Beat the eggs lightly, strain slowly into the butter and sugar mixture. Stir and cook until the mixture thickens. Do not let it boil. Remove from heat when it is thick enough (see page 45). Pot, cover and store.

Fruit Paste (Pâté de fruits)

You might like to turn some of your fruit cheese into the delectable French pâté de fruits. This is how to do it. Make your fruit cheese then, instead of potting it, spread a thin layer 5mm (¼in) thick on a lightly oiled metal baking tray or shallow tin. Let it dry out completely in a dry airy place, or in a very cool oven, if you can spare it. This may take up to 4 days.

Turn the paste over after 48 hours and dry out the other side. It is essential for it to be absolutely dry right through.

Cut it into squares or rectangles, coat with granulated sugar, store in a tin box with a well-fitting lid, with a sprinkling of sugar and waxed or greaseproof paper between each layer.

This keeps well for up to a year and improves with age if kept away from all humidity.

Quince cheese makes an excellent fruit paste. Black currants and damsons, give a good flavour, and greengages, plums and apples are also successful – in fact any fruit cheeses can be used. Serve as sweetmeats at the end of a meal.

47

Fruit cheese, butters, curds

Fruit cheeses, butters and curds
Delicious to eat but most of them are unbuyable, so you have to make them at home. Here, from l. to r. are: plum gumbo (in a pot and on a plate) dried peach curd, spicy apple butter, lemon curd, dried apricot curd (in an old-world mould) and cranberry butter. They're well worth making.

Candied, crystallised & glacé fruits

Candied, crystallised and glacé fruits can be prepared easily at home, and the results are well worth while, being juicier and fresher than many bought fruits. The process is not difficult, but it does take a considerable time, so when planning to make boxes of mixed fruits for gifts, allow 12 to 14 days if you are using tinned fruit or 15 to 18 days for fresh fruit.

Candied is the general term for fruit soaked in a sugar syrup over a period of time.

Crystallised is the term used to describe the rougher 'sparkly' appearance or finish when the candied fruits are rolled in caster or fine granulated sugar.

Glacé is the term used when the candied fruits are dipped in a very heavy syrup; when dried, this gives a clear crisp, glassy appearance.

Candied fruits

Briefly, the candying process consists of soaking the fruit in a hot syrup and gradually increasing the sugar content until the syrup has a honeylike consistency; in this way the fruit is gradually impregnated with sugar. The slow increase to a stronger syrup allows the water present in all fruits to be extracted and the sugar to penetrate. If the process is hurried in any way, the fruit will tend to shrivel and be tough and chewy in texture.

Equipment

Knife for peeling.
Cherry stoner for cherries.
Silver fork for apricots, plums, etc.
Cooking tongs.
Measuring jug.
Scales.
Saucepans.
Bowls of various sizes.
Hydrometer (optional).
Waxed paper.
Small cardboard or **wooden boxes**.

As you will see no special equipment is required for candying fruits, although if you own a hydrometer it can be used to check the density or strength of the syrup in which the fruit is being candied. This will help to guard against increasing the strength of the syrup too rapidly, but careful weighing of the sugar and strict adherence to the timetables should ensure success.

Choosing and preparing fruit

Tinned or fresh fruits may be used; the best are those with a pronounced flavour, as very delicate flavours may be masked by the large amount of sugar absorbed by the fruit.

All fruits, tinned or fresh, should be of good quality, and fresh fruit in particular should not be under- or over-ripe, as this will affect both flavour and texture.

Tinned fruit is a good choice for the beginner as this fruit has already absorbed a certain amount of sugar from the syrup in the tin. This speeds up the process a little and there is less likelihood of the fruit shrivelling. Of the tinned fruits, apricots, pineapple, pears and peaches are the most success-ful, but other fruits are also suitable.

With fresh fruits, apricots, peaches, pears, fleshy plums, figs, greengages and cherries are all suitable. Cherries should be stoned (a cherry stoner is useful), pears and peaches peeled and halved or quartered, and cores and stones removed. Apricots, plums and gages should be pricked lightly all over with a silver fork before use – their stones need not be removed as they will slip out easily after the first two or three processings.

Whether using tinned or fresh fruit, different fruits should **not** be candied in the same syrup, because the flavours will mix.

Method using tinned fruits

Quantities given are sufficient for about 500g (1lb) drained fruit.

Open the tin of fruit, drain the syrup into a measuring jug, and put the fruit into a bowl large enough to hold it when completely covered with syrup.

Make the syrup up to 250ml ($\frac{1}{2}$ pint) with water, place in a saucepan and add 200g (8oz) granulated or caster sugar. Heat gently, stir till the sugar is dissolved, bring to the boil and pour over the fruit. The fruit should be immersed completely in syrup; a small plate or saucer placed on top of the fruit in the bowl will help to keep it submerged. Allow the fruit to stand for 24 hours.

At the end of this time, pour off the syrup into a pan and add 50g (2oz) sugar. Heat gently, stir till the sugar is dissolved, bring to the boil, pour over the fruit. Allow to stand for a further 24 hours. Repeat this process twice more at 24-hour intervals, adding 50g (2oz) sugar each time.

On the fifth day, drain the syrup into a pan, add 75g (3oz) sugar; heat gently, and stir until the sugar is dissolved. Now add the fruit, bring to the boil and simmer gently for 3–4 minutes. Return the fruit and syrup to the bowl and leave for 48 hours or longer.

Repeat this process and if the syrup when cool has the consistency of thick, but clear honey, leave the fruit to soak for 3 or 4 days. Fruits vary a little in their capacity to absorb sugar, and the density of the syrup in tinned fruit varies with the different kinds of fruit, cherries and plums and pineapple usually being in a thinner syrup. If the syrup at this stage seems thin, boil it once more with another 75g (3oz) of sugar, add fruit and simmer for 3–4 minutes. Gentle boiling of the fruit in the final stages helps to make it plump and juicy.

When the fruit has been soaking for 3 days or longer (it will keep for up to 2 weeks in the heavy syrup), drain off the syrup and place the pieces of fruit on a wire rack or cake tray, which should stand over a plate so that the syrup is caught as it drains off.

Put the wire tray of fruit in a very cool oven (110°C, 225°F, Gas Mark $\frac{1}{4}$) and turn the fruit occasionally during the drying process, which will take about 12 hours at this temperature. The tray of fruit can equally well be placed in an airing cupboard, but in this case the drying process may take 2–3 days.

The fruit is dry enough when the surface is no longer sticky. Pack in wooden or cardboard boxes, using waxed paper to separate the layers. The box or container must not be sealed or airtight, as this may cause the fruit to go mouldy.

Store in a cool, dry place for up to one year, but it is best eaten within six months.

Method using fresh fruit

Quantities given are for about 500g (1lb) of fruit.

Place the prepared fruit (see opposite) in sufficient boiling water to cover it and cook gently until it is just tender. Care is required as over-cooking will spoil the shape and texture, too little cooking will give poor colour and tough texture.

Take 250ml ($\frac{1}{2}$ pint) of water in which the fruit was cooked and add 150g (6oz) of granulated or caster sugar. Heat gently, stir till the sugar is dissolved, bring to the boil, pour the boiling syrup over the fruit and leave for 24 hours. As with tinned fruit, take care that the fruit is completely immersed in the syrup.

At the end of this time, drain the syrup into a pan and add 50g (2oz) of sugar, stir till dissolved, bring to the boil, pour over the fruit again and leave for 24 hours. Repeat this last process five times more, after which the procedure is the same as for tinned fruits, the eighth day for fresh fruits being the same as the fifth day for tinned fruits.

Crystallised and glacé finishes

To produce a crystallised finish to your fruit, dip each piece of finished candied fruit quickly into boiling water (using a fork or cooking tongs). Shake off any excess moisture, then roll each piece in caster or fine granulated sugar. Allow to dry off before packing.

A glacé finish necessitates making a further fresh syrup. Dissolve 500g (1lb) sugar in 150ml ($\frac{1}{4}$ pint) water heating gently, bring to the boil and boil for one minute.

Have candied fruit ready, dip pieces in boiling water, again using fork or cooking tongs, shake off excess moisture.

Pour a small quantity of syrup into a **hot** cup or small basin, dip pieces of candied fruit quickly into it, then place on a wire tray. When the syrup in the cup appears cloudy, a fresh portion of hot syrup should be used. Keep the main portion of syrup hot and use a pan with a tightfitting lid to prevent evaporation of syrup.

When all the fruits have been dipped, place the tray in a warm place, either in the oven or an airing cupboard, but the temperature must not exceed 110°C, 225°F, Gas Mark $\frac{1}{4}$. Turn the fruit once or twice during the drying process. It is dry when the coating has hardened – if the coating is broken, the fruit underneath will be tacky. The packing for crystallised and glacé fruits is the same as for candied fruits. Syrups left over after candying fruits are delicious used as sauces.

Processing Timetable Guidelines

Day	Sugar to add	Method	Time for soaking in syrup
One	**Tinned Fruit** 200g (8oz) sugar to 250ml ($\frac{1}{2}$ pint) water and fruit syrup	Dissolve sugar in drained syrup and water, bring syrup to boil, and pour over fruit	24 hours
	Fresh Fruit 150g (6oz) sugar to 250ml ($\frac{1}{2}$ pint) cooking liquid		
Two	50g (2oz)	Dissolve sugar in drained syrup, bring syrup to boil and pour over fruit	24 hours
Three	50g (2oz)	As Day Two	24 hours
Four	50g (2oz)	As Day Two	24 hours
	For **Fresh Fruit** the above process should be repeated on 3 more days. The procedure is then as below.		
Five or Eight	75g (3oz)	Sugar dissolved, fruit added, simmered for 3–4 minutes, then returned to bowl	48 hours
Seven or Ten	75g (3oz)	As above until consistency of thick clear honey when cold	3 or 4 Days
Eleven or Fourteen		Fruit dried in oven or airing cupboard	

Recipes

What can go wrong

Tough, dry or shapeless fruit. If the process is hurried, fruit will be tough and lack juiciness. If using **fresh** fruit, take great care with initial cooking, as fruits can lose their shape if overcooked.

Mouldy or shrunken fruit. As with all preserves, storage is important. An airtight box or container may cause fruit to go mouldy. Boxes should be kept in a cool, dry place. Excessive heat will cause fruit to shrink.

Burns and scalds. Always take care when working with hot sugar syrup, avoid splashes on hands or arms.

Candied Peel, simple method

50g (2oz) sugar to each whole orange or lemon
Water

Fruit should always be washed thoroughly before halving or quartering and removing pulp. Place the peel in a saucepan, cover with water. Simmer gently till peel is tender, generally 1½–2 hours, adding more water if necessary. Add the sugar, stir until dissolved and bring to the boil. Leave for 24 hours in the uncovered pan. At the end of this time re-boil the contents of the pan and simmer gently for 4 minutes. Leave for a further 24 hours (uncovered). Then bring to the boil and simmer gently until the peel has absorbed nearly all the syrup.

Drain, place on a wire tray and dry as for candied fruit in an airing cupboard or very cool oven.

Alternative method of preserving orange peel

Scrub the orange skins in hot water before peeling them from the fruit. Do not take any pith, but do not peel so thinly that you lose the essential oils from the skin. Cut the peel into slivers. Layer peel and sugar (granulated or caster) in a jar until the jar is full, put on the lid and shake well. During the first two weeks, shake the jar occasionally and turn it upside down now and again. Twist-top jam jars are good for preserving peel in this way and if stored in a cool, dark and dry place, the peel will keep its colour and flavour for at least six months.

This method does not work as well with lemon as orange peel. It is a quick and easy way of preserving orange peel, but candied peel (see above) is better when the peel is required for purposes of decoration on cakes, cold sweets etc, or for baking on top of Madeira cakes.

Marrons Glacés

1kg (2lb) sweet chestnuts
500g (1lb) granulated sugar
500g (1lb) glucose
Vanilla essence
Water
500g (1lb) extra sugar for glacé finish

Snip tops of chestnuts, put a few at a time into boiling water and scald for 2–3 minutes. Peel carefully while hot (reheating when necessary), taking care to remove all brown inner skin. When all the nuts are prepared, place in a large pan, cover with cold water, cover pan and bring to simmering point. Simmer very gently until tender, this usually takes from 30–45 minutes.

Meanwhile make a syrup from 500g (1lb) sugar, 300ml (½ pint) water, 500g (1lb) glucose. Bring this syrup to the boil, add the drained chestnuts and bring back to boiling point (in an uncovered pan). Remove from heat but leave the pan in a warm place if possible, replacing the lid.

Next day, reboil the syrup and chestnuts (without the lid on the pan). Again, leave the pan in a warm place overnight, replacing the lid. Repeat this process on the third day, adding about 6 drops vanilla essence before heating the syrup.

Lift the chestnuts out very carefully and drain on a wire rack or tray over a plate. Then follow the same drying process as for fruits, though it may not take quite so long.

For glacé finish, follow the directions given for glacé fruits, using an extra 500g (1lb) sugar and 150ml (¼ pint) water to make the syrup.

Marrons glacés can be packed as for candied fruits, but wrap individual chestnuts in aluminium foil if they are to be kept for three to four months. Do not keep them longer than six months if you want them at their best.

Glacé Grapes

200g (8oz) green grapes
200g (8oz) golden syrup
50g (2oz) unsalted butter
100g (4oz) demerara sugar

Melt the butter in a pan, add the syrup and sugar, stir till dissolved. Bring to the boil and boil gently till a little tested in cold water will harden. Then remove the pan from the heat.

While the mixture cools a little, wipe the grapes, making certain they are clean and dry, and cut them into clusters of 2 or 3. Dip the clusters, one cluster at a time, into the mixture and hang them on string or something similar to set.

The grapes can be served at the end of a meal, or they can be used to decorate cold sweets.

These grapes will not keep very long.

Crystallised Angelica

Angelica stems
100g (4oz) salt
600g (1½lb) sugar
500ml (1 pint) water
Extra caster sugar
These quantities of sugar and water should be enough for about 500g (1lb) angelica

Choose young stems, cut them into suitable lengths and place in a heatproof glass bowl. Cover with the salt dissolved in 1·75 litres (3½ pints) boiling water and leave in the covered bowl for 24 hours. Remove stems from the water, peel carefully, refresh

Crystallised and glacé fruits
Angelica, pears, apricots, cherries, pineapple and figs: all suitable for decorating cakes and puddings, and for eating as sweets, except angelica which is better used for decoration.

in cold water and leave to drain. Make a syrup with the sugar and water and boil gently in an uncovered pan for 10 minutes. Place stems in boiling syrup and simmer gently for 20 minutes.

Remove from syrup and leave to drain on a wire tray for 3 days. At the end of this time, reboil in the same syrup for a further 20 minutes. Lift out, drain and dry in an airing cupboard or somewhere similar for 3–4 days. Roll in caster sugar, store in airtight jars.

Recipes for candied, crystallised

Crystallised Tomatoes

9 or 10 medium-sized ripe but not over-ripe tomatoes

300g (12oz) sugar
500ml (1 pint) water

Wash and dry the tomatoes and cut 4 small slits near the base of each one. Squeeze out as many seeds as possible by pressing the tomatoes down gently, without breaking them. Bring the water to the boil, add the sugar, stir till dissolved, then boil for 10 minutes in an uncovered pan.

Add the tomatoes to the syrup and simmer gently for about 10 minutes, turning occasionally. Remove from the syrup, drain well, roll in caster or granulated sugar, then leave to dry in an airing cupboard or somewhere similar for 48 hours.

It is important not to use over-ripe tomatoes in this recipe. Tomatoes will not keep as long as other candied or crystallised fruits, but they look very attractive cut up and scattered over savoury or sweet salads.

Crystallised Flowers

The most suitable flowers for crystallising are those with good bright colouring and a fairly flat shape. Violets, prim-roses, polyanthus, carnation and rose petals, pansies, forget-me-nots, sweet peas and fruit blossom are all good. There are two methods, and properly stored, the flowers keep equally well whichever is used.

The second method, using gum arabic, produces a stiffer finished product – a little less fragile – but all crystallised flowers should be handled with care.

First Method

Make certain the chosen flowers are clean and dust free. Use a small artist's paint brush to paint the flowers with white of egg. Do this carefully back and front of flowers, as any bare spots will shrivel and may cause

mould. Dredge lightly with cas-ter sugar, back and front, and lay on a wire rack covered with greaseproof paper. Dry in an airing cupboard or a very cool oven for 24 hours, turning once or twice to prevent sticking.

Second Method

Steep 10ml (2 teaspoons) gum arabic in 30ml (2 tablespoons) rose or orange flower water (both these ingredients are available from most chemists) in a screwtop jar for 2–3 days.

Shake the jar occasionally and stir before use. The mixture will be rather sticky. Paint the flowers back and front as in Method 1.

Dredge with caster or granu-lated sugar and dry in an airing cupboard or a very cool oven for 24 hours, turning occasionally to prevent sticking.

When dried, all crystallised flowers should be stored in boxes or tins with tight-fitting lids, between layers of waxed paper.

Keep in a cool, dry place.

Violet or Rose Petal Ice-cream

50g (2oz) crystallised violets or rose petals
500ml (1 pint) double cream, whipped
100g (4oz) fresh brown breadcrumbs (not wholemeal)
100g (4oz) demerara sugar

Serves 6

Crush the crystallised flowers with a rolling pin and mix thoroughly in a bowl with the crumbs and sugar. Fold this mixture gently but thoroughly into the cream. Place in a freezer tray, freeze till firm. Turn out into a bowl, beat for about 2 minutes, then freeze again. The ice-cream can be prettily decor-ated with whole crystallised flowers when served.

Soufflé en Surprise

75g (3oz) chopped candied fruits (any mixture)
1 sponge cake, Victoria or fatless
Block of vanilla ice-cream
3 egg whites
175g (6oz) caster sugar

Serves 6

Glacé cherry
Dip candied fruit in boiling water and shake off moisture.

Make a meringue in the usual way with the egg whites and sugar. Place the sponge cake on a heatproof dish. Remove the ice-cream from the refrigerator, place on top of the sponge and sprinkle with the chopped fruits. Cover completely with mer-ingue and 'flash' in a hot oven (220°C, 425°F, Gas Mark 7) for 3–4 minutes. Serve at once.

Fruity Fudge

50g (2oz) chopped candied fruits
400g (1lb) granulated sugar
50g (2oz) butter
125ml (¼ pint) evaporated milk
100ml (4floz) fresh milk
Small pinch salt

Makes about 48–50 pieces

Put sugar, butter and milks into a heavy-based pan, heat gently till the butter and sugar are dissolved. Bring to the boil, and boil steadily, stirring occasionally, until the tem-perature reaches 113–118°C,

& glacé fruits

235–245°F, or when a little of the mixture dropped into cold water forms a soft, pliable ball. Remove from the heat, add the salt and chopped fruits; beat until the mixture becomes thick and creamy (it takes on a 'grainy' appearance).

Pour into a greased tin measuring approximately 20 × 15cm (8 × 6in).

Mark into squares and leave to set.

Tutti-Frutti Ice-cream

50–100g (2–4oz) chopped candied fruits (for real 'tutti-frutti' a mixture of fruits should be used, but you can make a good ice-cream with one fruit, such as pineapple)
500ml (1 pint) vanilla ice-cream (bought or home-made)

Serves 6

Soften the ice-cream slightly (soft-scoop types may not need softening to incorporate the fruit). Mix the chopped fruits in thoroughly, pack into a mould or freezer tray and re-freeze.

Caramelled Cream and Apricots

200–300g (8–12oz) candied apricots, roughly chopped
250ml (½ pint) double cream, stiffly whipped
150g (6oz) demerara or caster sugar

Serves 4

Place the apricots in a shallow ovenproof dish. Spread the cream over the fruit and refrigerate for at least 2 hours, more if possible. Cover the cream completely with sugar and place under a very hot grill for about 2 minutes, until the sugar has caramelised (dissolved and turned golden brown). Watch carefully at this stage as the dish may need to be turned.

Refrigerate again and serve cold.

Apricots, pineapple or peaches, or a mixture of fruits, are suitable for this dish.

Light Christmas Cake

This cake makes a change from the dark, more traditional type, and homemade candied fruit gives the cake a lovely moist, but light texture.

225g (8oz) candied or glacé cherries
175g (6oz) candied pineapple
75g (3oz) candied angelica
50g (2oz) candied orange or lemon peel
50g (2oz) chopped walnuts
225g (8oz) sultanas (pale ones)
225g (8oz) self-raising flour
225g (8oz) butter
175g (6oz) caster sugar
4 eggs
45ml (3 tablespoons) brandy or sherry (optional)
Grated rind and juice of 1 lemon
Pinch salt

Makes 12–14 slices

Soak the sultanas in the brandy or sherry (if used) overnight. Sift the flour and salt together. Chop the cherries, pineapple, angelica and peel, and mix with a little of the flour. Cream the butter, add the sugar and cream again till light and fluffy. Add the lemon rind and juice and beat again. Add the eggs, one at a time, adding about a tablespoon of flour after each egg. Now add the cherries, pineapple, peel, angelica, nuts, and flour. Mix thoroughly and fold in the sultanas and brandy.

Grease and line a 20cm (8in) cake tin, using three thicknesses of greaseproof paper and allow the paper to stand about 5cm (2in) above the tin. Tie a band of thick brown paper outside the tin, also 5cm (2in) above the top.

Bake the cake at 180°C, 350°F, Gas Mark 4 for the first 20 minutes. Turn the heat down to 170°C, 325°F, Gas Mark 3 for a further 20 minutes. At the end of this time, place a piece of greaseproof paper over the cake to prevent it browning too much, reduce the heat to 150°C, 300°F, Gas Mark 2 for the remainder of the cooking time, or until a skewer inserted in the centre comes out clean (3–3½ hours in all).

Granny's Gingerbread

100g (4oz) candied lemon or orange peel, or a mixture of both
225g (8oz) self-raising flour
10ml (2 teaspoons) ground ginger
75g (3oz) granulated sugar
100g (4oz) butter or margarine
15ml (1 level tablespoon) golden syrup
2 egg yolks
Egg white and extra granulated sugar for top of gingerbread

Makes about 12 squares

Mix the dry ingredients, except the peel, thoroughly. Melt the butter or margarine and syrup together (do not boil), cool slightly then add the beaten egg yolks and mix well. Stir this into the dry ingredients – the texture will be soft and doughy. Press half this mixture into a greased oblong tin, about 18 × 15cm (7 × 6in). Sprinkle the peel over, then press the remainder of the mixture on top. Paint the top thickly with egg white, and sprinkle with granulated sugar.

Bake at 170°C, 325°F, Gas Mark 3 for 30–35 minutes. The combination of ginger and peel is delicious, and the texture is really moist.

Apple and Lemon Crisp

50g (2oz) candied lemon peel, chopped
450g (1lb) stewed sweetened apple
2 egg whites
100g (4oz) caster sugar

Serves 4–5

Put the stewed apple in a shallow heatproof dish. Sprinkle the lemon peel over the surface of the apple. Make the meringue in the usual way with egg whites and sugar, and spread over the apple and lemon mixture, covering the mixture completely. Bake at 180°C, 350°F, Gas Mark 4 for 30–40 minutes, till the meringue is crisp and golden brown. Serve either hot or cold with cream.

Home freezing

In the following chapters Mary Norwak goes into detail on every aspect of freezing including how to freeze, thaw and use all the foods you could possibly want to preserve, from fruit and vegetables (with recommended varieties) to fish, poultry, game, meat and dairy products. The tables on all these subjects are a ready reference for the experienced 'freezer' as well as the beginner.

Home freezing

The assets of freezing

Freezing is a quick, safe method of preserving food so that it remains fresh and palatable for weeks or months. Food for freezing must be fresh and of high quality, and if carefully packed, it will retain colour, texture and flavour, with little loss of nutritional value. Freezing is the only food preservation method which results in a preserved product with the flavour and texture of the raw material, unlike preservation by drying, heat treatment, or with the addition of salt, vinegar or sugar.

A home freezer offers great convenience to the housewife, saving considerably on shopping time, and often on cooking time. It is also possible to save money with a freezer by bulk-buying and batch-cooking, but most freezer-owners find they eat better food for the same expenditure.

The freezer can help large families – they can cut food bills by careful bulk-buying, and by buying seasonal food at bargain prices for home freezing, and batch-cooking is more worthwhile with a large family to cope with, plus the casual guests who are usually part of a large family. On the other hand, single people or couples on their own can find that a freezer saves shopping time, and provides balanced, healthy meals when the weather is bad or there is illness.

A family which includes a working mother, or many working members, also benefits from a freezer. Shopping expeditions are tiring and expensive for a working woman, and often shopping hours do not coincide with free time from office or factory. The temptation is to buy quickly-prepared but expensive food, or snacks which are not nourishing. With a freezer, planned shopping and cooking can be arranged for the weekend, and evenings will not be spoiled by frantic emergency shopping or meal preparation.

But the families which really benefit most from the freezer are those who enjoy gardening and cooking. The freezer takes care of all the glut crops, and provides storage space for some exotic crops such as asparagus and artichokes which cannot otherwise be easily preserved at home. The keen cook will find she can have all sorts of ingredients, such as fish, meat, cream, vegetables and fruit, including unusual and special ones, always available, so she need not waste time searching for an elusive green pepper, or seafood for a garnish, in neighbourhood shops. Her skills will be tested and well-rewarded by batch-baking, and entertaining need never be nerve-racking.

How to use your freezer

Using a freezer is not complicated or difficult, but it is worth considering a few basic points.

Planning the freezer contents

The freezer is an expensive piece of equipment, taking up space and costing money to run, and it should therefore be used as an asset to the kitchen, serving as a general shop in the home. It should be filled with a wide variety of food, which is eaten frequently and not saved from season to season, or year to year, and gardening, shopping and cooking should be planned with this in mind.

Home-grown and market produce should be frozen at peak periods when quality is high and prices are low. Using seasonal food as the basis of a freezer plan, it is wise to see where the greatest family consumption lies. The correct proportion of space can then be given to meat and fish, fruit and vegetables, home-cooked dishes and commercial packs. In general, one-third meat, poultry and fish; one-third fruit and vegetables; one-third home-cooked dishes and commercial packs is about right for most families.

Ensuring good quality

Food for the freezer must be of high quality, because the freezer will not magically transform poor food into high-quality food with a good flavour. Food must be completely fresh, and should be frozen as quickly as possible after picking or purchase. Only small amounts of food should be prepared at a time, using clean utensils in a cool place. Packaging materials should be clean and dry, and food must not be left around in a kitchen when it is ready for the freezer.

The correct packaging must be used to see that fresh food does not lose moisture or absorb air which will cause deterioration in colour, texture and flavour.

Organising your freezer

It is wise to pack food in a variety of portion sizes, such as two-portion, four-portion or entertaining-portion containers, as this will avoid wastage when the food is served. All food must be sealed and labelled, and should be recorded as this will help the regular use of stocks. A regular turnover is also encouraged by a tidy freezer, with each type of food kept together, and a special basket for odd items to be used up quickly. Supplies should be run down in the late spring to leave space for fresh summer crops. Defrosting can take place then.

To freeze

It is most important that the packaged food is frozen quickly. Most freezers now have a special fast-freeze compartment for this purpose, but otherwise food to be frozen must be placed along the bottom and sides of a freezer at its coldest setting. Slow-freezing brings about a breakdown in food cells which will spoil the texture of many foods, particularly meat. To speed up freezing, fresh food should be well-chilled before being put into the cabinet so that it does not raise the temperature of the freezer, nor warm surrounding food.

To thaw

However good the freezing process has been, food will be spoiled if incorrectly thawed. Some foods, such as thin cuts of meat or fish, and vegetables, can be cooked straight from the freezer. Other foods should be thawed slowly, preferably in the refrigerator in their original wrappings, loosened slightly. In emergency, food may be thawed under cold running water, but hot water or excess heat must be avoided or the texture and flavour of the food will be spoiled.

Type of freezer

A food freezer must be capable of operating continuously at $-18°C$, $0°F$, and it must be capable of freezing fresh food to this temperature without any significant change in the temperature of the food already stored in the freezer. A food freezer will also store frozen food for many months. An efficient freezer is one which has a compartment which can be reduced to $-21°C$, $-5°F$, for quick freezing, which is essential for preparing high-quality frozen food from fresh.

A conservator is only a storage cabinet for food which has already been frozen, and it cannot be adjusted to sufficiently low temperatures for freezing food at home. This is the type of cabinet used for storing ice-cream, and it is often sold second-hand by shops. It can be useful for storing frozen food or animal food if there is space in the home for a second freezer.

A chest freezer is excellent for bulk storage, but must be fitted with dividers and baskets so that it can be operated efficiently without wastage of space. It is most suitable for placing in a garage or outhouse, but the cabinet may be difficult to fit into a kitchen. A short person may have a little difficulty in using a chest cabinet and reaching items at the bottom, and baskets may be heavy and awkward to lift.

An upright freezer is most convenient for the kitchen, but it is wise to check the safety of the floor as weight is concentrated in a very small area. This kind of freezer is easy to pack and organise, and nobody need risk a strained back lifting heavy food. It is also easier to defrost and clean, and the contents are easier to see. But an upright freezer may be a little more expensive to run than a chest freezer as cold air escapes more easily from an open door than from a lid, and the motor may have to work a little harder to chill the cabinet.

A refrigerator-freezer is extremely useful for installation in small areas and specially-designed kitchens, although the freezer space may not be large enough for some families. This type of cabinet can be useful as a second freezer, and is worth considering when an old refrigerator has to be replaced. It can be used to store food which is going to be used reasonably quickly, leaving a chest freezer to cope with the bulk storage of meat and home-grown produce. (A good arrangement may be to have a large chest freezer outside, and a smaller – probably upright – freezer in the kitchen.)

The easiest type of dual cabinet to use is one with equal-sized refrigerator and freezer, but some refrigerators have a small freezer on top. This must be marked with a four-star symbol which indicates a food freezer, rather than three stars or less which indicate the length of time frozen food may be stored in the frozen food compartment of a refrigerator.

Star marking

A freezer should be prominently and permanently marked with a four-star symbol, and the weight of food which can be frozen daily should be stamped on the rating plate. This international symbol has a fourth star which is larger and of a different colour, and indicates that the cabinet is suitable for freezing a stated quantity of food to $-18°C$, $0°F$, or below, within 24 hours, and for the storage of pre-frozen food at this temperature.

The frozen food compartment on a refrigerator is marked with stars which indicate the recommended storage times for packets of commercially frozen foods.

* (one star) operates at $-6°C$, $21°F$, and stores bought frozen food for one week and ice-cream for one day.
** (two star) operates at $-12°C$, $10°F$, and stores bought frozen food for one month and ice-cream for two weeks.
*** (three star) operates at $-18°C$, $0°F$, and stores bought frozen food for three months and ice-cream for one month.

Capacity

The size of a freezer is given in cubic feet and/or litres. To calculate the metric capacity of a freezer, multiply the number of cubic feet by 28·30. The maximum **storage capacity** of a freezer is calculated by multiplying each cubic foot by 25 to give storage capacity in lbs per cu ft. In practice, this amount is reduced by irregularly shaped packages, and lightweight packs which take up a large area.

The **freezing capacity** indicates the amount of fresh food which can be successfully quick-frozen within a 24-hour period and this is usually about one-tenth of the total storage capacity.

Choosing the correct size

The size of freezer chosen will depend on the number of people in the family, the space available for the freezer, and the amount of food which will be home-grown or bought at advantageous prices. Generally a capacity of 56·6 litres (2cuft) is recommended to store food for each member of the family, plus the same amount of additional space. In practice, this means that a freezer with 226·4 litre (8cuft) capacity would be the minimum size for a family of three people.

If the freezer is to be kept in the kitchen or other inside room, this will affect the size of the cabinet chosen, but a larger freezer can be bought to store in a garage or outhouse, and the cost will be repaid by a greater capacity for bulk purchases.

If it is planned to grow a lot of fruit and vegetables, provision must be made for the large quantity of produce which can be grown in quite a small garden. Meat also takes up a great deal of space, and a busy working household may consume a large supply of bulk-bought convenience food. It is therefore wise to make an estimate of the annual amount of food likely to be bought or grown before making a final decision on the size of the freezer to choose. **59**

Packing meat
Meat packed in small, usable
portions should be separated by
two layers of greaseproof paper or
foil or freezer film, so that single
items can be taken out by prizing
between the layers. They are then
packed in bags, (see page 63).

Home freezing

Special features

An upright freezer must be well supplied with shelves and additional storage space in the door. A chest freezer should come equipped with baskets, but extra baskets and dividers can be bought. A lock is also best fitted to a freezer to prevent pilferage if the cabinet is stored away from the house, or if children are likely to open it.

Most freezers now have a control panel which indicates whether the motor is functioning normally, according to the colour of the light shown. Make sure that this panel can be easily seen and the lights identified, and also that adjustment switches are easily accessible.

A fast-freeze compartment is now fitted to most chest freezers, divided from the main cabinet by a panel. The fast-freeze switch cuts out thermostatic control so that the motor runs continuously to keep the cabinet cold. Heat is thus removed from the fresh food as quickly as possible, and stored food does not rise in temperature. Upright freezers sometimes have special shelves for fast freezing. There should be a light on the control panel which indicates when the fast-freeze compartment is in action and the motor is running continuously.

Insurance

A freezer contains a great deal of expensive food, and it is worth taking out insurance against loss or damage. Special policies can be issued for the freezer and its contents, or a special clause can be inserted into a comprehensive policy for household contents. But the policy proposal should always be studied carefully, as it is common practice to exclude loss of power caused by strikes or industrial action. Some suppliers of freezers offer insurance, which may also include servicing arrangements, or a special policy can be arranged by an insurance broker.

Running costs

The cost of running a freezer will be affected by the size of the cabinet and its design, the warmth of the room in which the freezer stands, the number of times the cabinet is opened daily, and the length of time it is open. The amount of fresh food being frozen will also affect running costs, and so will the temperature of the food when it is put into the freezer. A little more power may be used by an upright freezer since the cold air is more likely to drop out of an open door than from the top-fitted lid of a chest. A well-packed freezer is more economical to run as the packages provide insulation. It is wasteful and expensive to use power to chill air in large empty spaces. Smaller freezers below 283 litres (10cuft) tend to use slightly more electricity in proportion to their size than the larger ones. As an approximate guide to the power used by an upright freezer under average conditions with the cabinet more than three-quarters full, 56·5 litres capacity (2cuft) will consume 4 units weekly. A freezer of 283 litres capacity (10cuft) will consume 17 units weekly.

Installing the freezer

Before using the freezer, be sure that it is installed in the correct position. It should be in a dry, cool and airy place, such as a large airy larder, utility room, spare room or passage, a dry garage or outhouse, or a cool part of the kitchen. The freezer should never be put next to a cooker, boiler or radiator, in an unventilated cupboard, a damp place, or in direct sunlight in a sunroom or conservatory. For convenience in packing and unpacking, it should be in good natural or

Freezing fish
Fish must be fresh-caught.

artificial light, and have a table nearby.

The freezer should be away from the wall, and preferably raised on wooden blocks or bricks so that there is an airspace beneath the floor of the cabinet. The controls should be set by the supplier and the machine tested before use. It is best to clean the inside of the cabinet with warm water, dry thoroughly, and switch on to chill for 12 hours before use.

Defrosting

The freezer needs no further attention, except for defrosting once or twice a year, when frost is about 5mm ($\frac{1}{4}$in) thick and food stocks are low. The day before defrosting, put on the fast-freeze switch, so that food packages are very cold. Take food from the freezer and pack closely in the refrigerator, or wrap in layers of newspapers and blankets and keep in a cold place.

Disconnect the freezer from the point. Put papers or towels on the bottom and scrape the sides with a plastic or wooden spatula, but not with sharp tools or wire brushes. A bowl of warm water may be placed in the base to spread melting ice, but heaters or hair-dryers must not be used. Leave the cabinet open and mop up moisture often. When all the ice has melted, wash the cabinet inside with a little bicarbonate of soda and warm water, rinse with clean water and dry. Switch the control to the coldest setting and run the machine for 30 minutes. Replace the packages after checking wrappings. Put food to be used up quickly in a basket near the top. Return to normal setting after three hours, but do not freeze any fresh food for 24 hours after defrosting.

Power failure

Food in the freezer will remain frozen for at least 12 hours, and will keep better in a well-insulated cabinet full of food. If the warning light indicates a power failure, check if the switch has been turned off by mistake, or if a fuse has blown. If the power failure is general, inform the local Electricity Board. Do not touch the freezer motor or open the lid or door. When power has been restored, check the condition of packages and cook any food which has thawed. Many items such as meat and vegetables can be made into casseroles which can be re-frozen, provided they have not spoiled. Leave the door or lid closed for at least two hours after the supply is restored.

Packaging

Food in the freezer must be prevented from drying out, which will happen if air is introduced to the food or moisture leaves it. Food must also be protected from cross-flavouring and smells, and delicate foods must be protected from chipping or bruising. Packaging must be clean and dust-free, and should prevent the passage of air and moisture. It must also be waterproof and greaseproof and free of smell. Packaging must also be durable so that it will not split or burst and will be resistant to low-temperature over a long period. Sheet foil, foil dishes, sheet polythene and heavy-gauge polythene bags, and plastic rigid containers are all suitable for freezer packaging.

Packing and sealing

Food is best packed in usable portions. These may be for individual servings, two-portion, four-portion, family-size or entertaining sizes, and most families will find a variety of pack sizes useful. It is better to use small, rather than large, packs for most cooked dishes, as it is always easy to put two or more packs together for a meal, but a too-large pack can be wasteful.

Many items can be packed before freezing, but if fruit and vegetables are open-frozen before packing, they remain free-flowing and easy to shake out of bags or boxes. To open-freeze, fruit and vegetables should be spread out on trays without wrapping and frozen until hard, but no longer, then tipped into a bag or rigid freezer container, and sealed. Special trays are available for open-freezing, but the lids of large freezer containers can be used instead. Small fish, such as whitebait, may be frozen this way, and the method is also suitable for iced cakes or delicate dishes which are easily smudged or broken if packed before freezing.

Small pieces of meat or fish, or cake layers – in fact any items that may be packed together but taken out individually – should be separated with two layers of greaseproof paper, foil or freezer film, so that single items can be taken out by prizing between the layers. They should then be packed in bags, and any protruding bones of meat or poultry should be padded with twists of foil to prevent causing damage to packs.

Bag packing can be used for most fresh food. Fill the bags carefully, making sure food goes right down into corners, and try to avoid soiling the edges of the bags. Take out air by squeezing, sucking through a straw, or using a special pump, and close the bag, as close to the food as possible, with a wire twist or a heat-sealing machine.

Box packing is suitable for fruit and vegetables, and for liquid or semi-liquid foods such as stews. The boxes should be filled carefully to prevent soiling, and headspace must be left above the food to allow for expansion at low temperatures. This space should be about 2·5cm (1in) above the food. When fruit in syrup is packed, the space above the fruit should be lightly filled with a little crumpled foil or freezer paper so that the fruit does not rise above the syrup and discolour.

Wrapping is suitable for large pieces of meat or fish, and for cakes. Foil is a good wrapping material as it can be moulded close to the food to exclude air. Polythene sheeting can also be used. The food should be placed in the centre of the wrapping material, and the two sides drawn together and folded neatly downwards to bring the wrapping as close to the food as possible, pressing out air. This fold should be sealed with freezer tape, and the ends folded over like a parcel to make them close and tight. All folds must be sealed to keep out air.

Home freezing

Filling the freezer
It is most important to keep the freezer tidy, and the packages neatly stacked and close together. For this reason, many items should be made as square as possible for easy storage. When packing polythene bags, put them into empty cartons or boxes before filling with food. After freezing, the bags can be removed from the boxes and will be neat and easy to pack into the freezer. Small quantities of sauces, syrups, baby foods and chopped herbs such as parsley and mint, can be frozen in ice-cube trays. The frozen cubes can then be packed in polythene bags for easy storage, and will eliminate a number of small untidy pots.

Labelling and recording
All packages must be labelled, as it is very difficult to identify items once the packages have become slightly frosted. Use labels with freezer gum which will not peel off in the icy conditions of the cabinet, or tie-on labels. Always write in wax crayon, Chinagraph pencil or freezer pen as anything else will fade in the freezer. Apart from naming the food and giving the date of freezing, it is helpful to put the weight or number of portions, and any additional information about seasonings needed during reheating – in the case of fruit, note if it is to be frozen in a dry sugar pack or an unsweetened pack.

A freezer record is important, to keep a check on food available and length of storage period. This can be a book, plastic shopping list or card index, and should allow space to record when food is removed from the freezer. This will help to maintain a regular turnover of stock while food remains of high quality.

Preparing fruit for freezing
Fresh top-quality fruit is essential for freezing, and when possible the correct varieties should be chosen as these have been tested under freezing conditions for flavour and texture. It is best to process small quantities of fruit as they ripen, rather than waiting for a full crop to mature.

While most people want to freeze home-produce, it is also possible to process many fruits purchased from shop or market when in season, cheap and plentiful. Pineapple, grapes, apricots, peaches and melons are all very good frozen and give considerable variety to winter meals. Citrus fruit freezes well, but varies little in price throughout the year and may not be worth freezer space. Bananas and avocado pears do not freeze particularly well, and are normally in plentiful supply in shops and markets.

It is certainly not necessary to use only one method of preserving fruit in the freezer. The traditional syrup pack (prepared fruit frozen in a sugar and water syrup) is in fact not particularly useful and only worth considering for apricots, pears, peaches and plums which tend to discolour unless kept in syrup. Fruit may be frozen raw and unsweetened, or with dry sugar or syrup. Fruit purée is useful for all sorts of puddings and can be made from both raw and cooked fruit. Fruit may also be prepared and frozen as syrup, juice, pie fillings, ices, crumbles, sponges, pies, puddings and sauces.

Freezer packs for fruit
Fruit may be packaged in polythene bags or rigid containers, according to the way in which it has been processed. The fruit may be prepared in three ways after cleaning and grading, ie putting fruits of the same size together; a mixture of large and small fruits in the same pack will freeze and thaw unevenly.

Unsweetened pack
This pack should not be used for fruit which discolours badly, eg peaches or pears, as sugar helps to retard the action of the enzymes which cause darkening. But the unsweetened pack is very useful for fruit which will be used later for pies, puddings and jams, and of course unsweetened fruit is preferred by many people with cereals or with cream. Clean the fruit well, removing stalks or stems. Wash, if necessary, in ice-chilled water, drain and dry well on absorbent paper. Open-freeze soft fruit such as raspberries, strawberries and currants before packing. Tougher fruit such as gooseberries may be packed before freezing.

Dry sugar pack
Soft juicy fruit can be packed in dry sugar, and this is also suitable for halved stoned fruit and pineapple slices. Either mix the fruit and sugar together before packing, or pack fruit and sugar in layers, starting with fruit and ending with a layer of sugar. The usual proportion of sugar and fruit is 125g (4oz) sugar to 500g (1lb) fruit. If only a little fruit is available, perhaps at the end of the season, freeze some mixed packs such as raspberries/ currants/strawberries, or apple slices/halved plums/blackberries in a dry sugar pack to make delicious fruit salads. Sweetened fruit can be eaten as soon as it is thawed.

Syrup pack
Non-juicy fruit and fruit which discolours easily are best packed in syrup made from white sugar and water. Honey may be used, but gives a strong flavour to the fruit, and brown sugar will colour the fruit. The sugar must be dissolved in boiling water and then chilled completely before using. For proportions of sugar to water, see page 69. Most fruits freeze well in a light or medium syrup, according to taste. The fruit should be packed into a rigid container and then covered with syrup. To prevent fruit rising and discolouring, a piece of greaseproof paper or Cellophane should be crumpled down on the fruit to fill the headspace. **65**

Home freezing: Fruit

Added lemon juice, citric acid powder or vitamin C (ascorbic acid) – both the latter obtainable from chemists – also helps to prevent discoloration. A little pure vanilla essence may be added to syrup for pears which otherwise tend to be flavourless when frozen.

Purée
Fruit for purée should not be over-ripe or bruised. Raw berries such as raspberries and strawberries, and ripe peaches, may be sieved, sweetened to taste and frozen at once. Other stone fruit, gooseberries and currants should be cooked in just enough water to cover, then sieved and sweetened to taste. Purée should be stored no longer than 3–4 months.

Syrup
Fruit syrup is useful for sauces and drinks and is more easily frozen than bottled. Use a standard recipe for preparing syrup and freeze in small rigid containers or ice-cube trays. Turn out the frozen cubes, wrap in foil, or freezer film for citrus fruits, and then pack in polythene bags for easy storage. One cube of syrup is enough for a drink or one portion of sauce.

Juice
Apple and citrus fruit juices may be frozen. Apple juice must not be sweetened as fermentation sets in very quickly. It should be prepared in the proportion of 1kg (2lb) apples to 300ml ($\frac{1}{2}$ pint) water, strained through a jelly bag or cloth, and cooled completely before being frozen in a rigid container, leaving headspace. Citrus fruit juice should be extracted, strained and frozen without heat treatment. Lemon and lime juice are best frozen in ice-cube trays (see syrup packing), because smaller quantities are normally used, but orange and grapefruit juice can be packed in larger containers.

Discoloration
Fruit which contains a lot of vitamin C does not darken so quickly when peeled. Other fruit needs the addition of lemon juice, citric acid powder, or vitamin C to prevent darkening. Use 15ml (1 tablespoon) lemon juice or 2·5ml ($\frac{1}{2}$ teaspoon) citric acid powder, or 2–3 × 100mg vitamin C tablets, to each 500g (1lb) syrup pack of fruit. (Dry sugar packs should not be used for fruits which discolour, if possible do them in syrup.) Fruit purée is subject to darkening as air is incorporated in the fruit during sieving, and it should only be stored 3–4 months. Fruit which discolours quickly should be thawed in the covered container in the refrigerator and eaten immediately it is thawed, or it should be cooked from frozen.

Thawing and serving
Fruit collapses quickly and loses texture if thawed in a warm place, or left too long when thawed. It is best to thaw in the refrigerator in the covered container. Fruit should be served when just thawed with a few ice crystals remaining. If fruit is to be cooked, it is best put into water or syrup while still frozen and cooked at once. If a dish such as Peach Melba is being prepared from frozen fruit, ice-cream and sauce, the fruit should be left in the covered container in the refrigerator until immediately before serving or it will discolour and spoil the dish.

Guidelines for freezing fruit
1 Freeze fruit in a variety of ways. Unsweetened fruit is useful for making pies, puddings and jam; sugar-sweetened fruit can be eaten as soon as thawed. Fruit need only be preserved in syrup if it is likely to discolour – for instance, peaches and apricots. Fruit purée is useful for turning quickly into mousses, ices or fools, and seems to keep the full flavour of such fruit as strawberries.
2 Grade fruit carefully for size before freezing. Small fruit is useful for jam-making, or for cooking and sieving. If fruit is a mixture of large and small in a pack, freezing and thawing will be uneven and less satisfactory.
3 Always be sure to add lemon juice or citric acid or vitamin C to packs containing fruit which is low in vitamin C and which discolours easily, eg peaches and apricots, and be sure that the fruit is kept under the packing syrup so that no air can discolour it.
4 Thaw fruit slowly in its container in the refrigerator and eat when slightly frosty, or cook while still frozen. This helps to prevent fruit collapsing or discolouring.
5 If frozen fruit is used for jam, allow $\frac{1}{10}$th more fruit to sugar than in a normal recipe, as there is a very small loss of pectin in the freezer.

What can go wrong
Discoloration. Browning of pale fruit occurs when air comes in contact with the flesh. The fruit skin is a natural protector of such fruit as apples, pears, peaches and apricots, but when it is removed the fruit quickly turns brown. Such fruit must be prepared quickly and protected from air during freezing. The addition of vitamin C will prevent discoloration.

Dark purée. This can result from over-long storage. During the sieving process, air is incorporated in the food cells which causes discoloration. Fruit purée should be stored no longer than 3–4 months, as against 12 months for most whole fruit.

Flabby fruit. This is the result of using a very heavy syrup. Most fruit freezes well in a light or medium syrup.

Poor flavour and texture. This may occur if the wrong variety of fruit has been used for freezing. It is easy to select the correct varieties for home produce, but important to check the varieties when buying from farm or shop.

Slushy fruit. This is also caused by freezing the incorrect varieties of fruit, or by using too much sugar in the processing, or by thawing for too long in a warm temperature. Strawberries particularly are subject to these problems.

Packing
Halved, stoned fruit may be packed
in dry sugar.

Home freezing: Fruit

Fruit	Varieties specially recommended
Apples	Bramley's Seedling (for purée)
Black currants	Blacksmith; Boskoop Giant; Laxton's Giant; Malvern Cross; Wellington
Gooseberries	Careless
Greengages	Cambridge Gage; Comte d'Althan's Gage; Jefferson
Plums	Victoria and others
Raspberries	Lloyd George; Malling Enterprise; Malling Jewel; Malling Promise; Norfolk Giant
Red currants	Red Lake
Strawberries	Cambridge Favourite; Cambridge Late Pine; Cambridge Rival; Cambridge Vigour; Royal Sovereign; Talisman

Note: Other varieties are, of course, usable, but may be less successful.

Other fruit worth freezing
Apricots
Blackberries
Blueberries and Bilberries
Cherries
Cranberries
Currants (White)
Damsons
Figs
Grapefruit
Grapes
Lemons
Limes
Loganberries
Mangoes
Melons
Nectarines
Oranges
Peaches
Pears
Pineapple
Pomegranates
Quinces
Rhubarb

Fruit not usually worth freezing because they
are readily available, are **avocado pears** and
bananas. They can be frozen, however, and
instructions are given on pages 70 and 71.

SYRUP TABLE

Sugar	Water	Type of Syrup
100g (4oz)	500ml (1 pint)	very light syrup
175g (7oz)	500ml (1 pint)	light syrup
275g (11oz)	500ml (1 pint)	medium syrup
400g (1lb)	500ml (1 pint)	heavy syrup
625g (25oz)	500ml (1 pint)	very heavy syrup

Vitamin C content in fruit
Fruits which are a good source of vitamin C are
rose hips, black currants, oranges, limes, lemons,
grapefruit and strawberries. Cooking tends to destroy
vitamin C in fruit but there should be little loss in
freezing if the fruit is prepared carefully according to
the instructions.

Avocado with lemon
To prepare an avocado pear for the
freezer, cut the pear in half, remove
the stone and rub the cut sides
with lemon juice to prevent
discoloration. Other methods are
described on the following page.

Home freezing: Fruit

Fruit	Preparation	Storage Life	Serving
Apples	Peel, core and drop in cold, lightly salted water. Cut in twelfths or sixteenths. Use dry sugar *or* medium syrup pack. Pack in bags or rigid containers.	12 months	Cook from frozen. Put in pies or puddings.
	Or cook apples and freeze as sweetened purée.	4 months	Use for sauce, ices or puddings.
Apricots	Peel, halve, stone, and pack in dry sugar, *or* slice in medium syrup pack. Pack in bags or rigid containers.	12 months	Thaw in covered container in refrigerator for 6 hours.
	Or sieve very ripe fruit, sweeten and freeze as purée.	4 months	Use for sauce and ices.
Avocado Pears	Cut in half, remove stones, and rub cut sides with lemon juice, wrap each in freezer film and pack in polythene bags.	2 months	Thaw in wrappings in refrigerator for 6 hours and serve.
	Or slice and dip in lemon juice and freeze in rigid containers.		
	Or mash each avocado with 15ml (1 tablespoon) lemon juice and pack in small rigid containers.		Thaw in container in refrigerator for 6 hours, season and add chopped onion or garlic to serve as spread.

Note: Thawing instructions are usually for a 500g (1lb) pack. Larger packs would take longer.

Fruit	Preparation	Storage Life	Serving
Bananas	Mash 750g (1½lb) bananas with 250g (8oz) sugar and 50ml (3 tablespoons) lemon juice. Pack in small containers.	2 months	Thaw in container in refrigerator for 6 hours, and use in cakes or sandwiches.
Blackberries	Wash and dry dark glossy ripe fruit. Open-freeze berries *or* use dry sugar pack.	12 months	Thaw in refrigerator for 6 hours and serve raw or cooked.
	Or sieve ripe raw or cooked fruit and freeze as purée.	4 months	
Blueberries	Wash and drain and crush slightly as skins toughen when frozen. Open-freeze berries *or* use dry sugar pack *or* heavy syrup.	12 months	Thaw in refrigerator for 6 hours. Use raw, cooked or in pies and puddings.
Cherries	Chill in water for one hour and remove stones. Use dry sugar pack, *or* medium syrup (sweet cherries) ; *or* heavy syrup (sour cherries). Do not use waxed containers as cherry juice remains liquid when frozen and may leak.	12 months	Thaw in refrigerator for 6 hours and serve raw or cooked.
Cranberries	Wash and drain firm glossy berries. Pack unsweetened, *or* cook and freeze as sweetened purée.	12 months 4 months	Cook berries in water and sugar while still frozen, or thaw purée in refrigerator for 6 hours.
Currants	Prepare black, red and white currants in same way : strip from stems, wash and drain. Pack unsweetened, *or* in dry sugar pack, *or* in medium syrup, *or* as cooked sweetened purée.	12 months 4 months	Cook currants while still frozen, or thaw purée in refrigerator for 6 hours to use for sauce, ices, drinks or puddings.
Damsons	Wash in chilled water, freeze whole or halve and remove stones. Pack in heavy syrup, *or* as cooked sweetened purée.	12 months 4 months	Thaw in refrigerator for 6 hours.
Figs	Wash sweet ripe figs, remove stems and do not bruise. Pack in medium syrup.	12 months	Thaw in refrigerator for 6 hours.
Gooseberries	Wash in chilled water and drain. Use ripe fruit to freeze for pies, but slightly under-ripe fruit for jam. Pack unsweetened for jam, *or* in medium syrup, *or* as cooked sweetened purée.	12 months 4 months	Cook gooseberries while still frozen, or thaw purée in refrigerator for 6 hours to use for sauce, ices or puddings.
Grapefruit	Peel, remove all pith and cut into segments. Use dry sugar pack *or* heavy syrup.	12 months	Thaw in refrigerator for 6 hours.
Grapes	Small seedless grapes may be frozen whole ; peel, seed and halve large grapes. Pack in light syrup.	12 months	Thaw in refrigerator for 6 hours.
Greengages	Wash in chilled water, and dry. Halve and stone. Pack in medium syrup.	12 months	Thaw in refrigerator for 6 hours.
Lemons and Limes	Peel, or leave unpeeled, cut in slices and pack in light syrup. **Or** use dry sugar pack. Separate with double layers of paper if using them for drinks	12 months	Put into drinks while frozen.

Home freezing: Fruit

Fruit	Preparation	Storage Life	Serving
Loganberries	Wash in chilled water and dry. Open-freeze or use dry sugar pack or heavy syrup or as cooked sweetened purée.	12 months 4 months	Thaw in refrigerator for 6 hours.
Mangoes	Peel ripe fruit, remove stones, slice and pack in heavy syrup. Add 15ml (1 tablespoon) lemon juice to 1 litre (2 pints) syrup.	12 months	Thaw in refrigerator for 6 hours.
Melons	Peel and cut into balls or cubes. Toss in lemon juice and pack in light syrup.	12 months	Thaw in refrigerator for 6 hours and serve while still frosty.
Oranges	Peel and divide into sections or slices and use dry sugar pack or light syrup.	12 months	Thaw in refrigerator for 6 hours.
Peaches and Nectarines	Fruit discolours easily, so work quickly. Peel, remove stones, cut in halves or slices and brush with lemon juice. Use medium syrup, or sieve very ripe fruit and freeze as sweetened purée, adding 15ml (1 tablespoon) lemon juice to 500g (1lb) fruit.	12 months 4 months	Thaw in refrigerator for 6 hours.
Pears	Peel ripe juicy pears, quarter and remove cores. Dip pieces in lemon juice and poach in light syrup for $1\frac{1}{2}$ minutes. Cool, and pack in fresh light syrup.	12 months	Thaw in refrigerator for 6 hours.
Pineapple	Peel ripe, golden fruit, remove core, and cut in slices or chunks. Use dry sugar pack or light syrup.	12 months	Thaw in refrigerator for 6 hours.
Plums	Wash in chilled water and drain. Halve and stone. Pack in medium syrup. Or halve and stone very large ripe eating plums and use dry sugar pack.	12 months	Thaw in refrigerator for 6 hours.
Pomegranates	Halve ripe fruit, scoop out juice sacs and pack in heavy syrup.	12 months	Thaw in refrigerator for 6 hours.
Quinces	Peel, core and slice. Simmer in light syrup for 20 minutes. Cool and pack in fresh light syrup.	12 months	Thaw in refrigerator for 6 hours.
Raspberries	Open-freeze or use dry sugar pack or pack in light syrup. Or sieve ripe fruit and freeze as sweetened purée.	12 months 4 months	Thaw in refrigerator for 6 hours.
Rhubarb	Wash in cold water and trim sticks. Blanch 1 minute and wrap in polythene, or chop and pack in medium syrup or freeze cooked sweetened purée.	12 months 4 months	Cook sticks while still frozen, or thaw syrup pack or purée in refrigerator for 6 hours.
Strawberries	Grade ripe, mature firm fruit. Open-freeze or use dry sugar pack or medium syrup. Or sieve ripe fruit and freeze as sweetened purée.	12 months 4 months	Thaw in refrigerator for 6 hours.

Home freezing: Vegetables

Preparing vegetables for freezing

Only young, tender and fresh vegetables are worth freezing, preferably processed as soon as they are picked. Vegetables from shops are rarely worth freezing, except for exotics such as peppers and aubergines. Bulk-bought vegetables are worth processing if you and your family have picked them yourselves and prepared them quickly, but it is not worth buying ready-picked sacks of vegetables from farms or markets as they may be old and stale, and there is much wastage.

Nearly all vegetables freeze well, except crisp salad greens and radishes which lose their texture. Root vegetables and potatoes can be stored by other means, and greenstuff stands well in the garden so is rarely worth freezing. A few vegetables, such as celery, tomatoes and cabbage, may be frozen but are not suitable for serving in salads when they have been blanched.

Blanching

Very few vegetables (eg tomatoes, mushrooms and herbs) can be frozen without blanching. One or two others (old potatoes, marrow, red cabbage) are better frozen after complete cooking. All other vegetables must be blanched, ie subjected to heat treatment, for a short time to retard the enzyme action which causes loss of colour, flavour and nutritive value. For short-term storage up to three months, vegetables may be put into the freezer without blanching, but will quickly deteriorate after that time. For blanching, a large saucepan is necessary, holding at least 5 litres (8 pints) water. A blanching basket is also essential, although a nylon wine-straining bag, or a wire salad or chip basket (if the holes are not too large – it may not do for peas) will serve well.

Before blanching, vegetables must be cleaned and trimmed, and graded for size, as they will be poorly processed if large and small sizes are mixed. Only blanch 500g (1lb) vegetables at a time, or heat will not penetrate the mass. Put 5 litres (8 pints) water in the saucepan and bring to the boil. Put in the basket of vegetables and cover with a lid. Bring back to the boil as quickly as possible

(within one minute) and time as soon as the water boils again. Time very accurately (see pages 78–83) and remove blanching basket at once. Tip the vegetables into a large bowl of ice-chilled water (running water from the tap is not cold enough). Chill for exactly the same length of time as blanching, drain and open-freeze or pack at once.

It is most important to time blanching carefully as over-blanching results in loss of flavour and crispness. Under-blanching results in colour change and loss of nutritive value.

Vegetables can be spread out on trays and open-frozen, then packed in large bags or rigid containers, from which they can easily be shaken as needed for use. This method is particularly suitable for peas and beans. Vegetables may be packed in bags or containers, but delicate asparagus and spiky artichokes are best in containers; smelly vegetables need overwrapping.

Well-frozen vegetables can be completely ruined by careless serving. Sweetcorn must be thawed before cooking, but other vegetables should be cooked from frozen in a little boiling water until only just tender. They can also be steamed or cooked in butter, without water, in a covered casserole in the oven.

Vegetables	Varieties specially recommended
Asparagus	Connover's Colossal; Martha Washington
Beans, Broad	The Sutton; Suttons Exhibition; Imperial Green Windsor; Masterpiece; Green Longpod
Beans, Dwarf	The Prince; Masterpiece; Sprite; Flair
Beans, Runner	Enorma; Streamline; White Stringless; Achievement; Fry; Long as Your Arm
Beetroot	Boltardy; Detroit Little Ball
Broccoli	Purple Sprouting
Brussels Sprouts	Peer Gynt; Citadel; Fasolt; Roodnerf Seven Hills
Cabbage	April; Greyhound; Autumn Supreme; Durham Early; Hispi; Chinese Cabbage Pe-Tsai
Calabrese	Green Duke; Express Corona
Carrot	Nantes Tip Top; Amsterdam Forcing; Pioneer; Scarla
Cauliflower	All the Year Round; Reading Giant; Walcheren
Courgette	Golden Zucchini
Leek	Musselburgh
Pea	Sweetness; Greenshaft; Vitalis; Feltham First; Kelvedon Wonder
Spinach	Sigma Leaf
Sweetcorn	First of All; North Star
Tomato	Sigmabush: Marmande

Preparing an artichoke for freezing

First it is necessary to remove the choke. Pull apart the top leaves of the vegetable until you see the fibrous choke, then with a small sharp knife, cut it out. Further instructions are given on page 78.

Other vegetables worth freezing

Globe Artichokes	Florence Fennel	Peppers
Jerusalem Artichokes	Mushrooms	Potatoes (New)
Aubergines	Onions	Red Cabbage
Celery	Peas (Edible Pods)	and Herbs

Vegetables not usually worth freezing, because they can be stored in other ways, are: **Cucumber, Kale, Kohl rabi, Marrow, Parsnips, Potatoes (Old), Pumpkin, Turnips.** They can be frozen, however, and we give instructions.

Home freezing: Vegetables

Guidelines for freezing vegetables

1 Only use fresh young vegetables, and process quickly after picking. If using home-grown produce pick and process in small quantities and do not wait until the whole crop is ready.

2 Avoid large sacks of picked vegetables from markets and farms which can be stale and so wasteful, and difficult to process quickly.

3 Grade vegetables for size so that blanching heat penetrates evenly, and the vegetables freeze evenly.

4 Time blanching and cooling very accurately to avoid over-blanching, otherwise vegetables will start to cook.

5 Make sure cooling water is ice-chilled with plenty of ice-cubes or blocks, and do not try to cool under running tap water.

6 Use blanching water for a number of items – it can be used six or eight times for the same kind of vegetable before changing, but the cooling water warms up, so make sure it is ice-cold for each fresh batch of blanched vegetables.

7 Pack vegetables carefully to prevent damaging delicate ones, and overwrap smelly items such as onions.

8 Cook frozen vegetables lightly for serving so that they remain crisp and fresh-tasting.

Red cabbage and cauliflower

Red cabbage can be shredded and cooked before freezing. Cool and pack in a rigid container. When preparing cauliflower heads lemon juice should be added to the blanching water.

What can go wrong

A smelly freezer. This results from poorly wrapped vegetables. Onions and greenstuff are best overwrapped in an extra polythene bag to prevent smells spreading to other foods and flavouring them.

Pale, soft greenstuff. Over-blanched green vegetables may be pale and soft. Blanching must always be carefully timed, and vegetables must be cooled quickly in ice-chilled water before draining and packing.

Tough, stringy vegetables. These were probably too old for processing. Only fresh young produce should be frozen.

Watery vegetables. Vegetables, particularly runner beans, may be watery if they have been cut too small and thin and/or blanched too long. For very watery kinds of vegetables, which need little water for cooking, pack when blanched, in boil-in-bag bags. These bags can go into boiling water for reheating without the vegetables touching the water.

Poorly-flavoured vegetables. Poor flavour may occur if the wrong variety was used for freezing. Research by seedsmen has resulted in recommended vegetables which will not lose colour, flavour or texture in the freezer.

Note: All vegetables are cooked from frozen, unless other instructions are given.

Home freezing: Vegetables

Vegetable	Preparation	Blanching Time	Storage Life	Serving
Artichokes (Globe)	Remove coarse outer leaves and stalks. Cut out 'chokes' and wash heads. Put 15ml (1 tablespoon) lemon juice in blanching water. Blanch, cool and drain upside-down. Pack in rigid containers to avoid damage to packages.	7 minutes	12 months	Cook in boiling water 5 minutes.
Artichokes (Jerusalem)	Peel and slice. Soften in butter and cook in chicken stock. Sieve and freeze as purée.		3 months	Make into soup with milk and cream, and seasoning to taste.
Asparagus	Remove woody portions and scales and wash well. Grade for size and cut in 15cm (6in) lengths. Blanch according to size – 2 minutes will be enough for thin spears, up to 4 minutes for thick spears. Cool, drain and pack in rigid containers.	2–4 minutes	9 months	Cook 5 minutes in boiling water.
Aubergines	Peel and cut in 2·5cm (1in) slices. Blanch, chill and drain. Pack in bags or rigid containers. Only use medium-sized and tender aubergines.	4 minutes	12 months	Thaw for 15 minutes and fry.
Beans (Broad)	Shell small young beans. Blanch, cool, drain. Pack in bags. *Or* open freeze, then pack in bags.	1½ minutes	12 months	Cook 8 minutes in boiling water.
Beans (Dwarf)	Top and tail. Leave small beans whole; cut large ones into 2·5cm (1in) slices. Blanch, cool and pack in bags.	3 minutes (whole beans) 2 minutes (cut beans)	12 months	Cook 7 minutes in boiling water (whole beans); 5 minutes (cut beans).
Beans (Runner)	Top, tail and string. Do not shred, but cut in pieces. Blanch, cool and pack in bags.	2 minutes	12 months	Cook 7 minutes in boiling water.
Beetroot	Use very young, under 7·5cm (3in) in size. Cook completely in boiling water, rub off skins, pack in boxes whole, diced or sliced.		6 months	Thaw 2 hours in container in refrigerator. Drain and add dressing.

Vegetable	Preparation	Blanching Time	Storage Life	Serving
Broccoli and Calabrese	Use green, compact heads with tender stalks. Trim stalks and remove outer leaves. Wash and soak in salt water 30 minutes. Wash again, grade for size, and blanch according to size – 3 minutes will be enough for thin spears, up to 5 minutes for thick spears. Cool, drain and pack in bags or rigid containers, alternating heads to prevent damage.	3–5 minutes	12 months	Cook 8 minutes in boiling water.
Brussels Sprouts	Use crisp compact heads. Clean and wash and grade. Blanch according to size – 3 minutes for small heads and 4 minutes for medium heads. Cool, drain and pack in bags.	3–4 minutes	12 months	Cook 8 minutes in boiling water.
Cabbage (Green)	Wash crisp young cabbage and shred finely. Blanch, cool, drain and pack in bags.	1½ minutes	6 months	Cook 8 minutes in boiling water (do not use raw).
Cabbage (Red)	Shred and cook completely to favourite recipe with apples, vinegar and spices. Cool and pack in rigid container.		6 months	Thaw for 2 hours and re-heat in low oven in casserole.
Carrots	Wash and scrape very young carrots. Blanch, cool, drain and pack in bags. Carrots may be left whole, diced or sliced.	3 minutes	12 months	Cook 8 minutes in boiling water.
Cauliflower	Wash firm compact heads with close white flowers. Break into sprigs. Add 15ml (1 tablespoon) lemon juice to blanching water. Blanch, cool, drain and pack in bags.	3 minutes	6 months	Cook 10 minutes in boiling water.

Home freezing: Vegetables

Vegetable	Preparation	Blanching Time	Storage Life	Serving
Celery	Scrub crisp young stalks and remove strings. Cut in 2·5cm (1in) lengths. Blanch, cool, drain and pack in bags. Celery may also be packed in rigid containers with blanching water, leaving headspace.	2 minutes	6 months	Braise or use for soups or stews. Do not use raw.
Cucumber	Cut in thin slices and pack in rigid containers with equal quantities white vinegar and water, adding 2·5ml (½ teaspoon) sugar and 5ml (1 teaspoon) black pepper to 500ml (1 pint) liquid.		2 months	Thaw in container in refrigerator. Drain and season with salt.
Fennel (Florence)	Use crisp young stalks and scrub well. Blanch and keep blanching water. Cool fennel and drain. Pack in rigid containers with blanching water.	3 minutes	6 months	Simmer 30 minutes in blanching water. Slip hard cores from roots when cooked.
Herbs (Mint, Parsley, Chives, Basil)	Only freeze tender-leaved herbs. Wash and pack sprigs in bags or chop with just enough water to moisten and pack into ice-cube trays, freeze and store herb cubes in bags.		12 months	Thaw in colander, drain and use as fresh herbs. Or stir frozen cubes into soups, crumble frozen leaves into stews.

Vegetable	Preparation	Blanching Time	Storage Life	Serving
Kale	Wash young, tender kale. Remove dry or tough leaves. Strip leaves from stems. Blanch, cool and drain. Chop leaves and pack into bags.	1 minute	6 months	Cook 8 minutes in boiling water.
Kohl rabi	Use young, small, tender and mild-flavoured kohl rabi. Trim, wash and peel. Freeze whole or dice. Blanch, cool, drain and pack in bags.	3 minutes (whole) 2 minutes (diced)	12 months	Cook 10 minutes in boiling water.
Marrow and Courgettes	Do not peel young marrows or courgettes. Cut marrow in 1·25cm ($\frac{1}{2}$in) slices. Blanch, cool, drain and pack in bags.	3 minutes	6 months	Fry in oil.
	Large marrows may be peeled, seeded, cooked until soft and mashed to freeze as purée in rigid containers.		6 months	Reheat gently with butter.
Mushrooms	Wipe well but do not wash or peel. Pack in bags.		3 months	Add frozen mushrooms to dishes before cooking. Do not sauté in butter.
Onions	Peel, chop, blanch, cool and drain. Pack in bags and overwrap to prevent smell affecting other food.	2 minutes	2 months	Add frozen onions to dishes before cooking.
Parsnips	Trim and peel young parsnips. Dice or cut in narrow strips. Blanch, cool, drain and pack in bags.	2 minutes	12 months	Cook 15 minutes in boiling water.
Peas	Shell young, sweet peas. Blanch, cool, drain. Pack in bags. *Or* open-freeze, then pack in bags.	1 minute	12 months	Cook 5 minutes in boiling water.
Peas (Edible Pods-Mange-tout)	Wash flat tender pods, remove ends and strings. Blanch in small quantities, cool, drain and pack in bags.	$\frac{1}{2}$ minute	12 months	Cook 7 minutes in boiling water.

Parsley in cubes
Parsley, like other tender-leaved herbs, can be moistened and packed into ice-cube trays. Freeze, then store the cubes in freezer bags.

Home freezing: Vegetables

Vegetable	Preparation	Blanching Time	Storage Life	Serving
Peppers	Wash well, remove stems and caps, take out seeds and membranes. Halve or slice. Blanch, cool, drain and pack in bags.	2 minutes (slices) 3 minutes (halves)	12 months	Thaw 1½ hours at room temperature.
Potatoes	Slightly undercook new potatoes. Drain, toss in butter and pack in boil-in-bag bags.		3 months	Put bag in boiling water. Take off heat and leave 10 minutes.
	Cook and mash old potatoes and pack in bags.		3 months	Reheat in double boiler.
	Make potatoes into croquettes or Duchesse Potatoes. Cook, cool and pack in rigid containers.		3 months	Thaw 2 hours and heat for 20 minutes at 180°C, 350°F, Gas Mark 4.
	Fry chips in clean fat for 4 minutes, without browning. Cool and pack in bags.		3 months	Fry in deep fat.
Pumpkin	Peel, seed and cook until soft. Mash and freeze as purée in rigid containers.		6 months	Reheat in double boiler, *or* thaw 2 hours to use as pie filling.

Vegetable	Preparation	Blanching Time	Storage Life	Serving
Spinach	Remove stems from young tender spinach. Wash leaves very well. Blanch and shake the basket so that leaves remain separate. Cool, drain and press out moisture. Pack in bags or rigid containers.	2 minutes	12 months	Melt a little butter and cook frozen spinach 7 minutes.
Sweetcorn	Remove leaves and threads from fresh tender corn. Grade for size. Blanch according to size – 4 minutes will be enough for small cobs, 6 minutes for medium cobs and 8 minutes for large cobs. Cool, drain and pack in bags. *Or* blanch cobs and scrape off kernels. Pack in rigid containers.	4–8 minutes	12 months	Thaw in wrappings in refrigerator, and cook 10 minutes in boiling water. Cook 10 minutes in boiling water.
Tomatoes	Wipe, cut in halves and open-freeze, *or* wipe, grade and pack in small quantities in bags. Core and quarter tomatoes, and simmer in own juice for 5 minutes. Sieve, cool and freeze as purée in rigid containers.		12 months 12 months	Fry, grill or bake from frozen. Add to soups, stews, or sauces.
Turnips	Peel small, young turnips. Cut in dice, blanch, cool, drain and pack in bags.	2½ minutes	12 months	Cook 10 minutes in boiling water.

Home freezing: Fish

Fish for freezing
Must be very fresh. Small fish can
be left whole but the heads and
tails of large fish should be
removed. They can then be frozen
in one piece or cut into steaks. All
fish should be gutted.

Preparing fish for freezing

Only freeze very fresh fish as soon as it has been caught, and do not freeze fish from a shop. As soon as the fish have been caught, the scales should be scraped off with a sharp knife, and the fins removed. Small fish can be left whole, but large fish need their heads and tails removing. They can then be frozen in one piece, or cut through into steaks. All fish should be gutted and all blood and waste matter washed away. Flat fish should be skinned and filleted. Wash white fish in salt water, but only use fresh water for fatty fish. Shellfish must be very fresh-caught, and cooked at once before freezing.

Freezing methods

There are four methods of preparing fish for freezing, the first two being most often used.

Dry pack

Separate the fish with double layers of freezer film and pack in polythene bags or a rigid container, excluding air. Freeze quickly.

Brine pack

This should not be used for fatty fish, as the combination of fat and salt in the freezer may result in rancidity. Dip prepared fish into cold salt water – 15ml (1 tablespoon) salt to 1 litre (2 pints) water. Drain, wrap and seal. Brine-dipped fish should not be kept longer than three months.

Acid pack

This pack helps to preserve the flavour and whiteness of the fish. Use citric acid powder in water, allowing one part to one hundred parts water (5ml/500ml; 1 teaspoon/1 pint). Dip prepared fish in this solution, drain, wrap and seal.

Solid ice pack

Freeze small fish, fish steaks or fillets in water in freezer containers until solid. Pieces of fish should be separated by two layers of freezer film before freezing. Wrap ice blocks in foil or polythene to store.

Glazed whole fish

A large fish, such as salmon, may be needed whole when cooked, but is difficult to pack for the freezer. To overcome the problem, the fish may be glazed and stored whole. Clean the fish and place it unwrapped against the freezer wall in the coldest part of the freezer. When frozen very hard, dip fish quickly into very cold water so that a thin coating of ice forms. Return to freezer for one hour, then repeat process. Continue until ice is about 5mm ($\frac{1}{4}$in) thick and then wrap in polythene sheeting. The fish may be kept unwrapped for two weeks if preferred.

Guidelines for freezing fish

1 Only freeze freshly-caught fish, never buy from the shop for freezing. Prepare and freeze as soon as caught, as even a short delay can affect flavour.
2 Shellfish **must** be freshly-caught and cooked **at once** before freezing as they stale very quickly. Cooked fish (except for shellfish) is rarely worth freezing as it becomes dry and tasteless. Leftovers may be mixed with a sauce, or made into fishcakes or fish pie for freezing. Fish which is reheated loses flavour and nutritive value.
3 Fish should not be stored longer than necessary. Flavour and texture will be lost in long-term storage. Keep fatty fish (haddock, halibut, herring, mackerel, salmon, trout, turbot) only up to four months; white fish (cod, plaice, sole, whiting) up to six months; shellfish up to one month and smoked fish up to three months.
4 Thin pieces of fish can be cooked straight from the freezer, but fish for frying will taste better if thawed first. Large pieces of fish and whole fish should be thawed in wrappings in the refrigerator, which will take a considerable time – 5–6 hours per 500g (1lb).

What can go wrong

Stale-tasting fish. These were left too long before freezing. Fatty fish, such as mackerel, are likely to deteriorate in flavour very quickly and should be processed as soon as caught.
Dry tasteless fish. This is the result of air being left in the pack. Wrappings should be pressed very close to the fish before freezing.
Poor-textured fish. The texture is also affected by air left in packs, and by overcooking. Fish must only be cooked long enough to become tender.

85

Home freezing: Fish

Fish	Preparation	Packing	Storage Life	Serving
Crab	Put in cold water or court bouillon, cover and bring to boil; simmer 20–30 minutes depending on size. Cool in cooking liquor and drain. Clean crab and take out edible meat. Pack into boxes or bags. If preferred, scrub shells and use for packing crabmeat.	Polythene bags. Rigid containers. Scrubbed shells inside bags.	1 month	Thaw in container in refrigerator for 3 hours.
Fatty Fish (Haddock, Halibut, Herring, Mackerel, Red Mullet, Salmon, Trout, Turbot, Whitebait)	Clean; fillet, or cut in steaks, or leave whole. Put 2 layers of freezer film between pieces to separate. Wrap and exclude all air, keeping pack shallow. Freeze quickly. Large fish may be prepared in solid ice pack.	Polythene bags. Rigid containers.	4 months	Thaw in wrappings in refrigerator for 3–4 hours. Small pieces of fish may be cooked while frozen. Large fish need 5–6 hours per 500g (1lb).
Lobster and Crayfish	Cook as for crab (above), cool and split. Remove flesh and pack.	Polythene bags. Rigid containers.	1 month	Thaw in container in refrigerator for 3 hours.
Mussels	Scrub and clean very well to take fibrous matter off shells and remove grit. Discard any which do not close when tapped. Put in large pan and cover with damp cloth. Put over medium heat for 3 minutes until they open. Discard any which do not open. Cool in pan and remove from shells, saving juices. Pack in containers, covering with juices.	Rigid containers	1 month	Thaw in container in refrigerator for 3 hours and use as fresh fish.
Oysters	Open oysters, remove from shells, and save juices. Wash fish in salt water – 5ml (1 teaspoon) salt to 500ml (1 pint) water. Pack in containers, covering with juices.	Rigid containers.	1 month	Thaw in container in refrigerator for 3 hours. Serve raw on scrubbed shells, or cooked.
Prawns	Put in cold, fresh water and boil 5 minutes. Cool in cooking water. Take off shells and pack prawns tightly.	Polythene bags. Rigid containers.	1 month	Thaw in container in refrigerator for 3 hours. Serve cold or use for cooking.
Scallops	Open shells, remove fish. Wash fish in salt water – 5ml (1 teaspoon) salt to 500ml (1 pint) water. Pack in salt water, leaving 2·5cm (1-in) headspace.	Rigid containers.	1 month	Thaw in container in refrigerator, drain and cook. Serve on scrubbed shells.
Shrimps	Put in cold, fresh water and boil 5 minutes; cool in cooking water. Take off shells and pack shrimps tightly.	Rigid containers. Polythene bags.	1 month	Thaw in container in refrigerator for 3 hours.
	Freshly cooked shrimps may be covered in melted spiced butter for freezing.	Rigid containers.	1 month	Thaw in container in refrigerator for 3 hours to serve with toast or salad.

Fish	Preparation	Blanching Time	Storage Life	Serving
Smoked Fish (Bloaters, Eel, Haddock, Kippers, Mackerel, Salmon, Sprats, Trout)	Pack in layers with 2 sheets of freezer film between each layer, keeping pack shallow.	Polythene bags.	3 months	Thaw in wrappings in refrigerator for 3 hours to eat cold. Cook haddock or kippers while frozen.

Fish	Preparation	Blanching Time	Storage Life	Serving
White Fish (Cod, Plaice, Sole, Whiting)	Clean, fillet or cut in steaks, or leave whole. Put freezer film between pieces to separate. Wrap and exclude all air, keeping pack shallow. Freeze quickly.	Polythene bags. Rigid containers.	6 months	Thaw in wrappings in refrigerator 3—4 hours; more if large. Small pieces of fish may be cooked while frozen.

Home freezing: Poultry & game

Preparing poultry for freezing

All birds to be frozen should be in perfect condition, and they must be starved for 24 hours before killing. Cold and hygienic conditions are essential throughout the preparation. After killing, birds must be hung and bled well. Dry-plucking is best, as scalding in water will increase the risk of freezer-burn or grey spots during storage. Whichever plucking method is followed, the skin should, if possible, not be damaged. The oil glands of ducks and geese must be removed, as they will taint the poultry flesh in the freezer. After plucking, the inside should be drawn and cleaned, then the bird should be cooled in a larder or refrigerator for 12 hours.

A whole bird should be trussed for easy packing, but poultry halves or joints can be frozen. Joints should be wrapped in freezer film before being packed into polythene bags for storage, and any protruding bones must be protected with foil.

A whole bird must never be stuffed for the freezer, nor should giblets be left inside. They have a short storage life of only two months and must be packed separately. Giblets should be cleaned and washed, dried and chilled, and packed in polythene bags. Livers may be packed separately for use in pâté or an omelette.

Thawing poultry

Poultry must be completely thawed before cooking, as food poisoning can result when the heat of cooking cannot penetrate to the frozen centre of the bird where bacteria may be present. It is best to thaw poultry slowly and evenly in the refrigerator, and this will take 5–6 hours per 500g (1lb), or up to 30 hours for a chicken weighing 2–2½kg (4–5lb). A turkey weighing 4½kg (9lb) will take two days, and a large bird will take as much as three days. Once the bird has been thawed, it may be stored for up to 24 hours in a refrigerator, but no more. All kinds of poultry should be thawed in opened freezer wrappings.

Preparing game for freezing

Young birds and animals which have been well shot are best frozen raw, but older or badly-shot birds are best cooked in pies, pâté or casseroles before freezing. Game must be hung for the required length of time before freezing, as it will go bad very quickly if hung after freezing. It is also very important to pluck or skin game before freezing, as the task becomes very unpleasant and difficult if game has been frozen and thawed

Grouse, pheasant and partridge should be drawn before freezing, and any waterfowl fed on fish, but blackcock, plover, quail, snipe and woodcock are not drawn. Hares and rabbits have to be bled and cleaned before freezing, while venison is jointed like beef.

Game must be kept cool between shooting and freezing, with care taken to remove as much shot as possible, and to clean the shot wounds. Birds should be hung to individual taste, plucked and drawn (if necessary), then the cavity washed and drained and the body wiped before continuing to pack and freeze like poultry.

Thawing game

Thaw all game in opened freezer wrappings in the refrigerator, allowing five hours for each 500g (1lb). As soon as the game has thawed and is still cold, start cooking so that juices are not lost.

Guidelines for freezing poultry and game

1 Always prepare poultry and game in cold and hygienic conditions, and see that it is hung in a cool airy place.

2 Be sure to hang game for the preferred time as it must not be hung after freezing.

3 Never put poultry or game in the freezer without plucking or skinning, trimming off heads, feet, etc, and drawing (except for the few birds which are cooked with their 'innards' intact, see above).

4 Prepare poultry and game in the form in which it is most likely to be used, ie whole for roasting, jointed for casseroles and pies, as this will save tedious preparation at the time of cooking.

5 Pack any giblets or stuffing separately and use within two months.

What can go wrong

Tough poultry and game. This results from lack of hanging, or because the bird or animal was too old and should have been cooked before freezing.

Grey patches on flesh. These are known as freezer-burn, and mean that packaging has been inadequate and air has been allowed to reach the poultry in the freezer. This is not a dangerous condition but is unsightly and may indicate that the flesh has dried out in the freezer. It is best to choose a 'juicy' method of cooking rather than a dry method like grilling or roasting.

Food poisoning. If poultry is not completely thawed, preferably in a refrigerator, before cooking, food poisoning can be caused.

Home freezing: Poultry & game

Bird	Preparation and Packaging	Storage Life	Serving
Chicken	Hang and cool, pluck and draw. Truss or cut in joints. Chill for 12 hours. Pack in polythene bag, removing air. Separate joints with freezer film. Pack giblets separately.	12 months	Thaw in opened wrappings in refrigerator for 5–6 hours per 500g (1lb).
Duck	Hang and cool, pluck and draw. Remove oil glands. Chill for 12 hours. Pack in polythene bag, removing air. Pack giblets separately.	6 months	Thaw in opened wrappings in refrigerator for 5–6 hours per 500g (1lb).
Goose	Hang and cool, pluck and draw. Remove oil glands. Chill for 12 hours. Pack in polythene bag, removing air. Pack giblets separately.	6 months	Thaw in opened wrappings in refrigerator overnight. A large bird will need 24 hours.
Guinea Fowl	Hang and cool, pluck and draw. Truss and chill for 12 hours. Pack in polythene bag, removing air.	12 months	Thaw in opened wrappings in refrigerator overnight. Lard this dry bird before roasting.
Turkey	Hang and cool, pluck and draw. Truss or cut in joints. Chill for 12 hours. Pack in polythene bag, removing air. Pack giblets separately.	12 months	Thaw in opened wrappings in refrigerator for 2 days (small birds) or 3 days (large birds).
Giblets	Clean, wash, dry and chill. Pack in polythene bag, removing air.	2 months	Thaw in opened wrappings in refrigerator for 3 hours.
Livers	Clean, wash, dry and chill. Pack in polythene bag, removing air.	2 months	Thaw in opened wrappings in refrigerator for 3 hours.

Game	Preparation and Packaging	Storage Life	Serving
Grouse (12th August–10th December) **Partridge** (1st September–1st February) **Pheasant** (1st October–1st February)	Remove shot and clean wounds. Hang by neck, in feathers, in cool place, for time according to taste (about 7 days in cool conditions). Pluck, draw and truss. Pack in polythene bag, removing air.	6 months	Thaw in opened wrappings in refrigerator, allowing 5 hours for each 500g (1lb).
Hare and Rabbit	Clean shot wounds, behead and bleed, collecting hare's blood for cooking. Hang for 24 hours in a cool place. Cut in joints. Separate with freezer film and pack in polythene bag. Pack hare's blood in rigid container.	6 months	Thaw in opened wrappings in refrigerator, allowing 5 hours for each 500g (1lb).
Pigeon	Remove shot and clean wounds. Prepare and pack as poultry.	6 months	Thaw in opened wrappings in refrigerator, allowing 5 hours for each 500g (1lb).
Blackcock, Plover, Quail, Snipe, Woodcock	Remove shot and clean wounds. Pluck but do not draw. Pack in polythene bag, removing air.	6 months	Thaw in opened wrappings in refrigerator allowing 5 hours for each 500g (1lb).
Venison	Clean shot wounds, and keep carcass cold. Behead, bleed, skin and clean. Wash and wipe flesh. Hang in a cool place for 5 days. Joint and pack in bags, removing air. Only freeze good joints, and cook other pieces before freezing.	8 months	Thaw in opened wrappings in refrigerator for 4 hours. Take off wrappings and put into marinade. Continue thawing, allowing 5 hours for each 500g (1lb). Lard before roasting.

Venison Marinade
This dry meat is greatly improved if thawed in marinade. Mix 250ml (½ pint) red wine, 250ml (½ pint) vinegar, 1 large sliced onion, parsley, thyme and bay leaf. Pour over partly-thawed meat, and turn venison often while marinading.

Home freezing: Meat

Preparing meat for the freezer

Bulk supplies of meat may be bought from a butcher, farmer or frozen food supplier, but it is expensive to buy and must be chosen with great care. Meat must be frozen with the needs of the family in mind – some families will eat economy cuts, others only eat steaks and roasts. If a family has little time for cooking, considerable effort and fuel may have to be used to make the economy cuts palatable, and this will offset the apparent cheapness of the purchase.

The meat must be of high quality and hung properly (beef 8 to 12 days; lamb 5 to 7 days; pork chilled only). Nothing will improve the texture of poor meat or give it good flavour. Discuss with the supplier how much meat is in a bulk purchase and whether the price is for the carcass weight, or for prepared meat without excess fat, bones, etc, as there can be a considerable difference. Some butchers will give a price reduction if a certain amount is spent, so that one need not buy a whole carcass for economy.

Ask for meat to be cut to individual requirements, so that there is a mixture of large and small joints, steaks and chops, cubed and minced meat, and sausages. For preference, ask the butcher to pack, label and freeze the meat as he has the facilities to freeze a large quantity down to a low temperature very quickly, which is essential for good meat. Meat will take less space in the freezer if boned and rolled and joints such as leg of lamb can be cut in two pieces for smaller families. Time will be saved if some meat is frozen as cubes or mince and packaged in small amounts which will not take long to freeze. Be sure to ask the butcher to separate steaks, chops and sausages with two layers of freezer film and to pack in small amounts, as large lumps of meat are difficult and wasteful to thaw and prepare.

Packaging meat

If meat is to be wrapped and frozen at home, use strong polythene bags or foil, so that air cannot enter the packages and affect the fat which can cause rancidity. Pad bones with twists of foil so that they cannot damage packaging, and overwrap very large pieces of meat with extra polythene or brown paper (and with muttoncloth if your butcher can supply it) so that they will not suffer if the initial packaging becomes split. Air must be completely excluded from packages and the wrappings pressed close to the meat. Label each package with the name of the joint and its weight.

Fast freezing

It is most important that meat is frozen quickly or it will become tough. Only freeze $1\frac{1}{2}$kg (3lb) meat per 28·3 litres (1cuft) freezer space at one time, and set the fast-freeze switch the day before freezing begins. If a lot of meat is being frozen, freeze offal first, then pork, lamb and finally beef. Keep unfrozen meat in a very cold place or refrigerator until it can be frozen.

Thawing and cooking

Thaw meat slowly in opened wrappings in the refrigerator to avoid loss of juices which will make the meat tough. Thin cuts of meat and mince can be cooked from frozen, but may be tough. As soon as meat is fully thawed it can be cooked as fresh meat.

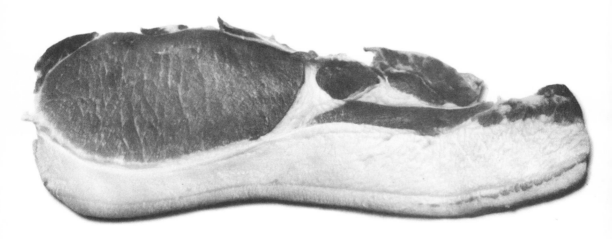

Guidelines for freezing meat

1 Only buy meat which the family likes. There is no advantage in buying a carcass if only the roasting and grilling meats will be used, and the economy cuts which need long and careful cooking are disliked. It is better to buy only the better cuts in a good selection if possible; families on a tight budget can buy a selection of economy cuts.

2 Make sure that meat for the freezer is of high quality and properly hung by the butcher. The freezer will not transform poor meat and make it more tender or palatable.

3 Freeze meat quickly at the lowest possible temperature. Slow-frozen meat will be tough and stringy. It is best to ask the butcher to package and freeze a carcass as he has greater space and the equipment to reach low temperatures.

4 Thaw meat slowly in the refrigerator to avoid loss of juices, and cook carefully. It is possible to cook frozen joints, but the procedure takes a long time, and much care, and involves the use of a meat thermometer. For really good meat, thaw completely and cook as usual.

5 Avoid combining salt and fat which will react together under freezing conditions to cause rancidity. The storage life of fat, salt meat is very limited.

6 To get full value from a carcass, make use of the large quantity of suet and fat which is included, and the bones. Cook the bones to make stock for freezing. Package the suet to freeze and use in puddings, and render down fat to make dripping which can be frozen and used for frying and for pastry-making – but remember that suet and fat have a storage life of about one month maximum.

What can go wrong

Off-flavours. These can sometimes be detected in offal, and are caused by poor packaging which has allowed the entrance of air, or by prolonged storage.

Rancidity. This is caused by the reaction of salt and fat in freezing conditions, and salt fat meat should be stored no longer than one month.

Dry meat. Poor or damaged packaging, which has allowed the entrance of air or the passage of moisture from the meat, can result in dry meat.

Tough meat. Toughness is caused by slow-freezing, quick thawing or poor cooking. The meat may also be of poor quality before freezing, or has not been hung properly.

Packaging bacon
At this stage the wrapping should be pressed tight against the meat so that all air is excluded. Label and add weight.

Home freezing: Meat

BEEF

Cuts	Uses
Topside	Roasting; Pot Roasting
Top Ribs	Roasting; Grilling in thin slices
Fore Ribs, Wing Ribs Back Ribs	Roasting
Rump	Roasting in the piece; Grilling in slices
Fillet	Roasting in pastry case; Grilling as Fillet, Tournedos or Châteaubriand
Sirloin	Roasting; Grilling as Sirloin, Entrecôte, Porterhouse or T-bone

Economy Cuts

Top Rump	Pot Roasting
Thick Flank	Pot Roasting
Flank	Pot Roasting (boned and rolled)
Brisket	Slow Roasting (de-fatted and rolled); Pot Roasting
Silverside	Pot Roasting
Shin	Stewing; Stock-making
Leg	Stewing; Stock-making
Neck and Clod	Stewing; Stock-making
Chuck and Blade	Stewing; Pies; Puddings
Skirt	Stewing; Pies; Puddings

LAMB

Cuts	
Shoulder	Roasting; Cubed for Pies, Casseroles, Kebabs
Leg	Roasting
Loin	Roasting (on bone, or boned and rolled); Chops
Saddle (Double Loin)	Roasting

Economy Cuts

Best End of Neck	Roasting; Cutlets; Stewing
Middle Neck	Stewing
Scrag End of Neck	Stewing
Breast of Lamb	Roasting (boned, rolled and stuffed); Stewing

PORK

Cuts	
Leg	Roasting
Loin	Roasting; Chops
Shoulder	Cubed for Pies, Casseroles, Kebabs

Economy Cuts

Blade	Roasting
Spare Rib	Roasting
Hand and Spring	Roasting (boned, rolled and stuffed)
Belly	Roasting (boned); Grilling in thin slices; Pâté

OFFAL

Hearts	Casseroles
Kidneys	Frying; Grilling; Casseroles; Pies; Puddings
Sweetbreads	Frying; Braising
Tongue	Boiling (serve hot or cold)
Liver	Frying; Grilling; Casseroles

HAM AND BACON

Joints	Boiled or baked (serving hot or cold)
Rashers	Frying; Grilling; Casseroles

Home freezing: Meat

Meat	Preparation	Storage Life	Serving
Joints	Trim surplus fat and bone and roll if possible to save space. Pad any sharp bones. Pack in foil or polythene bag, removing air. Freeze quickly.	12 months (beef) 9 months (lamb) 6 months (pork)	Thaw in opened wrappings in refrigerator for 5 hours per 500g (1lb).
Steaks and Chops	Pack in usable portions and quantities. Separate pieces with two layers of freezer film and pack in polythene bag, removing air. Freeze quickly.	12 months (beef) 9 months (lamb) 6 months (pork)	Thaw in opened wrappings in refrigerator for 5 hours per 500g (1lb), or cook thin cuts from frozen, using low heat to start.
Cubed Meat	Pack in usable quantities. Trim meat of fat and gristle, and cut in neat pieces. Press tightly into polythene bags, removing air. Freeze quickly.	2 months	Thaw in opened wrappings in refrigerator for 4 hours per 500g (1lb).
Minced Meat	Only freeze high-quality mince without fat. Pack tightly in bags and do not salt. Remove air. Freeze quickly. Or shape mince into flat cakes, separate with two layers of freezer film and pack in polythene bags or rigid containers. Remove air. Freeze quickly.	2 months	Thaw in opened wrappings in refrigerator for 4 hours per 500g (1lb). Cook from frozen.
Hearts, Kidneys, Sweetbreads, Tongue	Wash and dry well, and remove blood vessels and pipes. Wrap in freezer film and pack in polythene bags or rigid containers. Tongue may also be cooked and frozen whole, wrapped in polythene. Freeze quickly.	2 months	Thaw in opened wrappings in refrigerator for 5 hours per 500g (1lb).
Liver	Pack whole or in slices separated by two layers of freezer film. Wrap in polythene bags, removing air. Freeze quickly.	2 months	Thaw in opened wrappings in refrigerator for 5 hours per 500g (1lb).
Tripe	Cut in 2·5cm (1in) squares. Pack tightly in polythene bags or rigid containers, removing air. Freeze quickly.	2 months	Thaw in opened wrappings in refrigerator for 5 hours per 500g (1lb).
Sausages and Sausage Meat	If making your own sausages, leave out salt in preparation. Pack in usable quantities. Separate layers of sausages with two pieces of freezer film. Pack tightly in polythene bags, removing air. Freeze quickly.	2 months	Thaw in opened wrappings in refrigerator for 4 hours. Sausages may be cooked from frozen over low heat.
Bacon	Freeze vacuum-packed bacon for preference. Otherwise, pack portions in polythene bags, removing air. Freeze quickly. Smoked bacon will keep longer than unsmoked, as constituents in the smoke act as anti-oxidants and retard rancidity caused by action of salt on fat.	6 months (vacuum-packed) 5 weeks (home-packed)	Thaw in opened wrappings in refrigerator for 24 hours.
Ham and Delicatessen Meats	Freeze vacuum-packed for preference; cooked meat will dry out quickly if home-packed, because air may enter. For home-packing, separate slices with two layers of freezer film; pack tightly in polythene bag or rigid container.	1 month	Thaw in opened wrappings in refrigerator for 4 hours.

Home freezing: Dairy produce

It is not necessary to keep large supplies of dairy produce in the freezer, since it is always available easily from shops. The price of dairy produce does fluctuate a good deal, however, and this makes it worth while to freeze supplies when prices are low. The freezing of small quantities of eggs and cheese can also save waste of egg yolks and whites, or cheese ends.

Choose high-quality, fresh dairy produce, if possible buying direct from the producer. For economy, buy fresh cracked eggs from farms, and look out for rich cream and farmhouse cheeses in country markets.

Buy cheese from a reliable supplier and make sure it has been well kept and has just reached a peak of maturity before freezing. Avoid freezing small pieces of cheese sold pre-packed in thick polythene which can 'sweat' in the shop.

As with all frozen food, dairy produce must be absolutely fresh and clean before being frozen. Make sure all cartons and containers are scrupulously clean, and wash eggs before cracking them so that no dirt contaminates the contents. Work in a cool atmosphere and freeze food quickly.

Choose packaging carefully to exclude as much air as possible.

Milk
Long-life packs eliminate the need for freezing milk. Only **homogenised** milk can be frozen, as it will not separate when thawed. The milk must be packed in a waxed carton or rigid freezer container, leaving 2·5cm (1in) headspace. It should be thawed at room temperature and used quickly after thawing.

Cream
Only cream containing over 40 per cent butterfat can be frozen, which means cream sold as double cream, or that which comes from Channel Island cows. The cream must be **pasteurised** and should be frozen in a waxed carton or rigid freezer container, leaving 2·5cm (1in) headspace. Channel Island cream may be frozen without treatment, but double cream is best whipped and sweetened. Allow 25g (1oz) sugar to 500ml (1 pint) cream. The sweetened whipped cream can be frozen in bulk, or piped in rosettes, open-frozen, and packed in rigid containers. Cream should be thawed at room temperature and lightly beaten with a fork to make it smooth. Rosettes of whipped cream will thaw in 15 minutes, and should be placed on cakes or puddings while still frozen, just before serving.

Butter
Both salted and unsalted butter may be frozen, but salted butter has a limited storage life of three months, since salt and fat react together at low temperature to cause rancidity. Unsalted butter will store for 6 months. Blocks of butter should be left in greaseproof wrappings, and packed in polythene bags for freezer storage. Butter should be thawed in the refrigerator, and enough can be thawed for one week's use.

Margarine
Treat margarine as butter for freezing.

Yogurt
Homemade yogurt and natural yogurt are not suitable for freezing. Fruit-flavoured yogurt may be frozen in the cartons in which it is purchased. It is really better to buy commercially-frozen yogurt for freezer storage.

Cheese
Hard cheese such as traditional English and Dutch varieties are best frozen in wedges weighing about 250g (8oz), but they may be a little crumbly when thawed. Smaller slices may be frozen, divided by 2 layers of freezer film. Grated hard cheese should be frozen in small amounts in polythene bags.

Blue cheeses freeze well, particularly Stilton, but foreign varieties crumble when thawed. These strongly-flavoured cheeses should be over-wrapped for freezing to avoid any cross-flavouring of foods.

Soft cheeses such as Brie and Camembert may be frozen when at the peak of maturity, in their own wrappings, with an over-wrapping of foil or polythene.

All cheese should be fully ripe when frozen, so that it has developed maximum flavour. Cheese is best thawed overnight in wrappings in the refrigerator, and it should then be left to come to room temperature before serving. Grated cheese may be used for topping dishes while still frozen.

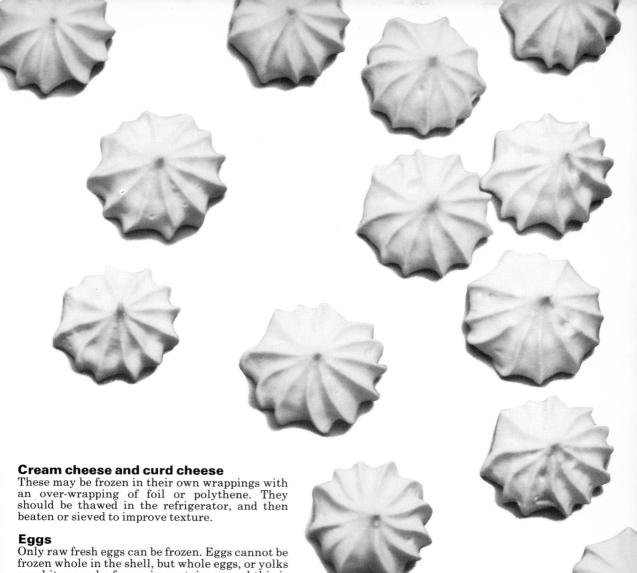

Cream cheese and curd cheese

These may be frozen in their own wrappings with an over-wrapping of foil or polythene. They should be thawed in the refrigerator, and then beaten or sieved to improve texture.

Eggs

Only raw fresh eggs can be frozen. Eggs cannot be frozen whole in the shell, but whole eggs, or yolks or whites can be frozen in containers, and this is particularly useful when yolks or whites are left over from a cooking session. Whole eggs and egg yolks need the addition of salt or sugar (as appropriate for use) to prevent coagulation, but egg whites need no pre-freezing treatment.

Whole eggs should be lightly whisked to combine white and yolk without incorporating air bubbles. Add 2·5ml ($\frac{1}{2}$ teaspoon) salt or 5ml (1 teaspoon) sugar to each egg. Pour into container and seal, labelling carefully to show whether salt or sugar has been added. When cooking with these eggs, 1 whole egg measures 50ml (2floz). Whole eggs are best thawed quickly in the covered container, under running cold water – this will take about ten minutes.

Egg yolks should be mixed well, adding 2·5ml ($\frac{1}{2}$ teaspoon) salt or 5ml (1 teaspoon) sugar to two yolks. Individual plastic butter or jam pots, or sections of a plastic egg-box can be used to freeze separate egg yolks. Larger quantities can be packaged in small freezer containers for making butter cream, custard and mayonnaise. Label containers with the number of yolks packaged,

Freezing cream
Rosettes of cream, if frozen, can be placed on cakes or puddings straight from the freezer. They will thaw in 15 minutes.

and whether salt or sugar is added. Thaw egg yolks in the container, under cold running water, and use at room temperature.

Egg whites need no additions or whisking. The containers should be labelled with the number of whites frozen. Single egg whites can be frozen in ice-cube containers, unmoulded and stored in polythene bags, for use in jelly, sorbet, etc. Larger quantities are useful for meringues and icings, and can be packed in small freezer containers. Allow egg whites to thaw at room temperature for one hour before use. 1 egg white measures 40ml ($1\frac{1}{2}$floz).

99

Home freezing: Dairy produce

Guidelines for freezing dairy produce

1 Make sure that milk is homogenised and cream is pasteurised. Cream should be double cream or Channel Island cream.

2 Avoid freezing home-made or farm-produced yogurt, or natural yogurt produced by manufacturers. Only fruit yogurt will freeze successfully, and it is really better to buy ready-frozen yogurt for storage.

3 Only raw fresh eggs can be frozen, and these cannot be frozen in the shell. Whole eggs and yolks need the addition of salt or sugar.

4 When freezing any liquid, such as milk, eggs or cream, leave a headspace (2·5cm/1in) in the container to allow for expansion on freezing, but no more or air will affect the contents.

What can go wrong

Tasteless, soapy cheese. This is caused by thawing cheese too quickly. Semi-frozen cheese will also be soapy and tasteless – serve at room temperature.

Rubbery egg whites. This is what happens if you freeze hard-boiled eggs. Only raw fresh eggs can be frozen, so Scotch Eggs or pies containing eggs should not be frozen. Chopped hard-boiled egg whites should not be included in recipes, but they can sometimes be added during thawing.

Lumpy eggs. Thawing eggs under warm water will partly cook them, and make them lumpy. They should be thawed under very cold running water.

Watery cream. Cream with a low butterfat content will not freeze successfully – it will be watery. Cream for freezing must be 'double' quality. Even rich cream may look lumpy and separated on thawing, but this is quickly put right by light beating with a fork.

Dairy produce in the freezer
It's worth freezing dairy produce if you buy when prices are low — they tend to fluctuate with the seasons — but it must be of the highest quality. Eggs are frozen raw without the shell and you can save odd yolks and whites by putting them in the freezer. Only homogenised milk and double cream can be frozen and they should be stored in waxed cartons or rigid containers. Hard cheeses are best frozen in large wedges as they tend to crumble when thawed, but blue cheese, especially Stilton, freezes well. All cheeses, particularly Brie and Camembert should be fully ripe when frozen.

Home freezing: Dairy produce

Food	Preparation and Packaging	Storage Time	Thawing and Serving
Butter or Margarine	Overwrap blocks in polythene or foil.	3 months (salted) 6 months (unsalted)	Transfer to refrigerator enough for one week's use.
Cheese	a) Cut hard cheese in 250g (8oz) portions. Divide pieces with freezer film and wrap in foil or polythene, excluding air.	3 months	Thaw in wrappings in refrigerator overnight. Cut in smaller pieces while still slightly frozen to avoid crumbling.
	b) Cut blue cheese in portions and pack as hard cheese. Overwrap carefully to prevent cross-flavouring.	3 months	Thaw in wrappings in refrigerator overnight.
	c) Soft cheeses, such as Brie and Camembert, can be left in wrappings, but overwrapped to prevent drying-out.	3 months	Thaw in wrappings in refrigerator overnight.
	d) Grate hard cheese and freeze in 50g (2oz) quantities in polythene bags.	3 months	Sprinkle on dishes while frozen, or thaw for 1 hour before adding to sauce.
	e) Leave cream and curd cheese in wrappings, but overwrap in foil or polythene.	3 months	Thaw in wrappings in refrigerator overnight, then beat or sieve to improve texture.

Food	Preparation and Packing	Storage Time	Thawing and Serving
Cream	Use pasteurised cream, over 40 per cent butterfat.		
	a) Freeze Channel Island cream in cartons, leaving 2·5cm (1in) headspace.	6 months	Thaw in container at room temperature.
	b) Whip double cream to soft peaks adding 25g (1oz) sugar to 500ml (1 pint) cream. Pack in cartons, leaving 2·5cm (1in) headspace.		Thaw in container at room temperature.
	c) Pipe rosettes of whipped cream on trays, open-freeze and pack in rigid containers.		Put on cakes or puddings, while still frozen, 15 minutes before serving.
Milk	Freeze homogenised milk only in cartons, leaving 2·5cm (1in) headspace.	1 month	Thaw at room temperature and use quickly.
Yogurt	Freeze fruit-flavoured yogurt only in cartons in which it is purchased.	3 months	Thaw in refrigerator overnight.
Whole Eggs	Blend lightly with a fork. Add 2·5ml ($\frac{1}{2}$ teaspoon) salt or 5ml (1 teaspoon) sugar to each egg. Put into rigid container, labelling if salt or sugar added.	6 months	Thaw under cold running water for 10 minutes.
Egg Yolks	Mix with a fork. Add 2·5ml ($\frac{1}{2}$ teaspoon) salt or 5ml (1 teaspoon) sugar to 2 yolks. Pack small quantities in plastic butter or jam pots, and larger quantities in rigid containers, labelling if salt or sugar added.	6 months	Thaw under cold running water for 10 minutes.
Egg Whites	Do not mix or add salt or sugar. Pack single whites in ice-cube containers, unmould and store in polythene bags. Pack larger quantities in rigid containers, labelling with number packed.	6 months	Thaw at room temperature.

Cooking for the freezer

All of us are aware of the convenience of having food already cooked and waiting in the freezer. It does away with all our food worries and leaves us happy and confident that we can cope with whatever emergency arises. But it is easy to get carried away with the idea – and make two of everything – one for the freezer – whether or not it is the ideal freezeable dish. Some cooked dishes taste as good as freshly-made when you take them from the freezer, but others can suffer, lose flavour and texture and simply don't compare with their originals. Katie Stewart feels strongly about this and in the following chapter she has taken particular care to choose those dishes which react well to freezing, all of which she recommends from her own experience. She also gives recipes for sauces which can be used in different ways so as to extend the variety and avoid the monotony of too many identical dishes. The family tea is taken care of, too, with recipes for scones and cakes which come out of the freezer as fresh as on the day they were made.

Cooking for the freezer

No two cooks ever use their freezer in the same way. Each must, by trial and error find out how it can best be used to fulfil their own personal requirements. Like any other piece of kitchen equipment, a freezer should be used sensibly; it must be a help and not an expensive waste of time or money. There is no point in freezing food for the sake of filling the freezer. You must freeze only the food that the family like and will enjoy eating and ignore other items however tempting.

Let your freezer help when it comes to planning menus, particularly for parties, but balance dishes from the freezer with freshly prepared foods so that meals are seasonal and have a certain amount of variation.

The use of a freezer should be carefully planned so that there is a regular turnover of the contents. Don't continually keep food 'for another time'. You must freeze food and then plan on using it. The storage life of foods in your freezer is based on quality. The low temperature in a freezer retards bacterial spoilage but only slows down enzymatic changes which are responsible for the deterioration of colour and flavour. Fresh food has a longer storage life, usually from one season to the next, than cooked foods, which may contain fat, spices and other strong flavours. As a general rule, only freeze as many cooked dishes as you expect to use up within two months. Food kept past the recommended storage time is perfectly safe to eat, but will suffer from an increasing deterioration of flavour, texture and appearance.

Quality is important

The quality of the food you freeze is very important because you only take out what you put in. Ingredients for a recipe must be very fresh and carefully prepared. The quicker food is frozen the better the quality and flavour later on.

All cooked food must be cooled first. When cold, cooked dishes should be, if possible, chilled in the refrigerator before freezing. Put foods in the coldest part of the cabinet where they will freeze quickly; usually around the sides, on the base of the cabinet or in direct contact with the shelves. Some freezers have a 'fast-freeze' section, and this should always be kept clear so that fresh foods can be frozen there. A 'fast-freeze' speeds up the process of freezing by keeping the motor running continuously. When foods are frozen, switch off 'fast-freeze' and transfer the items to the main part of the cabinet for storage.

Always freeze foods in amounts that you will use at one time. You cannot thaw cooked food and then refreeze it and it can be difficult, sometimes impossible, to separate out small quantities from a larger pack, so consider how and in what quantities your recipes will be the most useful. Remember that air in a freezer is very dry. It will absorb moisture from uncovered or badly wrapped food and the result will be a drying out of the item, accompanied by a change in flavour – a condition known as 'freezer burn'. All dishes to be frozen must be wrapped in moisture- and vapour-proof material to minimise this drying effect and to

reduce any risk of cross flavouring between foods. Make use of the foil containers, polythene bags and waxed cartons, which are specially made for home freezing. In some cases 'open-freezing' is recommended. This means that items are frozen uncovered until hard (about 1–2 hours), and then packed. Open-freezing can be useful when you want a loose pack of individually frozen items or when you have something very fragile or squashable which is easier to wrap when hard.

Most important, too, is the careful labelling of everything, giving as much information as possible – name, date of freezing, number of servings and how long a dish needs to be reheated for serving. At the time of preparation you may feel you will recognise items, but it is surprising how difficult this becomes later when food is frozen. Often labels are the only clues to contents.

Cooks tend to disagree on which foods will freeze and which will not. The truth is that you can freeze anything, it is the texture and condition of the item when thawed that is the criterion by which you judge it, for freezing brings about a change in texture. All foods contain a certain amount of water and on freezing the water forms ice crystals within the structure of the food. On thawing, moisture escapes from ruptured cell tissues and causes collapse of the cell structure. The faster food is frozen the smaller the ice crystals. Slow freezing means large ice crystals. This is why you should freeze foods at the lowest possible temperature and not too many at one time. Too many fresh foods in the cabinet at the same time naturally raise the temperature inside and slow down the rate of freezing. They may also cause the temperature of already frozen foods to rise.

Foods with a low water content, such as baked bread and cakes, will freeze and thaw with no noticeable change in the texture. On the other hand, watery fruits and vegetables will lose their structure and on thawing become limp, which is why they are often better frozen when made up into a recipe. Ideally a dish, when thawed, should taste as good as it did before it went into the freezer. It is up to the individual to judge which recipes freeze and thaw to their satisfaction. For instance, hard-boiled eggs do not freeze successfully because the white becomes rubbery.

Remember, nothing comes out of the freezer crisp and for this reason salad vegetables are not suitable either. Many of one's own recipes can be adapted for the freezer, but usually finishing touches, like the stirring in of a liaison of egg yolk and cream, are best left to the reheating stage, because of the danger of overheating. The addition of a garnish which looks fresh and pretty is best made just before serving. There is no real need for 'freezer recipes' as such – it is really a question of sorting out those which are suitable for freezing from those which are not.

Get the timing right when thawing foods and reheating them from the frozen state. Either process nearly always takes longer than one expects. It is far safer and often leads to a better end product in the long run to thaw pre-cooked dishes overnight in the refrigerator before reheating them. In the refrigerator foods thaw safely and can then be reheated as if fresh. This is where planning is important, because frozen foods are not always a source of 'instant' meals.

The recipes in this section have been selected mainly on the basis that they freeze, thaw, and serve with good results.

In other cases, they have been chosen because they have varied uses – this applies particularly to the selected sauces – and therefore increase the variety of items that can be served from the freezer; you have to be very careful that the same foods don't come out of the freezer with monotonous regularity. Lastly, recipes have been selected where the freezer can extend their life, and this applies very much to the section on home baking. Here you must select products that might stale quickly after baking – there is no point in freezing cakes that keep well anyhow.

Guidelines for cooking for the freezer

1 Select recipes for freezing, giving priority to those which produce the best results and are the greatest use in menu planning.
2 Ingredients used for freezing recipes must be fresh and carefully prepared. Freeze food in serving quantities that will be convenient to use at one time.
3 Allow cooked foods to become quite cold, then put in the coldest part of the cabinet to ensure speedy freezing. Place the foods in your 'fast-freeze' compartment if you have one.
4 Pay attention to careful wrapping and use of correct containers. Label all items for identification later.
5 Plan on using food in the freezer so that there is a regular turnover of the contents. Use items within the recommended storage time for best results.
6 Work out menus in advance so that foods from the freezer can be given correct thawing or cooking times. Thaw foods in the refrigerator when possible.
7 Experiment with your own recipes and new ideas, so that menus which include cooked dishes from the freezer do not become monotonous.

What can go wrong

Dry patches. Areas on the surface of frozen foods which appear light in colour and dehydrated are the result of poor wrapping which has allowed air in the freezer to reach the contents. They are due to a loss of moisture, known as freezer burn. Wrap foods more carefully.

Change of flavour. The flavour of dishes that are well seasoned or heavily spiced may intensify during storage. Use less seasoning or spices during preparation and add extra when dishes are being reheated. Foods can also be affected by inadequate wrappings allowing stronger flavours of some dishes to transfer to others in the freezer. Use recommended freezer wrappings to safeguard against this and wrap highly flavoured foods especially well. Flavour can also be affected if items suffer from freezer burn (see above). Seal all packages carefully. Take care when open-freezing items and do not leave unwrapped longer than necessary.

Separation of sauces. Sauces should be stirred while reheating to achieve a smooth consistency. This may also apply to meat or poultry in sauces – stir well if consistency is uneven. The use of cornflour as the thickening agent in the first place will give best results.

Burst cartons. This results when insufficient headspace has been allowed for the expansion of liquid ingredients on freezing. Always leave at least 2·5cm (1in) headspace between the level of any liquid ingredients and the top of the container before sealing, to avoid this.

Cooking for the freezer: Soups

Soups are practical to freeze because they are rarely made in small quantities. You can choose almost any recipe, but those which freeze best are pulse soups and soups made using a purée of vegetables. Any recipe made using a stock from a chicken carcass or beef bone will have a very good flavour and when it is prepared, some of the stock can be frozen with soup making in mind – but it is more practical to make the soup when the stock is available and freeze the soup.

For a really smooth soup, use an electric blender, for a slightly more granular texture use a sieve, or for a coarser result use a Mouli-légumes or food mill, where the ingredients are rubbed through a mesh by turning a handle.

It is important to freeze soups in the right quantities for serving and 500ml (1 pint) cartons (two servings) and 250ml ($\frac{1}{2}$ pint) are useful, if you need more, several cartons can be taken out. Cool soup as quickly as possible and leave 2·5cm (1in) headspace in cartons to allow for expansion. Always thaw, or at least partially thaw, soup in the refrigerator, or in a cool larder, so that it can easily be removed from the carton without tearing it. Or dip the carton quickly in hot water. Then the cartons can be washed and used again.

French Onion Soup

400g (1lb) onions, thinly sliced
1 litre (2 pints) stock
25g (1oz) butter
25g (1oz) cornflour
Salt and freshly milled pepper
50ml (4 tablespoons) cold water

Grated hard cheese (see recipe)
Thin slices of French bread, lightly buttered on both sides

Serves 4–6

Melt the butter in a large saucepan and add the onions. Cover with a lid and cook very gently, with no liquid added, for 30–40 minutes, or until the onions are softened; stir occasionally. Remove the pan lid and continue to fry for a further 5–10 minutes, or until the onions are golden brown, but take care that they do not burn. Stir occasionally while the onions are browning. Add the stock. Cover and simmer until the onions are tender, about a further 20–30 minutes. Blend the cornflour with the cold water and stir into the contents of the saucepan. Bring to a simmer, stirring all the time. Cook for a further 2–3 minutes then check the seasoning.

To freeze: Cool quickly. Pour into waxed cartons and freeze. Prepared slices of buttered French bread can also be frozen in a freezer bag. Grated hard cheese should be kept separately – see opposite.

To serve: Thaw in the refrigerator or a cool larder, or dip the carton quickly in hot water. Bring the soup slowly back to the boil. Arrange the buttered French bread on a greased baking tray, heap grated hard cheese on one side of each slice,

and put it in a moderately hot oven (190°C, 375°F, Gas Mark 5) for 3–5 minutes, or under a hot grill until the bread is crisp and the cheese melts. Place a teaspoon of grated cheese in each individual hot soup bowl and pour in the soup. Float the cheesy bread on top and serve.
Recommended storage life: 2 months.

Parsnip Soup with Curry

400g (1lb) parsnips, peeled and cut in pieces
200g (8oz) potatoes, peeled and cut in dice
1 large onion, finely chopped
5ml (1 teaspoon) curry powder
1 litre (2 pints) stock
25g (1oz) butter
Salt and pepper

Serves 6

Melt the butter in a good-sized saucepan and add the onion. Fry gently for 3–5 minutes to soften the onion, then stir in the curry powder. Fry for a further few moments to draw the curry flavour. Add the prepared parsnips and potatoes and toss in the onion and butter. Stir in the stock and bring to a simmer. Cover with a lid and cook gently for about 40 minutes or until the vegetables are quite soft. Pass the vegetables and liquid through a soup mill or a sieve, or blend to a purée in an electric blender. Check the seasoning.
To freeze: Cool quickly. Pour into waxed cartons and freeze.
To serve: Thaw in the refrigerator or a cool larder, or dip the carton quickly in hot water. Bring back to boiling point. Serve hot.
Recommended storage life: 2 months.

Soups of all kinds
Soup is useful to freeze as it is easy to make in quantity. Cool it and pack into suitably sized waxed cartons.

Watercress Vichyssoise

2 bunches watercress
1 large onion, chopped
400g (1lb) potatoes, peeled and cut in dice
1 litre (2 pints) chicken stock
250ml ($\frac{1}{2}$ pint) milk
25g (1oz) butter
1 bay leaf
Salt and freshly milled pepper

Serves 8

Wash both bunches of watercress in cold water, nip the leaves off one bunch and set aside for the garnish, if liked. Trim and cut up the remaining leaves, and the stalks from both bunches. Melt the butter in a large saucepan and add the onion, potato and bay leaf. Cover and cook gently for about 5 minutes to soften the vegetables. Stir in the chicken stock and bring to a simmer. Cover and cook for about 15 minutes, or until the vegetables are quite tender. Add the watercress leaves and stems. Bring back to the boil, simmer for one minute and draw off the heat. This brief cooking of the watercress ensures a fresh flavour and a good colour. Discard the bay leaf and add the milk. Pass the liquid and vegetables through a soup mill or a sieve, or purée in an electric blender. Check the seasoning, and add the garnish of finely chopped watercress.
To freeze: Cool quickly. Pour into waxed cartons and freeze.
To serve: Thaw in the refrigerator. Serve cold or reheat.
Recommended storage life: 2 months.

Soup garnishes from the freezer
Very finely chopped parsley can be packed into ice-cube trays and, with just enough water to moisten, frozen into 'parsley cubes'. At any time one can be stirred into soup to provide a parsley garnish – often very important with clear soups or broths.

Parmesan or grated hard cheese keeps well in a freezer bag – but take out of the freezer in time to thaw and regain flavour before using.

Tiny dice of white bread are useful for bread croûtons. Keep plenty in a freezer bag and take out as many as are needed at a time. Fry in hot butter until crisp and golden.

Cream for adding to any soup recipe should be stirred in after the soup has been reheated.

Freezing parsley
Frozen parsley cubes can be stirred into soup for a garnish.

Cooking for the freezer: Fish

Dishes made with cooked fish are excellent for freezing. But remember that fish is very perishable and so must be very fresh and must be dealt with promptly. Neither the raw fish for cooking, nor the cooked fish for freezing, must be left at room temperature, nor must it be kept for more than a few hours in the refrigerator before using.

Fish Cakes

**1kg (2lb) fresh cod or
  haddock fillet**
**About 250ml (½ pint) milk and
  water – see recipe**
**1kg (2lb) cooked mashed
  potato (without milk or
  butter)**
**30ml (2 tablespoons) finely
  chopped parsley**
Squeeze lemon juice
3 eggs
Dried breadcrumbs
1 bay leaf
**Salt and freshly milled
  pepper**

Makes 18–20 fish cakes

Cut the fish into convenient sized pieces and place in a saucepan. Add the bay leaf, a seasoning of salt and pepper and sufficient mixed milk and water partly to cover the fish – about 250ml (½ pint). Cover with a lid and poach gently for about 15 minutes or until the fish is tender. Lift from the pan and when cool enough to handle,
flake the fish removing all skin and bone. Place the fish in a mixing basin and add the cooked mashed potato (potatoes should be well dried over the heat before mashing). Season with salt and pepper, add the parsley, lemon juice and one of the eggs, lightly mixed. Blend the ingredients together and then turn out on to a clean working surface. With floured hands, shape the mixture into a roll and set aside in a cool place to firm up.

Place the remaining 2 eggs in a shallow dish and whisk with a fork to break them up. Put plenty of dried breadcrumbs on a plate. Divide the fish cake mixture into 18–20 equal portions. Using a palette knife, round up each one into a neat flat fish cake. Turn fish cakes first in the lightly beaten egg and then in the breadcrumbs. Pat the coating on firmly.

To freeze: Chill in the refrigerator, then open-freeze on a flat baking sheet until firm. Place in a freezer bag for storage.

To serve: Allow to thaw in the refrigerator for 1–2 hours. Fry in hot shallow fat for about 8 minutes, turning to brown both sides. Or cook from frozen – start cooking slowly to thaw fish-cakes. Serve hot, allowing about 2 per person.

Recommended storage life: 2 months.

Smoked Haddock au Gratin

**500g (1lb) smoked haddock
  fillet**
**500g (1lb) well seasoned
  creamed potato**
250ml (½ pint) milk
65g (2½oz) butter
25g (1oz) plain flour
5ml (1 teaspoon) lemon juice
Slice lemon
25g (1oz) Gruyère cheese
1 bay leaf
Few parsley stalks
Few peppercorns
Salt and pepper

Serves 6

110

It is important to follow either the imperial or the metric weights and measures in any one recipe. Do not mix them.

Rinse the fish and cut into convenient sized pieces. Place in a saucepan with the milk, slice of lemon, bay leaf, parsley stalks and peppercorns. Add a little water if necessary so that the liquid covers the fish. Cover with a lid and simmer gently for 15 minutes. Then strain off the liquid and measure 250ml ($\frac{1}{2}$ pint) for the sauce. Leave the fish to cool for a moment, then carefully remove the skin and any small bones. Break the fish into flakes.

quite firm. Then wrap and store.
To serve: Thaw in the refrigerator for 2–3 hours. Place near the top of a moderately hot oven (190°C, 375°F, Gas Mark 5) for about 20 minutes or until well heated and brown. Serve hot as a first course.
Recommended storage life: 2 months.

Kipper Mousse

450g (1lb) boned kipper fillets
150ml ($\frac{1}{4}$ pint) double cream
Juice of 2 lemons
40g (1$\frac{1}{2}$oz) butter (for sauce)
125g (4oz) unsalted butter
250ml ($\frac{1}{2}$ pint) milk
25g (1oz) plain flour
1 bay leaf
Freshly milled pepper

cover with a circle of greaseproof paper to prevent a skin forming. Leave until quite cold.

Flake the kipper flesh into a basin. Add the unsalted butter and beat both well together. To make a smooth purée, pass both through a mouli food mill, or press through a coarse sieve. Add to the cold sauce and beat to a smooth mixture. Check the seasoning, adding plenty of freshly milled pepper if needed. Lightly whip the cream and fold into the mixture.
To freeze: Spoon the mixture into a foil dish and spread level. Rough the surface up with the prongs of a fork. Chill in the refrigerator then freeze, tightly enclosed in a freezer bag.
To serve: Thaw overnight in the refrigerator. Serve with hot toast.
Recommended storage life: 2 months.

Melt 40g (1$\frac{1}{2}$oz) butter in a saucepan over a low heat and stir in the flour. Gradually mix in the reserved fish liquid. Bring to the boil, stirring well to make a smooth sauce. Cook for 2–3 minutes and then draw off the heat. Check the seasoning and stir in the lemon juice. Fold in the flaked fish. Have ready 6 scallop shells, or fluted china baking dishes, well buttered. Pipe a border of creamed potato around the edge of each one, or arrange a border of potato and rough it up with a fork if you have no piping bag. Pile the fish mixture in the centre. Sprinkle with the grated cheese.
To freeze: Allow to cool, then chill in the refrigerator. Top each portion with a flake of butter and open-freeze until

Serves 6

Separate the kipper fillets, pull away the skin from the back of each one. Marinate in the lemon juice for several hours, turning the fish occasionally. Meanwhile prepare a white sauce to bind the mixture. Heat the milk in a saucepan with the bay leaf and infuse for 10 minutes. Melt the butter in a saucepan and stir in the flour. Cook gently for a few moments and then gradually stir in the hot infused milk. Discard the bay leaf. Bring to the boil, beating well to make a smooth sauce. Cook for 1–2 minutes then draw off the heat. Pour the sauce into a small bowl and

Preparing fish cakes for the freezer
Shape the cooked mixture into a roll (see recipe). Whisk 2 eggs. Put egg and breadcrumbs on plates. Divide roll into 18–20 equal portions and round off into flat cakes. Dip cakes in egg and breadcrumbs and pat on coating firmly.

Cooking for the freezer: Cheese

Dishes based on cheese can be very useful for snacks or family suppers. This pizza has a tasty cheese and tomato topping on a simple bread dough and is a dish that freezes and reheats very well.

There are a number of quiche recipes that freeze very well, particularly those which include vegetables. Always reheat quiche before serving because it makes the pastry crumbly and more pleasant to eat. Ratatouille flan would make a good vegetarian lunch or supper dish.

Pizza

500g (1lb) plain flour
10ml (2 teaspoons) dried yeast
10ml (2 teaspoons) salt
2·5ml (½ teaspoon) caster sugar
15ml (1 tablespoon) oil
300ml (½ pint) water, hand hot (43°C, 110°F)

For the topping

500g (1lb) strong Cheddar cheese, grated
793g (1lb 12oz) tin tomatoes, drained
Two 50g (1¾oz) tins anchovies
12 black olives, cut in half
1 onion, cut in rings
30–45ml (2–3 tablespoons) olive oil
10ml (2 teaspoons) dried mixed herbs
Salt and freshly milled pepper

Serves 6

Sift the flour and salt into a basin. Stir the dried yeast and sugar into the hand hot water and leave in a warm place for about 10 minutes, or until frothy. Make a well in the centre of the flour and pour in the yeast liquid and the oil. Mix to a rough dough in the basin. Turn out and knead for about 5 minutes, or until the dough is smooth. Replace dough in the mixing basin and set aside in a warm place, covered with a cloth, until risen and doubled in size.

Turn out the risen dough and press all over with the knuckles to knock out the air. Divide the dough in half and roll out to an oblong shape, then press each piece of dough over the base of a well-buttered 33cm (13in) by 23cm (9in) by 1·5cm (½in) baking (biscuit) tin. Brush each piece of dough all over with a little olive oil. Spoon the cut up tomatoes equally over each one. Then add the onion rings, sprinkle with the cheese and season with salt and pepper and herbs. Decorate with the drained anchovy fillets and garnish with the black olives. Allow to rest in a warm place for about 15 minutes. Then put in a hot oven (220°C, 425°F, Gas Mark 7) for 25 minutes.

Freezing a pizza
Cut into portions before freezing.

It is important to follow either the imperial or the metric weights and measures in any one recipe. Do not mix them.

To freeze: Cool, then cut into 12 portions. Open-freeze until firm, then enclose in freezer bags and store.

To serve: Put the required number of pizza portions on a baking sheet to thaw at room temperature, about one hour. Place in a moderate oven (180°C, 350°F, Gas Mark 4) and reheat for 15 minutes. Serve warm with a green salad.

Recommended storage life: 1 month.

Ratatouille Flan

Shortcrust pastry, made with 125g (4oz) self-raising flour

For the filling
500g (1lb) courgettes, sliced
1 small green pepper, deseeded and finely sliced
3 tomatoes
1 medium-sized onion, chopped
3 eggs, lightly beaten
50g (2oz) hard cheese, grated
30ml (2 tablespoons) oil
5ml (1 teaspoon) caster sugar
Salt and freshly milled pepper
1 clove garlic (optional)

Serves 4

Roll out the pastry and use to line a 20cm (8in) flan ring set on a baking tray, or a quiche tin with a loose base. Set aside while preparing the filling.

Heat the oil in a medium-sized saucepan and add the onion and green pepper. Fry gently for 5 minutes to soften the vegetables. Then add the garlic (if using), crushed to a purée with a little salt, and the courgettes. Scald and peel the tomatoes, halve them, remove any seeds, and chop coarsely. Add to the pan with the sugar and seasoning of salt and pepper. Cover and cook gently for 30 minutes or until the vegetables are quite soft. Draw off the heat and allow to cool until the hand can be comfortably held against the sides of the pan. Stir in the eggs and recheck the seasoning. Pour the mixture into the pastry flan. Sprinkle the grated cheese on top. Set above the centre in a moderately hot oven (190°C, 375°F, Gas Mark 5) and bake for 40 minutes, until the pastry is cooked and the filling is seen to be thoroughly set.

To freeze: Remove the flan from the baking tin and cool on a wire tray. When quite cold, open-freeze until firm, then wrap or place in freezer bag.

To serve: Allow to thaw at room temperature for 3–4 hours. Slide on to a baking tray and heat through in a moderate oven (180°C, 350°F, Gas Mark 4) for 15–20 minutes. Serve warm with salad.

Recommended storage life: 2 months.

Cooking for the freezer:

Meat dishes that take time to prepare are the ones to choose for the freezer. Often these are less expensive recipes that can be very good for a dinner party or a buffet supper. The many recipes made with pasta, such as lasagne, or stuffed and rolled cannelloni, are good examples. Meat and poultry cooked and served in gravies or sauces are also excellent, because they can usually be reheated without any further attention.

Try to avoid bulky items including a lot of bone that would be difficult to pack, and for chicken dishes, use a chicken jointed off the carcass rather than chicken portions. A recipe like chicken fricassée, which can be served in alternative ways, is particularly useful, since there is a danger of monotony when too many of the same dishes are cooked for the freezer.

Experiment with your own meat or chicken casserole recipes. You should avoid over-cooking these for freezing so reduce the cooking time by 30 minutes. Thaw before reheating, or reheat from frozen very gently in a saucepan.

Other useful items include the cooked filling for a steak and kidney pie, frozen in the dish for baking (using the method in the Lasagne recipe), or in foil pie plates. Rolled-out pastry tops can be frozen separately. All cooked meats to serve cold are good for the freezer and your own galantines, terrines, pâtés and meat loaves will be excellent.

Some special dinner party recipe that is spicy in flavour and contains garlic will be perfectly satisfactory if cooked and frozen one week to be served the next. For longer storage, reduce amounts of spices or seasoning, and omit garlic.

Lasagne

250g (8oz) lasagne
500g (1lb) lean minced beef
425g (15oz) tin peeled
　tomatoes
170g (6oz) tin concentrated
　tomato purée
1 medium-sized onion,
　chopped
Two 226g (8oz) cartons
　cottage cheese
2 eggs
100g (3oz) grated Parmesan
　cheese
30ml (2 tablespoons) oil
5ml (1 teaspoon) salt
Freshly milled pepper
1 clove garlic, peeled
　(optional)

Serves 6

Heat 1 tablespoon oil in a saucepan and add the onion and meat. Fry gently until the meat loses its red colour, then drain off the fat. Crush the garlic (if using) to a purée with a little of the salt and add to the contents of the pan with the rest of the salt and seasoning of pepper. Stir in the tomatoes and their juice and the tomato purée. Cover and cook gently for one hour to achieve a fairly thick meat sauce. Cook the lasagne in a large pan of boiling salted water (with 1 tablespoon oil added) for about 15 minutes or until just tender – during the

first few minutes, stir to make sure the leaves do not stick together. Drain the lasagne in a colander and separate out the pieces to cool. Sieve the cottage cheese into a bowl, add the eggs with a seasoning of salt and pepper and mix well. To assemble the lasagne: Line a 33cm (13in) by 23cm (9in) by 5cm (2in) baking dish with foil (easiest to do this if foil is moulded over the outside of the baking dish first). Place half the cooked lasagne over the base of the dish. Spread with half the cottage cheese and then half the meat sauce. Sprinkle with half the grated cheese. Repeat the layers, ending with the grated cheese.

Stuffed peppers
Frozen Bolognese sauce (page 119) can be used as a stuffing for green peppers. Thaw sauce in refrigerator and reheat gently.

114

Meat & poultry

To freeze: Chill in the refrigerator and then freeze in the dish until firm. When solid, dip dish in cold water and lift out the contents in the foil – this releases the dish for other uses. Place the lasagne in a freezer bag and store.

To serve: Remove the foil wrapping and replace the lasagne in the original baking dish. Allow to thaw overnight in the refrigerator. Place in a moderate oven (180°C, 350°F, Gas Mark 4). The freshly cooked dish takes 40 minutes to heat through, but when it has come from the refrigerator allow an extra 15 minutes. To cook from frozen, allow $1\frac{3}{4}$ hours in a moderate oven (180°C, 350°F, Gas Mark 4). Lasagne should be bubbling hot. Before cutting, allow the lasagne to stand for 10 minutes – the filling sets slightly and this makes the dish easier to serve.

Recommended storage life: 2 months.

Chicken Fricassée

1 oven-ready chicken, about
    $1\frac{1}{2}$ kg (3lb)
500ml (1 pint) chicken stock,
    see recipe
150ml ($\frac{1}{4}$ pint) double cream
50g (2oz) plain flour
75g (3oz) butter
2 egg yolks
Squeeze lemon juice
15ml (1 tablespoon) salt
Few peppercorns
1 onion, stuck with a clove
2–3 stalks celery, cut up
1 bay leaf
Salt and freshly milled
    pepper

Serves 6

Place the chicken, breast downwards, in a saucepan just large enough to take it. Add sufficient cold water to cover half the chicken. Add the 15ml (1 tablespoon) salt, peppercorns, onion with clove, celery and bay leaf. Bring to a simmer, cover with a lid and cook gently for $1\frac{1}{2}$ hours. Remove the chicken from the pan and allow to cool.

Measure 500ml (1 pint) of the stock and check the seasoning, adding salt and pepper if needed.

Melt 60g ($2\frac{1}{2}$oz) of the butter in a saucepan stir in the flour. Cook gently for a moment, then gradually add the hot chicken stock. Bring to the boil, stirring all the time, to make a smooth sauce. Simmer for a few moments and check the flavour. Blend the cream and egg yolks in a basin. Stir in a little of the hot sauce, mix and return to the saucepan. Remove from heat. Stir to blend, add the lemon juice and remaining butter. This enriched sauce should have a good flavour and a creamy colour.

Lift the chicken flesh from the carcass and cut into chunky pieces. Place in rigid or foil containers – one or more, according to how you may use the mixture. Strain over the sauce. Tap the container so that the sauce runs to the base and leave 2·5cm (1in) head space. Cool.

To freeze: Chill then freeze until firm in the closed container.

To serve: Thaw and reheat gently; do not allow to boil. Or turn the frozen mixture into a double boiler and cook until well thawed and well heated. As the mixture thaws, break the pieces of chicken apart with a fork – takes about 30–40 minutes from frozen. Use as a filling for pancakes or vol-au-vent cases, or serve with hot boiled rice.

Recommended storage life: 2 months.

Cooking for the freezer:

Chicken with Peperonata Sauce

1 oven-ready chicken, about
   1½kg (3lb), cut into six
   portions
2 medium-sized green
   peppers, de-seeded and
   finely sliced
425g (15oz) tin peeled
   tomatoes
2 medium-sized onions,
   sliced
Few black or green olives
5ml (1 teaspoon) caster sugar
15ml (1 tablespoon) oil
50g (2oz) butter
1 bay leaf
Salt and freshly milled
   pepper
1 clove garlic (optional)

Serves 6

Melt the butter and oil in a large frying pan and add the chicken pieces. Fry gently, turning to brown the chicken on all sides. Lift from the pan and place in a suitable foil freezer container. Add the onion and green pepper to the hot fat in the pan. Cover with a lid and fry gently until the vegetables are tender and soft, about 10 minutes. Crush the garlic (if using) to a purée with a little salt and add to the softened vegetables with the tinned tomatoes and juices. Season with salt and pepper and add the bay leaf and sugar. Bring to a boil and draw off the heat. Remove the bay leaf. Spoon the peperonata sauce over the chicken joints. Place in a moderate oven (180°C, 350°F, Gas Mark 4) and cook for 45 minutes. No extra liquid will be required – the vegetables provide plenty of juice. Check the seasoning, add the olives and allow to cool.

To freeze: Chill, then freeze until firm in the container covered with a suitable lid.

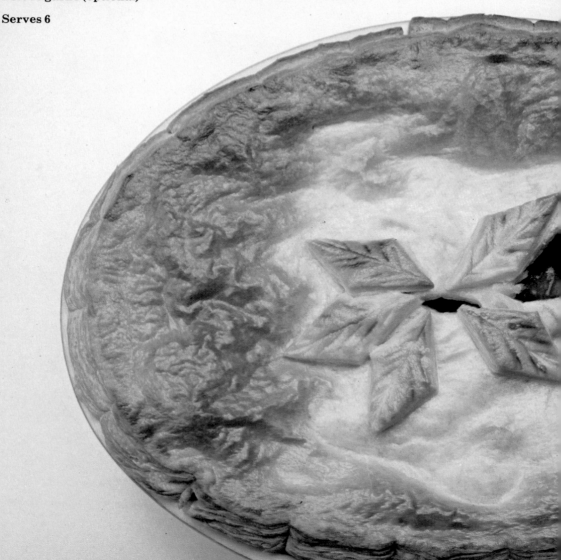

Meat & poultry

To serve: Thaw contents in the refrigerator overnight and reheat in the foil container, in a moderate oven (180°C, 350°F, Gas Mark 4) for about 40 minutes, or until simmering. Or put the frozen contents into a heavy saucepan. Thaw over a low heat for 40 minutes, or until hot through. Stir occasionally to prevent the chicken from sticking to the pan.
Recommended storage life: 2 months.

Moussaka

1kg (2lb) aubergines
500g (1lb) lean minced beef
2 large onions, chopped
150ml (¼ pint) red wine
10ml (2 teaspoons) concentrated tomato purée
125ml (about 4floz) oil
Cooking salt
5ml (1 teaspoon) salt
Freshly milled pepper

For the topping
25g (1oz) butter
25g (1oz) plain flour
250ml (½ pint) milk
1 egg

Serves 6

Steak and kidney pie
A steak and kidney mixture can be cooked and frozen in a dish or foil plate and later combined with a prepared pastry top which has been frozen separately.

Leave the aubergines unpeeled, but discard the stalks. Slice them thinly. Sprinkle layers of aubergine with cooking salt in a colander and leave for about one hour to draw the juices. Rinse the aubergine slices and pat dry. Then fry to brown them on both sides in about 100ml (3floz) of the oil – cook them in batches if necessary. Drain on kitchen paper.

Heat the remaining oil in a saucepan and add the onion. Cook gently for 3–5 minutes to soften the onion. Add the meat and cook until the meat loses all red colour. Stir in the 5ml (1 teaspoon) salt, a seasoning of pepper, the tomato purée and the wine. Cover and cook gently for 25–30 minutes. Arrange layers of aubergine and meat mixture in a 1 litre (2 pint) foil freezer dish, beginning and ending with a layer of aubergine. Set aside while preparing the topping.

Melt the butter over low heat and stir in the flour. Cook gently for a few minutes, then gradually stir in the milk. Bring to the boil, stirring well all the time, to get a smooth sauce. Season with salt and pepper and simmer for 1–2 minutes. Draw off the heat, cool for a moment and then beat in the egg. The addition of egg helps to form a topping which will remain on the surface of the moussaka. Pour the sauce topping over the moussaka.
To freeze: Allow to cool, then cover with the container lid and freeze.
To serve: Thaw slowly overnight in the refrigerator. Uncover, place in the centre of a moderately hot oven (190°C, 375°F, Gas Mark 5) and cook for 45 minutes. Or cook from frozen in a moderate oven (180°C, 350°F, Gas Mark 4) for 1½ hours. Moussaka should be bubbling and the top golden brown. Serve hot with salad.
Recommended storage life: 1 month.
Note: To freeze moussaka in a smart serving dish for a party, follow the method given in the lasagne recipe, using a foil lining. Make extra sauce if you use a shallow, wide dish.

117

Cooking for the freezer: Sauces

A ready-made sauce can considerably reduce kitchen preparation time. The most useful to have on hand are those that can be served with a number of different foods, therefore increasing the range of dishes that can be produced from the freezer. Most sauces can be frozen satisfactorily. Mayonnaise and egg-based sauces such as béarnaise and hollandaise sauce are the exceptions.

A basic white sauce, espagnole (or brown sauce), both of which are included in many recipes or can be used as bases for other sauces, are very useful to have on hand. Prepare these sauces in the usual way, using cornflour to thicken instead of white flour. Once made, allow to cool, stirring occasionally to prevent a skin forming.

Other useful freezer sauces include apple sauce and cranberry sauce.

Freeze sauces in small amounts that will be suitable for using at one time.

The recipes in this section can be frozen in waxed cartons (leave 2·5cm/1in headspace, cover and freeze), or in strong freezer cooking bags or 'boil-in-bag' bags, when they can be quickly thawed by immersing and reheating in boiling water.

Curry Sauce

1 large onion, finely chopped
1 cooking apple, peeled and cut in dice
60ml (4 tablespoons) curry powder
750ml (1½ pints) stock
30ml (2 tablespoons) sweet chutney or apricot jam
50g (2oz) soft brown sugar
75g (3oz) butter
50g (2oz) sultanas
Juice of 1 lemon
1 bay leaf
2·5ml (½ teaspoon) salt
25g (1oz) cornflour
30ml (2 tablespoons) water

Makes ¾ litre (1½ pints) sauce

Melt the butter in a saucepan and add the onion. Cook gently for 3–5 minutes to soften the onion. Then add the apple. Stir in the curry powder and cook for a moment to draw the flavour. Stir in the stock and bring to the boil. Add the chutney or jam (having cut up any large pieces of fruit), the sugar, salt and bay leaf. Cover with a lid and simmer for 30 minutes. Strain the mixture for a smooth curry sauce, or if a sauce with pieces of fruit and onion is preferred leave it as it is, but remove the bay leaf. Stir in the blended cornflour and water, the lemon juice and sultanas. Bring to the boil, stirring all the time until thickened. Cook for a moment and draw off the heat.
To freeze: Cool, stirring occasionally to prevent a skin forming. Freeze in waxed cartons leaving 2·5cm (1in) head space or in strong freezer cooking bags, tied down.
To serve: Thaw and reheat. Or reheat gently from frozen to simmering point. Cooked meat, cut in thin slices, pieces of cooked chicken, flaked cooked fish, prawns, or cooked rabbit can be brought just to the boil in the curry sauce and simmered for 3–4 minutes before serving. For curried eggs, arrange halved hard-boiled eggs in a hot dish and pour the hot curry sauce over. Serve with a border of boiled rice, lemon slices and parsley.
Recommended storage life: 3 months.

Savoury Orange Sauce

2 large oranges
100g (4oz) granulated sugar
30ml (2 tablespoons) wine vinegar
250ml (½ pint) chicken stock
45ml (3 tablespoons) thick orange marmalade
30ml (2 tablespoons) cornflour
45ml (3 tablespoons) water

Makes about 500ml (1 pint) sauce

Measure the sugar into a dry saucepan. Place over low heat and allow to melt to a golden caramel brown, stirring all the time so that the sugar melts evenly. Draw off the heat and add 30ml (2 tablespoons) water – take care, for the mixture boils furiously with the addition of a cold liquid. Replace the pan over the heat and stir to make a caramel syrup. Add the vinegar, stock and the orange marmalade. Thinly pare the rinds from the oranges, using a vegetable peeler. Reserve the rinds and add the orange juice to the sauce. Bring to a simmer, cover and cook gently for 20 minutes. Finely shred the orange rind and blanch in boiling water for 5 minutes, then drain. When the sauce is cooked, strain and return to the pan. Add the blanched rinds and stir in the cornflour blended with 15ml (1 tablespoon) water. Bring to the boil, stirring all the time. Cook for a moment and then draw off the heat.
To freeze: Cool, stirring occasionally to prevent a skin forming. Freeze in waxed cartons, leaving 2·5cm (1in) head space; or in strong freezer cooking bags, tied down.
To serve: Thaw and reheat. Or reheat gently from frozen to simmering point. Use orange sauce to serve with roast duck, to pour over pork chops, or with boiled bacon or gammon.
Recommended storage life: 4 months.

Fresh Tomato Sauce

1½kg (3lb) ripe tomatoes
2 large carrots, diced
2 medium-sized onions, chopped
50g (2oz) butter
2 streaky bacon rashers, chopped
15ml (1 tablespoon) sugar
Salt and freshly milled pepper
30ml (2 tablespoons) concentrated tomato purée
1 litre (1½ pints) stock
Bouquet garni of bay leaf, thyme and parsley stalks
Juice of 1 lemon
50g (2oz) cornflour
150ml (¼ pint) water

Makes 1½ litres (2 pints)

It is important to follow either the imperial or the metric weights and measures in any one recipe. Do not mix them.

Skin the tomatoes, halve them, scoop out and discard the seeds. Melt the butter in a saucepan, add the bacon and cook for a moment until the fat runs. Add the carrot and onion and cook gently for about 5 minutes to soften the onion. Add the tomatoes and continue cooking, covered with a lid, for a further 10 minutes to soften the tomatoes and draw the juices. Stir in the sugar, a seasoning of salt and pepper, the tomato purée, stock, and add the bouquet garni. Recover the pan and simmer the contents gently for 30–40 minutes, or until the vegetables are quite soft. Remove the bouquet garni and press the liquid and vegetables through a sieve. Return to the saucepan and stir in the cornflour blended with the water. Add the lemon juice and stir until boiling and thickened. Check the seasoning.
To freeze: Cool, stirring occasionally to prevent a skin forming. Freeze in waxed cartons, leaving 2·5cm (1in) head space; or in strong freezer cooking bags, tied down.
To serve: Thaw and reheat. Or reheat gently from frozen to simmering point. Tomato sauce is excellent with meat, fish or chicken and can be used in any recipe (particularly pasta dishes) that calls for tomato sauce. This sauce can also be thinned down with a little extra stock and served as a rich tomato soup.
Recommended storage life: 6 months.

Barbecue Sauce

1 small onion, chopped
63g (2¼oz) tin concentrated tomato purée
50g (2oz) soft brown sugar
5ml (1 teaspoon) Worcestershire sauce
Juice of ½ lemon
15ml (1 tablespoon) oil
2·5ml (½ teaspoon) salt
Freshly milled pepper
10ml (2 teaspoons) made mustard
15ml (1 tablespoon) cornflour
250ml (½ pint) water

Makes 400ml (¾ pint) sauce

Heat the oil in a saucepan and add the onion. Cook gently for 3–5 minutes or until the onion is tender. Measure the seasoning, sugar, cornflour, mustard, Worcestershire sauce, lemon juice, tomato purée and water into a mixing basin. Blend well and then add to the onion in the pan. Stir to mix and bring to the boil, stirring all the time. Lower the heat to a simmer, cover and cook gently for 5 minutes. Draw the pan off the heat.
To freeze: Cool, stirring occasionally to prevent a skin forming. Freeze in waxed cartons leaving 2·5cm (1in) head space; or in strong freezer cooking bags, tied down.
To serve: Thaw and reheat. Or reheat gently from frozen to simmering point. Use barbecue sauce for basting kebabs, pour it over grilled or fried pork chops or chicken joints before serving. It can also be used as a cooking sauce for chicken portions – excellent for drumsticks.
Recommended storage life: 2 months.

Bolognese Sauce

500g (1lb) lean minced beef
425g (15oz) tin tomatoes
30ml (2 tablespoons) concentrated tomato purée
1 medium-sized onion, finely chopped
1 clove garlic, peeled
150ml (¼ pint) red wine
150ml (¼ pint) stock
Pinch mixed dried herbs
30ml (2 tablespoons) oil
5ml (1 teaspoon) salt
Freshly milled pepper

Makes 500ml (1 pint) sauce

Heat the oil in a medium-sized saucepan. Add the onion. Cover and cook gently for 3–5 minutes to soften the onion. Crush the garlic to a purée with a little salt, then add to the pan. Stir in the minced beef and cook gently until the meat loses all red colour. Add the salt, pepper, the tomatoes and their juice, the concentrated tomato purée, herbs, stock and wine. Bring to a simmer. Cover with a lid and cook gently for 40 minutes. Stir occasionally. If you would like the consistency to be thicker, remove the lid and boil to reduce the liquid.
To freeze: Cool quickly. Freeze in waxed cartons, leaving 2·5cm (1in) head space; or in strong freezer cooking bags, tied down.
To serve: Thaw sauce slowly in the refrigerator or a cool larder, then reheat until simmering. Or reheat gently from frozen to simmering point. Serve hot over pasta, in pancakes, or use as a stuffing for cabbage leaves or green pepper shells.
Recommended storage life: 2 months.

Cooking for the freezer: Desserts

Desserts that really save time are those that require no more than to be removed from the freezer and allowed to thaw before serving. Such are the recipes here. Useful too are prepared and baked cases for fruit and dessert flans as these take no time to fill and finish.

Homemade ice-creams are easy to prepare and lovely to serve. For a stunning dinner party dessert use an ice-cream bombe mould for freezing your prepared mixture.

Traditional family suet and sponge puddings freeze perfectly if cooked in foil pudding basins. Allow to thaw and then reheat by steaming for about one hour before serving.

Make your own fruit crumble recipe and freeze uncooked. Or make crumble toppings and freeze separately to use with frozen fruits.

Fruit pies can be baked before freezing, or frozen raw and baked before serving. Foil pie plates are convenient to use for these but do not let the fruit touch the foil; line the plates with pastry.

Lemon Cheesecake

500g (1lb) cottage cheese
14g (½oz) envelope gelatine
3 large eggs
75g (3oz) caster sugar
Finely grated rind and juice of 1 large lemon
150ml (¼ pint) double cream
50ml (3 tablespoons) water

For the crumb base
8 digestive biscuits
15ml (1 tablespoon) caster sugar
50g (2oz) butter

Serves 8

Measure the water into a saucepan, sprinkle in the gelatine and allow to soak for 5 minutes. Stir over low heat until the gelatine has dissolved, then draw off the heat. Separate the eggs, placing the yolks in one basin and the whites in a second larger basin. Add the sugar and grated lemon rind to the yolks and beat well. Sieve in the cottage cheese and mix. Add the strained lemon juice to the dissolved gelatine and then stir the lemon and gelatine mixture into the cottage cheese, egg and sugar. Blend well. Lightly whip the cream and stiffly beat the egg whites. Fold both into the cheesecake mixture and blend gently but evenly together. Pour into a 20cm (8in) round deep cake tin, ungreased but lined on the base with a circle of greaseproof paper.

To make the crumb base
Crush the digestive biscuits and mix with sugar. Melt the butter in a saucepan and stir in the crumb mixture. Mix well, using a fork, and then sprinkle the crumb mixture evenly over the cheesecake, pressing the crumbs down very lightly – when turned out this will become the base.

It is important to follow either the imperial or the metric weights and measures in any one recipe. Do not mix them.

Chill for several hours or until set firm.

To freeze: Loosen round the sides of the mixture with a palette knife and turn out on to a baking sheet. Peel away the paper from the top. Open-freeze until firm. Then place inside a large freezer bag and tie down.

To serve: Remove frozen cheesecake on to a serving plate and thaw in the refrigerator for 2–3 hours. Serve chilled. This recipe is particularly nice served with the black currant sauce given on page 123.

Recommended storage life: 2 months.

Specially good for freezing
To make lemon cheesecake takes time and it is best to make it when you have time and attention to spare. It is ideal for freezing as it does not deteriorate in flavour or texture. Particularly good with black currant sauce (page 123).

Cooking for the freezer: Desserts

Coffee Brandy Cake

150g (6oz) plain flour
2·5ml (½ teaspoon) salt
10ml (2 teaspoons) baking
  powder
125g (5oz) soft brown sugar
2 eggs
90ml (6 tablespoons) corn oil
60ml (4 tablespoons) milk
30ml (2 tablespoons) coffee
  essence

For the syrup

100g (4oz) granulated sugar
125ml (¼ pint) strong black
  coffee, made by stirring
  10ml (2 teaspoons) instant
  coffee into 150ml (¼ pint)
  boiling water
30ml (2 tablespoons) brandy

For the decoration

170ml (6floz) carton double
  cream
25g (1oz) sugar
Toasted flaked almonds or
  chopped hazelnuts

Serves 8

Sift the flour, salt and baking
powder into a large mixing
basin. Add the soft brown sugar.
Separate the eggs, cracking the
yolks into a small basin and the
whites into a larger one. Add the
corn oil, milk and coffee essence
to the yolks and mix with a fork.
Pour into the centre of the dry
ingredients and using a spoon,
mix to a smooth batter. Whisk
the egg whites until stiff and
fold into the mixture. Pour the
cake batter into a greased and
lined 22cm (8½in) by 4cm (1½in)
sandwich tin. Place above the
centre in a moderate oven
(180°C, 350°F, Gas Mark 4) and
bake for 40–45 minutes. Turn
out, remove lining, and allow to
cool.

   Measure the sugar and coffee
for the syrup into a saucepan.
Stir over low heat to dissolve the
sugar, then bring to the boil and
simmer for 5 minutes to concentrate the flavour. Draw off
the heat and stir in the brandy.
Replace the cake in the original
baking tin and prick holes all
over the surface with a skewer
or fork. Spoon the hot syrup
over the cake and leave to soak
for an hour or so. Turn the cake

out on to a baking sheet.
   Whisk the cream, adding the
sugar, until thick, and swirl all
over the top and sides of the
cake to cover it.
To freeze: Open-freeze as a
whole cake, or cut into serving
portions. Then place inside a
freezer bag for protection during storage.
To serve: Remove the cake
from the wrapping while it is
still frozen and allow to thaw on
a plate in the refrigerator for 2–3
hours. Before serving, sprinkle
with toasted flaked almonds or
chopped toasted hazelnuts.
Recommended storage life: 2
months.

Sweet Pastry for Freezer Flans

500g (1lb) plain flour
300g (10oz) butter or
  margarine
75ml (5 tablespoons) milk
60g (2oz) caster sugar

Makes four 8in flan cases

Sift the flour into a mixing
basin. Blend the fat on a plate to
soften and add to the flour – rub
in until fine and crumbly. Mix
the sugar and cold milk in a
small basin. Add to the dry
ingredients and, using a knife,
mix to a rough dough in the
basin. Turn out on to a lightly
floured working surface and
knead for a moment to make a
smooth pastry dough. Cover
with a polythene bag if possible
and leave to rest for 20 minutes.
   Divide the pastry into 4 equal
portions and keep each piece of
pastry covered to prevent a skin
forming on the surface of the
dough. Using one piece of pastry
at a time, roll out to a circle and
use to line a 20cm (8in) flan ring
set on a baking tray (or a quiche
or flan tin of the same size). Line
with a circle of greaseproof
paper and a few 'baking beans'
(dried haricot beans) to hold the
pastry down in the centre. Bake
in a moderately hot oven (190°C,
375°F, Gas Mark 5) for 15
minutes. Then remove paper and
beans and return the flan to the
oven for a further 10 minutes.
Repeat this procedure with the
three remaining pieces of pastry.

Two flans can, of course, be
cooked at the same time if tins
are available.
To freeze: Remove the flan
cases from the baking tins and
cool on a wire rack. Place in
rigid containers or freezer boxes
to prevent crushing, and freeze.
To serve: Allow to thaw at
room temperature for one hour.
Then use for fruit flans or
desserts – such as lemon meringue pie – which require a
baked pastry case.
Recommended storage life: 3
months.

Chocolate Ice-Cream

150g (6oz) plain chocolate
3 egg yolks
250ml (½ pint) double cream
50g (2oz) caster sugar
50ml (4 tablespoons) water

Serves 6

Measure the sugar and water
into a saucepan. Stir over low
heat until the sugar has dissolved, then bring to the boil.
Simmer for 2–3 minutes.
Meanwhile break the chocolate
into the goblet of an electric
blender. Add the hot syrup,
cover and blend on high speed
for a few moments or until the
chocolate is melted and smooth.
Add the egg yolks, cover and
blend again for a few moments
to mix. Whip the cream until
thick, add the chocolate mixture
and fold both together gently
but evenly.
To freeze: Pour into a polythene freezer container of
about 1 litre (1½ pint) capacity.
Turn sides to centre as they
begin to freeze. When quite firm,
cover with the lid for storage.
To serve: Remove container
from freezer to refrigerator
about 30 minutes before serving.
Recommended storage life: 2
months.

Orange Slices in Caramel Syrup

6 large oranges
Juice of ½ lemon
150g (6oz) granulated sugar
125ml (¼ pint) water

Serves 6

It is important to follow either the imperial or the metric weights and measures in any one recipe. Do not mix them.

Mark the peel of each orange in quarters. Pour boiling water over the oranges and allow to stand for 5 minutes to loosen the skins. Drain and peel off the orange skins – most of the white pith should come away as well. Scrape the surface of each peeled orange with a sharp knife to remove any remaining traces of white pith. Slice the oranges thinly and remove any pips.

Select a few of the best pieces of orange peel. Cut away the white pith and then shred the peel finely. Place the shredded peel in a saucepan, cover with cold water and bring to the boil. Drain and replace peel in the pan. Re-cover with cold water and bring to the boil again. This time, cover the pan and cook gently for 20 minutes or until the peel is very tender. Drain and reserve.

Measure the sugar into a dry saucepan and stir over low heat until the sugar has melted and turned to caramel. Draw off the heat and add the 125ml ($\frac{1}{4}$ pint) water – take care, since the mixture will boil up furiously with the addition of a cold liquid. Lower the heat to a simmer, replace the pan over the heat and stir until the caramel has dissolved and formed a syrup. Add the cooked orange peel and simmer gently for about 5 minutes, or until the peel is glazed and candied looking. Add the lemon juice. Pour over the orange slices and leave until cold.

To freeze: Put the orange slices and syrup into a rigid plastic container. Cover and freeze.

To serve: Allow the orange slices to thaw in the closed container for 2–3 hours at room temperature. Pour into a glass serving bowl. These are very nice served with a lemon water ice.

Recommended storage life: 3 months.

Dessert Sauces

Dessert sauces made with fruit can be extremely useful to serve with ice-cream or homemade yogurt. Black currants, which are usually plentiful but not popular (unless made up into desserts), can provide a delicious sauce with a beautiful colour and a very good flavour.

Black Currant Sauce

1kg (2lb) black currants
375g (12oz) granulated sugar
1 litre (1$\frac{1}{2}$ pints) water
15ml (1 tablespoon) cornflour
15ml (1 tablespoon) water

Makes 1$\frac{3}{4}$ litres (2$\frac{1}{2}$ pints) sauce

Strip the black currants from the stems. Measure the sugar and 1 litre (1$\frac{1}{2}$ pints) water into a saucepan and stir over low heat to dissolve the sugar. Add the black currants and bring to a simmer. Cook gently for about 15 minutes or until the fruit is quite soft. Draw off the heat and pass the liquid and fruit through a sieve to make a purée. Discard all pips and skins remaining in the sieve. Return the purée to the saucepan. Stir in the cornflour blended with 15ml (1 tablespoon) water and bring to the boil, stirring all the time, until the mixture has thickened. The cooked mixture should have a thin sauce consistency. Draw off the heat and leave to cool, stirring occasionally to prevent a skin forming. Check the sweetness.

To freeze: Pour into 250ml ($\frac{1}{2}$ pint) waxed containers – these provide a useful serving quantity. Freeze.

To serve: Thaw slowly in the refrigerator, or cool larder.

Recommended storage life: 6 months.

Freezing flan cases

Bake flan cases as described in the recipe opposite, remove from baking tins, cool on a wire rack, place in a rigid container to prevent crushing and freeze.

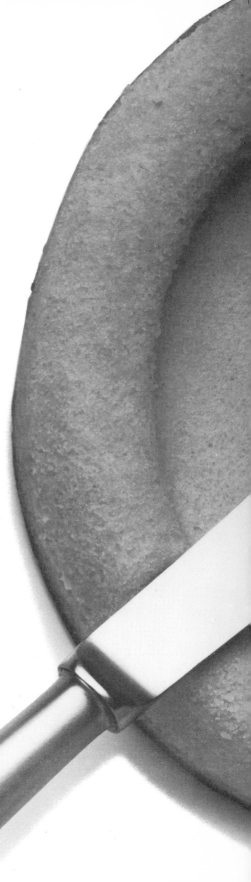

Orange slices in caramel syrup

Cooking for the freezer: Baking

Most baked foods freeze extremely well, but avoid taking up valuable space with recipes that keep well anyhow – instead go for layer cakes, scones, and sponges that stale soon after baking, because the freezer will keep them beautifully fresh for another day. Take care to allow all items to become quite cold before freezing. Avoid glacé icings on cakes – they are inclined to go thin on thawing; instead use a buttercream or fudge icing – and where cakes are decorated or in any way fragile, 'open-freeze' them until firm, before packing.

Chocolate Cake

125g (4oz) self-raising flour
5ml (1 teaspoon) baking powder
125g (4oz) quick creaming margarine
125g (4oz) caster sugar
2 eggs
25g (1oz) cocoa powder
30ml (2 tablespoons) boiling water

For the chocolate fudge icing

75g (3oz) icing sugar
25g (1oz) cocoa powder
40g (1½oz) butter
30ml (2 tablespoons) water
50g (2oz) caster sugar

Makes one 18cm (7in) sandwich

This cake is made using the modern quick mix method and for this the new soft easy creaming margarine must be used. All ingredients must be at room temperature. Sift the flour and baking powder into a basin. Add the sugar and margarine. Crack in the eggs. In a small basin, blend the cocoa powder and boiling water to a smooth paste. Add this to the mixing basin and, using a wooden spoon, stir to blend the ingredients and then beat well for 1 minute to get a soft cake mixture. Divide this mixture equally between two greased and lined 18cm (7in) sponge cake tins and spread level. Bake in the centre of a moderate oven (180°C, 350°F, Gas Mark 4) for 25 minutes. Turn the cake layers on to a wire rack, remove the lining paper and leave them to cool.

Sift the icing sugar and cocoa powder for the chocolate icing into a basin. Measure the butter, water, and caster sugar into a saucepan. Stir over low heat until the sugar has dissolved and the butter has melted, then bring just to the boil. Pour at once into the sifted ingredients and mix to a smooth chocolate icing. Allow the icing to cool until it is thick enough to coat the back of a wooden spoon. Sandwich the cake layers with some of the icing and spoon the remainder on top. Leave until set firm.

To freeze: Open-freeze the cake as a whole, or cut in portions. When firm place in a freezer bag for storage.

To serve: Remove the cake from its wrapping while still frozen and allow it to thaw on a plate at room temperature.

Recommended storage life: 2 months.

Oven Scones

500g (1lb) plain flour
1·25ml (¼ teaspoon) salt
10ml (2 teaspoons) bicarbonate of soda
20ml (4 teaspoons) cream of tartar
90g (3oz) butter
90g (3oz) sugar
1 egg made up to 300ml (½ pint) with milk

Makes 24 scones

Sift the flour, salt, bicarbonate of soda and cream of tartar into a large basin. Rub in the butter and stir in the sugar. Lightly mix the egg and milk and pour all at once into the dry ingredients. Using the blade of a knife, mix quickly to a rough dough in the basin. Turn out on to a lightly floured working surface and pat or roll out to a thickness no less than 1·5cm (½in). Cut into squares with a floured sharp knife or stamp out rounds with a 5cm (2in) plain or fluted cutter – flour the cutter each time it is used. This mixture will make about 24 scones, depending on the thickness of the dough – use up all the trimmings.

Cooking for the freezer: Baking

Place the scones on a floured baking tray and then dust them with flour. Place above centre in a very hot oven (220°C, 425°F, Gas Mark 7) and bake for 10 minutes, or until risen and lightly brown – the sides should feel springy when pressed.

To freeze: Cool on a wire rack until quite cold then pack into freezer bags and tie down.

To serve: Remove from wrappings, thaw at room temperature, then warm through in a moderate oven (180°C, 350°F, Gas Mark 4) for 3–5 minutes. Or warm through from frozen for 5–10 minutes.

Fruit scones: Add 125g (4oz) cleaned currants or sultanas after rubbing in the butter, then follow the recipe.

Wheatmeal scones: Use 250g (8oz) wholemeal flour and 250g (8oz) plain flour. Sift the plain flour, salt and raising agents, then add the wholemeal flour and follow the recipe.

Cheese scones: Follow the recipe for oven scones, omitting the sugar. After rubbing in the butter, add 160g (6oz) finely grated hard cheese and a pinch of cayenne pepper.

Recommended storage life: 2 months.

German Streusel Cake

225g (8oz) green gooseberries, rhubarb or sharp-flavoured apples, weighed after preparation

For the crumble topping
75g (3oz) self-raising flour
50g (2oz) butter
50g (2oz) caster sugar

For the cake base
180g (6oz) self-raising flour
Pinch salt
125g (4oz) butter
125g (4oz) caster sugar
2 eggs
2·5ml ($\frac{1}{2}$ teaspoon) vanilla essence
15ml (1 tablespoon) milk
Icing sugar for serving

Serves 8

Prepare the crumble topping. Sift the flour into a basin and rub in the butter. Add the sugar and continue to 'rub in' until the mixture becomes a little 'short' and crumbs are coarse.

Sift the flour for the cake base with the salt on to a plate. Cream the butter and sugar until light. Lightly mix the eggs and vanilla essence and then gradually beat into the creamed mixture. Add a little of the sifted flour with the last few additions of egg, then fold in the remaining flour with the milk to make a smooth consistency. Spoon the cake mixture over the base of a buttered 21·5cm (8$\frac{1}{2}$in) spring clip pan (this is a tin that opens from the sides and is available in most specialist cook shops). A 20cm (8in) cake tin with a loose base could be used if necessary.

Prepare the fruit: Top and tail the gooseberries, cut the rhubarb into 2·5cm (1in) lengths, or peel and slice the apples. Cover the cake mixture with the prepared but uncooked fruit. Then sprinkle the crumble or 'streusel' mixture over the fruit. Place the cake in the centre of a moderate oven (180°C, 350°F, Gas Mark 4) and bake for 1$\frac{1}{4}$ hours. Allow the cake to cool before removing the tin by opening the sides (or pushing up the base).

To freeze: Loosen the cake from the tin base and open-freeze until firm. Then place in a freezer bag for storage.

To serve: Remove the cake from the wrapping while still frozen and allow to thaw at room temperature. Sprinkle the top of the cake with sieved icing sugar before serving. Serve as a cake, or as a dessert with cream. The recipe has a particularly moist and delicious flavour because the fruit is cooked in the cake mixture; it can be seen quite clearly in a layer across the middle.

Recommended storage life: 2 months.

Doughnuts

500g (1lb) plain flour
5ml (1 teaspoon) salt
60g (2oz) butter
60g (2oz) caster sugar
15g ($\frac{1}{2}$oz) dried yeast
150ml ($\frac{1}{4}$ pint) water, hand hot 43°C, 110°F
1 egg made up to 150ml ($\frac{1}{4}$ pint) with warm milk
Red jam – see recipe
Caster sugar for serving

Makes 24 doughnuts

Sift the flour and salt into a mixing basin. Cut in the butter and rub into the mixture. Stir 5ml (1 teaspoon) of the sugar into the hand hot water and add the dried yeast. Set aside in a warm place until frothy – about 10 minutes. Add the remaining sugar to the mixed egg and milk and blend well. Stir the yeast liquid and the sweetened egg and milk into the flour mixture. Mix to a soft dough in the basin. Turn the dough out on to a clean working surface and knead for about 5 minutes, or until the dough is smooth. Replace the dough in the mixing basin, cover and leave in a warm place to rise until almost double in size – takes about one hour.

Turn the risen dough out and press lightly all over with the knuckles to even out the texture. Roll up and, using a knife, cut into 24 pieces of equal size. Shape each piece into a ball, then flatten slightly with a rolling pin. Spoon about 2·5ml ($\frac{1}{2}$ teaspoon) firm set red jam into the centre of each. Gather the edges of the dough over the jam, pinch well to seal and turn doughnuts over (seal underneath) on to greased and floured baking trays. Leave in a warm place, covered with a cloth until puffy looking – about 15 minutes.

Fry the doughnuts in hot oil until golden brown – turn them over as they cook – takes about 3–5 minutes. Lift out with a draining spoon and place on crumpled absorbent kitchen paper.

To freeze: Leave until quite cold. Then place in freezer bags.

To serve: Remove the number of doughnuts required and allow to thaw at room temperature. Place on a baking tray and heat through in a moderate oven (180°C, 350°F, Gas Mark 4) for 5 minutes or until hot. Roll in caster sugar and serve at once.

Recommended storage life: 1 month.

Brandy Snaps

50g (2oz) butter
50g (2oz) plain flour
5ml (1 teaspoon) ground
    ginger
125g (5oz) caster sugar
50g (2oz) golden syrup

Makes 24 brandy snaps

Slice the butter into a warm mixing basin and beat until softened. Sift in the flour and ground ginger, add the sugar and syrup and beat all the ingredients together until smooth and pale coloured. Turn out on to a floured working surface and shape the soft dough into a fat roll, handling it as little as possible. Wrap in foil or waxed paper and leave in a cool place for one hour before using.

Cover 2–3 baking sheets with silicone-treated paper cut to fit. Smear the corners of the baking sheets with fat to hold the paper in position. Roll teaspoons of the brandy snap mixture into small balls and flatten slightly. Place on the paper-lined sheets, spaced well apart (few baking sheets will take more than 5 brandy snaps). Set in the centre of a moderately hot oven (190°C, 375°F, Gas Mark 5) and bake for 10 minutes, or until bubbling and golden brown. Cool for 1 minute then lift from the tray with a palette knife, turn over and quickly wrap loosely round greased wooden spoon handles or cone-shaped tins. Slip off when cool and crisp – about 1–2 minutes. You will have to use the wooden handles many times. If the brandy snaps harden while awaiting their turn on the baking sheet, replace in the oven for a moment to soften.

To freeze: Leave until quite cold and then place in a polythene freezer box that has a good airtight seal.

To serve: Remove from container and allow to thaw at room temperature for 1 hour. Then fill with brandy flavoured cream, whipped and slightly sweetened. For all 24 brandy snaps 250ml ($\frac{1}{2}$ pint) double cream and 30ml (2 tablespoons) brandy will be required.

Recommended storage life: 1 month.

Pickles, Chutneys and Sauces

Pineapple Chutney

Red Tomato Chutney

Apricot and Orange Chutney

Gooseberry Chutney

Beetroot Chutney

Pickles are a traditional English dish as old as Shakespeare ('a plague o' these pickle herring') and seem to have been continually popular ever since. Chutney on the other hand came from India, no doubt via the army, sometime in the nineteenth century. There it was traditionally eaten with curry and was soon adopted 'at home' where it became a seasonal occupant of the store cupboard. The Indians used sweet mangoes with acid flavouring from lemons and bitter herbs for their chutneys, mixed with hot seasoning from spices and chillies. Nowadays we have a much wider variety of ingredients and uses; all kinds of vegetables and fruits are included, from beetroot and peppers to gooseberries, blackberries, apples and apricots. Chutneys are no longer restricted to curries but are served as a special extra, along with pickles, with hot or cold meat, pies and pasties, with cheese, and in sandwiches. And a sharp pickle is delicious with evening drinks.

While Mary Norwak provides a fund of unusual recipes here, don't forget that it's fun occasionally to experiment on your own and invent new variations depending on what you have in the garden or what you can get from the market or 'pick-it-yourself' places or from friends and neighbours.

Pickles, chutneys and sauces are easy to make, and surplus produce can be transformed into delicious relishes by variations of spices and unusual combinations of ingredients. It is easy to use up produce which is slightly damaged or bruised and unfit for table use or freezing, but seasonal bargains such as peaches or citrus fruit can also be used. There is no need to make an enormous amount of one kind of chutney; it is far better to experiment and produce small quantities of different kinds to tempt family appetites. Pickles and sauces can have many interesting variations according to the amount and type of raw materials available. As a result, the store cupboard can be full of a far wider range of spicy relishes than can ever be found in the shops.

They are usually served with cold meats, plain hot roast or grilled meats, as a traditional accompaniment to English cheeses and with spiced foods and curries. The sharp, sweet-sour flavours and fruitiness contrast well with rich meat such as pork, enliven plainer cold meats and mellow the heat of spicy foods.

The vegetables and fruit are preserved by cooking in vinegar and sugar, and in some cases they are brined in wet or dry salt. In addition, a range of spices is used to give zest to the other ingredients.

It is a false economy to use cheap vinegar, as vinegar is the chief preservative in pickles or chutneys. Vinegar should contain at least 5 per cent acetic acid to be effective, and branded vinegars contain 5–7 per cent. Draught vinegar sometimes has an acetic acid content of only 3 per cent, and should be avoided. Malt vinegar is widely used and is suitable for pickles, chutneys and sauces, but it has a strong flavour and colour. White distilled vinegar has a better appearance in pickles, especially when pickling spiced fruit. Wine vinegar and cider vinegar may be used for more delicately flavoured pickles, and where spicing is light, but they are more expensive. Spiced vinegar is often required and may be prepared a month ahead of the main pickling season so that it is already well-flavoured when needed.

Sugar may be white, demerara or soft brown. White is best for pickles which need no colouring, but demerara and soft brown sugar give both colour and flavour to chutney. Golden syrup is not suitable for chutney because of its flavour and also because it may crystallise during storage. Dried fruits such as dates, sultanas, raisins and apricots provide flavour and consistency in chutney as well as adding sweetness.

Spices should always be fresh, whether whole or ground. Ground spices blend in with chutney and the flavour can be easily adjusted, but whole spices should be used for pickles as they can be easily removed (ground spices will make the pickling vinegar cloudy and result in a less attractive appearance). Whole spices are also preferable for making spiced vinegar which will have a sediment if ground spices are used. When using spices whole, it is best to put them in a piece of muslin and bruise them slightly with a weight to release flavour. The piece of muslin can then be tied into a bag-shape and suspended in the hot vinegar or pickle.

Equipment for making pickles, chutneys and sauces

The equipment for making all types of vinegar based pickles is simple, but it is essential that the correct items are used or acid may affect both the equipment and the finished cooked product. A large **preserving pan** or big saucepan is necessary, as quantities of raw materials are often large and there must be room for the raw materials to cook without boiling over. A stainless steel or aluminium pan is best, but unchipped enamel may be used. Iron, brass or copper must not be used for vinegar mixtures.

Accurate **scales** are necessary for measuring ingredients. As with all other branches of cookery, accuracy will give good results, although some variation can be made in the amount of spices used, according to taste. In addition, a **large bowl** may be needed for brining, a **long-handled wooden spoon** for safe stirring, and a **sharp stainless knife** for cutting.

If a mixture has to be strained or sieved, a **hair or nylon sieve** should be used, and a **jelly bag** is best for straining spiced vinegar and ketchups. Metal strainers should never be used. If a jelly bag is not available, a well-boiled tea-towel is suitable. Small pieces of **double muslin** are useful for tying up whole spices, or a well-boiled handkerchief can be used.

Pickles and chutneys must be stored in **wide-mouthed jars with vinegar-proof lids**. Jam jars with twist-on or screwtop lids can be used, or old pickle jars which have been sterilised, or preserving jars which have acid-proof lids. The important thing to be stressed is that uncoated metal should not be allowed to touch the finished pickle – the metal should either be coated with lacquer or lined with a vinegar-proof card disc – these are found in commercial pickle jars which can be used again. Coffee jars with plastic lids are very suitable for pickles, but jars should never be covered with brown paper or transparent jam covers as these allow the volatile vinegars to escape. Porosan tied tightly will make a satisfactory covering. Jars must always be completely clean and can be sterilised with hot water to which a small amount of Milton or Campden solution has been added (obtainable from chemists – follow the directions given). Sauces and ketchups are best stored in sterilised bottles (preferably used sauce bottles) with screwtop lids which are vinegar-proof. Disposable mineral water bottles can also be used. It is important to **label** jars and bottles as soon as they have been filled, cooled and cleaned. Pickles and chutneys can look very similar after storage, and a clear label and date of preservation will ensure easy identification and also provide a ready check on the length of time for which pickles have been stored and avoid over-long keeping.

Pickles

Vegetables and fruit pickled in vinegar, with the addition of sugar, salt and spices, are delicious accompaniments to cold meat, fish and cheese. While pickled vegetables are often thought of as sharp and mouth-twisting, they can be subtly sweet-and-sour, and pickled fruit with a hint of spice is particularly delicious.

Method
Vegetables for pickles are brined to draw out some of their water, as otherwise this dilutes the vinegar during storage and reduces the preservative quality. This brining is not necessary for vegetables which are cooked for some time (eg for chutney) as the cooking will drive out excess moisture. Fruit is not brined before pickling because it contains acids which are lacking in vegetables, and is usually lightly cooked before pickling in spiced vinegar.

Salt for pickling should be block salt which has to be grated or crushed. Ordinary table salt contains a chemical to keep it free-running, and it may cloud the vinegar.

Vegetables may be dry-brined or wet-brined. For dry-brining, the prepared vegetables are layered with dry salt sprinkled between the layers. Wet-brining means dissolving salt in water and pouring this over the prepared vegetables.

Dry brining
About 75g (3oz) salt will be needed for each 750g (1½lb) vegetables. The layers should be put in a large bowl and sprinkled well with salt, then the bowl covered with a cloth or paper to keep out any impurities. After 24 hours in a cold place, the fluid should be drained off in a colander for about an hour. Surplus salt should be rinsed from the vegetables under running cold water and they should then be drained well before processing further.

Wet brining
Vegetables should be put in a large bowl and covered with a solution of salt and water, allowing 200g (8oz) salt to 2 litres (4 pints) water. Approximately 500ml (1 pint) brine should be used for each 400g (1lb) prepared vegetables, and the brine should be enough to cover the vegetables in the bowl. A lightly weighted plate should be put on top to keep the vegetables under the brine for 24 hours, although onions, shallots and gherkins do not need such long brining. The liquid should be drained from the vegetables and the vegetables should be rinsed before further processing.

Spiced vinegar
Spiced vinegar is essential for many pickles and this may be prepared at least one month before use to extract full flavour from the spices, although it can be made only two hours before use. A good basic mixture for spiced vinegar is 15g (½oz) stick cinnamon, 15g (½oz) blade mace, 15g (½oz) allspice berries, 8g (¼oz) peppercorns and 8g (¼oz) whole cloves to each 2 litres (4 pints) vinegar. If liked, 2 or 3 bay leaves may be added, or a little grated horseradish, or a couple of peeled garlic cloves. When white vinegar is used, it is best to use white peppercorns and to omit cloves as these will discolour the vegetables.

If vinegar is made well ahead of use, put the spices into clean jars and cover with cold vinegar. Seal the jars or bottles and keep them in a cold place for at least one month, but two if preferred, and shake them at least once a week. Drain off the vinegar carefully for use, and for a very clear vinegar, strain through a jelly bag.

A second method for preparing spiced vinegar is to put the liquid into an ovenware or china bowl over a saucepan of hot water, or into an aluminium or unchipped enamel saucepan. Add the spices tied in muslin. Bring vinegar very slowly to simmering point, keeping it covered so that flavour is not lost. Take off the heat and leave to stand for 3 hours so the flavour of the spices goes into the vinegar. Remove the muslin bag. Use the vinegar hot or cold as required. Cold vinegar will keep pickles crisp when they are made with uncooked brined vegetables.

Ready-prepared spiced vinegar may sometimes be available in shops. This is a timesaver, but you can more easily adjust the flavour of homemade spiced vinegar.

For fruit pickles, the spiced vinegar is usually sweetened, allowing about 500g (1lb) sugar and 625ml (1 pint) vinegar to 1½kg (3lb) fruit.

Preparing pickles
Prepare the vegetables by peeling, trimming and cutting them up, removing any bruised or damaged parts. Only perfect vegetables should really be used for pickles, and the imperfect ones can be used up for chutney. Marrow and red cabbage are normally dry-brined, cucumber can be either wet or dry-brined, and other vegetables are usually wet-brined.

Vegetable pickles may be made by brining raw vegetables, draining and rinsing them and packing them firmly into jars up to 2·5cm (1in) from the rim, then filling the jar with vinegar (usually spiced) before sealing tightly with a vinegar-proof lid.

Cooked vegetables should also be packed firmly but without pressing tightly or their shape will be spoiled. The vegetables should then stand for an hour to allow any water to drain to the bottom of the jar, and this liquid should then be drained off and hot spiced vinegar poured in.

Fruit may be whole, or cut in halves, quarters or slices. It is normally lightly cooked in sweetened spiced vinegar, then drained and packed in jars. The syrup is then cooked a little longer and poured over the fruit while hot.

Storage times
Vinegar-preserved pickles keep a long time, but vegetables will usually be ready to eat after about two weeks and do not need a long maturing time. Raw vegetable pickles should be eaten within a year, and red cabbage is really only at its best for six months. Pickled fruits should be kept for two

months before using. All pickles are best kept in a cool, dark, dry place. Avoid over-large jars, so that opened jars are not kept too long.

Guidelines for making pickles
1 Use good-quality vegetables and fruit, and remove any blemishes carefully. Do not process if soft and slushy.
2 Make up spiced vinegar carefully, and weigh all ingredients.
3 Brine vegetables as directed, drain off all liquid and rinse before further processing.
4 Always use clean sterilised jars and vinegar-proof covers, and store in a cool, dark, dry place.

What can go wrong
Pickles with poor-keeping qualities. These may have been packed in unclean jars, or poorly stored. They may also be under-brined with too little salt, or for too short a time so that water in the vegetables themselves reduces the strength of the vinegar and affects its preserving qualities.
Fermentation, mould or white speckles. Any of these conditions indicate that something is seriously wrong, and the pickle should be thrown away. It may be due to weak vinegar or imperfect brining, or if a bad piece of fruit or vegetable should have been included, the deterioration may have spread.

Pickling vegetables
1 Select vegetables which are in perfect condition and prepare according to recipe.
2 a) For dry salting put vegetables into a large bowl in layers with dry (block) salt between the layers. Cover to keep out impurities, and leave for 24 hours.

2 b) For wet brining, put vegetables in a large bowl, cover with a solution of salt and water as prescribed, adding a weighted plate to keep them under the brine. Leave for 24 hours. 3 Drain well and rinse under running water, pack into jars. 4, 5 Add spiced vinegar and seal with metal lids.

Pickling fruit
1 Prepare fruit as recipe requires.
2 Put sugar and vinegar into pan, hanging spice bag from handle. Add fruit simmer till tender. 3 Lift out fruit and pack in warmed jars. Remove bag, boil up liquid till syrupy, pour over fruit and seal at once.

Recipes for pickles

Clear mixed pickles
The shallots, cauliflower and cucumber have been prepared, brined overnight, then drained and packed into jars to within 2.5cm (1in) of the rims. Now the spiced vinegar is poured in to the jar.

It is important to follow either the imperial or the metric weights and measures in any one recipe. Do not mix them.

Mustard Pickle

1 medium-sized marrow
1 medium-sized cauliflower
1 cucumber
400g (1lb) button onions
400g (1lb) French beans
25g (1oz) block salt
1 litre (2 pints) vinegar
   (see page 129)
250g (10oz) sugar
50g (2oz) flour
50g (2oz) mustard
15g (½oz) turmeric
15g (½oz) ground ginger
15g (½oz) ground nutmeg

Yield: about 4kg (8lb)

Chop the marrow into 2·5cm (1in) chunks without peeling, but remove seeds and pith. Break the cauliflower into small pieces. Chop the cucumber and beans, and peel the onions. Mix all the vegetables together in a bowl and sprinkle with salt. Cover with water and leave to soak overnight. Drain off the water. Mix all the dry ingredients with a little of the vinegar to a smooth paste. Put the vegetables into a saucepan with the remaining vinegar and simmer until just tender. Add a little of the boiling vinegar to the blended ingredients, then return to the pan of vegetables. Simmer for 10 minutes, stirring all the time, until thick. Put into warmed jars while hot.

Clear Mixed Pickles

400g (1lb) shallots
400g (1lb) cauliflower
1 large cucumber
25g (1oz) block salt
1½ litres (3 pints) spiced
   vinegar (see page 130)
15g (½oz) pickling spice

Yield: about 1½kg (3lb)

Peel the shallots. Break the cauliflower into sprigs. Peel the cucumber and cut into cubes. Mix all the vegetables, put into a bowl and sprinkle with salt. Leave overnight. Drain off the liquid and pack the vegetables into jars. Pour over the spiced vinegar, put a few spices in each jar. Seal tightly (see page 129), keep a few months before use.

Crisp Pickled Onions

1kg (2lb) small onions or
   shallots
50g (1½oz) block salt
1¼ litres (2 pints) spiced
   vinegar (see page 130)

Yield: about 1kg (2lb)

Peel the onions or shallots and put on a shallow dish. Sprinkle with salt and leave overnight. Put the onions or shallots into a colander, rinse under cold water and drain well. Pack into jars, arranging with the handle of a wooden spoon so that there are no large spaces. Fill up with cold spiced vinegar and seal tightly (see page 129).
   Keep 3–4 weeks before using.

Pickled Beetroot

8 medium-sized beetroot
1 litre (2 pints) vinegar
15g (½oz) black peppercorns
15g (½oz) allspice berries
5ml (1 teaspoon) grated
   horseradish
5ml (1 teaspoon) block salt

Yield: about 1kg (2lb)

Cook the beetroot and cool. Take off the skins and slice the beetroot. Pack in jars. Put the vinegar, spices, horseradish and salt into a saucepan. Bring to the boil, and then cool. When cold, pour over the beetroot and seal (see page 129) at once.

Pickled Green Tomatoes

1kg (2lb) green tomatoes
250g (8oz) onions
125g (4oz) block salt
250g (8oz) sugar
625ml (1 pint) white vinegar

Yield: about 1kg (2lb)

Wipe the tomatoes. Do not peel them, but cut across in slices. Peel and slice the onions thinly. Arrange the tomatoes and onions in a bowl in alternate layers, and sprinkle layers generously with salt. Leave for 24 hours, then drain off the liquid completely and rinse. Put the sugar and vinegar into a saucepan and heat gently until the sugar has dissolved. Put in the tomatoes and onions and simmer until soft but not broken. Put into warm jars and seal at once (see page 129).

Pickled Red Cabbage

1kg (2lb) red cabbage
125g (4oz) block salt
1¼ litres (2 pints) spiced
   vinegar

Yield: about 1kg (2lb)

Remove the coarse outer leaves from the cabbage and then shred the cabbage finely, removing the coarse stem. Put the cabbage in a large bowl in layers with the salt. Cover and leave for 24 hours. Drain the liquid from the cabbage and rinse it under cold running water. Drain cabbage well and pack fairly loosely in clean cold jars, filling them half full. Cover with cold spiced vinegar. Press down the cabbage slightly and fill the jar up with more cabbage. Cover with vinegar and seal (see page 129). Keep at least a week before use. **133**

Recipes for pickles

Pickled Mushrooms

400g (1lb) button mushrooms
500ml (1 pint) white vinegar
5ml (1 teaspoon) block salt
2·5ml (½ teaspoon) white
   pepper
Small piece root ginger
1 small onion, sliced

Yield: about 400g (1lb)

Wipe the mushrooms, discard stalks, but do not wash or peel them. Put into a pan with the vinegar and add the other ingredients. Simmer until mushrooms are tender. Lift the mushrooms out with a slotted spoon and pack into warmed jars. Bring the vinegar to the boil and pour over the mushrooms. Seal tightly (see list of equipment on page 129).

Pickled Cucumbers

1kg (2lb) ridge or green-house cucumbers
1¼ litres (2 pints) water
175g (6oz) block salt
50g (2oz) sugar
1¼ litres (2 pints) spiced vinegar
Bay leaves

Yield: about 1kg (2lb)

Use young cucumbers with soft skins. Do not peel them, but wipe them, cut in half, and then in quarters lengthwise. Boil the water and salt together, leave until cold and then pour over the cucumbers. Leave for 24 hours. Put the sugar and spiced vinegar into a saucepan and heat gently until the sugar has dissolved. Lift the cucumbers out of the salt brine, and rinse them in cold water. Drain and leave to dry for 2 hours. Pack upright in preserving jars, and cover with cold vinegar syrup. Put a bay leaf in each jar and seal tightly (see page 129). Keep 2–3 weeks before using.

Pickled Eggs

12 hard-boiled eggs
1 litre (2 pints) white vinegar
15g (½oz) root ginger
15g (½oz) mustard seeds
15g (½oz) white peppercorns
2 chillies

Yield: about 1½kg (3lb)

Cool the eggs and shell them. Simmer the vinegar with the bruised ginger, mustard seeds and peppercorns for 5 minutes. Strain and leave to cool. Arrange the eggs upright in a wide-mouthed jar, and put the chillies on top. Cover with vinegar and seal tightly (see page 129). Keep for 2–3 weeks before using.

Apple and Pepper Pickle

2kg (4lb) eating apples
1kg (2lb) green peppers
2¼ litres (3½ pints) cider vinegar
150g (5oz) soft brown sugar
25g (1oz) juniper berries

Yield: about 2kg (4lb)

Peel the apples, remove the cores, and cut them into rings. Remove the stalk and cap from each pepper and scoop out the seeds and membrane. Cut the peppers into rings. Pack the apples and peppers in layers in hot jars. Bring the vinegar, sugar and juniper berries to the boil, stir, and pour over the apples and peppers at once. Seal tightly (see page 129). Leave for about 6 weeks before using.

Spiced Oranges

6 thin-skinned oranges
375ml (¾ pint) white vinegar
350g (14oz) sugar
10ml (2 teaspoons) cloves
7·5cm (3in) cinnamon stick

Yield: about 750g (1½lb)

Wipe the oranges but do not peel. Slice across in thin rounds. Put into a pan with water to cover and simmer for 45 minutes until the peel of the fruit is tender. Drain the fruit. Put the vinegar, sugar and spices into a pan and bring to the boil. Reduce to simmering point, and add the orange rings a few at a time. When they are all in the pan, cook gently until the rind becomes transparent. Lift out the orange rings with a slotted spoon and pack into warmed jars. Boil syrup for 5 minutes until it starts to thicken and pour over the fruit. Put one or two of the cloves into each jar and seal (see page 129) at once.

Pickled Peaches

2kg (4lb) small ripe peaches
1kg (2lb) sugar
625ml (1 pint) white vinegar
25g (1oz) cloves
25g (1oz) allspice berries
25g (1oz) cinnamon stick

Yield: about 2kg (4lb)

Wash the peaches and wipe them dry. Put the sugar and vinegar in a saucepan and dissolve the sugar over gentle heat. Put the spices into a piece of muslin, crush them, and tie the muslin bag so that it hangs in the saucepan. Put in the fruit and simmer until tender but not soft. Drain the fruit with a slotted spoon and pack into warmed jars. Remove the spice bag, and boil up the liquid for 10 minutes until syrupy. Cover the fruit, seal (page 129) at once.

Recipes for pickles

Pickled Walnuts

Green walnuts
500g (1lb) block salt
5 litres (8 pints) water
Spiced vinegar

The walnuts will be ready to use in early July. They should be used before the shells start to form in the green outer casing. This can be tested by pricking with a needle and if any shell can be felt, the walnuts are too old for pickling. The shell begins to form opposite the stalk about 5mm ($\frac{1}{4}$in) from the end. Make up a brine in the proportion of 500g (1lb) salt to 5 litres (8 pints) water and cover the green walnuts, leaving them to soak for 5 days. Drain off the brine and make a new batch of the same strength. Cover the walnuts again and leave for 7 days. Drain well and spread them out on a tray in the air for 24 hours, when they will be black (it is a good idea to turn the nuts a few times during this process so that they blacken evenly). Put into jars and cover with hot spiced vinegar. Seal and leave for a month before use.

Walnut stains are very difficult to remove so it is a good idea to protect clothing and hands while working.

Spiced Prunes

400g (1lb) large prunes
375ml ($\frac{3}{4}$ pint) cold tea,
    without milk
500ml (1 pint) white vinegar
400g (1lb) sugar
2·5cm (1in) cinnamon stick
5ml (1 teaspoon) cloves
10 allspice berries
Blade of mace

Yield: about 600g (1$\frac{1}{2}$lb)

Put the prunes into a bowl, cover with tea and leave to soak overnight. Simmer in the tea until the prunes are plump. In another pan, boil the vinegar and sugar with the crushed spices tied in a muslin bag which hangs in the pan, for 5 minutes. Add the prunes and cooking liquid and simmer for 5 minutes. Lift out the prunes with a slotted spoon and pack them into warmed jars. Remove the spice bag, boil the syrup, pour over the prunes, and seal at once (see page 129).

These are particularly good with fat meats such as pork.

Spiced prunes
Prunes soaking in a bowl of tea, ready for spicing. Next they will be simmered in the tea until they are plump, then cooked with vinegar, sugar and spices. The spices are cinnamon stick, cloves, allspice berries and a blade of mace. They will be hung in the pan in a muslin bag.

It is important to follow either the imperial or the metric weights and measures in any one recipe. Do not mix them.

Pickled Pears

2kg (4lb) cooking pears
1kg (2lb) sugar
625ml (1 pint) white vinegar
25g (1oz) cloves
25g (1oz) allspice berries
25g (1oz) root ginger
25g (1oz) cinnamon stick
Rind of ½ lemon

Yield: about 2kg (4lb)

Peel the pears, cut them into quarters and core. Put the sugar and vinegar in a saucepan and dissolve the sugar over gentle heat. Put the spices and lemon rind into a piece of muslin, crush them, tie the muslin bag so that it hangs in the pan. Add pears to vinegar and sugar and simmer until tender. Lift out the pears with a slotted spoon and pack into warmed jars. Remove the spice bag, and boil up the liquid for 10 minutes until syrupy. Cover the fruit and seal (see page 129) at once.

Spiced Plums

1kg (2lb) cooking plums
625ml (1 pint) white vinegar
750g (1½lb) sugar
2·5cm (1in) cinnamon stick
5ml (1 teaspoon) cloves
10 allspice berries
Blade of mace

Yield: about 1½kg (3 lb)

Wipe the plums and prick them four times each with a needle. Put into a bowl. Put the vinegar and sugar into a saucepan. Put the spices into a piece of muslin, crush them, and tie the muslin bag so that it hangs in the saucepan. Boil together for 10 minutes. Pour vinegar and sugar over the plums and add the spice bag and leave overnight. Drain off the liquid and boil for 10 minutes. Pour over the fruit again and leave for 12 hours. Put into a saucepan with the plums and bring to the boil. Remove the spices and lift out the plums with a slotted spoon. Pack them into preserving jars. Boil the syrup again, pour it over the plums and seal (see the list of equipment on page 129) at once.

Chutneys

The spices give variety
It is the spices used in making chutney that provide limitless variations in flavour with the result that every chutney, even when made from the same recipe, has its own individuality. Hot flavours come from the peppers, chillies and ginger, while the blandness of cloves, cinnamon, nutmeg and mace helps to produce a mild chutney. The exotic cardamom on the other hand, is highly aromatic. You can buy spices at good grocers, delicatessens and supermarkets. The measuring spoons (below) in metric and imperial are useful for small quantities of spices.

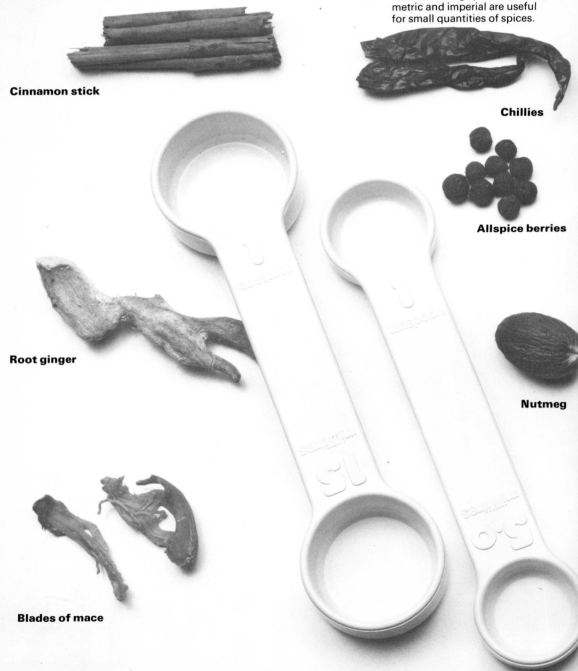

Cinnamon stick

Chillies

Allspice berries

Root ginger

Nutmeg

Blades of mace

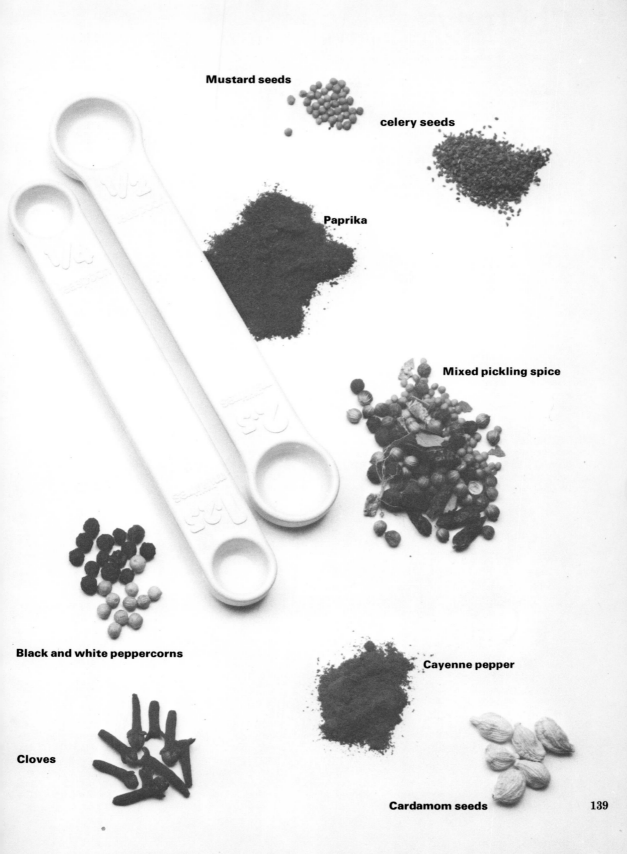

Mustard seeds

celery seeds

Paprika

Mixed pickling spice

Black and white peppercorns

Cayenne pepper

Cloves

Cardamom seeds

139

Chutneys

Chutney is a mixture of fruit and/or vegetables cooked with vinegar, sugar and spices to the consistency of jam. The vegetables and fruit should be cut into small pieces and cooked until soft but still identifiable. Chutney mixtures can be rubbed through a sieve and cooked to make sauce.

Chutney can be made from bruised or imperfect fruit or vegetables, but the bruises or poor parts must be cut away. Apples, plums, etc, can always include some windfalls. The fruit or vegetables must never be over-ripe, rotten or mouldy. A chutney mixture often includes dried fruit such as raisins or dates which give sweetness, texture and flavour. Onions are often added as well, and sometimes garlic, which should be chopped finely. Brown sugar gives flavour and a rich colour to chutney.

Spices play a most important part in chutney-making because they provide endless variations in flavour. Any basic chutney recipe can be varied to suit individual tastes, according to whether a hot, mild or aromatic mixture is preferred. Cayenne, ginger and chillies provide hot flavours; cayenne and chillies must be omitted if a mild chutney is needed. Cloves, cinnamon, nutmeg, and mace are delicious in mild chutney, and cardamom seeds are highly aromatic. A ready-mixed curry powder is useful to give extra heat. Ground spices may be used, but it is worth looking for fresh supplies, as spices which have been kept for a long time can become stale and musty, and it is best to buy only small quantities of those which are not in general use.

Chutney spices should be used with care and measured accurately as they can deaden other flavours. It is best to make up a recipe exactly, but when the chutney has been stored, taste carefully to see if additions or deletions are perhaps needed when the recipe is made again. The flavour of chutney cannot be judged by smelling or tasting when it is still hot.

For equipment needed see page 129.

Spices used in chutney
Cinnamon stick
Root ginger
Allspice berries
Black and white peppercorns
Mustard seeds
Celery seeds
Nutmeg
Chillies
Cayenne pepper
Mixed pickling spice
Blades of mace
Cloves
Paprika
Cardamom seeds
These spices are available at delicatessens and good grocers and supermarkets.

Method
Select fruit and vegetables carefully for chutney-making. Over-ripe produce should not be used. Cut away any part which is bruised or damaged, and discard any mouldy fruit or withered vegetables. Wipe fruit and wash vegetables, and peel or skin if necessary. Cut them into small pieces (use a stainless knife) and put into a preserving pan, or a large pan with a lid if the fruit or vegetables are of a rather dry type and the mixture might evaporate too quickly.

(For the kinds of vinegar to use, see page 129.)

Add the spices and remaining ingredients, and then cook very gently to soften the main fruit and vegetables. This can take from 1–4 hours, but usually takes about $2\frac{1}{2}$ hours, and long slow cooking is essential to break down tough fibres and bring out flavour. When this cooking is neglected, the chutney is colourless and watery.

Continue cooking slowly without a cover, until the mixture looks like thick jam. It must be stirred often to prevent sticking, and burning. The chutney will look thick at this stage, but it will also thicken slightly as it cools.

For vegetables and fruit with skins which may toughen, such as gooseberries, plums, oranges, add the spices and enough of the given amount of vinegar just to cover, and cook very gently until very soft. Then add the remaining vinegar and the sugar and continue cooking, stirring frequently, until of the required consistency.

Sealing
Jars for chutney should be clean and hot, with lids which are proof against the action of vinegar. These may be plastic, coated metal or lined metal, or the lacquered tops of preserving jars (see page 129). Paper covers or transparent jam covers are useless for chutney as they allow the mixture to evaporate, but Porosan may be used. Jars should be well-filled with the hot mixture to within 1·25cm ($\frac{1}{2}$in) of the rim. Lids should be put on at once and jars wiped clean with a wet cloth. Chutney should preferably be stored in a cool, dark, dry place.

Yield of chutney recipes
It is difficult to calculate exactly the yield of a chutney recipe, as much will depend on the final thickness of the chutney. An approximate weight of the finished product can be arrived at by adding the weights of fruit or vegetables, dried fruit and sugar in the recipe. In most of the recipes, allow about 450g (1lb) for wastage of such items as apple peelings and cores, onion skins and other trimmings, and discount the weight of spices and most of the weight of liquid which will evaporate during cooking.

A variety of different chutneys is better in the store cupboard than a large amount of only one kind. If some recipes seem to yield too much, quantities can be halved, or divided into three or four parts, except for the vinegar where slightly more than a half, a third, or a quarter of the original quantity should be used, as it will evaporate during cooking.

For small quantities of chutney, use a covered pan or the mixture will dry out before it is fully cooked.

Storage time

Most chutneys are best stored for at least six months before eating, so that the flavours can blend and mature. A well-made chutney will keep at least two years, and even after four years it will be delicious if properly stored.

Guidelines for making chutney

1 Make up a standard recipe exactly if it is a first-time brew of chutney, but after a little experience, vary the fruit and vegetables used or change the quantity or mixture of spices.

2 For a finer chutney mixture, and also to save time, mince fruit and vegetables instead of chopping. Dried fruit can go through the mincer as well. A plate should be put under the mincer to catch juices.

3 It is better to over-cook, rather than under-cook chutney before the sugar is added, to drive out excess moisture, but the mixture must not become dry and sticky. As the cooking time is rather long, it may be necessary to leave the kitchen during cooking. It is best to turn off the chutney and start cooking again later as the flavour will be spoiled if the chutney sticks to the pan, or extra vinegar has to be added to counteract dryness.

4 Always allow for long storage of chutney as the flavours mature and improve. Be sure to keep it in an airy place which is cool, dark and dry.

5 Be sure to use vinegar-proof covers for jars.

What can go wrong

Colourless, watery chutney. This results from under-cooking. Good chutney should be of the same thickness as jam, and rich in colour.

Fermentation or mouldy chutney. This may also result from under-cooking which leaves too much water in a mixture, or from using unclean jars or covers, or putting too little vinegar.

Dry chutney. Chutney which becomes dark on top during storage has been kept in too warm a place, or the cover has not been airtight.

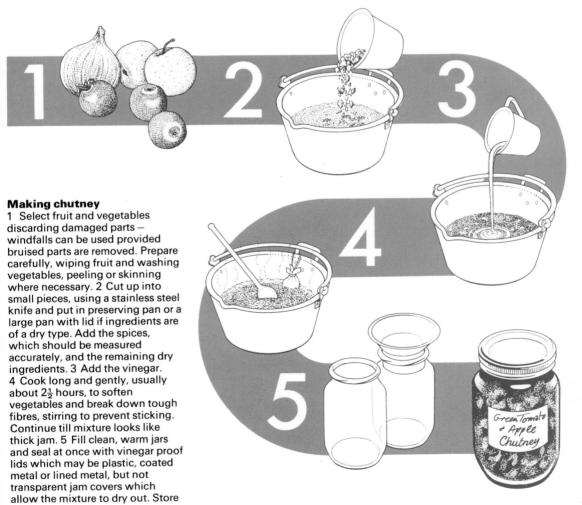

Making chutney

1 Select fruit and vegetables discarding damaged parts – windfalls can be used provided bruised parts are removed. Prepare carefully, wiping fruit and washing vegetables, peeling or skinning where necessary. 2 Cut up into small pieces, using a stainless steel knife and put in preserving pan or a large pan with lid if ingredients are of a dry type. Add the spices, which should be measured accurately, and the remaining dry ingredients. 3 Add the vinegar. 4 Cook long and gently, usually about 2½ hours, to soften vegetables and break down tough fibres, stirring to prevent sticking. Continue till mixture looks like thick jam. 5 Fill clean, warm jars and seal at once with vinegar proof lids which may be plastic, coated metal or lined metal, but not transparent jam covers which allow the mixture to dry out. Store in a cool, dark, dry place.

Recipes for chutneys

Autumn Chutney

2kg (4lb) cooking apples
1kg (2lb) pears
1½kg (3lb) red tomatoes
2kg (4lb) soft brown sugar
250g (8oz) sultanas
250g (8oz) seedless raisins
1¼ litres (2 pints) vinegar
5ml (1 teaspoon) ground
  mace
5ml (1 teaspoon) cayenne
  pepper
5ml (1 teaspoon) ground
  cloves
5ml (1 teaspoon) pepper
30ml (2 tablespoons) salt
5ml (1 teaspoon) ground
  ginger

Yield: about 5kg (10lb)

Peel the apples and pears, core and cut into small pieces. Skin the tomatoes and chop them. Put the apples, pears, tomatoes and all the remaining ingredients into a preserving pan. Stir well and simmer for 2 hours until tender, golden brown and thick. Stir occasionally to prevent sticking. Put into hot jars, cover and seal.

Beetroot Chutney

1kg (2lb) beetroot, cooked
2 medium-sized onions,
  chopped
500g (1lb) cooking apples
250g (8oz) granulated sugar
625ml (1 pint) vinegar
15ml (1 tablespoon) lemon
  juice
2·5ml (½ teaspoon) ground
  ginger
2·5ml (½ teaspoon) salt

Yield: about 1½kg (3lb)

Peel the beetroot and cut it into small cubes. Peel and core the apples and chop them finely. Mix the onions, apples, sugar, vinegar, lemon juice, ginger and salt, and bring to the boil. Simmer for 30 minutes. Add the beetroot and simmer for 15 minutes. Put into hot jars, cover and seal.

Green Tomato Chutney

2½kg (5lb) green tomatoes,
  sliced
500g (1lb) onions, chopped
500g (1lb) soft brown sugar
1¼ litres (2 pints) vinegar
250g (8oz) seedless raisins
250g (8oz) sultanas
15g (½oz) pepper
25g (1oz) salt

Yield: about 4kg (8lb)

Put the tomatoes and onions into a bowl with the pepper and salt. Mix well and leave to stand

Garden apples
These are a valuable chutney ingredient. Cooking apples are usually best – they can include windfalls; imperfect fruit is usable, so long as bruised or bad parts are cut away.

It is important to follow either the imperial or the metric weights and measures in any one recipe. Do not mix them.

overnight. Put the sugar and vinegar into a preserving pan and bring to the boil. Add the raisins and sultanas and bring to the boil. Simmer for 5 minutes. Add the tomatoes and onions and continue simmering for one hour until tender, golden brown and thick. Stir occasionally to prevent sticking. Put into hot jars, cover and seal.

Green Tomato and Apple Chutney

2kg (4lb) green tomatoes
500g (1lb) cooking apples
750g (1½lb) onions, chopped
250g (8oz) seedless raisins
500g (1lb) soft brown sugar
625ml (1 pint) vinegar
15g (½oz) ground ginger
15g (½oz) salt
12 red chillies

Yield: about 3½kg (7lb)

Cut up the tomatoes without peeling. Peel and core the apples and chop them. Put all the tomatoes, apples, onions and raisins in a preserving pan. Add the sugar, vinegar, ginger and salt. Tie the chillies into a piece of muslin and suspend in the pan. Bring to the boil, stir well, and simmer for one hour until thick and golden brown. Remove the bag of chillies. Put into hot jars, cover and seal.

Red Tomato Chutney

500g (1lb) red tomatoes
125g (4oz) cooking apples
250g (8oz) onions, chopped
500g (1lb) seedless raisins
125g (4oz) soft brown sugar
300ml (½ pint) vinegar
10ml (2 teaspoons) salt
10ml (2 teaspoons) ground ginger
Pinch of cayenne pepper

Yield: about 1½kg (3lb)

Skin the tomatoes and chop the flesh. Peel and core the apples, and chop them. Put all the tomatoes, apples and onions into a preserving pan with the other ingredients. Stir well and simmer for one hour until thick and golden brown. Put into hot jars, cover and seal.

Marrow and Tomato Chutney

1½kg (3lb) marrow
500g (1lb) red tomatoes
250g (8oz) cooking apples
250g (8oz) onions, chopped
1 red pepper
1 green pepper
125g (4oz) dates, stoned
200g (6oz) seedless raisins
500g (1lb) sugar
625ml (1 pint) vinegar
75g (3oz) salt
15g (½oz) mustard seed
10ml (2 teaspoons) ground ginger
10ml (2 teaspoons) ground allspice
5ml (1 teaspoon) ground cinnamon
5ml (1 teaspoon) ground mace

Yield: about 3kg (6lb)

Peel the marrow and remove seeds and pith. Chop the flesh in small cubes and arrange in a large bowl with the 75g (3oz) salt in layers. Cover and leave in a cool place for 24 hours. Drain the marrow thoroughly through a colander. Then rinse. Skin the tomatoes, chop them roughly.

Peel, core and chop the apples. Remove the stems, seeds and membranes from the peppers and chop the flesh. Put all the ingredients except the marrow and sugar into a preserving pan and cook over low heat for 1½ hours until tender. Stir in the sugar, and when it has dissolved, stir in the marrow cubes. Simmer for one hour until the marrow is soft and most of the liquid has evaporated. Stir occasionally to prevent sticking. Put into hot jars, cover and seal.

Pineapple Chutney

1 medium-sized pineapple
250g (8oz) granulated sugar
300ml (½ pint) cider vinegar
5ml (1 teaspoon) ground cinnamon
5ml (1 teaspoon) ground cloves
5ml (1 teaspoon) ground ginger
15ml (1 tablespoon) curry powder

Yield: about 500g (1lb)

Peel and core the pineapple and cut the flesh in small pieces. Put any pineapple juice with the sugar and vinegar into a preserving pan and bring to the boil. Add the spices and simmer for five minutes. Add the pineapple and cook for ten minutes on low heat, stirring well. Put the chutney into hot jars, cover and seal.

Blackberry Chutney

3kg (6lb) blackberries
1kg (2lb) cooking apples
1kg (2lb) onions, chopped
1kg (2lb) soft brown sugar
1¼ litres (2 pints) vinegar
25g (1oz) salt
50g (2oz) mustard (dry powder or mustard seed)
50g (2oz) ground ginger
10ml (2 teaspoons) ground mace
5ml (1 teaspoon) cayenne pepper

Yield: about 4kg (8lb)

Wash the blackberries and put them into a preserving pan. Peel and core the apples and chop them. Add to the blackberries with the onions, sugar, vinegar, seasoning and spices. Simmer for 1¼ hours until thick, stirring well. Put the chutney into hot jars, cover and seal.

Plum Chutney

1½kg (3lb) plums
500g (1lb) carrots, minced
500g (1lb) seedless raisins
500g (1lb) soft brown sugar
625ml (1 pint) vinegar
25g (1oz) garlic, chopped
25g (1oz) chillies, chopped
25g (1oz) ground ginger
40g (1½oz) salt

Yield: about 2kg (4lb)

Cut up the plums and remove the stones. Put into a preserving pan with the carrots and vinegar and simmer until soft. Add the remaining ingredients and simmer for one hour until thick and soft. Stir occasionally to prevent sticking. Put into hot jars, cover and seal.

Recipes for chutneys

Using the mincer
To make a finer chutney mixture – or to save precious time – the fruit and vegetables can be minced instead of chopped. Here gooseberries are being put through the mincer – with a plate strategically placed under the machine, to catch the juices.

Cherry Chutney

1½kg (3lb) eating cherries
250g (8oz) seedless raisins
125g (4oz) soft brown sugar
50g (2oz) honey
300ml (½ pint) vinegar
10ml (2 teaspoons) ground
  mixed spice

Yield: about 1kg (2lb)

Stone, then chop, the cherries. Put into a preserving pan with the other ingredients. Heat gently and stir until the sugar has dissolved. Bring to the boil and boil for 5 minutes. Reduce the heat and simmer for 30 minutes, stirring all the time until thick. Put into hot jars, cover and seal.

Gooseberry Chutney

2kg (4lb) gooseberries
500g (1lb) soft brown sugar
1¼ litres (2 pints) vinegar
500g (1lb) onions, finely
  chopped
750g (1½lb) seedless raisins
125g (4oz) mustard seeds
50g (2oz) ground allspice
125g (4oz) salt

Yield: about 3½kg (7lb)

Mix the sugar with half the vinegar and boil until a syrup forms. Add the onions, raisins, bruised mustard seeds, spice and salt. Top and tail the gooseberries. Boil them in the remaining vinegar until tender. Put the two mixtures together, and simmer for one hour until tender, golden brown and thick. Stir occasionally to prevent sticking. Put into hot jars, cover and seal.

Recipes for chutneys

Apple and Date Chutney

2½kg (5lb) cooking apples
625ml (1 pint) vinegar
250g (8oz) dates, stoned
250g (8oz) sultanas
250g (8oz) onions, minced
500g (1lb) demerara sugar
15ml (1 tablespoon) salt
15ml (1 tablespoon) ground
   ginger
6 chillies, chopped (optional)
5ml (1 level teaspoon)
   mustard seed (optional)

Yield: about 3½kg (7lb)

Peel and core the apples, and cut them into small pieces. Put the vinegar into a preserving pan with the sugar, salt, ginger, and chillies and mustard seed (if using), and bring to the boil. Add the apples, onions, dates and sultanas and simmer for at least one hour until golden brown and thick. The apples make a lot of juice, and the chutney should not be runny. Put into hot jars, cover and seal.

The chillies do, of course, make the chutney very hot, and may be omitted if preferred.

Grape and Apple Chutney

1kg (2lb) grapes
1kg (2lb) cooking apples
250g (8oz) seedless raisins
625g (1¼lb) soft brown sugar
300ml (½ pint) cider vinegar
150ml (¼ pint) lemon juice
2·5ml (½ teaspoon) ground
   allspice
2·5ml (½ teaspoon) ground
   cloves
2·5ml (½ teaspoon) ground
   ginger
2·5ml (½ teaspoon) salt
Pinch of ground cinnamon
Pinch of paprika
Grated rind of ½ lemon

Yield: about 2½kg (5lb)

Cut the grapes in half and remove the seeds. Peel and core the apples, and chop them. Put all the ingredients into a preserving pan and bring to the boil. Simmer for one hour until soft, golden brown and thick, stir occasionally to prevent sticking. Put into hot jars, cover and seal.

Banana Chutney

1kg (2lb) ripe bananas
250g (8oz) dates, stoned
250g (8oz) seedless raisins
250g (8oz) demerara sugar
500ml (¾ pint) vinegar
300ml (½ pint) syrup from
   canned fruit
1 lemon
125g (4oz) crystallised ginger,
   chopped
10ml (2 teaspoons) salt
20ml (4 teaspoons) curry
   powder

Yield: about 1½kg (3lb)

Peel the bananas and cut them into small pieces. Chop the dates and put them into a preserving pan with the bananas. Grate the lemon rind and squeeze out the juice. Add to the pan with the vinegar. Cover the pan and cook gently for 1½ hours. Take off the lid and stir in the raisins, sugar, fruit syrup, ginger, salt and curry powder. Simmer for 30 minutes, stirring well, until thick. Put into hot jars, cover and seal. The canned syrup can come from one fruit or a mixture.

Rhubarb Chutney

1kg (2lb) rhubarb
250g (8oz) onions, chopped
750g (1½lb) soft brown sugar
250g (8oz) sultanas
625ml (1 pint) vinegar
15g (½oz) mustard (dry
   powder or mustard seed)
5ml (1 teaspoon) ground
   mixed spice
5ml (1 teaspoon) pepper
5ml (1 teaspoon) ground
   ginger
5ml (1 teaspoon salt
Pinch of cayenne pepper

Yield: about 2kg (4lb)

Wipe the rhubarb (this can be young or old – it is a good way of using old rhubarb) and cut into 2·5cm (1in) lengths. Mix with the onions in a preserving pan and add all the ingredients. Stir well and simmer for one hour until soft, golden brown and thick. Stir occasionally to prevent sticking. Put into hot jars, cover and seal.

Dried Apricot Chutney

500g (1lb) dried apricots
750g (1½lb) onions, chopped
500g (1lb) granulated sugar
2 oranges
250g (8oz) sultanas
1¼ litres (2 pints) cider vinegar
10ml (2 teaspoons) salt
2 garlic cloves, crushed
5ml (1 teaspoon) mustard
   (dry powder or mustard
   seed)
2·5ml (½ teaspoon) ground
   allspice

Yield: about 2½kg (5lb)

Put the apricots into a bowl and just cover with water. Leave to soak overnight, drain and chop finely. Put the apricots and onions into a preserving pan with the sugar. Grate the rind from the oranges and squeeze out the juice. Add the orange rind and juice to the pan with the sultanas, vinegar, salt, garlic, mustard and allspice. Simmer gently for one hour until tender, golden brown and thick. Stir the chutney occasionally to prevent sticking. Put the chutney into hot jars, cover and seal.

Damson Chutney

1½kg (3lb) damsons
500g (1lb) cooking apples
250g (8oz) onions, chopped
250g (8oz) dates, stoned
250g (8oz) soft brown sugar
625ml (1 pint) vinegar
15g (½oz) ground ginger
15g (½oz) mustard
15g (½oz) salt
2·5ml (½ teaspoon) pepper
2·5ml (½ teaspoon) ground
   cloves

Yield: about 1½kg (3lb)

Put the damsons into a preserving pan and simmer in their own juice until soft. Take out the stones. Peel and core the apples, and cut them in pieces. Put the apples, onions, dates, sugar, vinegar, seasoning and spices with the damsons. Simmer for 2 hours until soft and thick. Stir occasionally to prevent sticking. Put the chutney into hot jars, cover and seal.

Pear Chutney

2kg (4lb) pears
750g (1½lb) soft brown sugar
500g (1lb) seedless raisins
2 oranges
300ml (½ pint) white vinegar
5ml (1 teaspoon) ground
 cloves
5ml (1 teaspoon) ground
 cinnamon
5ml (1 teaspoon) ground
 allspice

Yield: about 3kg (6lb)

Peel and core the pears and chop
them. Grate the orange rind and
squeeze out the juice. Put the
pears, sugar, raisins, orange
rind and juice into a preserving
pan with the vinegar and spices.
Bring to the boil and then
simmer for one hour until thick
and golden brown. Stir occasionally to prevent sticking.
Put into hot jars, cover and seal.

Apricot and Orange Chutney

500g (1lb) dried apricots
250g (8oz) sugar
125g (4oz) sultanas
300ml (½ pint) white vinegar
1 orange
1 garlic clove
3 peppercorns

Yield: about 750g (1½lb)

Put the apricots into a bowl and
just cover with water. Leave to
soak overnight and then drain
off the liquid. Put the fruit into a
preserving pan with the sugar,
sultanas, chopped garlic clove
and peppercorns. Grate the rind
from the orange and squeeze out
the juice. Add to the pan and
bring to the boil. Stir in the
vinegar and simmer for 45
minutes until thick. Put into hot
jars, cover and seal.

Orange Chutney

6 thin-skinned oranges
250g (8oz) onions, chopped
500g (1lb) dates, stoned
625ml (1 pint) vinegar
10ml (2 teaspoons) ground
 ginger
10ml (2 teaspoons) salt

Yield: about 2kg (4lb)

Peel the oranges and remove the
pips. Chop the oranges and put
into a preserving pan with their
juice, the onions and the dates.
Add the vinegar, ginger and salt
and stir well. Cook for one hour
until golden brown and thick.
Put into hot jars, cover and seal.

All kinds of fruit
Almost any garden or hedgerow
fruit can be used for chutney, and
so can all-the-year round imported
fruits, like oranges.

Sauces and ketchups

Both sauces and ketchups can be made at home, and sauce-making is a useful way of using up surplus produce. A **sauce** pours from a bottle, but is thickened because the ingredients are rubbed through a hair or nylon sieve. Sauces are made to be used cold to accompany either hot or cold dishes. A **ketchup** is made by straining through a very fine sieve or jelly bag to give a thin, almost clear liquid without any solid matter left in it. Ketchup is most often used as an additive to recipes (eg casseroles, pâtés) rather than served at table like sauce.

While there are many special recipes for sauces, it is possible to make sauce from any favourite chutney recipe. The chutney mixture should be rubbed through a sieve about two-thirds of the way through cooking time, and then cooked again, but it should not be made as thick as chutney, so do not simmer the mixture to reduce its consistency for quite as long.

Preparing sauces and ketchups

Most sauces and ketchups are based on a single fruit or vegetable with onions, spices, vinegar and sugar, but a mixture of fruit and vegetables can be used. The finished sauce should be smooth. with a bright colour and a distinct flavour. A ketchup should be thin and almost clear, but may leave a little sediment in the bottles after storage.

Usually cut-up fruit and vegetables have to be simmered in vinegar until soft. After sieving, or straining, the purée is spiced and sweetened and then simmered again until smooth and creamy. Sauces should not be as spicy as chutney, but extra mustard, pepper or ginger can be added to the recipe if liked.

When the sauce is smooth and creamy, it should be poured at once into hot sterilised bottles (see bottling chapter, page 162) and the tops put on immediately. Sauces and ketchups should then be sterilised in a water bath as they may otherwise ferment in storage.

Sterilisation

Put the filled sauce bottles into a large preserving pan on a rack or thick wad of newspaper. Screw the tops on tightly and then release one half-turn. Cover the bottles with hot, not boiling water, and bring to simmering point, 88°C, 190°F. Keep this temperature for 30 minutes. Take out the bottles and screw the tops on tightly at once.

Storage

Sauces and ketchups should be stored in a cool, dark place. Provided they are sterilised, they will keep for some time, but it is best to use them before the new crops come. They can be used at once – they do not need time to mature.

Guidelines for making sauces and ketchups

1 Follow the recipes carefully, weighing out the ingredients exactly, and timing the cooking so that the sauce does not become too thick.
2 Use good-quality ingredients and make sure that fruit and vegetables are carefully wiped or washed, according to recipe.
3 Be sure that all equipment is vinegar-proof, and is clean. Sterilise all jars or bottles before filling.
4 Fill bottles with hot sauce (with the exception of tomato sauce which is cooled), screw on tops at once, and sterilise in a water bath.
5 Store sauces in a cool, dark place.

Making sauces
1 Prepare fruit and/or vegetables according to recipe. 2 Simmer in vinegar until soft. 3 Put through sieve, return purée to clean pan, add spices, sugar and vinegar as required. 4 Simmer till smooth and pour at once into hot, sterilised bottles and tighten tops. 5 Wrap in newspaper against bumping, put in pan, release tops half a turn. Cover bottles to neck in hot, not boiling water and simmer as required. Take out and screw tops on tightly.

What can go wrong

Fermentation or mould. This indicates that the sauce may have been stored in a warm place, or the covers were not airtight. The sauce should be thrown away without tasting. Sauces may also deteriorate in this way when there is too much liquid left in the mixture because it has not been cooked long enough.

Deterioration of tomato and mushroom sauces. This will always occur if they are not sterilised after bottling. All sauces should be sterilised for 30 minutes in a water bath, but tomato and mushroom sauces are particularly likely to deteriorate.

Sauce separating during storage. It may not have been cooked quite long enough so that it still has a watery appearance. Separation does not mean that the sauce is unfit to use. Shake the bottle before using to restore even smoothness.

Failure of sauce to keep. If the bottles are not completely clean when filled, and/or the covers are not clean, the sauce will not keep.

Sauce darkening at top. This happens, particularly with tomato sauce, if the lids are not airtight.

Recipes for sauces

Tomato Sauce

2kg (4lb) red tomatoes
4 large onions
500g (1lb) demerara sugar
625ml (1 pint) vinegar
50g (2oz) peppercorns
25g (1oz) salt
15g (½oz) cloves
10ml (2 teaspoons) cayenne
   pepper

Yield: about 750ml (1½ pints)

Slice the tomatoes and onions. Put into a preserving pan with the other ingredients and stir well. Simmer gently for 2 hours until thick and soft, stirring occasionally. Rub through a fine sieve, leaving nothing but seeds, skin and spice in the sieve. Put into a clean pan, bring to the boil and boil for 5 minutes. Leave until cold and pour into screwtop bottles. Sterilise for 30 minutes in a water bath.

Good with fish and chips, sausages and grills.

Green Tomato Sauce

1kg (2lb) green tomatoes
125g (4oz) shallots
15g (½oz) celery seed
1 lemon
10ml (2 teaspoons) turmeric
5ml (1 teaspoon) ground
   allspice
2·5ml (½ teaspoon) ground
   ginger
2·5ml (½ teaspoon) ground
   cinnamon
250g (8oz) sugar
300ml (½ pint) vinegar

Yield: about 750ml (1½ pints)

Cut up the tomatoes into small pieces and put in a saucepan with the chopped shallots, celery seed and chopped lemon. Cover the pan and simmer very gently for about 40 minutes until the tomatoes and shallots are soft. Put through a sieve and return to a clean pan. Add the remaining spices, sugar and vinegar. Stir over low heat until the sugar has dissolved. Bring to the boil and simmer for 45 minutes until thick and smooth. Put into hot bottles, while hot, and seal, Sterilise for 30 minutes in a water bath.

Used in the same way as Tomato Sauce, but spicier – more popular with adults than with children.

Blackberry Sauce

3kg (6lb) blackberries
625ml (1 pint) vinegar
5ml (1 teaspoon) salt
25g (1oz) sugar
5ml (1 teaspoon) mustard
2·5ml (½ teaspoon) ground
  cloves
2·5ml (½ teaspoon) ground
  nutmeg
2·5ml (½ teaspoon) ground
  cinnamon

Yield: about 1½ litres (3 pints)

Clean the blackberries and put into a pan with just enough water to cover. Simmer until the berries are soft and strain through a sieve, pushing through as much pulp as possible. Put the purée into a clean pan with the remaining ingredients. Stir over low heat until the sugar has dissolved. Bring to the boil and simmer for 15 minutes. Put into hot bottles, while hot, and seal. Sterilise for 30 minutes in a water bath. Serve with ham.

Rich Fruit Sauce

3½kg (7lb) tomatoes
3kg (6lb) cooking apples
1kg (2lb) onions
500g (1lb) dates, stoned
1½kg (3lb) seedless raisins
1½kg (3lb) soft brown sugar
2 litres (3 pints) white vinegar
15ml (1 tablespoon) salt
10ml (2 teaspoons) ground
  mixed spice

25g (1oz) mustard seeds
15g (½oz) cloves
2·5ml (½ teaspoon) cayenne
  pepper
10ml (2 teaspoons) ground
  ginger
3 red chillies
2 blades mace

Yield: about 3 litres (6 pints)

Either red or green tomatoes may be used, or a mixture of both. Slice the tomatoes. Peel, core and chop the apples, and chop the onions and dates. Put all the ingredients except the sugar into a preserving pan and simmer for one hour until vegetables are soft. Put through a sieve and return to a clean pan

with the sugar. Stir over low heat until the sugar has dissolved. Bring up to the boil, then simmer for 45 minutes until thick. Put into hot bottles, while hot, and seal. Sterilise for 30 minutes in a water bath.

Good with cheese, and any cold roast meats, especially pork.

Spicy Sauce for Meats

500ml (1 pint) vinegar
2 shallots, chopped
30ml (2 tablespoons) anchovy
  essence
45ml (3 tablespoons) walnut
  ketchup (see page 153)
30ml (2 tablespoons) soy
  sauce
Pinch of salt

Yield: about 500ml (1 pint)

Mix all the ingredients together and put into a screwtop jar. Shake the bottle twice a day for a fortnight. Strain and bottle.

Add a dash to chilled tomato juice, tomato soups and sauces, beef casseroles and stews.

Recipes for sauces & ketchups

Cranberry Sauce

1kg (2lb) cranberries
250g (8oz) onions, chopped
250g (8oz) sugar
300ml (½ pint) vinegar
2·5ml (½ teaspoon) ground
  cloves
2·5ml (½ teaspoon) ground
  cinnamon
2·5ml (½ teaspoon) ground
  allspice
2·5ml (½ teaspoon) pepper
15ml (1 tablespoon) salt
250ml (8floz) water

Yield: about 1 litre (2 pints)

Put the cranberries, onions and
water into a saucepan, cover
and simmer for 30 minutes until
the cranberries are soft. Put
through a sieve and return the
purée to a clean pan. Stir in the
sugar, vinegar, spices and salt.
Stir over low heat until the
sugar has dissolved. Bring to the
boil and simmer for 20 minutes.
Put into hot bottles while hot,
and seal. Sterilise for 30 minutes
in a water bath.
  Traditional accompaniment
to turkey, but good with most
poultry and game.

Gooseberry Sauce

1kg (2lb) gooseberries
375g (12oz) seedless raisins
500g (1lb) onions
250g (8oz) soft brown sugar
625ml (1 pint) vinegar
5ml (1 teaspoon) mustard
15ml (1 tablespoon) ground
  ginger
30ml (2 tablespoons) salt
Pinch of cayenne pepper
10ml (2 teaspoons) turmeric

Yield: about 750ml–1 litre
  (1½–2 pints)

Top and tail the gooseberries.
Put them through a mincer with
the raisins and onions. Put into
a preserving pan with the
remaining ingredients. Bring
slowly to the boil, stirring
occasionally, and simmer for 45
minutes. Put through a sieve
and return to a clean pan.
Simmer for 15 minutes, stirring
occasionally.
  Put into hot bottles, while
hot, and seal. Sterilise for 30

minutes in a water bath.
  Try this with oily fish such as
mackerel, and rich meats, such
as pork, goose, duck.

Hot Plum Sauce

1kg (2lb) plums
250g (8oz) sugar
625ml (1 pint) vinegar
5ml (1 teaspoon) salt
5ml (1 teaspoon) ground
  ginger
2·5ml (½ teaspoon) cayenne
  pepper
8 cloves

Yield: about 1 litre (2 pints)

Cut up the plums and put with
the stones and all the ingredients into a preserving pan,
Stir well and bring to the boil.
Simmer for 30 minutes and then
sieve. Return to a clean pan.
Simmer for 30 minutes, stirring
occasionally. Put into hot
bottles, while hot, and seal.
Sterilise for 30 minutes in a
water bath.
  Especially good with pork and
ham, or a little may be added to
sweet-sour sauces.

Damson Sauce

2kg (4lb) damsons
250g (8oz) onions, chopped
625ml (1 pint) vinegar
25g (1oz) salt
15g (½oz) ground ginger
15g (½oz) ground allspice
15g (½oz) ground nutmeg
15g (½oz) mustard
250g (8oz) sugar

Yield: about 1 litre (2 pints)

Cut up the damsons and put into
a preserving pan with the
stones, onions, vinegar, salt and
spices. Simmer for 45 minutes
until the onions are soft. Put
through a sieve, stir in the sugar
and return to a clean pan.
Dissolve the sugar over low heat
and bring to the boil. Simmer for
one hour, stirring occasionally.
Put the hot sauce into hot
bottles and seal. Sterilise for 30
minutes in a water bath.
  Use as Hot Plum Sauce; but
you will find that this recipe is
less 'hot' and rather more sharp
and spicy.

Keeping Mint Sauce

250ml (½ pint) vinegar
150g (6oz) demerara sugar
125ml (¼ pint) mint, finely
  chopped

Yield: about 500ml (1 pint)

Measure the mint after chopping by pressing it down in a
measuring jug. Boil the vinegar and sugar together for 2
minutes, stirring well so that the
sugar dissolves. Add the chopped mint, stir well and leave
until cold. Put into screwtop
jars. For use, stir well, take out
the required amount and add a
little extra vinegar.
  Use with hot or cold lamb.

Hampshire Store Sauce

1 litre (2 pints) vinegar from
  pickle jars
2 medium-sized onions,
  chopped
6 medium-sized tomatoes
6 apples

Yield: about 1 litre (2 pints)

This is made from the various
spiced vinegars saved from such
pickles as walnuts, onions and
gherkins. Put the vinegar into a
preserving pan with the onions.
Chop the tomatoes and apples,
including the skins, and add to
the pan. Simmer for 45 minutes
until the onions are soft. Put
through a sieve and return to a
clean pan. Simmer for 15
minutes and put the hot sauce
into hot bottles. Seal, and
sterilise for 30 minutes in a
water bath.
  This is a thin sauce – add a
tablespoonful to quick sautés,
and to sauces for meat or fish.

Elderberry Ketchup

2kg (4lb) ripe elderberries
1¼ litres (2 pints) vinegar
5ml (1 teaspoon) peppercorns
2·5ml (½ teaspoon) ground
  cloves
5ml (1 teaspoon) ground
  mace
15ml (1 tablespoon) salt
8 shallots

Yield: about 1 litre (2 pints)

Clean the elderberries and strip them from their stems. Put into a preserving pan with the vinegar. Bring to the boil very slowly and simmer for 15 minutes. Strain off the liquor while it is hot and return to a clean pan. Add the spices, salt and peeled shallots. Bring to the boil and simmer for 10 minutes. Take out the shallots, and pour the ketchup into hot bottles. Seal, and sterilise for 30 minutes in a water bath.

Complements lamb and fish.

Mushroom Ketchup

$1\frac{1}{2}$kg (3lb) mushrooms
75g (3oz) salt
5ml (1 teaspoon) peppercorns
5ml (1 teaspoon) allspice
2·5ml ($\frac{1}{2}$ teaspoon) ground mace
2·5ml ($\frac{1}{2}$ teaspoon) ground ginger
2·5ml ($\frac{1}{2}$ teaspoon) ground cloves
Pinch of ground cinnamon
500ml (1 pint) vinegar

Yield: about 750ml ($1\frac{1}{2}$ pints)

Break the mushrooms into small pieces, sprinkle with the salt and leave in a bowl for 12 hours. Rinse the mushrooms in fresh water, drain and mash with a wooden spoon. Add the vinegar and spices and simmer with a lid on for 30 minutes. Strain through a sieve. Pour at once into hot bottles. Seal and sterilise for 30 minutes in a water bath.

Best used with chicken and fish dishes, only a small quantity needed.

Raspberry Ketchup

2kg (4lb) raspberries
625ml (1 pint) cider vinegar
5ml (1 teaspoon) salt
5ml (1 teaspoon) mustard
2·5ml ($\frac{1}{2}$ teaspoon) ground mixed spice
400g (12oz) sugar

Yield: about 1 litre (2 pints)

Use ripe but not over-ripe fruit. Put into a saucepan with the vinegar and simmer for 15 minutes. Strain through a sieve,

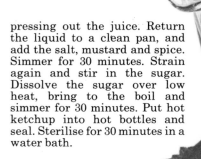

pressing out the juice. Return the liquid to a clean pan, and add the salt, mustard and spice. Simmer for 30 minutes. Strain again and stir in the sugar. Dissolve the sugar over low heat, bring to the boil and simmer for 30 minutes. Put hot ketchup into hot bottles and seal. Sterilise for 30 minutes in a water bath.

Walnut Ketchup

80 green walnuts
$1\frac{1}{2}$ litres (3 pints) vinegar
225g (8oz) onions, chopped
150g (6oz) salt
15g ($\frac{1}{2}$oz) peppercorns
15g ($\frac{1}{2}$oz) allspice berries
12 cloves
6 blades mace

Yield: about 2 litres (4 pints)

The walnuts must· be picked before the shells have formed inside the green casing. To test, (see Pickled Walnuts, page 136). Split the nuts and crush in a

bowl, or mince them coarsely. Put all the other ingredients into a saucepan and bring to boiling point. Pour over the nuts. Cover and leave in a cold place for 14 days, stirring once or twice each day. Strain the liquid through a jelly bag or clean piece of fabric, leaving it to drip for 2–3 hours. Put the liquid into a clean pan, bring to the boil, and then simmer without a lid for one hour. Put into hot jars or bottles and seal. Sterilise for 30 minutes in a water bath.

For nutty flavour, add a little to beef, pork or game casseroles. **153**

Bottling

Bottling is coming into its own again. It's been in the doldrums for the last 25 years or so since the arrival on the market of the wonder home-freezer which resulted in many freezer-buyers dropping bottling altogether. But now continually rising prices have stirred up an interest in conservation of all kinds; people are growing more fruit and vegetables themselves and are able also to buy them cheaply from the 'pick-it-yourself' farms and so the need for bottling as well as freezing has gradually become apparent again. Bottling is extremely economical and jars can be stored on the shelves for free, with no electricity bills looming. Most of the

equipment is already in the kitchen and the new improved jars and rings are widely available – you can even buy them in the supermarkets in the fruit season. Processing the material has to be done accurately and there are several methods of doing it, the overall object being efficient sterilisation and air-tight sealing. In the following chapters Dr Susan Passmore, an expert on the subject, describes clearly and in detail the various methods available.

Bottling

Preserving in bottles is an effective and rewarding method of fruit preservation, which is becoming popular again with home gardeners and families using the 'pick-your-own' facilities of commercial growers. The recommended methods, which must be followed accurately, may seem complicated when compared with simpler methods like home freezing, but the skills of packing and processing can be rapidly acquired to produce first-class preserves. Most of the basic equipment can be found in the kitchen and bottled fruit is stored 'free' in a cupboard rather than an expensive, power-consuming food freezer, and can save valuable space in a small freezer.

Some fruits benefit from the added sweetness from bottling in syrup, and bulk quantities of common fruits, like apples, are preserved more cheaply as bottled pulps or purées than by freezing. Delicious fruit syrups or squashes, and liqueurs, or fruit preserved in spirits can also be made at home with simple utensils.

How it all began

The preservation method of sealing food in jars and heating it is attributed to a French chef called Nicolas Appert, who developed the method in 1809 to help supply the armies of Napoleon with wholesome food. But the method had been used by housewives for preserving fruit as far back as 1680. This original method involved sealing the foods in glass bottles with corks and heating them slowly in an oven or kettle – Appert's important contribution was working out the processing times to preserve different foods. The fundamentals of modern home bottling are still the container, the seal and the heating time, and of course the vast food canning industry also grew from this pioneer work.

How it works

Although Appert had developed the correct processes for bottling, he did not know **why** food treated by his methods stored for longer than unprocessed food. The underlying principles were explained later in the century when Louis Pasteur showed that heat inactivated the micro-organisms which cause food to deteriorate. This, combined with the hermetic seal which prevented entry of new micro-organisms, kept the food. Heating the food thoroughly so that heat penetrates to the centre of the pack is therefore extremely important to destroy the majority of the micro-organisms, but the heating must not be too prolonged or the food texture will suffer. Thorough heating will also destroy the chemical enzymes which occur naturally in the foods and cause colour, flavour and aroma changes if left active in stored foods.

Apart from the heat treatment and efficient seal required for home bottling, the acidity (sharpness) of the food is very important as it helps control pathogenic micro-organisms which might grow in badly preserved foods and cause illness. All preservation methods must not only keep food free from spoilage, but also prevent the growth of these dangerous organisms. This is relatively simple in many methods, because most pathogens are not as resistant to the processing as the food spoilage organisms and are soon destroyed. Unfortunately bottling and canning have a *bête noir* in the form of a bacterium called *Clostridium botulinum*. This micro-organism causes the fatal disease botulism, and is quite capable of surviving boiling-water temperatures and thriving in the vacuum of bottles and cans, because it prefers to grow without air. Fortunately it cannot multiply in acid conditions and will present no hazard in most bottled fruits processed by home methods, although some less acid fruits (particularly tomatoes see page 172) need added citric acid as a safeguard.

What not to bottle

Vegetables, meat and fish are **not** sufficiently acid to prevent the growth of this organism, and these foods must be heat-treated much more severely, under pressure, to destroy the resistant cells and completely sterilise the food. Special pressure canners are used for bottling these foods and, as home models are no longer available, **home bottling of meat, fish and vegetables is no longer recommended** in this country and is not covered in this chapter. Home pressure cookers are not a satisfactory substitute because it is difficult to keep the required pressure constant throughout the processing time. Also the cookers heat and cool more rapidly than heavy pressure canners, which effectively shortens the processing and may allow unwanted micro-organisms to survive and multiply. All of these foods are better frozen to give safer preserves of better quality.

Bottling fruits

Acid fruits can be bottled to produce perfectly safe, good quality food which is completely free from spoilage or health hazard, and which is nutritionally good. Although heating destroys some heat-sensitive nutrients, they are retained quite well in bottled fruits provided processing is correct and the jars are not heated for too long. Finished jars should be stored in a cool, dark place to preserve colour and for maximum nutritional value, because some nutrients are destroyed by exposure to light. Only 30 per cent of the valuable vitamin C or ascorbic acid is lost from black currants which have been bottled and stored well.

All fruits can be bottled at home, either whole or as pulp or purée, but some are more worth while than others. In general, firmer fruits, like plums and apricots, are more successful bottled whole than softer berry fruits like strawberries which lose texture and are 'cooked' by the heat treatment. A supply of bottled fruit pulps and purées, such as apple or tomato, is useful to have in the store cupboard. Exactly what fruits are bottled depends on supplies available and family preferences. Methods for a wide range of fruits and pulps are given in this chapter.

Bottling fruit

An important part of bottling fruit is using correct bottles with suitable lids, rubber rings, or gaskets, and clip or screw fastenings. Bottling jars are usually known by their capacity, for example, English 1lb and 2lb jars or continental $\frac{1}{2}$ and 1 litre jars. In this chapter bottles are referred to by their accepted measures, with nearest metric or imperial equivalents in brackets, 1lb being taken as equal to $\frac{1}{2}$ litre.

These bottles are expensive to buy, but last for many years and can be used repeatedly once an adequate stock is collected.

The **Kilner type of bottle** is perhaps the best known and most widely sold. These squat shaped bottles are easy to fill as the fruit can be kept down under the shoulder of the jar (see picture). They are available in 1, 2 and 4lb ($\frac{1}{2}$, 1 and 2 litre) sizes, which will hold enough for modern family needs. They have metal lids with an integral rubber ring which can only be used once, or cheaper re-usable lids with separate rings are obtainable.

Bottling jars are also imported from Europe, for example the **'Le Parfait' brand** which are available in two shapes: the **'Bocaux'** which is Kilner shape with an 85mm mouth and the **'Terrine'** which is straight-sided (see picture) with a 100mm opening. Both have glass lids, separate rubber rings and spring clip closures like old-style lemonade bottles. They are fairly easy to pack and close, although the wide rubber ring may move off centre as the lid is clipped down. The spring clip should not be too strong or air will not be able to escape from the jar against the spring pressure during processing, but unsealed jars will show up when tested. The instruction booklets may recommend bottling meat and vegetables without pressure treatment, but this is contrary to official recommendations. However, the jars are perfectly acceptable for bottling fruit by the methods given here.

The bottles are available in a range of sizes.

They are expensive, but may also be used as storage jars and the 'Terrine' type may be used for freezing foods.

The **Fowler Lee type of jar** (see picture) is no longer made, but many can still be found. They are straight-sided and easy to pack with most fruits, producing excellent preserves for entering in shows. They have metal lids, separate square section rings and spring closures, which may still be found for the 23, 31, 36, 41 and 56 fluid ounce sizes, but the 12, 25 and 46 types, which require different sized rings, are obsolete.

Some hardware shops stock useful metal conversion lids and rings which fit popular brands of coffee jars – though unfortunately these tend to be in short supply. Both the 4oz and 8oz sizes can be used as 1lb ($\frac{1}{2}$ litre) and 2lb (1 litre) bottling jars. The lids are kept on during processing with either the metal screw lid from the coffee jar or with spring clips. Closures for rimmed jam jars are available, including 'Porosan' fruit preserving caps with replacable gasket rings. The modern jam jars which have twist-on tops with integral gaskets can also be used, if you are able to procure new lids to fit each time. With both these types the lids are placed on loosely and tightened down after processing, except for the oven method when they must be fitted afterwards. They are processed as for $\frac{1}{2}$ litre (1lb) bottles.

All the bottles mentioned, except the 'Le Parfait' types, may be used with a synthetic skin such as 'Porosan'. This is cut roughly to size and tied down over the jar with the special twine provided to form the seal, either before or after processing, depending on the method used. It has the added advantage that the pieces are re-usable.

Note: It may be possible to buy second-hand jars from jumble sales or junk shops, or beg some from relations and neighbours who have hoarded them away. But do make sure that rubber rings and closures are still made for some of the older types. Whatever type is used, the bottles should be clean and free from chips or cracks, especially around the rim. For more information, see Where to Buy Equipment.

Preparation equipment

Silver or stainless steel knives and peelers to prevent discoloration.

Spoons or packing sticks with flat sides and blunt ends to manoeuvre fruit into place.

For water bath methods

A large saucepan or other deep lidded vessel to submerge the jars.

A thermometer.

For the pressure cooker method

A home pressure cooker with weight to maintain 5lb pressure is suitable for processing bottled fruit, although it must be deep enough to hold the bottles on a rack in the pan.

For the oven method

Any type of cooker.

An oven thermometer for accuracy as temperatures may vary in different parts of the oven or in different ovens.

For all methods

A heatproof oven glove and strong pair of tongs are useful for handling hot jars after processing.

A wooden board to cool hot jars on to lessen the risk of cracking.

Fowler Lee preserving jar

Bottling fruit

Fruit should be prepared as in Table 2 (page 168).

It may be bottled in a sweet syrup, in water or, for apple slices, as a solid pack with no added liquid. Methods for tomatoes and fruit purées are different and are given on pages 172 and 171. Bottling fruit in water will probably result in poorer colour and flavour in the final product, but may be preferred in certain circumstances. A syrup will certainly give better flavour as the fruit absorbs the sweetness, and brandy or other spirits can be added for special preserves (see page 182). The fruit may shrivel or rise in the bottles if the syrup is too strong, and it is always best to use a medium strength syrup and add more sugar to taste when the pack is opened.

Syrup-making

Soft water is best for syrup-making, particularly for bottling rhubarb which may form a white deposit on storage in hard water. If soft water is not available, the water can be boiled before use or otherwise softened.

White, granulated sugar is the most usual sweetener for bottling syrup. A strength of 400g (8oz) sugar to 1 litre (1 pint) of water gives a medium syrup, but this can be varied according to personal taste. A stronger syrup of 600g (12oz) sugar to 1 litre (1 pint) of water can be used for tighter packs containing more fruit. These quantities will give 75–100g (2–3oz) sugar to each 500g (1lb) of packed fruit, in a normal pack of 300g

To get a tight pack
Rhubarb can be soaked in hot sugar syrup to reduce the volume. Pour over syrup to cover the prepared fruit and leave for 8-12 hours. The syrup draws the moisture from the fruit which can then be strained and packed. Reduce syrup before filling into packed bottles.

10oz) fruit to 200ml (6floz) syrup or a tighter pack of 375–425g (12–14oz) fruit to 125–75ml (4–2floz) syrup. Although less syrup is used in the tighter packs, it is stronger and contains more sugar in the smaller volume added to the packs.

Whatever proportions are used, the water and sugar should be measured carefully and the sugar dissolved in half of the water in a clean saucepan. This syrup should be brought to the boil and boiled for 1–2 minutes, before the remaining water, and any citric acid (5ml per litre or ½ teaspoon per pint) needed to acidify less acid fruits, is added. Hot syrup is used for the quick water bath method and the syrup must be boiling for the pressure cooker and oven methods, so the syrup should be ready when the fruit is packed. The jars can then be filled and processed with minimum delay. If the syrup is kept simmering, the saucepan should be covered to stop water evaporating away as steam and concentrating the syrup. For the slow water bath method the syrup should be prepared in advance, so that it is cool when required. Clear hazy syrup by filtering through muslin, cheesecloth or a jelly bag.

An advantage of using white sugar in making syrups is that it preserves and often accentuates the natural flavour and colour of the fruit, but the flavours can be altered if desired by using other sweetening agents. For example, honey or golden syrup, used in the same proportions as sugar, will impart their characteristic flavours. Brown sugars are normally not used in fruit bottling as their strong flavour tends to overwhelm the fruit, but a small proportion of the white sugar may be replaced with brown.

'Slimming' packs of bottled fruit can be made using saccharin, but this should not be added as a 'syrup' before bottling or bitter flavours will result. Instead the fruit is processed in water, and then warmed with the saccharin (dissolved in the liquid when the bottle is opened) so that the sweetness penetrates the fruit.

to ensure that these weights are bottled. Some fruits pack more tightly than others and have to be processed for longer times for thorough heat penetration, so it is advisable to follow the quantities in the Table as these correlate with the processing times given. Individual preparation of each fruit is also explained in the Table.

Usually packs of fruit are built up by forming a layer of raw fruit which covers the bottom of the jar, then successive layers are placed on top. Small, whole fruit such as berries, cherries or currants, can be packed in concentric rings around the circumference of the jar, and the centre filled with odd-sized fruit to form a neatly layered pack. The same pattern can be followed with slices, segments or chunks of fruits like apples, citrus fruits, rhubarb or pineapple. Halved apricots, peaches, pears and plums will pack in layers, but the layers may need overlapping to pack the required amount in the jars. Larger whole fruit like apricots and plums should be packed to fill as much space as possible, but the fruit should not be damaged or bruised by excessive handling or pressure.

Some fruits are not packed raw, either to make packing easier or to produce a better preserve. Apple slices can be preserved as a solid pack by scalding in boiling water for 1½–3 minutes or in steam for 3–5 minutes until they are tender. They should be packed tightly so that 475g (15oz) fit into ½ litre (1lb) bottles. Similarly, rhubarb and strawberries are soaked in hot sugar syrup to reduce their volume and give a tighter pack. Enough syrup to cover the prepared fruit is poured on and left for 8–12 hours for rhubarb and overnight for strawberries. The syrup draws moisture from the fruit, which can then be packed with 375–500g (12–16oz) fruit to ½ litre (1lb) bottles. The syrup is concentrated to the original volume by heating to drive off the absorbed moisture and may then be used in the packs of fruit. Hard fruits like cooking pears and quinces give a more

Packing a preserving jar

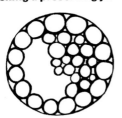   

Preparation and packing

Bottles should be washed thoroughly and rinsed and drained before filling, but they do not need drying as the fruit slips more easily over a wet surface during packing. Real works of art can be produced with even-sized fruit neatly packed, and this is desirable when preserves are to be exhibited in shows but is not necessary for everyday use. Table 2 (page 168) shows the approximate amounts of prepared fruit which should be packed into ½ litre (1lb) jars and careful packing will help

acceptable preserve if the fruit is tenderised first by simmering in syrup (200–300g per litre/4–6oz per pint), but they may still give disappointing results and are not really recommended.

However the fruit is packed, the jars should be filled to the brim as some shrinkage will occur during processing. When syrup is added before processing, the rubber ring should be fitted first and then the hot or cold syrup poured on carefully, jerking the jars to release trapped air bubbles until the jar is **full**.

Bottling fruit

Processing the packs of fruit is the most critical operation, for it is this which makes the food keep. As explained opposite, there are four methods of heat treatment and these are set out in Table 1 with temperatures and basic processing steps. It is vital that these instructions be followed closely, the temperatures maintained steadily and the times for different fruits (see Table 2) measured accurately. The processing will then be sufficient to ensure that heat penetrates to the centre of the pack to destroy enzymes and micro-organisms, but will not be too long and cook the fruit. If the jars are sealed correctly, the fruit should store well.

Very important
1 The recipes and methods, especially the proportions and timings, in this chapter have been worked out carefully and they should be followed closely to ensure good, safe preserves.
2 Both metric and imperial quantities are given and either one or the other should be followed. They are not conversions but separate metric and imperial recipes.

To prepare dessert pears
Peel, halve and core pears and remove fibres. Immerse in salted acid water to prevent browning.

Methods of bottling fruit
There are four methods. All have advantages and disadvantages, but the quick water bath method is the easiest and most useful, as all fruits and sizes of pack can be processed to give attractive results.

The slow water bath method gives packs of even better appearance but needs a thermometer.

The pressure method is much quicker and cheaper on power, but can give 'cooked' fruit.

The oven method can also give 'cooked' fruit, is heavy on power, difficult to control with varying oven temperatures and not recommended for tall packs, but requires no special equipment.

Finally, the choice of method depends on the fruit, size of pack and the equipment available, and perhaps even more on your own personal preference and skill with the different methods.

For a quick guide to the methods, see Table 1, page 164.

Slow Water Bath Method
The water bath can be a large saucepan, fish kettle or metal bin or boiler, but it must be deep enough to submerge the bottles completely or at least to the shoulder, and have a close-fitting lid. The bath should have a false bottom as the jars must not be directly in contact with the heat source. This can be made easily at home with chicken wire or wooden trellis. The jars should stand safely on this and may be separated with sheets of newspaper to stop them knocking together during processing. An accurate jam or bottling thermometer which reads up to 100°C, 212°F is essential for this method and it should be checked to see that it reads 100°C, 212°F in boiling water.

The cold bottles packed with fruit are placed on

a tray or plate to catch any liquid spilt during filling, then the rubber rings are fitted if jars with separate rings are being used. (For explanation of various types of bottle see page 158.) The rings should be soaked in warm water to soften them before use and dipped in boiling water before putting them on the jars. This is to make sure they lie quite flat and fruit pips are not trapped underneath. The bottles should be carefully filled to the brim with cold liquid and any air bubbles removed. When the bottles are **full** the lids are put on carefully and secured. Screw lids for Kilner jars and twist-on lids should be tightened down and then released a little to allow air and steam to escape during processing, but Le Parfait, Fowler Lee and other spring clipped types allow the air to come out against the pressure of the clip.

The bottles are placed in the water bath and covered with cold water. The water is then heated so that it reaches at least 55°C, 130°F in one hour and the necessary final temperature (see Table 2, page 168) in a further 30 minutes. This temperature should be maintained for the correct processing time depending on the type of fruit. The times given in Table 2 are suitable for $\frac{1}{2}$ and 1 litre (1 and 2lb) bottles, but $1\frac{1}{2}$ and 2 litre (3 and 4lb) sizes should be processed for an extra five minutes so that heat penetrates through the extra bulk to the centre. Careful regulation of the heat is necessary to keep the temperature steady, but this can soon be mastered with practice. If the water does heat up too quickly, the processing **must** still be carried on for the total recommended time ($1\frac{1}{2}$ hours plus specified time for each fruit) to ensure adequate heat penetration. The fruit will probably rise in the jars and the appearance may suffer because it has been at the higher temperature for a longer time, but it will be safely preserved.

Once processing is completed the jars are removed from the bath with tongs, or with a heatproof glove after dipping out the water, and put to cool on a wooden board or rack. Screw lidded jars should be tightened before leaving the jars undisturbed to seal while cooling.

Quick Water Bath Method

As the name suggests, this method is a faster version of the slow water bath method and the same equipment is required. A thermometer is not essential, but will help to control the process more accurately.

The bottles should be warmed before packing for this method, then fitted with rubber rings if necessary and filled with hot (60°C, 140°F) liquid to the brim. The lids should be fitted carefully, as in the previous method, before standing the bottles on the false bottom of the bath and submerging them in warm (38°C, 100°F) water. The water is heated to simmering (88°C, 190°F, if a thermometer is used) in 25–30 minutes and kept steadily simmering for the processing time. Again an extra five minutes should be allowed for larger bottles. When processing is over the jars should be removed, screw lids tightened and the bottles left to cool as in the slow water bath method.

Pressure Cooker Method

This is a very rapid method which can be used if a pressure cooker deep enough to hold the bottles and with a 5lb to the sq in ('low') pressure weight is available. About 2·5cm (1in) of water should be pre-heated in the pan so that it is hot when the bottles are ready for processing.

The fruit is packed into warm bottles and boiling liquid poured in carefully to within 2·5cm (1in) of the rims. Then rubber rings, lids and clips are fitted quickly, making sure that screwed lids are turned back to allow air to escape. The bottles should stand steady and separate on the rack in the bottom of the pan before it is closed. The cooker is heated until steam appears, when the weight is added and pressure brought up to 5lb to the sq in. This **must** take more than five and less than ten minutes for processing to be correct. The pressure should be maintained for the time given for the fruit in Table 2, then the cooker is removed from the heat and left to cool for ten minutes before it is opened and the jars removed. The total processing time is therefore: five to ten minutes coming to pressure + time held at pressure + ten minutes' cooling, and each stage should be timed accurately. When the bottles are removed from the cooker, place them on a wooden board or rack, tighten the screw lid firmly and leave the bottles until they are cool.

Oven Method

The oven should be tested and preheated to 150°C, 300°F, Gas Mark 2, for 15 minutes while the fruit is packed into warmed jars on a wooden board. Rubber rings are fitted, the bottles filled to within 2·5cm (1in) of the top with boiling liquid, and the lids rested on loosely without any fastenings. Saucers should be used as covers for jars with Porosan skin or lids or twist-on lids. The packed jars should be spaced out in the centre of the preheated oven on a baking tray lined with newspaper to absorb any liquid which boils out. Processing times (Table 2) vary for different fruits, packs and quantities. Finished bottles should be tightened or covered and left undisturbed on a wooden board to cool and seal.

Testing processed bottles

Where possible, bottled fruit should be tested next day to make sure a vacuum has formed. The fastenings should be removed from jars with metal or glass lids with rubber rings, and these are sealed if they can be lifted carefully by the lid. Some metal covers and Porosan skins are drawn in by the vacuum and this indicates an adequate seal. Jam jars with twist-on or Porosan lids cannot be tested after processing, but should be examined for signs of mould or fermentation when they are eventually opened. Contents of suspect jars should be discarded.

Sealed bottles should be wiped clean, labelled with names of contents and the date, and stored. Unsealed jars should be stored in a refrigerator and the contents used as soon as possible as reprocessing is rarely worth while.

Bottling fruit: Table 1

Process	Slow Water Bath	Quick Water Bath
Method	Start with cold water and raise to the required temperature in 90 minutes. Keep at temperature for time given for different fruits.	Start with warm (38°C/100°F) water and raise to simmering (88°C/190°F) in 25–30 minutes. Keep simmering for time given for different fruits.
Liquid	Cold. Add before processing.	Hot (60°C/140°F). Add before processing.
Comments	Good appearance. Thermometer required.	Good appearance. Thermometer not essential.

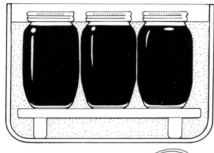

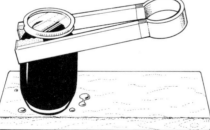

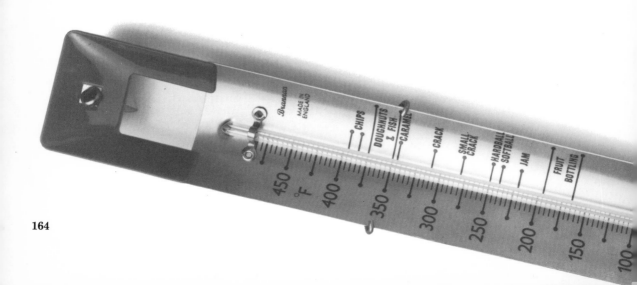

Pressure Cooker

Heat until steam appears then put on the weight and raise to 5lb pressure in 5–10 minutes. Keep at temperature for time given for different fruits. Cool for 10 minutes before opening.

Boiling. Add before processing

Pressure cooker must be deep enough to hold the jars and must maintain 5lb (low) pressure steadily.

Oven

Preheat the oven to 150°C, 300°F, Gas Mark 2, for 15 minutes. Process for times given according to type of fruit and quantity.

Boiling. Add before processing.

Not recommended for tall jars as the fruit will be processed unevenly. Check the temperature in different parts of the oven.

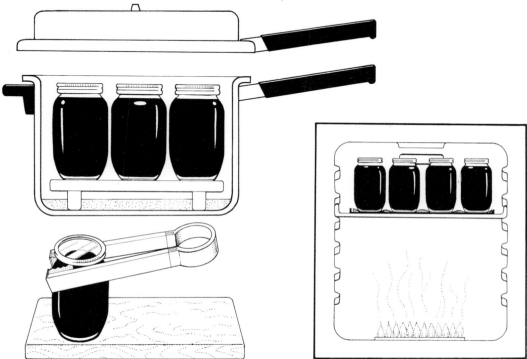

Guidelines for bottling fruit

1 Use purpose-made bottling jars or jam jars which are not chipped or cracked and have suitable covers.
2 Do not use chipped or cracked glass lids.
3 Check lacquered metal lids, discard any with scratches exposing the metal or it will react with the fruit acid.
4 Wash the jars carefully, rinse well, drain, but do not dry.
5 Make sure sealing rubber rings and gaskets are new, soft and pliable. Soaking in warm water softens some types.

6 Use good quality fruit, free from bruising and mould, and prepare carefully.
7 Pack the fruit carefully, to avoid damage, and neatly to give recommended weights in bottles.
8 Pack bottles as full as possible to allow for shrinkage during processing.
9 Have the packing liquid ready at the correct temperature so that packs can be filled when finished.
10 Acidify packs of less acid fruit.
11 Fill the bottles with liquid to the brim, twist gently to remove trapped air bubbles and top up if necessary.
12 Ensure bottle lids, especially screw types, are loose enough to vent air and steam before processing.
13 Pack boiling fruit pulps and purées into hot jars and fit hot lids immediately.
14 To stop bottles cracking during processing:
Use a false bottom in water baths or pressure cookers to keep bottles away from the heat source,

Stand bottles on asbestos, cardboard or newspaper for the oven methods.
Ensure times and temperatures are accurate for all heat processing methods for safety and to prevent overcooking.

15 Extend water bath processing times by five minutes (ten minutes for tomatoes) for $1\frac{1}{2}$ and 2 litre (3 and 4lb) bottles.
16 Use longer processing times for total loads above 2 litres (4lb) in the oven method.
17 Stand hot jars on a wooden board or other material which does not conduct heat.
18 Tighten down screw lids immediately after processing.
19 Leave bottles undisturbed overnight to cool and seal. Where possible, test seals the day after processing.
20 Store unsealed bottles in a refrigerator and use the contents as soon as possible, as reprocessing is rarely worth while.
21 Wipe and label sealed jars.
22 Store in a cool, dark cupboard with spring clips or screw bands removed.

Storage
If properly processed, bottled fruit should store well for 1–2 years. It can be kept much longer than this and used after many years without risk of food-poisoning, but the quality and nutritional value will deteriorate gradually during prolonged storage.

The bottles should be stored in a cool, dark, dry place to retain maximum quality. Storage in warm or light surroundings will affect the colour adversely and light may also destroy some nutrients. A moist atmosphere may cause the lid to rust through or allow mould to grow on the outside and around the rim of the bottle.

Screwbands or clips are removed from bottles when the seals are tested, and these should be washed to remove any traces of fruit or syrup. Spring clips should **not** be replaced on the bottles, as they will weaken gradually and be of no further use. Screwbands can be stored on the bottles, but they should be dried thoroughly, oiled and replaced very loosely to prevent rusting.

What can go wrong
Provided the methods are followed correctly, good quality preserves which store well should be produced. However, problems do occur sometimes and some common ones are listed below:

Jar not sealed
Damaged rim, lid, rubber ring or gasket,
piece of fruit trapped between lid and rim,
spring clip or screw band not tight enough,
underprocessing so no vacuum formed.

Poor colour fruit
Over- or under-ripe fruit,
discoloration during preparation or processing,
overprocessing, fruit stored in the light.
Poor colour at top of jar only – liquid not added immediately, not enough liquid added,
underprocessing.

Blue or purple – lid damaged exposing the metal.

Fruit risen
Over-ripe fruit,
pack too loose,
overprocessing or too rapid processing.

Cloudy liquid
Over-ripe or dirty fruit,
syrup not strained,
over-processing.

Air bubbles
Pack too tight,
bad filling with liquid.

Mould or fermentation
Over-ripe or damaged fruit,
underprocessing,
incorrect storage.

Specific methods
Water bath methods
Fruit discoloured at top $\Big\}$ jars not submerged.
mould in sealed jars
Oven method
Mould in sealed jars – too big a load.

Specific fruits
Apples – discoloured – delay in preparation or processing, underprocessing.
Gooseberries – shrivelled – fruit not pricked or trimmed to let syrup penetrate.
Grapefruit – white spots – under-ripe fruit (not harmful).
Pears – discoloured – delay in preparation or processing, underprocessing.
Rhubarb – white sediment – water too hard (not harmful).
Strawberries – risen – not soaked in syrup before packing, poor colour – no artificial colour added (see page 170).

Using bottled fruit preserves
Correctly processed bottled fruit will be sealed tightly and the vacuum seal must be broken when the fruit is required for use. Bottles with flush metal or glass lids and rubber rings can be prised open gently with the point of a knife, taking care not to damage the rim. A stream of air bubbles will enter the bottle when the seal is broken. Jam jar lids should open if twisted firmly, but if these or other seals are stubborn ease them by standing the bottles in hot water for a few minutes.

Bottled fruit, pulps and purées have many uses and the number of servings will vary with the use – as a rough guide, a $\frac{1}{2}$ litre (1lb) bottle holds about as much fruit as a medium-sized commercial can. Dessert fruits have been processed so that they are ready to serve either alone or incorporated in trifles, etc. Fruit for pies, such as apples, gooseberries or rhubarb, will soften to an acceptable texture with the extra cooking. If not given extra cooking in made-up dishes, simmer fruit gently, with extra sugar if needed, until tender. Fruit pulps and purées may be used for sauces, in recipes or with cereals, etc. Once opened, bottled fruit should be stored covered in a refrigerator and used in 2–3 days.

Bottling fruit: Table 2

Fruit	Preparation	Waste from 500g/1lb		Prepared fruit per ½ litre (1lb) pack	
Apples, slices	Peel, core and slice. Immerse in slightly salted water to prevent browning. Pack	125–175g	4–6oz	300g	10oz
Apples, solid pack	As above, but blanch 1½ min until tender before packing	125–175g	4–6oz	475g	15oz
Apricots, whole	Remove stalks, rinse in cold water	25–50g	1–2oz	300g	10oz
Apricots, halved	Cut round stone and twist halves apart. Pack quickly before fruit browns	50–250g	2–8oz	425g	14oz
Blackberries	Use only good fruit	25–50g	1–2oz	300g	10oz
Black currants	Remove stem and calyx	25–100g	1–3oz	375g	12oz
Cherries, whole	Remove stalks, rinse in cold water	25–100g	1–3oz	375g	12oz
Cherries, stoned	Stone and add juice to pack. For sweet cherries, add citric acid to syrup	50–150g	2–5oz	375g	12oz
Damsons	Remove stalks, wipe off bloom, rinse in cold water	25–50g	1–2oz	375g	12oz
Figs	Remove stems and peel. Add citric acid to syrup. Pack with equal weight of syrup	25–125g	1–4oz	250g	8oz
Gage plums	Remove stalks, rinse in cold water	25–50g	1–2oz	300g	10oz
Gooseberries	Prick skins or cut off small slice with 'tops and tails' to stop shrivelling in syrup	25g	1oz	375g	12oz
Grapefruit	Peel, cut segments free from pith. Remove pips	225–375g	7–12oz	375–475g	12–15oz
Lemons	As grapefruit	225–375g	7–12oz	375–475g	12–15oz
Loganberries	Remove hulls and damaged fruit	25–50g	1–2oz	375g	12oz
Mulberries	Remove over-ripe fruit, handle carefully	25–50g	1–2oz	375g	12oz
Oranges	As grapefruit	225–375g	7–12oz	375–475g	12–15oz
Peaches	Blanch for ½ min, cool in water to remove skins. Halve and stone	50–125g	2–4oz	275–375g	9–12oz
Pears, cooking	Peel, halve and remove core and fibres. Immerse in salted, acid water to prevent browning. Stew until tender in syrup	125–175g	4–6oz	250–375g	8–12oz
Pears, dessert	As cooking, but do not stew	125–175g	4–6oz	250–375g	8–12oz
Pineapple	Peel, remove ends and core. Cut into rings or segments	Variable		375g	12oz
Plums, whole	Remove stalks, rinse in cold water and wipe bloom from dark plums	25–50g	1–2oz	300g	10oz

For water bath methods, times should be increased by 5 minutes for larger (1½ and 2 litre/3 and 4lb) jars.
For oven method, the times depend on the quantity being processed.

Slow water bath	Quick water bath	Pressure cooker	Oven Quantity Processed	
			A = ½ litre–2 litres (1lb–4lb) B = 2½ litres–5 litres (5lb–10lb).	
			A	**B**
74°C 165°F 10 min	2 min	1 min	30–40 min	45–60 min
82°C 180°F 15 min	20 min	3–4 min	50–60 min	65–80 min
82°C 180°F 15 min	10 min	1 min	40–50 min	55–70 min
82°C 180°F 15 min	20 min	3–4 min	50–60 min	65–80 min
74°C 165°F 10 min	2 min	1 min	30–40 min	45–60 min
74°C 165°F 10 min	2 min	1 min	30–40 min	45–60 min
82°C 180°F 15 min	10 min	1 min	40–50 min	55–70 min
82°C 180°F 15 min	10 min	1 min	40–50 min	55–70 min
82°C 180°F 15 min	10 min	1 min	40–50 min	55–70 min
88°C 190°F 30 min	40 min	5 min	60–70 min	75–90 min
82°C 180°F 15 min	10 min	1 min	40–50 min	55–70 min
74°C 165°F 10 min	2 min	1 min	30–40 min	45–60 min
82°C 180°F 15 min	10 min	1 min	40–50 min	55–70 min
82°C 180°F 15 min	10 min	1 min	40–50 min	55–70 min
74°C 165°F 10 min	2 min	1 min	30–40 min	45–60 min
74°C 165°F 10 min	2 min	1 min	30–40 min	45–60 min
82°C 180°F 15 min	10 min	1 min	40–50 min	55–70 min
82°C 180°F 15 min	20 min	3–4 min	50–60 min	65–80 min
88°C 190°F 30 min	40 min	5 min	60–70 min	75–90 min
88°C 190°F 30 min	40 min	5 min	60–70 min	75–90 min
82°C 180°F 15 min	20 min	3–4 min	50–60 min	65–80 min
82°C 180°F 15 min	10 min	1 min	40–50 min	55–70 min

Bottling fruit: Table 2

Fruit	Preparation	Waste from 500g/1lb		Prepared fruit per ½ litre (1lb) pack	
Plums, halved	Treat freestone plums as apricots	50–100g	2–3oz	475g	15oz
Quinces	As cooking pears	125–175g	4–6oz	250–375g	8–12oz
Raspberries	Remove plugs, damaged fruit and maggots	25–50g	1–2oz	375–425g	12–14oz
Red currants	Remove stems. Rinse in cold water	25–100g	1–3oz	375g	12oz
Rhubarb	Remove base and leaves, wipe stems. Cut into 4cm (1½in) lengths	50–125g	2–4oz	300g	10oz
Rhubarb, tight pack	Prepare and pour on hot sugar syrup. Leave 8–12 hrs. Drain. Concentrate syrup before filling into packed bottles	50–125g	2–4oz	375–475g	12–15oz
Strawberries	Use medium even shaped fruit. Remove plug, rinse in cold water	25g	1oz	275g	9oz
Strawberries, tight pack	Prepare and pour on hot, coloured sugar syrup. Leave overnight. Drain. Concentrate syrup before filling into packed bottles	25g	1oz	500g	16oz
Whortleberries (Bilberries)	As black currants	25–50g	1–2oz	375g	12oz

Quinces from a Leicester garden
These fruits are still grown in English gardens and have a spicy and unusual flavour. They mix well with apples in pies, or can be stewed. Bottle as for cooking pears.

For water bath methods, times should be increased by 5 minutes for larger ($1\frac{1}{2}$ and 2 litre/3 and 4lb) jars.
For oven method, the times depend on the quantity being processed.

Slow water bath	Quick water bath	Pressure cooker	Oven Quantity Processed	
			A	B
82°C 180°F 15 min	20 min	3–4 min	50–60 min	65–80 min
88°C 190°F 30 min	40 min	5 min	60–70 min	75–90 min
74°C 165°F 10 min	2 min	1 min	30–40 min	45–60 min
74°C 165°F 10 min	2 min	1 min	30–40 min	45–60 min
74°C 165°F 10 min	2 min	1 min	30–40 min	45–60 min
82°C 180°F 15 min	10 min	1 min	40–50 min	55–70 min
74°C 165°F 10 min	2 min	1 min	30–40 min	45–60 min
82°C 180°F 15 min	20 min	3–4 min	50–60 min	65–80 min
74°C 165°F 10 min	2 min	1 min	30–40 min	45–60 min

A = $\frac{1}{2}$ litre–2 litres (1lb–4lb)
B = $2\frac{1}{2}$ litres–5 litres (5lb–10lb).

Information based on HMSO Bulletin 21, 'Home Preservation of Fruit and Vegetables'.

Fruit pulps and purées
Bottled pulped and puréed fruits are useful to have in the store cupboard for pies, recipes or subsequent jam-making. They are prepared in the same way by stewing the fruit, the main difference being that purées are sieved. Both can be preserved easily and quickly in bottling jars, either sweetened or unsweetened, by the same processing method. They are economical preserves as misshapen fruit can be used and tight packs are produced.

Pulps
Any fruit may be bottled as pulp, but apple, blackberry and apple, gooseberry and rhubarb are perhaps most popular. Fruit is prepared and heated with enough water to stop it burning, preferably in an aluminium or stainless steel saucepan, until it is cooked through. The boiling pulp is poured into hot bottling jars standing on a wooden board, and sealed **immediately** with rubber rings dipped in boiling water and hot lids. The packed jars are submerged in a hot water bath, making sure that they are standing well separated and steadily on the false bottom, and the water brought to the boil and held for five minutes. Then the bottles are removed on to a wooden board to cool and seal. Next day they should be tested and stored as for bottled fruit.

Purées
For purées, the fruit is prepared and cooked as for pulps, but is sieved when tender to give the smooth characteristic of a purée. The fruit must be sieved quickly or it will discolour as it is oxidised by the air incorporated during sieving. The purée is returned to the pan and brought back to the boil, before being filled into hot jars and sealed and processed like fruit pulps.

Bottling tomatoes

Tomatoes may be bottled whole in brine or as solid packs, using the same equipment as for other fruits and the processing methods shown in Table 3 (below).

For whole tomatoes, small or medium-sized fruits are rinsed in cold water and packed at the rate of 300g (10oz) in $\frac{1}{2}$ litre (1lb) bottles. Jars are filled to the rim with brine, either before or after processing, depending on the method. The brine is made with 10ml ($\frac{1}{2}$oz) salt and 7·5ml (2 teaspoons) citric acid **or** 65ml (5 tablespoons) lemon juice to 1 litre (2 pints) of water.

For solid packs the fruit should be scalded in boiling water for 10–20 seconds, dipped in cold water and peeled carefully. Small fruit may be packed whole, but to give a tight pack (500g/16oz to $\frac{1}{2}$ litre/1lb jars) larger fruit should be halved or quartered. During packing, 5ml (1 teaspoon) salt, 2·5ml ($\frac{1}{2}$ teaspoon) sugar and 2·5ml ($\frac{1}{4}$ teaspoon) citric acid **or** 10ml (2 teaspoons) lemon juice should be mixed thoroughly with the fruit in each bottle.

Packed bottles are processed for the times shown in Table 3 (below) and handled in the same way as other bottled fruits.

Tomato pulp and purée

These are prepared in virtually the same way as other fruit pulps and purées, the main difference being that they must be acidified and heat treated for a longer time.

For pulp, sound tomatoes are washed in cold water, peeled and then cooked until soft in a covered saucepan with a little water. Fruit for purée need not be peeled because sieving removes the peel. Before filling the boiling pulp or purée into bottles, 2·5ml ($\frac{1}{4}$ teaspoon) citric acid or 10ml (2 teaspoons) lemon juice must be added for each 500g (1lb) of cooked fruit. The bottles must be sealed with hot lids immediately and processed in the same way as other bottled purées in a hot water bath, except that they must be boiled for ten minutes instead of five.

Tomato juice

Tomato juice is really diluted tomato purée and the tomatoes are cooked down and sieved in the same way, so both recipes may be made from the same batch of tomatoes. Each litre (pint) of purée is diluted with 250ml ($\frac{1}{4}$ pint) of water and seasoned with 5ml ($\frac{1}{2}$ teaspoon) salt, 25g ($\frac{1}{2}$oz) sugar and pepper to taste. In common with other bottled tomato preserves, this juice must be acidified with 2·5ml ($\frac{1}{4}$ teaspoon) citric acid or 20ml (2 teaspoons) of lemon juice to each litre (pint). The finished juice should be returned to the pan and brought back to the boil, before filling into suitable bottles and sealing the bottles with hot lids. The bottles are processed like tomato pulp and purée in a boiling water bath for ten minutes.

Bottled tomatoes and tomato products

Tomatoes differ from other fruits in that they are bottled for savoury use with added salt or brine. They are also different because they are less acid and **must** be acidified as well as heat processed to make sure they keep. Cases of botulism have been traced to home bottled tomato products in the United States, but the preserves given here will be perfectly wholesome if these methods incorporating citric acid or lemon juice are followed carefully.

Table 3. Preparation and Processing for Bottled Tomatoes

Pack	Preparation	Waste from 500g/1lb		Prepared fruit per $\frac{1}{2}$ litre (1lb) pack	
Whole in brine	Use small, firm ripe fruit. Remove stems and rinse in cold water. Fill packed jars with brine with added citric acid or lemon juice.	25g	1oz	300g	10oz
Solid	Scald firm fruit in boiling water for 10–20 sec. Dip in cold water and remove outer skins. Halve or quarter and pack tightly adding salt, sugar and citric acid. No liquid is needed.	50–100g	2–3oz	500g	16oz

Slow water bath*	Quick water bath*	Pressure cooker	Oven† Quantity processed	
			A	B
88°C 190°F 30 min	40 min	5 min	60–70 min	75–90 min
88°C 190°F 40 min	50 min	15 min	70–80 min	85–100 min

* For water bath methods, times should be increased by 10 minutes for larger (1½ and 2 litre/3 and 4lb) jars.
† For oven method, the times depend on the quantity being processed:
A = ½ litre–2 litres (1lb–4lb)
B = 2½ litres–5 litres (5lb–10lb).

Bottling syrups and squashes

A variety of fruit juice preserves can be made easily and cheaply at home, with little or no special equipment and by simple methods. The fruit used should be ripe, as under-ripe fruit has a weak flavour and is not juicy enough. The juice is extracted, using either hot or cold treatments, prepared according to the product required, and is preserved by heating or adding sulphur dioxide in the form of Campden Fruit Preserving Tablets.

Syrups are clear, sweetened juices and are sometimes referred to as cordials. They can be diluted three or four times with water, soda or milk for drinks, or used undiluted for flavouring sauces and desserts or pouring over ice-cream. Economical ice lollies may be produced by diluting syrup with an equal volume of water and freezing the mixture in suitable moulds. Many fruits can be made into good syrups, but juicy, strong-flavoured ones such as black currants, raspberries, blackberries and citrus fruits give best results. Recipes are given for these and other fruit syrups, and for spiced syrups which make pleasant hot or cold drinks and are useful in sauces, desserts and cocktails.

Fruit squash differs from syrup because the juice is extracted in a different way so that it contains particles of fruit and is cloudy. Also, the fresh juice is diluted with water and more sugar is added than for syrups. Squashes are bottled mainly for drinks, and are very good substitutes for expensive commercial fruit squash when diluted four or five times with water. Citrus fruit squashes are most popular, but other acid fruits with good flavours may be used.

Extracted fruit juice, sweetened with a small amount of sugar, may be bottled for drinking undiluted. The fruits recommended for syrup-making are suitable for preserving as juices. Commercial apple juice is popular, but this is a difficult preserve to make at home as the juice often darkens unacceptably during extraction and processing.

Many of the recipes given here produce nutritious preserves as the fruits are good sources of vitamin C. This is particularly true of the rose hip syrup which can be taken daily to supplement vitamin C intake. To ensure maximum nutritional value and pleasing preserves, good quality fruit should be prepared and processed by the methods shown below.

Equipment and methods

The first step in making fruit juice preserves is extracting the juice. The fruit needs little preparation, apart from removal of damaged fruit and rough chopping for large or firm fruit, as peel, stems and seeds will be removed when the juice is strained. There are three basic methods of juice extraction – heating, cold treatments or pressure extraction – and which one is chosen depends on the fruit used, equipment and time available, and personal preference. Hot extraction methods are quicker than cold treatments for most fruits, but do tend to destroy the fresh flavour as a certain amount of cooking is involved. Extraction by pressure is really a modification of the cold process, except that the juice is forced out of the fruit rather than encouraged to flow out naturally. Juices are strained carefully for bottling as syrups or juices, but some fruit particles are included in squashes. To ensure good flavour, colour and vitamin C content, utensils made of iron, copper or zinc should not be used for extracting and preparing the fruit juices.

Hot extraction

For hot extraction methods, the fruit is heated to break it down and release the juice. Usually no water is added, although black currants need about 600ml ($\frac{1}{2}$ pint) and blackberries about 100ml (3 tablespoons) for each kilogram (1lb) of fruit. Exactly how the fruit is heated depends on the equipment available and the simplest way is to heat the fruit in a large pan, stirring all the time, and bring it quickly to the boil. The fruit is boiled for one minute and then crushed with a wooden spoon. The pulp is left to drip through **a scalded jelly bag or several thicknesses of butter muslin** and then pressed to remove any remaining juice, or strained carefully through **a fine sieve**.

Making syrups

Use ripe, juicy strong-flavoured fruits and extract juice by one of the three methods recommended and strain. 2 Add sugar and stir till completely dissolved. 3 Strain syrup into bottles and process by heat (as shown).

A better method is to use **a glass or earthenware bowl over a pan of hot water, or a double saucepan**, as the fruit may be overcooked and fresh flavour lost by direct heating. The fruit should be broken up and heated until the juice begins to flow, when it is crushed again before straining.

Special juice extractors, like large double saucepans, which steam the fruit to release the juice are available. The juice is collected as it runs out through a spout.

These hot methods are suitable for most fruits, except rose hips and apples, which are prepared using hot infusion methods (sée recipes) and citrus fruits which do not need heating to release the juice.

Cold extraction

Cold extraction takes longer than hot methods, but produces juice with a fresher flavour and needs no special equipment. The fruit is placed in a large glass or earthenware bowl and crushed. It is then either left to ferment slightly, which will release the juice, or a commercial pectin-destroying enzyme is added to break down the fruit tissues. For the fermentation method, the bowl of crushed fruit is simply covered and left in a warm room until gas bubbles begin to form on the surface of the pulp. This only takes about 24 hours for most fruits, although black currants may need three to five days as the skins are tough. The pulp is then strained as for the hot extraction methods.

A number of enzyme preparations are available from wine-making suppliers and one of these should be stirred into the bowl of crushed fruit, in the quantities directed by the manufacturer. Again the fruit is covered and left in a warm room, overnight for most fruits or about three days for black currants, before the juicy pulp is strained.

These cold extraction methods can be used for most fruits and produce juices with excellent fresh flavours.

Pressure extraction

Extracting juice from fresh fruit by hand or mechanical pressure also gives fresh-flavoured juices, as no heating is involved. These methods are especially suitable when making fruit squashes and pressed juice can also be strained for making syrup or juice.

Juicy citrus fruits are pressed by hand using **a lemon squeezer** and the fresh juice, with small pieces of pulp, bottled as squash. For better flavour, some of the oil from crushed rind is added to recipes for squashes or for syrups made with the strained juice.

A mechanical fruit press or electrical juice extractor may be used to obtain juice from firmer fruits like apples. A simple press can be made at home using a car jack to squeeze the fruit between strong boards against a rigid frame. Alternatively, the purpose-made extractors or extracting attachments for food mixers are fairly efficient and filter the juice as well.

A particularly good syrup
Blackberries make an exceptionally well-flavoured syrup, though you first have to collect a large amount of them. For full details see recipe on page 179.

Bottling syrups and squashes

Once the juice is extracted it is sweetened, if necessary, with varying amounts of sugar, depending on the preserve required. White, granulated sugar is normally used, although some recipes include honey, golden syrup or demerara sugar as the sweetener to give added flavour to weak fruit or spiced preserves. Saccharin can be used for 'diet' fruit juices but, like bottled fruit, the juice should be processed without the saccharin which is added when the bottle is opened. Artificial sweeteners cannot be used in syrups or squashes.

The amount of sugar added to fruit syrups depends on the fruit and the recipe. About 600g (12oz) sugar to each litre (pint) of juice is recommended. The sugar is added to cold, prepared juice and stirred, **without heating**, until it is completely dissolved. The syrup may need straining again before bottling, to make sure it is as clear as possible.

Prepared juice for squash is diluted with an equal or slightly larger volume of water and then about 800g (1lb) sugar is added to each litre (pint) of diluted juice. Citrus squashes are improved by added citric acid to give them extra tang.

Fruit juices may be bottled unsweetened, or with only a small amount of sugar to help retain the original flavour of the fruit, as they are usually drunk undiluted.

Bottling

Apart from the equipment for the juice extraction method and preparing the preserve, suitable bottles are required. **Convenient sized, clean bottles which can be sealed,** will fit in the water bath, and will stand moderate pressure are needed for heat processing fruit juice preserves.

Traditionally the bottles are closed with **corks** and sealed with **melted wax**, so bottles need not have caps. If sauce bottles are used, the metal or plastic screw tops can be fitted loosely to keep the corks in place during processing, otherwise they have to be tied down. Screw-topped, disposable soft drink bottles are most convenient to use, as the caps can be partially screwed on to keep them in place during processing, and then tightened down so that the built-in gasket makes the seal. These are also suitable for chemical processing which requires a tight seal, although the bottles need not be as strong because no heating or pressure is involved.

Processing methods

Bottled fruit syrups, squashes and juices can be processed by heat treatment like bottled fruit and pulps, or chemically preserved with sulphur dioxide in the form of Campden Tablets.

Heat processing

For heat processing the freshly-prepared syrup, squash or juice should be filled into clean bottles as quickly as possible and processed rapidly to prevent discoloration. The headspace in the bottles is important, because the liquid will expand during heating. For corked bottles the

liquid is filled to within 4cm ($1\frac{1}{2}$in) of the top and for screwtop bottles to 2cm ($\frac{3}{4}$in). The corks or tops should be sterilised in boiling water for 15 minutes before they are required, and fitted to the bottles, hot. Corks must be held in to prevent them blowing out during processing and the original bottle caps can be used for this purpose. Otherwise the corks must be wired in or secured with strong cloth tied over the cork with string. Screwtops with gaskets are just fitted on loosely.

The finished bottles are packed into a water bath with a lid and false bottom, and separated with wads of newspaper. Cold water is poured in carefully until it is above the level of the liquid in the bottles. The water is heated to 77°C, 170°F, and held at that temperature for 30 minutes, or, if no thermometer is available, to simmering (**not** boiling) point (88°C, 190°F) for 20 minutes. The bottles are removed with tongs or heatproof gloves to a wooden board, and screwtop bottles tightened immediately and left to cool. Corks may not push in straight after processing, but should once the bottles have cooled slightly. When corked bottles are cool, they are sealed by dipping into melted paraffin wax to cover the porous cork and 1cm ($\frac{1}{2}$in) of the neck.

The finished bottles should be wiped and labelled before storing in a cool, dark place. Most fruit juice preserves will keep for up to one year, but flavour and colour may deteriorate with prolonged storage. Citrus juice preserves deteriorate more rapidly and should be used within two months. Once opened, all these preserves should be kept refrigerated and used within two weeks.

Chemical preservation
Processing with Campden Tablets, which are available from chemists or wine-making suppliers, is a quicker method than heating the bottles. The sulphur dioxide generated by the tablets in acid preserves does not kill micro-organisms, but stops them from growing and spoiling the fruit. The bottles must be sealed tightly or the volatile preservative will leak away, allowing the dormant micro-organisms to grow again.

The same recipes can be used for making the preserves, except that 800g (1lb) sugar should be added to each litre (pint) of juice for chemically preserved syrups and strawberry syrup should be acidified with 10ml (1 teaspoon) citric acid to each litre (pint). Also the preservative will bleach the juices slightly, so artificial colouring may be added.

The Campden Tablets should be crushed with a wooden spoon in a glass or earthenware bowl and dissolved in 15ml (1 tablespoon) of warm water to each tablet. This solution is added at the rate of 30ml (1 tablespoon) per litre (pint) of prepared juice, before filling it into bottles. Bottles should be sealed tightly with waxed corks or lacquered metal lids with gaskets, wiped, labelled and stored. Ideally the preserves should be used within six months. Only very small amounts of sulphur dioxide are present and the preserves can be used direct from the bottle quite safely.

Note: Campden Tablets can also be used for a quick method of bottling firm acid fruits. Stone fruits, rhubarb and apple slices (normal packs) preserve well by this method, but soft fruits, cherries, pears and tomatoes are **not** recommended. The fruit is prepared and packed, then covered with Campden solution made from one tablet dissolved in 250ml ($\frac{1}{2}$ pint) of tepid water. Bottles should be sealed with glass or lacquered metal lids as the sulphur dioxide may react with exposed metal. The fruit is bleached by the preservative, but the colour will return if the fruit is heated before use to drive off the sulphur dioxide. Fruit preserved in this way can be used for stewing, pies or puddings.

Guidelines for bottling fruit syrups and squashes
1 Use sound, fully ripe fruit.
2 Extract the juice by a method suitable for the fruit and the required preserve.
3 Prepare and process the juice quickly to prevent discoloration.
4 Do not use iron, copper or zinc utensils. If you do, flavour, colour and nutritional value will be poor.
5 Completely dissolve the sugar in cold juice.
6 Clean the bottles thoroughly and rinse well.
7 Boil corks and lids for 15 minutes before use.
8 Fill bottles carefully leaving headspace for expansion.
9 Secure corks or fit screwtops loosely before processing.
10 Tighten down screwtops immediately after processing.
11 Seal corks with melted wax when preserves are cool.
12 Ensure quantities of Campden preservative are accurate.
13 Do not use metal utensils or unprotected metal tops with Campden Tablets.
14 Store in a cool, dark place.
15 Shake squash to distribute fruit pieces before use.
16 Decant syrups carefully so any sediment is not disturbed.
17 Store opened preserves in a refrigerator and use within two weeks.

What can go wrong
Sediment in syrup or juice.
Strainer not fine enough to trap all fruit particles.
Musty or off-flavour.
Fruit mouldy or tainted,
bottles not washed and rinsed.
Mould on cork or surface of liquid.
Old, badly-fitting or un-sterilised cork,
damaged or non-gasketed screwtop,
bottles not sealed immediately after they have been heat processed.
Discoloration in heat-processed preserves.
Juice extracted or prepared too slowly,
zinc, copper or iron utensils used,
over processing, bottles not sealed immediately or adequately, poor storage.

Recipes for syrups and squashes

The amounts of sugar required and the yields are difficult to assess for fruit juice preserves, as they depend on the fruit quality and the amount of juice extracted. Amounts of sugar are given as the weights added to each litre (pint) of juice and the yields are intended only as guidelines to the approximate number of bottles required. Both metric and imperial quantities are given, and either one or the other should be followed as they are separate recipes, **not** conversions.

A glut of apples

The time to choose to make apple juice and apple syrup is when you have too many apples. Juice and syrup use up considerable amounts of fruit and are popular with most families.

Black Currant Juice

3kg (5lb) black currants
30ml (3 teaspoons) pectin-destroying enzyme
150g (3oz) sugar to each litre (pint) of juice

Yield: about 2¼ litres (3 pints)

Remove damaged fruit. Crush the fruit with a wooden spoon in a large glass or earthenware bowl and mix in the enzyme. Cover the bowl and leave in a warm room for two to three days, stirring each day. Strain and press the pulp and measure the juice. Add the required amount of sugar to the cold juice, stirring until dissolved. Bottle and heat process.

Black Currant Syrup

3kg (6lb) black currants
1¾ litres (3 pints) water
600g (12oz) sugar to each litre (pint) of juice

Yield: about 4–5 litres (7–8 pints)

Remove damaged fruit. Heat the fruit and water in a saucepan and bring to the boil quickly, stirring all the time. Boil for one minute, crushing any whole fruit with a wooden spoon. Strain and press the pulp and measure the juice. Add the required amount of sugar and stir until completely dissolved. Bottle and heat process, **or** add extra sugar (200g per litre/4oz per pint) and process with Campden solution.

It is important to follow either the imperial or the metric weights and measures in any one recipe. Do not mix them.

Apple Syrup

3kg (6lb) cooking apples
1kg (2lb) dessert apples
500g (10oz) sugar to each litre (pint) of juice
Water

Yield: about 2–2½ litres (3–4 pints)

Chop the apples coarsely, removing any blemishes and submerge them in salted water (25g per litre/½oz per pint) until ready for use, to prevent browning.
Either: Drain and press the fruit as for apple juice recipe.
Or: Drain half the apples and put in a large pan. Cover with water and boil until the fruit begins to break down. Strain the pulp carefully and return the juice to the pan. Add the remaining apples and simmer for one hour.

Strain through a jelly bag overnight. Measure the juice, stir in the required amount of sugar. Bottle and heat process.

Apple Juice

5kg (10lb) cooking apples
1kg (2lb) dessert apples
500ml (¾ pint) water
150g (3oz) sugar to each litre (pint) of juice

Yield: about 3–4 litres (5–6 pints)

Chop the apples coarsely, removing any blemishes, and submerge them in salted water (25g per litre/½oz per pint) until ready for use, to prevent browning. Drain the apples. Press the apples once, then press the pulp again with the measured water, or use an electric juice extractor. Sweeten the measured juice, if desired, by stirring in the required amount of sugar. Strain through a scalded jelly bag to remove any scum before bottling. Preserve by heat processing. Apple juice preserves will almost inevitably darken during preparation.

Blackberry Syrup

3kg (6lb) blackberries
300ml (½ pint) water
600g (12oz) sugar to each litre (pint) of juice

Yield: about 2 litres (3 pints)

Remove any damaged fruit. Wash and drain the fruit if necessary, then crush it in a bowl over a pan of boiling water, in a double-saucepan or in a steam extractor, and add the water. Heat for about one hour until the juice begins to flow, then crush the fruit again. Strain the fruit pulp overnight through a scalded jelly bag and press out any remaining juice. Measure the cold juice and add the required amount of sugar. Stir until completely dissolved. Bottle and heat process, **or** add extra sugar (200g per litre/4oz per pint) and process with Campden solution.

Recipes for syrups and squashes

Apricot Syrup

1½kg (3lb) apricots, stoned
1¾kg (1½lb) sugar
1¾ litres (3 pints) water

Yield: about 2½ litres (4 pints)

Stir the sugar into the cold water to dissolve. Bring to the boil in a covered pan and add the apricots and the crushed kernels from a few stones. Cover and simmer until the fruit is tender. Strain through a scalded jelly bag and bottle. Heat process the syrup.

Lemon Syrup

½ litre (1 pint) lemon juice
   (from 10–18 lemons)
1¼kg (3lb) sugar
5ml (¼oz) citric acid
¾ litre (1½ pints) water

Yield: about 1¾ litres
   (4 pints)

Wash the lemons and grate the rind from half of them into the water in a large bowl. Squeeze the juice from all the fruit and add it to the water with the sugar and citric acid. Stir to dissolve the sugar and extract the oil from the rind. Strain the syrup through a scalded jelly bag. Bottle and heat process, **or** add Campden solution.

Loganberry Syrup

2kg (4lb) loganberries
600g (12oz) sugar to each litre
   (pint) of juice

Yield: about 1 litre
   (1½ pints)

Remove damaged fruit and any maggots. Place the fruit in a large glass or earthenware bowl and crush it with a wooden spoon. Cover the bowl and leave to ferment in a warm room for about 24 hours or until small bubbles of gas begin to form on the surface of the pulp. Strain and add the required amount of sugar. Stir to dissolve the sugar, then bottle and heat process, **or** add extra sugar (200g per litre/4oz per pint) and process with Campden solution.

Orange Squash

½ litre (1 pint) orange juice
   (about 8 oranges)
1kg (2¼lb) sugar
30ml (1oz) citric acid
¾ litre (1½ pints) water

Yield: about 2 litres
   (3–4 pints)

Wash the fruit. Peel or grate the rind very thinly from half the oranges and add to the water and sugar in a large saucepan. Stir to dissolve the sugar. Warm the syrup and crush the rind to extract the oil. Strain through a scalded jelly bag. Halve and squeeze all the fruit, using a lemon squeezer. Try to keep pips and larger pieces of pulp out of the juice. Mix the juice, strained syrup and citric acid thoroughly. Bottle and heat process **or** add Campden solution.

Orgeat Syrup

200g (4oz) sweet almonds,
   blanched and skinned
25g (½oz) bitter almonds,
   blanched and skinned
1½ kg (2lb) sugar
50ml (2 tablespoons) orange-
   flower water
2 litres (2 pints) water

Yield: about 3 litres (3 pints)

Dissolve the sugar in half the water in a large saucepan. Crush the almonds to a fine paste with a little of the remaining water, then carefully stir in the rest of the water and the orange-flower water. Add this diluted paste to the syrup and bring it slowly to simmering point. Allow to cool. Strain, bottle and heat process.

Raspberry Juice

2kg (4lb) raspberries
10ml (1½ teaspoons) pectin-
   destroying enzyme
150g (3oz) sugar to each litre
   (pint) of juice

Yield: about ¾ litre (1 pint)

Remove damaged fruit and any maggots. Crush the fruit with a wooden spoon in a large glass or earthenware bowl and mix in the enzyme. Cover the bowl and leave in a warm room overnight. Strain and press the pulp and measure the juice. Add the required amount of sugar to the juice and stir to dissolve. Bottle and heat process.

Spice Syrups
(cinnamon, cloves, ginger, mace or nutmeg)

1 litre (2 pints) water
800g (2lb) white or demerara
   sugar

Whole spice, crushed:
100g (4oz) cinnamon, cloves
   or mace
or
75g (3oz) nutmeg
or
50g (2oz) ginger
1 lemon or 1 orange

Yield: about 1½ litres
   (3 pints)

Finely peel or grate the rind from the lemon or orange and squeeze out the juice. Tie the rind with the chosen crushed spice in a muslin bag and put in a covered saucepan with the water. Bring to the boil and simmer gently for 30 minutes. Remove the bag and make up to one litre (2 pints) with the citrus juice and cold water. Stir in the sugar until it is completely dissolved and strain. Bottle and heat process.

It is important to follow either the imperial or the metric weights and measures in any one recipe. Do not mix them.

Strawberry Syrup

1kg (3lb) strawberries
600g (12oz) sugar to each litre (pint) of juice
10ml (1 teaspoon) citric acid to each litre (pint) of juice

Yield: about ½ litre (1 pint)

Heat the strawberries gently in a saucepan, stirring all the time, and bring to the boil. Boil for one minute, crushing any whole fruit with a wooden spoon. Strain and press out the juice. (NB An electric juice extractor may be used, instead of this process, to preserve the fresh flavour.) Measure the juice and add the required amount of sugar and the acid. Bottle and heat process, **or** add extra sugar (200g per litre/4oz per pint) and process with Campden solution.

Rose Hip Syrup

1kg (2lb) ripe rose hips
500g (1lb) sugar
3 litres (4½ pints) water

Yield: about 1¼ litres (2 pints)

Boil 2 litres (3 pints) of the water in a large aluminium or enamel pan. Mince the rose hips coarsely and add them immediately to the boiling water. Bring back to the boil, then allow to cool for 15 minutes before straining quickly through a scalded jelly bag. Return the pulp to the pan, add the remaining water and bring to the boil. Allow to cool for 10 minutes before straining again. Boil the juice down to one litre (1½ pints), add the sugar and boil for 5 minutes. Bottle the hot syrup and heat process in boiling water for 5 minutes.

Grapefruit Squash

1 litre (1½ pints) grapefruit juice (about 5 large grapefruit)
1¼kg (2½lb) sugar
20ml (½oz) citric acid
1 litre (1½ pints) water

Yield: about 3 litres (4 pints)

Wash the fruit. Peel or grate the rind very thinly from half the fruit. Add the rind and sugar to the water in a large saucepan and stir to dissolve the sugar. Warm the syrup and crush the rind to extract the oil. Strain through a scalded jelly bag. Halve and squeeze all the fruit using a lemon squeezer. Try to keep pips and larger pieces of pulp out of the juice. Mix the juice, strained syrup and citric acid. Bottle and heat process, **or** add Campden solution.

Sweet and sour
The sharpness of the loganberries and the sweetness of the sugar make a very acceptable sweet-sour syrup to add to desserts.

Bottling: fruit liqueurs

Unlike the other methods of bottling fruit, adding alcohol cannot be described as economical because the spirits used as the preservative are rather expensive. However, the results are delicious and are still cheaper than buying commercial products. They are more cheaply made using 'duty free' supplies from holidays abroad, but even so they are special occasion preserves.

The methods of adding alcohol to fruit vary from simply flavouring fruit bottled in syrup with spirit, to soaking whole, sweetened fruit in neat spirit to make liqueurs. 'Alcoholic' bottled fruit needs heat processing as only a small quantity of alcohol is added to each pack, but fruits steeped in neat spirit will keep because no spoilage micro-organisms can grow in such high concentrations of alcohol.

A water bath is needed to process fruit bottled in syrup, but otherwise only kitchen utensils are required. The bottles and crocks used for preparation and storage must have tight seals to stop the alcohol evaporating away, and wide-mouthed bottling jars are ideal. Liqueurs can be stored in the empty spirit bottles, but corked bottles give a tighter seal than screwcap types.

The basic ingredients are fruit, alcohol and sugar, and recipes using different fruits and spirits can be made up to suit individual tastes. It is essential to use good quality fruit, and types 'worthy' of the method, for example soft, dessert fruits like peaches, apricots and raspberries, are best. Liqueurs and whole fruit preserves need good quality spirits which will blend well with the fruit, but coarser spirits can be used for fruit bottled in syrup. White granulated or caster sugar is normally used so that the fruit flavour predominates, although brown sugar is sometimes added to orange liqueurs.

Flavouring bottled fruits with spirits
The preparation methods for flavouring bottled fruits with alcohol are virtually the same as for normal fruit bottling. Really only soft, dessert fruits like peaches, pears, apricots, cherries or berries are worth doing in this way, and they are prepared and packed as for bottling. The bottles used must have a seal, and small bottling jars or twist-top jam jars are recommended. A heavy syrup of 800g (1lb) sugar to a litre (pint) of water is used and $\frac{1}{4}$ litre ($\frac{1}{4}$ pint) of spirit (usually brandy) added to each litre (pint) of syrup. The filled bottles must be heat processed, because the amount of spirit is not sufficient to keep the fruit. The slow water bath method (see page 162) must be used as fiercer heating will evaporate the alcohol. Bottles are wiped clean, labelled and stored in a cool, dark place and will keep for up to one year.

Bottling whole fruits in spirits
Whole fruits preserved in neat spirit are very easy to make. Basically any fruit is submerged in any spirit with added sugar, but good quality dessert fruits will give best results. The fruit needs little preparation apart from hulling berries, peeling and thickly slicing peaches and pears, pricking small stone fruits and stoning and halving larger ones. Prepared fruit is packed in layers, mixing in an equal weight of dry sugar, and covered in a suitable spirit. Brandy is traditional, but whisky, rum, sherry or port may be used. Any glass or earthenware jars can be used, provided they have tight-fitting covers to stop the alcohol evaporating, and wide-mouthed bottles are easier to pack. Large jars of the preserve may be made, as portions can be removed and the jars resealed provided the spirit is topped up to keep the remaining fruit covered.

Making liqueurs
Liqueurs are made by steeping prepared and sweetened fruit in a spirit which 'matches' the fruit, for example cherries or peaches in brandy, sloes in gin and oranges in rum. Bottling jars are ideal for steeping but other vessels with good seals will do. The soaking extracts the flavour and colour from the fruit, and the time taken depends on the fruit. The jars should be left in a cool place away from direct sunlight to preserve the colour. No spoilage or fermentation will occur as no micro-organisms can grow in the high levels of alcohol and sugar. The flavoured, coloured spirit is then filtered or strained off and the highly alcoholic fruit can be eaten in small portions. To avoid losing some of the liqueur in an absorbent jelly bag, it is best to filter through butter muslin or a paper coffee filter as only small quantities are involved. The liqueur is then bottled, preferably in corked bottles of dark glass, and stored in a cool, dark place. A period of maturing will improve the liqueur as the flavour will mellow and smoothen.

Guidelines for fruit in alcohol
1 Use good quality fruit suitable and worthwhile for the method.
2 Use clean, non-metallic utensils and bottles.
3 Use good quality alcohol for whole fruit preserves and liqueurs, although coarser spirit can be used for bottling fruit in syrup.
4 Put fruit to steep in a cool place, away from direct sunlight.
5 Make sure fruit is always covered with spirit.
6 Store in a cool, dark place.

What can go wrong
Discoloration.
Delay during fruit preparation,
exposure to light during steeping or storage.
Liqueurs not smooth.
Poor quality spirit used, not matured.

Bottled Brandied Fruit

1¾–2kg (4–4½lb) fruit
400g (1lb) sugar
200ml (7½floz) brandy
500ml (1 pint) water

Yield: about 6 × ½ litre (1lb)
  bottling jars

Completely dissolve the sugar in
the water. Bring to the boil in a
covered saucepan and allow to
cool. Add the brandy. Prepare
the fruit:
Apricots: Skin, halve and stone
1¾kg (4lb) of fruit. Submerge in
slightly salted water (10ml per
litre/1 teaspoon per pint) to
prevent browning. Rinse, pack
and process without delay.
Cherries: Prick 2kg (4½lb) of
dessert fruit, or stone them if the
preserve will be kept longer
than two months.
Damsons: As cherries.
Peaches: As apricots.
Pears: As apricots.
Raspberries: Remove plugs,
damaged fruit and maggots.
  Pack the fruit in ½ litre (1lb)
bottling jars at the rate of 300g
(10oz) for peaches and pears or
375g (12oz) for other fruits.
Cover with the cold, brandied
syrup and process **only** by the
slow water bath method (see
pages 162–3).

Peaches in brandy
Expensive, but worth it; and
cheaper to make than to buy. For
how to do it, see above.

183

Recipes for fruit liqueurs

Mixed Fruit Preserve

Various fruits
Equal weight of sugar
Brandy, rum or whisky to
**   cover the fruit**

Prepare whatever fruit is available. The traditional French method uses fruits as they come into season (ie strawberries, cherries, raspberries, peaches, pears, apricots, grapes), making the preserve up throughout the summer. Use a large jar or earthenware crock with a tight cover to prevent evaporation. Pack the prepared fruit in layers with equal weights of sugar, then cover with brandy (or other spirit) and seal the jar. Add other fruit when available, ensuring that the fruit is always submerged in the brandy. Reseal after each addition.

Usquebaugh

(Irish – a strong cordial of spirits, raisins, spices and other ingredients.)

1 litre (2 pints) brandy
100g (4oz) stoned raisins
10g ($\frac{1}{2}$oz) stick liquorice,
**   sliced and bruised**
25g (1oz) sugar
7·5ml (1$\frac{1}{2}$ teaspoons) ground
**   cinnamon**
2·5ml ($\frac{1}{2}$ teaspoon) ground
**   mace**
2·5ml ($\frac{1}{2}$ teaspoon) ground
**   cloves**
1ml ($\frac{1}{4}$ teaspoon) ground
**   ginger**
Rind of small orange, grated
375ml ($\frac{3}{4}$ pint) water

Yield: about 1$\frac{1}{4}$ litres
**   (2$\frac{1}{2}$ pints)**

Add the spices and orange rind to the brandy in a jar or crock, cover and leave for three days. Boil the liquorice and raisins in the water and reduce to half the quantity. Cool and strain the liquid and add the sugar. Stir to dissolve the sugar. Filter the brandy and add the syrup. Traditionally the liqueur should be coloured green by adding an infusion of spinach, or yellow with saffron steeped in white wine. Bottle and leave to mature for at least one month.

Currant Shrub

(Arabic – a drink composed of acid fruit and sugar with spirit to preserve it.)

500g (1lb) red currants for
**   300ml ($\frac{1}{2}$ pint) of juice**
600ml (1 pint) rum
300ml ($\frac{1}{2}$ pint) sweet white
**   wine**
175g (6oz) sugar
Rind of small orange, grated
A little grated nutmeg

Yield: about 1$\frac{1}{4}$ litres
**   (2 pints)**

Extract the juice from the fruit by the cold enzyme method (see page 175). As only a small amount of juice is needed this liqueur can be made at the same time as red currant jelly. Measure out 300ml ($\frac{1}{2}$ pint) of strained juice and mix with the rum, orange rind and nutmeg. Seal tightly and leave for three days in a cool, dark place. Add the wine and sugar, stir to dissolve the sugar completely and filter the liqueur. Bottle and leave to mature.

French Cherry Brandy or Cherry Ratafia

(French – a spiritous liquor flavoured with the kernels of the fruit.)

500g (1lb) Morello cherries,
**   stoned**
250g (8oz) sugar
750ml (1 pint) brandy
Small piece of cinnamon
**   bark**
Pinch of coriander seeds

Yield: about 1 litre (1$\frac{1}{2}$ pints)

Mix the fruit and sugar in a jar or crock, cover loosely and leave for two to three days, shaking or stirring daily, until the juice begins to flow. Add the brandy, cinnamon, coriander and one or two crushed cherry kernels. Seal the jar tightly and leave for three months in a dark place, shaking occasionally. Filter and bottle the liqueur and leave to mature. The cherries can be eaten separately, with ice-cream or can be delicious when added to fruit salads.

Sloe Gin

500g (1lb) sloes
100g (3oz) sugar
1 litre (1$\frac{1}{2}$ pints) gin
Few drops almond essence

Yield: about 1$\frac{1}{4}$ litres (2 pints)

Remove stalks and prick the sloes all over. Mix the fruit and sugar in a jar or crock, cover loosely and leave for two to three days, shaking or stirring daily, until the juice begins to flow. Add the gin and almond essence. Seal the jar tightly and leave for three months in a dark place, shaking occasionally. Filter and bottle the liqueur and leave to mature for at least six months.

White Curaçao

(A liqueur flavoured with orange peel, sugar and cinnamon, originally from Curaçao.)

1 litre (2 pints) eau de vie
600g (1$\frac{1}{2}$lb) sugar
4 Seville (or sweet) oranges
5ml (1 teaspoon) ground
**   cinnamon or 5g ($\frac{1}{4}$oz) stick**
**   cinnamon**

Yield: about 1$\frac{1}{4}$ litres
**   (2$\frac{1}{2}$ pints)**

Peel or grate the rind from the oranges **very thinly** with no white pith. Add the rind and cinnamon to the brandy in a jar or crock, cover and leave for one week. Filter the liquor and stir in the sugar until completely dissolved. Bottle and leave to mature.

The best of the summer fruit
An old French (and German) custom that might do well to become an old English custom preserves the summer fruits as they come along month by month. They are packed in dry sugar in a jar and topped up with brandy, (see recipe top left). Then, come the winter one can enjoy a beaker full of the warm South, homemade.

Drying, Salting and Smoking

Drying, salting and smoking are ancient methods of preserving food and were practised in some form or other by primitive man. In recent centuries we have managed to improve on methods and equipment though the tools are still mostly very simple and easy to come by. **Drying** is useful in many respects, particularly for fruit and herbs and some vegetables and the recipes Beryl Gould-Marks gives for using them make it all worth while. **Salting** is a handy way of preserving fish and meat, if a freezer is not available and there is nothing more delicately flavoured than cured salmon – the Norwegian *gravlaks* – should a salmon come your way. Salted raw herring keeps in pickle for up to six months and is excellent as an hors d'oeuvre or a supper dish. **Smoking** is more complicated and some methods, such as hot smoking, are a cooking and flavouring process, not a way of preserving. But the cold smoking process, preceded by drying and salting, is indeed a good means of preservation and achieves the most subtle and unique flavours; smoked eel, smoked salmon, smoked ham or smoked goose-breast being regarded as delicacies all over the world. All these processes and how to carry them out are described clearly by Beryl Gould-Marks who has tested them personally.

Drying

Drying food for preservation, if it is to be safe and effective, means dehydrating it so that only a little moisture remains. This means the food keeps because moulds and bacteria need water to grow, and enzymes which may cause food to deteriorate remain largely inactive in dried foods. Drying can therefore arrest, or at least delay, decay and keep foods in a static condition.

Right from pre-history man has needed to store the results of harvest and hunt for winter food. Drying was one of his first methods. In hot countries sun and air have always been used, but in Britain this is only possible in periods of sun-drenched drought. The Red Indians dried buffalo or deer meat into strips of pemmican. In South East Asia fish is one of the chief sources of protein. Salted shrimps are dried in the sun, pounded, fermented and then compressed into cakes called *blachang* in Malaya. Curry lovers will have eaten Bombay duck – bummalo fish – dried in the sun.

Religion and Friday abstinence led to the production of dried fish in the hinterlands of Europe. Dried cod appears as *bacalao*, *bacalhau* and *baccalà* in Spain, Portugal and Italy. Stockfish, which is dried cod or ling, is the standard Christmas dish in Sweden.

In this country, many fruits, some vegetables and most herbs can be dried at home. They are good, sometimes nearly as good as fresh, but they do have a different flavour.

The decision to dry, or not to dry, as a method of food preservation depends on your particular circumstances. If you have fruit and vegetables in your garden, or can buy them at reasonable prices, and you have no room in your freezer or do not own one, drying is a good solution. Dried food takes up less space. Herbs are always worth dehydrating.

If you have an airy barn, attic or shed, with some economical heat source, drying is for you. Take advantage of the high season to buy the very freshest of fruit and vegetables you can get. Market during gluts, or go to a pick-it-yourself orchard and benefit from bargain rates. But remember that it is no good drying inferior fruit or vegetables. When decay has started nothing will arrest it. Use anything which is not first rate for other preserves, such as chutneys, or cook and eat it at once.

Equipment

Drying is a simple process requiring no expensive equipment. Food must be spread out so that warm air can pass all round it. So you need:

1 **Trays** – these may be:
   a) Slatted or perforated wooden trays – scrupulously clean seed or plant trays are excellent.
   b) Non-ferrous cake racks.
   c) The shelves of your oven.
   d) Any type of grid or wire netting.
   e) For apple rings and mushrooms, strings or wooden rods can be used.

2 **Cloth** – loosely woven cloth, ie butter muslin, cheesecloth or old (but clean) net curtains, to prevent food from touching the trays, without interfering with the flow of air or the evaporation of moisture.

3 **Heat source** to produce the ideal drying temperature of between 49°C (120°F) and 66°C (150°F). There must also be a flow of air. Suitable heat sources are:
   a) Gas ovens, good because the actual combustion draws in and circulates air. Even when the oven is turned off air continues to circulate by convection as the oven cools.
   b) Electric ovens – convection currents circulate. These are especially good if fan-assisted. Leave the door open.
   c) The plate heating rack or cupboard on any stove from solid fuel to electric – if enclosed, leave open.
   d) The oven or top of any solid fuel cooking stove, provided it is sufficiently cool.
   e) A fan heater or hair dryer turned to cool will dry with warm circulating air.
   f) Any warm area, above central heating, or in a ventilated airing cupboard.
   g) The sun is a possible source of heat and in a good summer could be used. Bring fruit and vegetables in at night.

Other equipment includes:
Stainless steel knives for slicing.
Non-metal bowl.
Wooden cutting board.
Wooden spoons.
Apple corer.
Potato peeler.
Glass jars, cartons, paper bags, plastic bags (for some vegetables only) for storing.

Dried fruit

The best fruits for drying are apples (both dessert and cooking), apricots, peaches, pears and grapes. Plums are less satisfactory, but can be dried. As they all need slightly different preparation they are dealt with separately.

Method and preparation

When the fruit is prepared it should be spread on trays lined with the loosely woven cloth, in single layers – the fruits should not touch each other. A 30cm (12in) square tray will take about ¾–1kg (1½–2lb) of fruit. Do not prepare more fruit than you can conveniently put to dry immediately. The temperature should be as near as possible to the ideal (49°C/120°F to 66°C/150°F). The drying process should never be hurried – it should be slow – sometimes taking several days. When fruit is thoroughly dry allow several hours for it to cool completely before packing and storing.

Apples

'Bramley's Seedling' apples are excellent for drying, because of their full flavour. Other suitable varieties are 'Grenadier', 'Russet', 'Lane's Prince Albert', 'Delicious' and 'Jonathan'.

The apples should be fully ripe and freshly picked if possible. Peel, removing any bruises or blemishes. If there is any sign of over-ripeness or woolliness, discard. Core them (with a corer) and cut into even slices or rings about 5mm ($\frac{1}{4}$in) thick. Put these, as they are prepared, into a salt water solution: 15ml (1 tablespoon) of coarse common salt to 1 litre (2 pints) of water. Make certain that all the slices are completely submerged. Put a plate on top to keep them submerged if necessary. Leave for 6–8 minutes. This prevents oxidation, and so discoloration. Alternatively, ascorbic acid (vitamin C) can be used, as it is one of the best anti-oxidants available. Dissolve 30ml (2 tablespoons) of crystalline ascorbic acid (available from chemists) in 500ml (1 pint) of boiled and cooled water. Then proceed as with salt solution.

Using sulphur is smelly, and not recommended.

Drain the rings or slices thoroughly, pat dry, then either spread on drying trays or thread on wooden sticks or string so that they do not touch one another. Hang up threaded rings in a dry airy room where they will dry slowly but surely. Or put rings or slices on trays to dry in a source of heat such as an oven. They are dry when they feel soft and springy. If they can be left in the oven, this will take 4–6 hours. If they are put in the oven when it is available, ie from time to time, it could take up to 3 days. They should lose about two thirds of their peeled and cored weight. Leave spread out for a few hours to cool and then pack in cartons or paper bags, seal loosely, label them, and store in a dry place out of direct light.

Drying apple rings
After cutting apples into rings and processing them as described above, dry them near a heat source on clean trays or seedboxes with slatted shelves – you can easily improvise them as in the photograph – or on wooden sticks or string hung in a dry, airy place. They are dry when soft and springy and can finally be stored in cartons or paper bags in a dry place.

Drying fruit

Apricots

Apricots have a great reputation, for in Hunza (India), the natives attribute their phenomenal long life to a diet of fresh and dried apricots. They are high in vitamin A and also contain a certain amount of vitamin C. Unfortunately apricots are expensive, so unless you grow them yourself, or can buy them in bulk (perhaps using some for other purposes, or sharing bulk with friends), it is not an economic proposition. Only dry fruit when it is ripe but without any tendency to over-ripeness. 'Moorpark' is a good variety for drying.

Home-dried apricots are delicious. Cut in half and remove stones. They need not be peeled, but if you wish to skin them, plunge them in boiling water for about $\frac{1}{2}$ minute, then dip in ice-cold water. The skins should come off easily. Dipping in an ascorbic acid solution (see apples above, but use half the amount of ascorbic acid) is optional. A degree of darkening due to oxidation is acceptable. Arrange the fruit on trays with the cut side up. This prevents the flavoured juice running out before it desiccates.

When completely dry, the apricots should have reduced their weight by two thirds, and will have shrunk and become leathery. No liquid should ooze out if you cut one in half. Cool, pack and store as for apples.

Grapes

English grown grapes are unfit for drying, except in unusually sunny years. They lack sugar. I find the best are the relatively cheap, small Cyprus seedless grapes (in season from mid-June onwards). As with other fruit, choose ripe ones.

Wash, dry and drain the grapes. Look them over and remove imperfect ones. Separate them. Spread them on trays and dry in warm circulating air. They will shrink and look like sultanas when ready. Cool and pack as for apples. Use like sultanas.

Peaches

You will probably have to buy peaches, so choose ones that are just ripe. Ones with yellow flesh dry well. 'Hale's Early' (freestone) are good for drying.

Do not peel if you are going to dry halves, but if you prefer to slice them you can peel them first (blanch in boiling water, like apricots). Wipe thoroughly and remove stones. Arrange peach halves on trays, cut side up; when they begin to dry you can invert them. They will take longer than apricots as the flesh is much denser, up to 24 hours. Slices will take about eight hours. Peaches are quite tough when dry. Cool, pack and store.

Pears

Only the best dessert pears are worth drying. 'Conference' and 'William's Bon Chrétien' are good varieties. They should be just ripe, never over-ripe. Pears ripen better off the tree, so pick them just short of perfection. Keep them in a dry airy room at about 21°C (70°F) until ready.

Wash and drain the pears. Remove stalks, cut in half lengthwise. Remove core, this is easily done with a small spoon. Large pears can be quartered. Put in salt water or ascorbic acid solution as for apples, but use half the amount of ascorbic acid. Spread on trays and dry in the usual way.

Plums

Red plums dry best – good ones are 'Belle de Louvain' and 'Pond's Seedling'. They will lose a lot of juice if you try to remove the stones so dry them whole.

Wash the plums, then drain and pat them dry. As they are very juicy they may take several days to dry. When really dry, they will look wrinkled like prunes. Cool, pack and store. Unfortunately they never have the flavour of the shop-bought prune, because prunes are a special variety with a high sugar content.

Plums are only worth drying if your own trees crop well.

To reconstitute dried fruit

Pour boiling water over the fruits; they should be well covered and as they swell and absorb the water it may be necessary to add a little more water, but for full flavour do not swamp them. Leave overnight. Cook gently the next day in the water they were soaked in, as this is full of goodness. Do not add sugar to taste until they are cooked – if it is added during cooking, it tends to harden the fruit.

Guidelines for drying fruit

1 Choose dry fresh fruit at its peak of perfection.
2 Ripe fruit dried at once keeps much of its flavour. Never hurry over drying. Fruit should be dried slowly – like drying out meringues. It may take several days to dry out thoroughly.
3 Fruit should be sliced or prepared to a size as uniform as possible, so that pieces dry at the same rate.
4 Drying trays must be well ventilated to carry the moisture away.
5 If new cheesecloth or butter muslin is used, wash and dry before use.
6 If heat is too fierce, the outside may be scorched and moisture sealed inside. Ideal drying temperature: 49°C (120°F) to 66°C (150°F).
7 Check that food is sufficiently dehydrated.
8 Leave to cool thoroughly before storing.
9 Pack in cartons or paper bags, loosely sealed, or in containers with loose-fitting lids.

What can go wrong

Mould and nasty smell.
This will happen if dried fruits are stored in damp conditions.
Perished fruit.
The fruit is insufficiently dried.
Scorched fruit.
The drying heat has been too fierce.
Sweating fruit.
If the fruit was not cold enough before packing and storing, it will sweat.

Recipes using dried fruit

Apple and Almond Tart

250g (8oz) dried apple rings,
  soaked overnight in just
  enough boiling water to
  cover
45ml (3 tablespoons) apricot
  jam, diluted with 150ml
  (¼ pint) water
Shortcrust pastry (made
  with 250g/8oz flour)

Topping
100g (4oz) ground almonds
100g (4oz) butter
100g (4oz) plain flour
100g (4oz) sugar, or more or
  less to taste
Pinch of cinnamon

Serves 6–8

Line a deep 25cm (10in) flan case
with pastry. Preheat a moderate
oven to 180°C, 350°F, Gas mark 4.
Drain the apple rings and cut in
half. Arrange them in concentric circles in the pastry case.
Cover with diluted jam.

To make the topping
Mix flour, sugar, almonds and
cinnamon well together. Rub in
the butter until it looks like
breadcrumbs. Cover the apples
with this mixture. Bake for
30–40 minutes until pastry and
apples are cooked and the top is
brown and crusty. This tart can
be served either hot or cold with
cream or ice-cream.

Dried Apricot Soup

250g (8oz) dried apricots,
  soaked overnight in 2½
  litres (4 pints) water
200g (6oz) sugar, or to taste
Juice of 1 small lemon
Pinch of cinnamon (optional)
30ml (2 tablespoons)
  cornflour, mixed to a thin
  paste with a little cold
  water

Serves 4–6

Add sugar and cinnamon (if
using) to the fruit and water in
which the fruit was soaked.
Simmer until the fruit is tender.
Strain off the liquid. Liquidise
the fruit or rub through a sieve.
Return it to the liquid. Heat it
gently, then slowly add the

blended cornflour, stir and cook
until it thickens. Cook for 3–4
minutes. Add lemon juice, taste
to see if there is enough sugar.
Serve cold; it can begin or end a
meal.

Hot Baked Peaches with Ice-cream

8 dried peach halves
Block of vanilla ice-cream
1 wineglass of sherry
30ml (2 tablespoons) brown
  sugar, or to taste
Grated rind and juice of 1
  large orange
50g (2oz) butter
Pinch of cinnamon

Serves 4

Soak the peaches overnight in
just enough boiling water to
cover. The next day, add the
sherry and orange juice.
  Heat the oven to 180°C, 350°F,
Gas Mark 4. Arrange the peach
halves, cut side down, in an
ovenproof dish. Cover with the
liquid they were soaked in and
the added sherry and orange
juice. Cover and cook for 15
minutes. Remove from the oven,
arrange the peaches, cut side up.
Mix the sugar, cinnamon, butter
and orange rind together. Put
some on each peach half. Cover
and cook until the peaches are
tender – about 30 minutes.
Remove cover, cook for 5 minutes longer, basting with the
sauce constantly.
  Divide the ice-cream into four
portions and put two hot peach
halves on each. Serve at once
with the liquid poured over.

Dried Fruit Custard Tart

500g (1lb) dried plums
250g (8oz) dried apricots
50g (1½oz) dried apples
3 bananas (fresh)
A little lemon juice
Shortcrust pastry (made
  with 250g/8oz flour)

Custard
2 large eggs
100g (4oz) caster sugar
250ml (½ pint) hot milk
30ml (2 tablespoons) rum

Serves 8

Soak the dried fruit overnight,
the next day cook until softened.
Drain. Cut the bananas into
rounds, cover with lemon juice
to prevent discoloration. Line a
deep 25cm (10in) flan case with
pastry, line the pastry with foil,
put dried beans on top. Bake for
10 minutes at 190°C, 375°F, Gas
Mark 5, until the pastry is set
but not cooked. Remove beans
and foil.

To make the custard
Beat the eggs and sugar together, gradually stir in the hot
milk, add the rum.

To assemble the tart
Drain the bananas. Arrange a
layer of dried fruit and bananas
in the pastry case, Pour in half
the custard. Now add another
layer of dried fruit and bananas.
Cover with the rest of the custard. Bake in the middle of the
oven at 230°C, 450°F, Gas Mark
8, for 15 minutes. Reduce temperature to 200°C, 400°F, Gas
Mark 6. Cook for 25–30 minutes
when the custard should have
set and the pastry be a nice
brown. Unmould and serve
when cold.

Roast Pork with Dried Apricots

450g–550g (1–1¼lb) pork tenderloin
100g (4oz) dried apricots, soaked overnight in 550ml (1 pint) boiling water
1 clove garlic, finely sliced
About 6 leaves of rosemary
Ground coriander
1 onion, chopped
1 carrot, chopped
30ml (2 tablespoons) sherry
Pepper and salt
Fat for frying

Serves 4

Brown the meat all over in hot fat. Make 2–3 slits in the joint and insert the slivers of garlic. Put the meat in an ovenproof dish, add the apricots and the water they were soaked in, and the rest of the ingredients. Cook in a moderate oven (180°C, 350°F, Gas Mark 4) for about 1½ hours, or a little longer if the meat is very thick. Cut across in thick slices and serve with the apricots and sauce.

Rabbit with Dried Red Plums

1 medium-sized rabbit, jointed, and the liver, finely chopped
150g (5oz) belly of pork, diced
15–20 dried plums
2 medium-sized onions, chopped
12 small onions
2 carrots, chopped
1 clove garlic, crushed
Bouquet garni
1 wineglass of red wine or cider
30ml (2 tablespoons) wine vinegar
15ml (1 tablespoon) sugar
2 dried sage leaves
Chopped parsley
30ml (2 tablespoons) flour
Pepper and salt
Fat for frying
250ml (½ pint) water

Serves 4–5

Put the rabbit in a dish with the plums, chopped onions, carrots, garlic, bouquet garni, sage leaves, pepper and salt. Cover with the wine or cider, water and vinegar. Marinate overnight in the refrigerator. The next day, remove the rabbit from the marinade and pat dry. Brown in the fat in a large saucepan, then remove and keep aside.

Remove the plums from the marinade and stone. Brown the pork and small onions in the saucepan. Sprinkle in the flour, stir and let it brown slightly, put back the rabbit, add the parsley, pour in the marinade, removing the bouquet garni and sage leaves. Cover and simmer gently for about one hour.

Add the plums and chopped liver. Continue simmering for half an hour longer. Adjust seasoning, add sugar.

Serve the rabbit and pork surrounded by the small onions and plums, pour the sauce over. Noodles go excellently with this dish.

Dried fruit and nuts
The selection shown here consists of, from the left, shelled walnuts, hazel nuts, figs, raisins and on the right, shelled almonds.

Drying vegetables

Packs of dehydrated mixed vegetables are on sale, so it does not really pay the housewife to dry root vegetables. They can be preserved by other methods, such as in sand or clamps. The simplest and most useful vegetables for drying are pulses, green beans, mushrooms, onions and pimientos.

Peas and beans

The easiest way to dry large marrowfat peas and other field varieties, and butter and haricot beans, is to let them stay on the vine, **if** the weather is fine, until the pods are withered and dry. If the weather is bad, pull up the plants and hang them in an airy, dry place, like an attic or porch. Shell when completely dry. Leave spread out for a few days to make certain, then store.

Young, tender green peas can also be dried, but the process is quite different. Shell them, but keep the best of the pods. Tie up the peas in a piece of muslin. Hold the top and lower them into boiling water for 1–2 minutes. Take them out and plunge them immediately into cold water to refresh. Drain thoroughly, put them in a dry cloth and shake to get them as dry as possible. Arrange a thin cloth on a drying tray, spread the peas evenly in one layer. Dry slowly at 60°C (140°F) increasing gradually to 71°C (160°F). Take care they do not discolour or scorch. When dry, they should be hard and look shrivelled. Leave to cool, pack in jars or small plastic bags and store.

Very few varieties of pea dry well, but 'Harrison's Glory' is quite satisfactory.

Fresh pea pods

These are well worth drying, a few put into a soup or stew give both colour and a subtle flavour. Wash them, blanch and refresh them as for green peas above. Dry in the coolest possible oven until slightly brown, but not burnt (they scorch easily). A good way to store pea pods is to hang them up in a muslin bag.

Garlic

Lift the bulbs in late summer or early autumn. Hang them to dry in plaits in an airy room or frostproof outhouse until you need them. The outside should dry but the cloves should remain fresh and moist.

Haricot beans

When young they can be used as runner beans, but if left on the vine till the beans are mature they are an excellent source of winter protein. They can be left to dry outside or they can be treated like young green peas. 'Comtesse de Chambord' is an excellent variety for drying – high in protein, carbohydrate, calcium and iron.

Runner and French beans

Wash, dry, top and tail, and string if necessary. Slice fairly thickly. Fine, small French beans can be dried whole. Blanch and refresh as for green peas. Dry, spread out on trays. Cool, pack in jars and store. All varieties of string bean can be dried.

Mushrooms and other edible fungi

If you know your fungi, but you **must** be able to identify them without any possibility of doubt, they are a most useful addition to the store cupboard. Near London, Polish friends of mine have gathered five different edible species including blewits, morels and ceps.

Choose the freshest you can buy, or preferably pick. There is no need to peel them, just wipe them thoroughly with a damp cloth, or if they are really dirty, wash them under running cold water. Remove stems as they hinder the drying of the caps. Do not waste the stems, they can be made into mushroom ketchup, or used in stews or casseroles.

Examine the caps carefully. Do not use any with the slightest blemish. Thread thin string into a larding needle, pass the needle through the centre of each cap, make a knot between them, so they cannot touch, and hang them up in an airy loft, attic or shed until they are completely dry. They become shrivelled looking and leathery.

Alternatively, they can be sliced finely and dried on trays in a cool oven. They become brittle when really dry. Cool, pack in jars.

To use, either soak for an hour before quick cooking, or add to soup, stews, etc, for slow cooking, without previous soaking.

Useful dried vegetables
Peas, haricot beans and butter beans are useful sources of winter protein. They are included here ranged from left to right between a garlic bulb, left, and some dried morels on the right.

Onions

Peel and cut into rings about 3mm ($\frac{1}{8}$in) thick. Try to cut them as evenly as possible. Arrange in single layers on trays and dry out in a slow oven (110°C, 225°F, Gas Mark $\frac{1}{4}$). Do not allow to scorch. When dry they should be quite crisp. Cool, pack in jars and store.

For use in slow-cooked dishes they do not need pre-soaking. They make the best crisp fried onions if put straight into the pan, but take care as they burn quickly.

Pimientos (peppers), green or red

Cut them in half, remove seeds and membranes. Cut into quarters. Steam for 10 minutes. Arrange on trays, dry in a very cool oven or plate rack. Turn over twice an hour. Do not allow them to burn or change colour. Cool thoroughly, pack in jars and store. Soaked for an hour they can be used in any recipes employing fresh sliced or chopped pimientos. All varieties dry well.

Red and green chillies

Both dry well. Wipe or wash and thread on strings through the stalks. Hang in a well ventilated area protected from the weather. Use with care as they are 'cayenne-hot'. Pack in jars.

To reconstitute dried vegetables

Soak dried vegetables in a little water, and they should become nearly like fresh vegetables. Dried legumes, that is pulses which come out of pods, should be soaked overnight. They usually absorb enough water to double their weight. They should be simmered slowly without salt, for salt toughens them. Add salt when they are nearly cooked.

Guidelines for drying vegetables

1 Pick prime vegetables in perfect condition.
2 Discard any inferior specimens.
3 Beans and peas dried on the vine should not be left out during bad weather, but dried under cover.
4 Some vegetables should be blanched and refreshed before drying. Follow instructions for individual vegetables.
5 Avoid scorching; the drying heat should not be too fierce.
6 Pack in glass jars or plastic bags and store in a cool, dry, dark place for up to one year.
7 To reconstitute, soak in a little cold water until nearly like fresh vegetables.

What can go wrong

Softness or sliminess. This is usually caused by faulty packing, and storing in a damp place.
Limpness and decay. The original drying was insufficient.
Deterioration. This occurs if damaged or inferior vegetables are used.

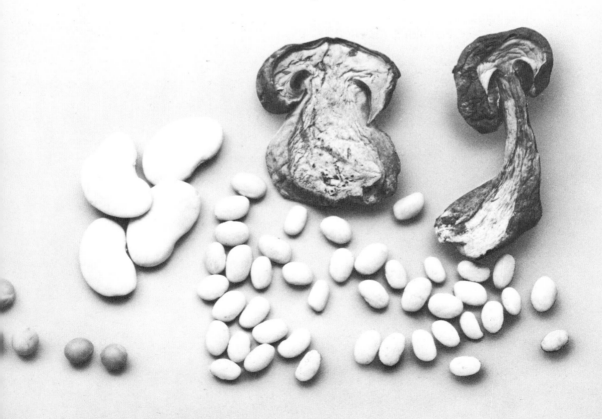

Recipes using dried vegetables

Baked Bean Feast

500g (1lb) dried haricot beans, soaked overnight in 1½ litres (3 pints) water
500g (1lb) salt belly of pork, cubed
100g (4oz) streaky bacon rashers
1 bay leaf
2 celery stalks, chopped
1 small onion stuck with 3 cloves
Chopped parsley
Pinch each of dried marjoram, thyme and chilli powder

Sauce

Bean liquid
30ml (2 tablespoons) tomato ketchup
30ml (2 tablespoons) tomato paste
2 onions, coarsely chopped
4 large tomatoes, peeled and chopped
150g (5oz) black treacle
125g (4oz) brown sugar
5ml (1 teaspoon) dry mustard
Pepper and salt
Chilli pepper to taste
5ml (1 teaspoon) Worcestershire sauce

Serves 4–6

Put the soaked beans in a large saucepan, if necessary add more water so that they are completely covered. Add the bay leaf, celery, onion, and herbs. Simmer for 1–1½ hours or until the beans are tender. To test, put a few beans on a spoon, blow on them; if they are cooked the skins will break. Drain well, remove onion and bay leaf, but keep the liquid. If you have a large brown earthenware casserole use it. Arrange layers of beans, salt pork and bacon in it.

To make the sauce

Mix all the ingredients for the sauce well together, bring to the boil, pour over the beans.

Heat the oven to 130°C, 250°F, Gas Mark ½. Cover the beans and bake for 5–6 hours until all is gooey, moist and succulent.

Both beans and sauce can be prepared in advance, and then refrigerated separately and mixed before cooking.

Green Pea Soup

Make this when you have some ham stock.

250g (8oz) dried green peas soaked overnight in 600ml (1 pint) cold water
15ml (1 tablespoon) dried mint, soaked with the peas
2 large onions, chopped
1 leek, chopped
6 dried pea pods
Bouquet garni
Pepper and salt
Ham stock

Serves 4

Heat the peas in the water they were soaked in, bring to the boil, add the vegetables, the pea pods, the bouquet garni and pepper to taste. Cover and simmer until tender. Remove bouquet garni. Liquidise, or rub through a sieve, thin down with ham stock. Reheat. Adjust seasoning, adding salt if necessary. Add a good knob of butter. Serve with fried croûtons of bread.

Haricots Panachés

The word panaché means mixed or variegated; a lovely name for a dish of white and green beans.

250g (8oz) dried haricot beans, soaked overnight
150g (5oz) dried French beans, soaked for 2 hours in warm water
Pepper and salt
Butter

Serves 4–6

Cook the haricot beans in the water they were soaked in, without salt, until tender (if salt is added when they are cooking it hardens the skins). Cook the French beans in boiling salted water until tender. Drain when cooked. Mix both kinds of beans together. Add some butter and pepper and salt to taste.

Serve with a main course, or leave to cool, mix the beans with oil and lemon juice and season to taste. If preferred, salted French beans may be used. See chapter on salting vegetables, page 208.

Scrambled Eggs with Mushrooms

50g (2oz) dried mushrooms
6 eggs
Pepper and salt
25g (1oz) butter
3–4 slices of hot buttered toast

Serves 3–4

Soak the mushrooms in a little cold water for 10 minutes. Drain, but keep the water. Slice the mushrooms and fry them in butter for 2–3 minutes. Add the water they were soaked in, season with pepper and salt. Cover the pan and cook gently for 10 minutes.

Break the eggs into a basin, heat lightly, season. Pour on top of the mushrooms, then stir and cook quickly until the eggs are lightly scrambled. Pile them on the toast, eat at once.

A Simple Pot-pourri

Pot-pourri is a colourful mixture of dried flower petals and herbs used to scent a room or linen cupboard. The fragrance of the ingredients is preserved by careful drying and enhanced by the addition of flower oils and spices. Pot-pourri is usually placed in pretty, open bowls or glass dishes so that the petals may be stirred lightly with the fingers as you pass and the scent is released, or as in traditional lavender bags the mixture may be used to fill sachets of fine material and placed in clothes drawers or among sheets and blankets.

To make pot-pourri, collect a selection of sweet smelling rose and other flower petals. Lavender, elderflowers, lime tree flowers, violets, pinks and carnations and lily of the valley are obvious choices but any others may be added. The greater proportion of petals should be from roses of all colours but especially from the heavily scented varieties. Some very dark red rose petals are included to improve the appearance as these retain their colour well when dried. Choose dry petals from flowers that are not quite fully opened, sprinkle on flat trays, sheets of paper or material, and spread out in a warm dry and dark place – a boiler room or airing cupboard is ideal. Make sure the petals are all separate and turn them gently at least once a day without bruising them. Leave until quite dry and brittle.

You can collect and dry flower petals as they come into season throughout the summer and store them or make the pot-pourri as you go along. To store the petals until enough have been collected, place them in dark airtight containers.

When you are ready to make the pot-pourri, sprinkle the dry petals in layers in a bowl with a selection of the following ingredients:

Mixed spices – a pinch of ground mixed spice or a few whole cloves, pieces of cinnamon stick, bruised allspice berries or grated nutmeg. The amount to add simply depends on how spicy you like the finished fragrance to be.

Leaves of flowers or dried herbs can be added if you prefer their scent. Thyme and rosemary are especially attractive but it is also nice to include some less usual herbs if available. Mint should only be added in small amounts as it can be overpowering.

Herbs and strips of thinly pared orange and lemon rind may be dried at the same time as the petals.

Mix in powdered orris root and a few drops of essential flower oils to add to the scent. These are obtainable from herbalists and some garden departments and shops.

If the mixed pot-pourri is not in use, store it in dark airtight containers. It is best brought out when required to scent a room rather than being left out all the time as light and air gradually weaken the fragrance and colours. If this does happen, you can add special oils to revive the mixture, but it should be freshly made each year.

197

Drying herbs

The months for harvesting may be variable according to weather and district – the best guide is to pick them just before they bloom.

When seeds are wanted, harvesting will be later. Wait until the seeds ripen.

Method and preparation
Fresh herbs in summer and dried in winter add an essential savour to many dishes. It is worth the little trouble it takes to preserve their evocative perfume for the cold weather.

Like the flowers used in perfume, it is best to pick them in the early morning of a sunny day just before they bloom. This is the moment when the amount of essential oil in the leaves is at its optimum – it is these oils which give flavour and scent.

Herbs should be air dried. Pick the youngest shoots, keeping the stalks long enough for them to be tied in bunches. Wash the herbs in cold running water, shake gently to dry. Spread out on blotting or other absorbent paper until no moisture is visible. Tie up loosely in bunches, so that all the sprigs can dry out thoroughly. Hang up, preferably in muslin bags, in a warm dry airy room – or in the sun.

Alternatively they can be dried on trays in the oven at a temperature between 43°C (110°F) and 54°C (130°F). First, tie them in muslin and blanch for one minute. Remove muslin, shake to get rid of as much moisture as possible. Then put them in the oven for about one hour.

When herbs are completely dry, strip from stalks, pulverise them, or leave as they are, and store in airtight containers, eg small glass jars, in a dry, dark place.

Drying stalks
Fennel stalks, bay twigs and grape vine cuttings can be dried to give character to barbecue cooking. The dried twigs are put on the smouldering embers to give off an aromatic smoke when cooking.

Drying seeds
Caraway, coriander, dill and fennel seeds dry well. Wait until the seeds are really ripe and ready to drop. Pick the stalks carefully. Shake them into a bag, or rub between the fingers till you have gleaned them all. Then dry out in the air.

To reconstitute dried herbs
Soak in a little water for 10 to 15 minutes for omelettes, salads and dishes which need little cooking. For mint sauce, soak in vinegar. Put dried herbs straight into soups and stews, when they will be cooked for a long time.

Parsley and Dill
Dry them this way if you want them to be a bright green. Wash them under running water, then dry in a moderately hot oven, 190–200°C, 375–400°F, Gas Mark 5–6, for a few minutes. Check frequently, on no account let them brown. When brittle rub between your hands, pack, store.

Guidelines for drying herbs
1 Pick herbs when they are at their prime on a dry sunny day.
2 If seeds are required, pick when fully ripe.
3 Air dry in suspended bunches or muslin bags, or dry on trays in the oven.
4 When herbs are completely dry, store in airtight containers in a dry, dark place.

What can go wrong
Bad colour. Past their prime when picked, or overheated when being dried in the oven.
Lack of flavour. Dried herbs kept too long.
Dried seed failure. Seeds are almost foolproof, unless they were not fully ripe when harvested.

How to use dried herbs
When using dried herbs, remember that their flavour is much more concentrated than in fresh ones, so use less volume. About 2.5ml ($\frac{1}{2}$ teaspoon) dried herbs is the equivalent to 15ml (1 tablespoon) of fresh. Do not keep dried herbs too long as they lose their flavour. A rough guide is to replace them when the new harvesting season comes around again.

Basil (sweet or bush)
Use in soups, especially Soupe au Pistou, stews and sauces. It is the traditional flavour for turtle soup. Goes well with tomatoes. Keeps its aromatic flavour when dried.

Bay leaves
Part of a bouquet garni. Pungent, so don't overdo it. Useful in many savoury dishes, marinades and court-bouillons. In Victorian times they were used in custards and blancmanges. If used on top of kebabs cooked under the grill, they burn to give an exotic smoky flavour. Whole leaves are usually dried and stored.

Bouquet garni
A sprig of thyme, parsley and bay leaf, and sometimes tarragon and sage, are tied together, or put in a small muslin bag. Add to soups, stews, casseroles, but remove before the dish is served. I often dry my bouquet garni herbs together in little sachets so that they are ready for use.

Caraway
Every part can be eaten, but only the seeds are dried. Add these to soups, stews, bread, puddings and cakes.

Chervil (Sweet Cicely)
Used in omelettes. Can be used instead of parsley.

Coriander
The pervasive flavour of the fresh leaves is very popular in Greek and Cypriot salads, but they do not dry well. On the other hand, the dried seeds are very aromatic, spicy without being hot. They are used from the Mediterranean to the Far East. They are an ingredient of curry. I keep mine in a pepper mill and use it in many soups and stews.

Dill
Extensively used in Scandinavia to decorate and flavour fish and meat dishes. Germans pickle gherkins with it. Dill has a slightly aniseed flavour. The seeds are used in soups.

Fennel
The ideal accompaniment for fish, much used in Provence. Dried twigs of fennel can be used in barbecuing fish.

Lemon balm
Has a pleasant lemon flavour. Used in salads.

Lovage
Can be used as a substitute for celery.

Marjoram
Often used in Italy with pasta dishes. Used for stuffing meat and poultry. Oregano is a variety of marjoram.

Mint
Dried mint can be added to new potatoes and green peas while cooking, and used to make mint sauce and jelly. It makes a good infusion for indigestion.

Parsley
Part of a bouquet garni. Use for sauces, stews, casseroles and egg dishes.

Rosemary
A small quantity goes well with pork, lamb and chicken.

Sage
Used in stuffings, particularly for pork, goose and duck and in sausages and rissoles. A very pervasive flavour.

Summer Savory
A strongly flavoured herb. Used in stuffings, goes well with pike and trout.

Tarragon
The French kind is superior to the Russian. Good with eggs, chicken and stuffed tomatoes. An ingredient in Sauce Tartare and Sauce Béarnaise.

Thyme
Part of a bouquet garni. Used in stocks, stews, casseroles, pâtés and many other savoury dishes.

Herbs you can grow easily
Left to right:
Rosemary, bay, parsley, thyme and sage.

Recipes using dried herbs

Basil and Garlic Sauce – il Pesto

This is a magnificent meridional sauce, originally from Genoa but now popular in the whole of Italy, Corsica and Southern France.

It is added to a soup of dried beans and potatoes to make 'Soupe au Pistou'. It can be served with pasta or salad.

30ml (2 tablespoons) dried
   basil, soaked for 15
   minutes in a little milk
3 cloves of garlic, chopped
25g (1oz) Parmesan cheese,
   grated
30–45ml (2–3 tablespoons)
   olive oil
Pepper and salt

Pound all the ingredients well together until they make a thick creamy paste. If necessary add more oil.

If adding to soup, mix in at the last moment, and do not let the soup boil again.

If adding to pasta, toss with the hot spaghetti, tagliatelle, etc, before serving.

Omelette aux Fines Herbes

Do not make too large an omelette, 2–6 eggs is ideal. A larger one may burn on the outside before it begins to cook in the centre.

5–6 eggs
15ml (1 tablespoon) dried
   herbs, soaked in 30ml
   (2 tablespoons) water for
   10–15 minutes. These can
   be parsley, tarragon, pinch
   of thyme, and chives, if
   liked
Butter
Pepper and salt

Serves 2

Break the eggs into a bowl, add pepper, salt, and herbs with water they were soaked in. Beat the eggs lightly. Heat a heavy pan, add just enough butter to grease it lightly, do not let it burn. Pour the eggs into the pan, stir briskly with a fork, especially round the edges where the omelette cooks first. As soon as the bottom sets, stop stirring and let the bottom brown. Tilt the pan and with a palette knife lift up the set mixture and let the liquid egg run underneath. Fold the omelette away from you and slide it on to a warm plate. Eat at once; it should be creamy, or 'baveuse' inside; if left, the eggs go on cooking.

Spaghetti alla Carbonara

Dried marjoram or oregano gives this dish a typical Italian flavour.

500g (1lb) spaghetti, cooked
   and drained
125g (4oz) fat bacon rashers,
   diced
15ml (1 tablespoon) dried
   marjoram or oregano,
   soaked for 15 minutes in
   just enough water to cover
2 cloves garlic, finely
   chopped
2 eggs, lightly beaten
15ml (1 tablespoon) olive oil
Parmesan or other dry
   grated cheese
Pepper

Serves 4–6

In a large saucepan, fry the bacon and garlic until the fat runs, and the bacon is crisp. Add the oil, let it heat then mix in the hot spaghetti, marjoram and pepper. Add the eggs, stirring in lightly until all the pasta is coated and the egg just set. Serve the dish at once with the grated cheese.

Tarragon Chicken with Suprême Sauce

1½–2kg (3½–4lb) roasting
   chicken, jointed
1 litre (2 pints) chicken stock
5ml (1 teaspoon) dried
   tarragon

Sauce
750ml (1½ pints) chicken stock
100g (4oz) butter
30ml (2 tablespoons) dried
   tarragon, soaked in a little
   of the stock
50g (2oz) plain flour
30ml (2 tablespoons) double
   cream
3 egg yolks
5ml (1 teaspoon) lemon juice
Pepper and salt to taste

Serves 4–6

Poach the chicken in the stock with the tarragon for 1–1½ hours, or until it is tender. Keep it hot while you make the sauce.

To make the sauce

Melt 75g (3oz) of the butter, stir in the flour, do not let it colour. Cook for 3–4 minutes, stirring all the time. Remove from heat, add hot stock, stir until smooth. Then cook slowly for 20 minutes. Now make the liaison. Beat the egg yolks and cream lightly together, add this to the sauce, stir gently and cook over a low heat until the egg yolks thicken the sauce. On no account let the sauce boil or it may curdle.

Gradually add small pieces of the remaining butter, stirring until they have melted. Add the lemon juice and the tarragon. Correct the seasoning. Arrange the chicken on a serving dish and cover with the sauce. Serve with boiled rice.

Note: For herb jellies, see Jellies chapter.

For the famous Scandinavian 'Gravlaks' dish using dill, see page 205 (Salting).

Drying nuts

Nuts are so commonplace that we seldom define and analyse what they are. They are fruits which have a skin, a hard shell and an outer husk. The husk may be a complete covering as in walnuts, almonds and chestnuts, or a leafy sheath, as in cob or hazel nuts. Nuts are rich in protein and fat, and in thiamine. Because of the amount of oil they contain they can quickly become rancid, so if you are not going to use them at once, they must be frozen, bottled or dried.

Most nuts are more digestible when fresh, especially walnuts; drying tends to toughen the fibres. But if you have a nut tree in the garden or hedgerows full of cob nuts, preserving the harvest may be well worth while. Most nuts, when ripe, fall and are easily collected.

Cob Nuts
The best come from Kent and they are usually ready early in October. You may be able to keep some until Christmas, but they do not keep longer than the end of December.

Remove any husks, arrange the nuts on a tray in a dry airy room. Inspect them for mildew and turn frequently. When reasonably dry, put them in net bags and hang in an airy place.

Sweet Chestnuts
When chestnuts are ripe the prickly husk usually opens, so that when they fall they are easy to take out. Wipe the nuts thoroughly with a dry cloth. Put alternate layers of dry sand and nuts in a box, put on the lid and keep in a cool place as they do in Perigord. Some people bury them in the garden. If you do this, put chestnuts and sand in a well sealed tin box. 'X' should mark the spot.

Another method is to hang them in loosely woven sacks in a cool dry place. If they shrivel, it is because they are too dry, and should be put in slightly damp sand for a few days – not too long or they will go mouldy.

Walnuts
The walnut tree is extremely ancient, and there are many varieties of *Juglandaceae* – Jupiter's nut. In England we chiefly grow the Iranian walnut, rather than the American black one. The walnut, like most nuts, falls from the tree when mature. It is wise to wait until they fall because they must be absolutely ripe before drying.

Remove the husks, remember that these contain a dark stain which is difficult to remove from the fingers or clothes, so wear an old pair of gloves and an apron. Clean the brown inner shells really thoroughly with a small hard brush. I prefer not to wash them in case the moisture penetrates.

Space them out on a tray in one layer, and let them dry out in an airy room – an electric fan helps drying. Turn occasionally. When they are as dry as possible the shells will be lighter in colour and lose some of their sheen. Hang them in net bags in a cool dry place. They should keep until the following spring, but watch them.

Walnut kernels
Shell the nuts carefully, try to keep the halves whole, remove the central membrane. The broken pieces are worth drying as they are useful for cakes and toppings. Arrange the kernels on trays and dry them out in a cool oven – take care that they do not scorch. When they look dry and are brittle when you break a piece, remove from the oven and let them cool. Store in a lidded container. Keep only for about three months.

201

Salting

Salting as a means of preserving food is almost as old as the process of drying, in the story of man's struggle to keep food edible for the stark days of winter. Without any knowledge of science his inventiveness led him to the discovery that salting delayed decay. It prevents the growth of most bacteria, yeasts and moulds and inactivates enzymes.

There are two main ways of salting, dry and wet.

Dry salting
Dry salt is rubbed into, and/or put between layers of food to preserve it. The salt draws out moisture from the food, and as the salt is dissolved in these exuded juices a brine is formed. In salting, and in brining, the food must be kept covered with brine at all times or it will spoil.

Wet salting or brining
Food is put into a suitable container and covered with brine. The strength of the brine depends on the food to be salted, but a salt solution of 500g (1lb) of salt to 3 litres (5 pints) of water prevents the growth of bacteria including those which are salt tolerant.

A third method used only for some vegetables is:

Light salting and fermenting
Vegetables are prepared, then lightly salted, kept in a warm place and allowed to ferment (see the recipe for Sauerkraut page 211).

Kinds of salt
There are two basic types of salt (Sodium chloride – NaCl): rock-salt, which is mined principally in Cheshire, and sea-salt which is made by evaporating sea water.

These are processed and treated to produce all the salts we buy. They vary in size of granule from blocks and coarse crystals to the extremely fine.

Additives are used to give flavour or to modify their performance.

1 Common, kitchen, cooking or block salt is the best for dry salting as it is pure, and sufficiently fine to cover and cling to the surfaces of food when rubbed in. It can be used for brining, too.

2 Rock- and sea-salt are usually sold in coarse crystals, which makes them the most suitable for brining, but not for dry salting. Sea-salt used to be called bay-salt.

3 Table salt is very finely ground and has magnesium carbonate and calcium phosphate added to prevent it absorbing moisture in damp weather. These make it flow smoothly, but the chemicals may cause deterioration if used in salting. It is also more expensive.

4 Iodised salt has iodine added. It is less common now than it was. It was used during war-time rationing to supplement the necessary intake of iodine. It must not be used in salting.

5 Flavoured salts. There are a number of salts on the market which have been given real or artificial flavours. There are garlic and onion salts and smoke-flavoured salts to which pyroligneous acid has been added to give the flavour of smoke. Do not use these for salting.

Equipment
Large containers with wide mouths. They can be glass jars, earthenware crocks or wooden barrels, depending on the food being salted. They must be large enough to hold the food to be salted comfortably. (Large sweet jars would be suitable.)

When it is necessary to press food down, as with meat and fish and brined vegetables, **a lid of wood** or other suitable material which fits into the top of the receptacle and acts like a 'piston'. *A saucer or plate with a weight* may be adequate.

A cutting board for preparing meat, fish and vegetables.

Wooden spoons.

Stainless steel knives suitable for fish, meat and vegetables.

A boning knife.

Scales, measuring cups and spoons.

Moistureproof lids, for vegetables. These can be glass with rubber seals, plastic, plastic lined metal or cork.

Saucepan for blanching vegetables.

Clean white cloths (cheesecloth, mutton cloth or old sheets).

Packaging material Cling film wrap, plastic bags, containers.

Cleaning earthenware crocks
These should be thoroughly washed, and then scalded with boiling water. If necessary, use a domestic bleach, in the proportions recommended by the manufacturer, to cleanse the crock. Rinse very thoroughly afterwards.

Cleaning wooden barrels
These should be scrubbed and scalded, then fill them with water and leave it in to swell the staves and make the barrels watertight.

Cleaning glass jars
These, with lids and rubber bands, usually only need to be thoroughly washed and dried, but if really dirty they can be sterilised (stand in large pan on a false bottom, cover with cold water, bring to boil, boil for 5 minutes).

Salted herrings
Fish to be salted must be fresh. Arrange the herrings in a small scoured barrel in layers with salt, bay leaves, peppercorns and an occasional chilli. The herrings are ready in three to four weeks.

Salting fish and meat

Salted pork, from lightly salted streaky pork to all kinds of bacon and ham, depends on salting for preservation and flavour. Greenback – unsmoked bacon – is cured entirely with salt and saltpetre. Smoked pork is first salted then smoked.

There are so many different kinds of ham that it is impossible to list them all. There are the smoked hams of Germany – Westphalian and katen-schinken from Schleswig Holstein. Parma and San Daniele from Italy and smoked hams from the Ardennes. These are mainly eaten raw. Honey and molasses cure ham from the United States. York and black skinned Bradenham hams have a special curing. Some recipes include beer and vinegar, but however different the recipes are, salt is the main preservative.

It is unusual nowadays for the housewife to cure a whole pig, but in my early youth my grandfather used to kill a pig around Michaelmas, and we would all help to rub a mixture of salt and saltpetre into the sides.

Homemade corned beef is infinitely better than the tinned bully on sale. Salt beef is as English as fog, and 'corned' is the old word for salted.

Method and preparation

Salt preserves by penetrating flesh and extracting moisture. It is an essential prelude to cold smoking, so this chapter should be read before attempting home smoking.

Methods of dry salting and brining are almost the same for most foods, but results are improved by following individual recipes.

Time in the curing bath depends upon size, thickness and weight. For meat count on a minimum of 25 days for dry salting, and a month for brining. Fish is done more quickly, but anchovies and herrings are kept for a long time in brine.

Potential health risks dictate clinical cleanliness. All animal foods can deteriorate until the salt has penetrated sufficiently to preserve them, therefore temperature control is very important.

Fish is fragile and should be kept from start to finish in a refrigerator. Meat is processed at a

Salting fish and meat

slightly higher temperature, and it should be kept at approximately 3°C, (38°F), that is in an outhouse or cool room, the whole time. At a lower temperature salt is not easily absorbed, at a higher one the food may go off. Curing was always done in the cold months. This was discovered empirically by the ancients, but is supported by modern scientists.

Fish is often brined before being dry salted. The brining draws out blood and other fluids, the fish is then drained, washed and dry salted. Meat is frequently dry salted before being put into a brine bath.

Dry salting

A proportion of salt and other ingredients is allowed to a given weight of food. This mixture is rubbed firmly into the flesh, so that it completely covers its surface, especially near the bone. Make sure pork is fresh; ideally it should have been killed within the previous 24 hours. Fish should be freshly caught. Beef should be in good mature condition.

The container should be cooled with ice-cold water or ice-cubes. Then it is filled with layers of food and salt, starting and ending with salt. Food should be pressed down and weighted, to prevent air pockets and stop the salt falling off. Usually salt draws out liquid and forms a brine. The food should be inspected periodically, turned over and more salt or brine added, according to individual recipes.

Brining

The specified ingredients can be dissolved in cold water, but I prefer to simmer the solution for 20 minutes, skim and cool. This dissolves salt, sugar and other soluble ingredients quickly and thoroughly, and helps spices to yield up their essential oils.

A good standard brine is 500g (1lb) salt to 3 litres (5 pints) of water, to which can be added sugar, spices and other ingredients.

Put the food in a thoroughly cleaned container, and pour the cold brine over to cover completely. Leave enough space to put in a non-metallic, weighted lid designed to keep the food submerged. The liquid should not come up to the rim, to avoid spilling. As some of the curing times are rather long for the amateur, I have given a Scandinavian way for speedy brining of ham (see opposite).

Salt injection

Professionals often inject brine into meat with a syringe, which is a quick method of getting deep penetration into large joints, but this requires considerable know-how, and is not recommended for home use.

Inspection

The brine bath should be examined once a week. If the texture of the brine has changed, if it has become sticky, discoloured or stringy, it should be drained off, the food washed. wiped, and put back in a fresh brine in an absolutely clean container.

Saltpetre (Potassium Nitrate)

Saltpetre is used in curing to give meat an attractive pink colour but it is inclined to harden the meat so sugar is also added to counteract this. It is obtainable from chemists. (See recipes.)

Storage

Store in a cool dry place, but do not keep earthenware crocks on a stone floor. Salted fish and meat can usually be refrigerated or frozen. Storage times are given in recipes.

Guidelines for salting meat and fish

1 Only preserve fish that is freshly caught and meat freshly killed.
2 Always prepare and handle food hygienically.
3 Always keep food in a cold, dry place while salting.
4 Use fine common salt for dry salting.
5 Rock- or sea-salt should be fully dissolved in boiling water and then allowed to cool for brining.
6 Never use salt that has additives, ie table, iodised or flavoured salt.
7 Use recommended proportion of salt to food or water.
8 Crocks or other containers used for salting should be large enough to hold food comfortably. They must be absolutely clean. For fish and meat there should be a headspace.
9 Food must be kept under the brine at all times to avoid contact with the air. Food should be pressed down so that there are no air pockets. Fish and meat should have a weight on top. This should not fit tightly but cover most of the surface of the container. Nothing metallic should be used.
10 Store in a cool dry place, but do not keep earthenware crocks on a stone floor, as this draws out the moisture.
11 Salted fish and meat can usually be refrigerated or frozen if liked.

What can go wrong

Deterioration. Never keep salted foods too long. In the old days salting was one of the only preserving methods known. One reads of HM's ships feeding the crew with salted pork alive with weevils, but this is to be avoided in the twentieth century. Do not exceed reasonable storage time (see recipes). Refrigeration or freezing lengthens keeping time.

Hardness of meat. This could be caused by too much saltpetre, or drying out during storage.

Fish and meat 'going off'. High protein and oily or fatty food is very susceptible. Absolute cleanliness must be observed at all times during processing. 'Going off' can also be caused by insufficient salt, air pockets forming during curing, food that was not really fresh when treatment commenced, or too high temperature during processing – meat is best cured in cold weather.

Over-saltiness. Salted food can be almost inedible if it is not washed, and soaked, to remove surplus salt. The exception to this is lightly salted food (which cannot be kept so long), ie *Gravlaks* and belly of pork.

Recipes using salted fish

Saltiness can make food unpalatable, so it should be washed under running water, soaked in fresh cold water, and cooked in fresh unsalted water. Flavour can be adjusted when done. The use of stock produced by cooking salt meat will depend on its taste. If it is too salty, the stock should be discarded. If more mildly flavoured, it can be used with water added if still rather salty) as a basis for soups – it is especially good with pulses and blander vegetables.

Fish to be eaten raw, like salted herrings, should be soaked for some time. Lightly salted fish like Scandinavian *Gravlaks*, and salted belly of pork do not need soaking.

If salted food is going to be smoked, it needs to be washed and air dried first. (see page 216).

Salted Herrings

2kg (4lb) herrings, scaled, cleaned and filleted
500g (1lb) salt
2–3 bay leaves, broken into small pieces
12–16 peppercorns
1–2 red chillies, chopped

Arrange layers of fish and salt, with bay leaves, peppercorns and chillies sprinkled here and there in a scoured small wooden barrel or an earthenware container. Weigh down, cover and keep in a cool place. They are ready in 3–4 weeks, but may be kept in the pickle for 6 months. As many as are wanted can be taken from the pickle.

Housewife's Herrings (Heringe Hausfrauenart)

4 herring fillets, salted
1 onion cut in rings
1 dessert apple, cubed
Pepper
Sour cream or milk

Serves 4 as an hors d'oeuvre or 2 as a main course

Well wash the herrings, soak them for one hour in a little water. Drain and cut them into 2·5cm (1in) lengths. Put them in a dish, sprinkle with pepper. Mix in the onion and apple. Cover with sour cream or milk. Marinate for 4–5 hours. Serve in the sour cream together with boiled potatoes.

Norwegian Cured Salmon (Gravlaks)

I first ate this in Norway, and each time I go to Scandinavia I order it. It is delectable.

In the old days the fish was salted, spiced, wrapped up and buried in the earth – hence the name *gravlaks*, which means buried salmon.

Today it is cured, put under a weight and kept in the refrigerator or a cold place. The salmon used must be very fresh.

1 whole salmon, beheaded, split in half and boned
To every 500g (1lb) salmon allow:
30g (1oz) salt
30g (1oz) caster sugar
6–9 white peppercorns
White pepper, freshly ground to taste
5ml (1 teaspoon) ground coriander
2·5ml (½ teaspoon) allspice
1 large handful fresh dill sprigs, or 15ml (1 tablespoon) dried dill, soaked

Leave the skin on the fish. Wipe it thoroughly with a clean cloth. Pat it as dry as possible. Mix together salt, sugar and spices. Rub them well all over the fish. Lay one piece of fish, skin side down, on the bottom of a shallow dish which should be covered with dill. Spread dill on both fillets, then lay the other piece of salmon on top, skin side up. Cover with greaseproof paper or foil. Put a heavy weight on top. Keep in a refrigerator or cold place for 2–3 days. It is now ready to eat, but it can be refrigerated for about a week. It is better that this dish is not frozen.

To serve

Remove spices and peppercorns and any excess surface salt from the fish. Arrange it on a dish or board, if possible decorated with fresh dill. Slice it on the slant, but in thicker slices than smoked salmon.

It is usually eaten raw, but thin slices can be fried and served with a spinach purée. It also makes a good filling for sandwiches.

Cured salmon is often served with a cold mustard sauce.

Mustard Sauce

60ml (4 tablespoons) olive oil
10ml (2 teaspoons) wine vinegar
15ml (1 tablespoon) made mustard
Pepper, salt and sugar to taste

Mix all the ingredients well together until they emulsify.

Quick Brine Cured Ham (Greenback)

For preliminary dry salting

For a 4–5kg (8–11lb) leg of pork:
350g (12oz) salt
125g (4oz) sugar
10ml (½ level tablespoon) saltpetre

For the brine

Enough water to cover the ham
For every 1 litre (2 pints) allow:
150g (6oz) salt
50g (2oz) sugar
5ml (1 teaspoon) saltpetre

To dry salt

Mix the salt, sugar and the saltpetre together. Rub them thoroughly into the ham, particularly round the bone. Put the ham in a container and keep in a refrigerator or cold place for 2–3 days. Take out and wipe well.

To brine

Bring the water to the boil, dissolve the salt, sugar and saltpetre in it. Let it cool. Pour over the ham and weigh down so that it is completely submerged. Leave in a refrigerator or cold place for 10–14 days.

Ham cured this way is designed to be eaten quickly, so it should be cooked within a week or kept in brine in a refrigerator or cold place for up to a month.

Recipes using salted meat

To cook brined ham

Wash the joint well. Soak for one hour in cold water. Put it in a saucepan, cover with fresh water, bring to the boil, pour off the water. Put the meat back again into a pan of cold water, bring to the boil. Skim, cover and simmer until tender, allowing 20 minutes for each 450g (1lb) and 20 minutes over. Drain or lift out and remove rind carefully. Serve hot or cold.

Both the following are good and economical lightly salted cuts, easy to make and to eat.

A Simple Way to Pickle Belly of Pork

Rub the belly well with plenty of salt. Place in crock, cover and weigh down. Leave for 25 days. Turn each belly over daily. If at any time the meat is not covered by salt or brine, add more salt. Leave in brine in a cool place or wrap in foil and refrigerate, for up to 3 weeks, or freeze (for up to 3 months).

To use
Remove from brine or refrigerator, wash well and cook.

Boiled Pickled Pork Belly

1kg (2lb) pickled pork
1 onion, sliced
1 carrot, sliced
1 small turnip, sliced
1 celery stalk, chopped
5–6 peppercorns
Pease pudding

Serves 4–5

Put the pork in cold water, bring to boiling point, skim. Add vegetables and peppercorns. Cover and simmer until tender. Allow 30 minutes per 450g (1lb) and 30 minutes over. Serve with the vegetables and heated pease pudding.

To Salt and Dry Pig's Cheeks

Allow 500g (1lb) common salt to 2 cheeks (chaps). Rub them well all over. Place in crock, cover and weigh down. Leave for 3 weeks. Turn over daily and make sure they stay under the brine. After the 3 weeks, hang up in a cool, dry, airy place until there is no moisture visible. Keeps in the refrigerator for 1–2 weeks, or in the freezer for up to 3 months.

To use
Soak for 3–4 hours.

Pig's Cheek

1 pig's cheek (soaked)
Dried breadcrumbs
    (raspings)

Serves 3–4

It is important to follow either the imperial or the metric weights and measures in any one recipe. Do not mix them.

Put the cheek into cold water, bring to the boil, simmer for about 2½ hours until tender. Remove from water, strip off rind. Coat with the crumbs. Serve cold cut in thin slices.

Corned Beef

Silverside, brisket or cheaper cuts of meats are good for corned beef.

When processing a large quantity of meat, cut joints to suit your family requirements.

For each 6kg (12lb) of beef after trimming and boning, allow: 500–700g (1–1¼lb) salt.

Put a layer of salt in a container. Rub the meat all over with the salt, put it in. If there are several layers of meat, cover each layer with salt, ending with salt. There should be plenty of space at the top as 2½ litres (4 pints) of liquid are added later. Cover, then leave for 24 hours. Make a well flavoured solution. To each 2½ litres (4 pints) of water allow:

250g (8oz) soft brown sugar
10ml (½oz) saltpetre
2 bay leaves
12 peppercorns
6 whole allspice
Small piece of cinnamon
   stick
3 whole coriander seeds
5ml (1 teaspoon) bicarbonate
   of soda

Dissolve the saltpetre, brown sugar and bicarbonate of soda in the boiling water. Add the spices. Pour it over the meat. Press the meat down so that it is completely submerged. Weigh it down, cover.

The bicarbonate of soda retards fermentation which could be caused by the sugar should the temperature rise above 3°C (38°F).

Keep the meat in the brine for 3–4 weeks in a refrigerator or cold place not exceeding 3°C (38°F).

If preferred the meat can now be removed from the brine, dried, packed and frozen. Before the advent of refrigeration it was kept in the brine for 2–3 months without apparent ill effect. Nowadays with our knowledge of hygiene we should take advantage of modern methods for complete security.

To cook

Wipe the meat, soak in cold water for one hour. Put it in a saucepan, add fresh cold water bring slowly to the boil, skim well.

Now add to each 2kg (4lb):

Bouquet garni
3 cloves
Cover and simmer gently. Allow 25 minutes for each 450g (1lb) and 25 minutes over. An hour before the joint is cooked add:

6 carrots, sliced
2 turnips, sliced
3 large onions, chopped

To serve

Arrange the meat on a hot dish, surround with the vegetables and pour over some of the stock. Suet dumplings go well with this, or boiled potatoes.

Scandinavian Christmas Ham

4–5kg (8–11lb) cured ham
1–2 bay leaves
6 whole allspice
9–10 peppercorns

Coating for ham
1 egg white
30ml (2 tablespoons) made
   mustard
45ml (3 tablespoons) brown
   sugar
Dried breadcrumbs
   (raspings)

Follow recipe for cooking brined ham (see page 206) until the ham has been brought back to simmering point, then add the bay leaves and spices. Cover and simmer until tender. Leave to cool in the liquid without a lid. The next day rinse the ham, remove rind.

To coat the ham
Mix together the egg white, mustard and sugar and spread all over the ham, then sprinkle with breadcrumbs. Bake at 200°C, 400°F, Gas Mark 6, for 30–45 minutes or until nice and brown.

To Cure an Ox Tongue

1 ox tongue weighing about
   3½–4kg (7–8lb)

For the brine
500g (1lb) salt
100g (4oz) soft brown sugar
5ml (1 teaspoon) black pepper
25g (1oz) juniper berries
10ml (½oz) saltpetre
2½ litres (4 pints) water

Make the brine by boiling all the ingredients together for 20 minutes. Skim. Let it get cold. Put the tongue in a scrupulously clean crock. Pour in the brine. Cover and weigh down so that it is completely submerged. Keep in the refrigerator. It will be ready in 10–14 days, but can be kept for 3–4 months in the brine in the refrigerator.

To Cook Cured Ox Tongue

1 cured ox tongue
1 large onion
1 large carrot
2 celery stalks
2 cloves
1 bay leaf
1 sprig of parsley
Pepper to taste
Jellying stock (aspic or
   consommé)
Water

Wash and soak the tongue in cold water for 3–4 hours. Put in a pan, cover with fresh cold water, bring to the boil, skim thoroughly. Add all the other ingredients except the jellying stock. Cover and simmer for about 4 hours or until the tongue is tender. Skim when necessary.

When the tongue is cooked, put it at once into cold water. When it is cool enough to handle, make a slit at the base, pull off the skin, get rid of the roots and small bones. Make sure none are left. Curl the tongue round tightly in a cake tin or mould. Cover with the jellying stock. Put a piece of foil or greaseproof paper on top, arrange a weight on this. Leave to cool and set overnight. To serve, turn out and slice as thinly as possible in rounds. **207**

Salting vegetables

This is a task that is only worth while if there is a glut, or threat of price increases, or you have no other way of storage.

Blanching and refreshing
Blanching and refreshing slows down or arrests the action of enzymes, and it also helps to preserve natural colour. Although it is not necessary to salting, it is a worthwhile operation. Fairly small quantities of the vegetable being processed should be tied in a cloth and plunged into boiling water, which must be brought back to the boil as quickly as possible. They should be heated through, but not at all cooked. Remove them, and plunge immediately into a bowl of ice-cold water. The whole process should be as quick as possible or the vegetables may become mushy. See freezing chapter for blanching times.

Dry salting
Dry salting is best for juicy vegetables, like runner beans. If not enough liquid is extracted from the vegetables, a brine solution must be added.

Choose young, fresh vegetables – young turnips, beans, cabbages, broccoli and small onions can be done like this. Allow 500g (1lb) common salt to each $1\frac{1}{2}$kg (3lb) of vegetables. Prepare them as for cooking. They may be blanched and refreshed, but this is not essential.

Put a thick layer of salt in the bottom of the crock. Then put alternate layers of vegetables and salt ending with salt. The proportions of salt to vegetables must be correct, and the salt must be **evenly** distributed.

Press down thoroughly so there are no air pockets. Cover and leave for 3–5 days, then add more vegetables to fill the jar – you have to do this because they shrink. As the salt draws out the moisture from the vegetables it makes a strong brine. If there is not enough at any time add some more salt. Seal with a moistureproof lid. Make certain that all the vegetables are submerged. Store in a cool dry place on wooden shelves for up to one year. Always discard any which do not look good.

In order not to open and close a large vessel, if you only use small quantities at a time, transfer the vegetables to smaller jars and pour in enough brine to cover them. Seal and store.

Brining vegetables
Onions, cauliflowers (cut into florets) and red or green pimientos (peppers) can be brined successfully.

This method is best for vegetables that have little juice. Choose fresh, young vegetables, without any blemishes. Trim, wash, wipe and peel when necessary.

Cold water is added to the salt to compensate for the lack of juiciness, so make a brine using 500g (1lb) common salt to 3 litres (5 pints) of water.

Put the vegetables into well cleaned crocks or preserving jars. Pour in the brine, put a weight on top to keep all the vegetables down. Examine them once a week to make sure they are all under the brine. Leave for 4–5 weeks, then remove the weight, cover and seal. Store in a cool dry place.

To use dry salted and brined vegetables
Wash and soak in several fresh cold waters for 2–4 hours to remove salt. Cook in unsalted boiling water until tender.

Guidelines for salting vegetables

These are the same as for fish and meat, **except:**

1 When dry salting vegetables, there should be no headspace in the container. Top up with more vegetables if necessary. There should not be a weight on top.

2 A moistureproof lid must be used for sealing either dry salted or brined vegetables.

What can go wrong

Slimy vegetables. Vegetables will be slimy if not enough salt was used, or if they were not completely submerged during salting.

Discoloration. Table or iodised salt will discolour vegetables.

Shrivelling. This can be caused by storing in too warm or too dry an atmosphere.

Salting runner beans
If you have a glut of runner beans, it's worth dry salting some. Choose a wide-mouthed jar, and be careful to use the correct proportion of salt to beans.

Recipes using salted vegetables

Salted Vine Leaves

Many people have grape vines in their gardens, but more often than not the grape harvest is negligible. There is a crop to be won however, which can make the famous Middle Eastern dolmades.

Choose the youngest and best leaves when they are still tender. Blanch them for about 5 minutes when they should be limp.

1 onion, finely chopped
A sprinkling of thyme
30ml (2 tablespoons) chopped parsley
Pepper and salt
15–30ml (1–2 tablespoons) oil for frying
1 × 396g (14oz) tin of tomatoes

Serves 6–8

Brined Pimientos (Peppers)

Choose red or green young pimientos without any blemishes. Wash, wipe and quarter them. Remove seeds and membranes. Now follow the instructions for brining vegetables (page 208).

Refresh immediately. Drain and weigh. To each 500g (1lb) of vine leaves allow:
125g (4oz) coarse common salt. Now follow the recipe for dry salted vegetables. To use, rinse under running water and then soak for 2–3 hours, changing the water once.

Stuffed Vine Leaves (Dolmades)

36–40 salted vine leaves, well rinsed and soaked for 2–3 hours
200g (8oz) minced lamb or beef
50g (2oz) cooked rice

Soften the onion in hot oil. Add meat, rice, herbs, pepper and salt to onion, stir and cook for a few minutes, stirring, until meat loses its red colour. Put 10ml (2 teaspoons) of the mixture on each leaf. Roll up, tucking in the ends to make a small neat packet. Put in a heavy pan, packed close together, layers can be separated by covering them with vine leaves. Pour the tinned tomatoes over. Cover and cook slowly on a low heat for 1–1½ hours. Serve hot or drain and serve cold as an hors d'oeuvre.

Salted vine leaves

If you have a vine it may not, in a cool climate, have edible grapes, but it will probably have leaves. These can be picked while still young, dry salted and used to make the delicious Dolmades or Stuffed vine leaves.

It is important to follow either the imperial or the metric weights and measures in any one recipe. Do not mix them.

Pimiento Salad

You will need the equivalent of 2 brined pimientos; wash thoroughly and soak overnight. Cook in boiling unsalted water until they are just tender. Drain well and cool.

2–3 large tomatoes, sliced
5–6 radishes, cut in circles
Chives, chopped
60–90ml (4–6 tablespoons) olive oil
Lemon juice to taste
Pepper
Lettuce leaves

Serves 4 as an accompaniment to meat or fish, or 2 as a snack meal.

Line bowl with lettuce leaves. Dice the pimientos, mix with the tomatoes, radishes and chives. Mix together oil and lemon juice, season with pepper, pour over the vegetables.

Arrange vegetables in the centre of the lettuce leaves just before serving.

Light Salted and Fermented Cabbage (Sauerkraut)

This is lightly salted cabbage which is allowed to ferment. It makes delicious, simple and easily prepared dishes. It has the reputation of being much more digestible than freshly cooked cabbage. Choose really fresh white cabbages.

For every 2½kg (5lb) cabbage allow:

50g (2oz) coarse common salt
10–12 juniper berries
5ml (1 teaspoon) caraway or cumin seeds
2 bay leaves

Wash the cabbage and divide it into 4. Remove cores. Hold the quarters firmly on a cutting board, shred finely with a sharp knife. Have a wooden tub, or a wide-mouthed jar or crock large enough to hold the cabbage. Make sure it is scrupulously clean. Put alternate layers of salt, spices and cabbage in. Press the cabbage down hard. Cover with a thin sterilised cloth, weigh down with a plate or other 'piston'. Fermentation should begin within 24 hours if the container is kept in a warm place, about 20°C (70°F). It is working when small bubbles appear on the surface. Remove scum daily and replace cloth and plate. Do this until fermentation ceases – about 3 weeks. It may be necessary to add more brine to keep the cabbage submerged, if so, add 25g (1oz) salt dissolved in 1 litre (2 pints) of water.

When the cabbage is ready (2–3 weeks) it should be a pleasant yellow. Use it up within 3 months. If you wish you can sterilise it and keep it in sealed jars. To do this pour off the brine, heat to boiling point. Add cabbage and bring back to simmering. Pack immediately into sterilised, heated preserving jars and process in a boiling water bath for 25 minutes. (See bottling chapter.)

Chinese cabbage can be shredded like sauerkraut; kohl rabi and young turnips can be cut into fine strips and then prepared as with sauerkraut.

Rhineland Garnished Sauerkraut
(Sauerkraut Garniert)

A well cooked and garnished sauerkraut makes a lusty meal. One of the best I have ever eaten was in Luxembourg. It can be as simple as you like, with just frankfurters, or slices of boiled bacon on top, or it can be sophisticated and varied with an assortment of pork products piled on it.

1kg (2lb) sauerkraut
4 frankfurters
4 thin pork chops fried until lightly browned and cooked
4 thin slices of smoked pork or 4 thin slices of cooked ham
Any other sausages you care to add
1 large onion, sliced
3 sharp apples, peeled, cored and sliced
3–4 juniper berries, crushed
250ml (½ pint) meat stock, or stock and white wine
1 clove garlic, crushed
5–10ml (1–2 teaspoons) sugar
1 bay leaf
Pepper
Fat for frying

Serves 4 hearty appetites

Rinse the sauerkraut under cold running water, while breaking it up with a fork. This helps to remove excess salt.

Fry onion in a little fat until it softens without changing colour. Check that there are no lumps in the sauerkraut. Add it to the onion. Put all the ingredients, except the meats, into a large saucepan. Cover with the stock and wine, stir thoroughly to mix. Cover and simmer slowly for 30–40 minutes, or until the cabbage is cooked, but still crisp. Taste and correct seasoning. Arrange the meats on top, cover and heat through very slowly. If you cook them too fast the frankfurters may split.

Serve as soon as everything is heated through – with boiled potatoes, German mustard and, preferably, chilled lager.

Smoking

In the days when food laden spits turned in front of roaring log fires, our ancestors hung meat, fish and fowl in the chimney to dry and smoke gently. And their forebears did the same over camp fires hundreds of years before. Even now this flavourful method of preserving is so little changed that it remains a link with the past. Nowadays food is often smoked for the taste and not to preserve it.

There are two basic forms of smoking, hot and cold.

Hot smoking is a delightful method of cooking. Scandinavian anglers cook their catch in their smoke box at the lakeside. I bought my first smoke box in Finland and use it for fish, meat, sausages and poultry. There is now an English hot smoke box available (see Where to buy equipment). Strictly, hot smoking is a type of barbecuing and **not** a method of preservation. Most dishes cooked this way are served hot, but they can be eaten cold. Unfortunately, they keep no longer than any other cooked food, but they can be refrigerated for 2–3 days.

Moist smoke cooking is a kind of hot smoking, imported from the United States, which combines smoke with steam – there is a moist smoker now available in this country (see Where to buy equipment). It pot roasts large joints, whole hams and turkeys of up to 12kg (25lb), giving them a smokey flavour. It does not preserve in any way.

For **cold smoking**, food is usually prepared by first salting and drying (see instructions in salting chapter, page 202), it then absorbs pyroligneous acid and other volatile substances produced by the controlled combustion of suitable woods. Salt, dehydration and smoke together prevent most causes of spoilage. In the past this was one of the best means of preservation.

Hot smoking

Food can be prepared as for grilling, and the cooking time is similar to that for grilling or frying. Smoking is best done out of doors.

Buy or make a smoke box large enough for your family (see opposite and Where to buy equipment). Mine is 28cm by 18cm (11in by 7in). This cooks comfortably for three, and at a pinch for four. It is like a Boy Scout's billy can – oblong, with a lid which slides on to close it, but does not prevent smoke escaping.

A layer of sawdust – from hickory, oak, apple or other hardwood – is spread on the bottom; do not use too much. Over this is put a combined drip tray and cover for the smouldering sawdust. Mine is a sheet of thin metal with bent down corners which act as legs; it must not touch the sawdust. It catches any drips which fall during smoking and prevents them from burning in the sawdust. Above this is a grid, also with legs, on which the food is put. Then the lid is slid on.

Put the box on a spirit stove, gas ring or any other heat source. The sawdust will soon smoulder. Adjust heat to keep it smouldering gently. The smoke will eddy round the drip tray, and the box becomes a miniature oven, while smoking the food.

Food should be turned over once at half cooking time. For example, a 250g (8oz) salmon cutlet will take about 20 minutes to cook, so open the box after 10 minutes, turn the food, close the box and continue smoking.

Equipment for hot smoking

Smoke box (bought, see Where to buy equipment; or improvised, see below), with drip tray, grid and lid.

Heat source and stand for smoke box – the stand, and often a windbreak, are supplied if you buy a commercial smoke box.

Kitchen tongs, or other utensil to turn food.

Hardwood sawdust, preferably hickory, oak or apple. This depends on supply (see Where to buy equipment).

To improvise a hot smoke box

Use any old lidded metal container which is large enough to hold the amount of food you plan to cook. The simplest way to improvise one is to use an old saucepan. Get a metal plate that will fit easily inside. Mount this on 1·5cm (½in) metal legs screwed underneath the rim of the plate. This makes an efficient drip tray because it will hold any drippings without overflowing.

Make a grill to hold the food by cutting down an old frying basket until its sides are about 4cm (1½in) high. Upside down, this will hold the food to be smoked. The saucepan lid will almost certainly let enough smoke escape and air enter. If it is to be used with a spirit stove, a secure stand must be invented.

For moist smoke cooking

A moist smoker – one can now be bought in this country (see Where to buy equipment).

Moist smoke cooking method

Charcoal is burned in a grate in a metal cylinder mounted on legs. If smoke is required small logs of hardwood are put on the charcoal.

Cooking may take as long as 12 hours. The maker's instructions tell how much charcoal must be put in to last that time without refuelling.

Above the fire is a pan containing water, wine or marinade. This boils and the steam blends with the smoke to envelop the food which is put on a grill above. The whole is topped by a dome.

All the condensed moisture drips back into the water pan making the gravy. The meat is being continually basted. The dome should not be removed during cooking, so after the initial work, there is no further labour.

Full instructions go with the equipment.

Guidelines for hot smoking

1 The smell of food-laden smoke is pervasive and lingers like stale cigarette smoke for days. All smoking is best done out of doors.

2 Cover the bottom of the box with a thin layer of sawdust. Do not use too much.

3 Put in the drip tray, it should not touch the sawdust.

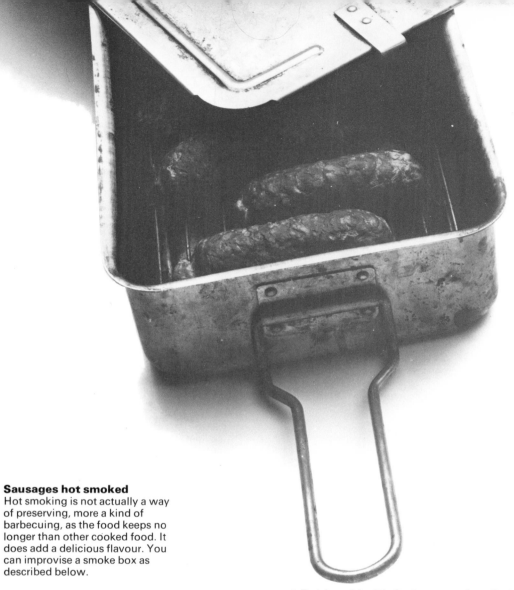

Sausages hot smoked

Hot smoking is not actually a way of preserving, more a kind of barbecuing, as the food keeps no longer than other cooked food. It does add a delicious flavour. You can improvise a smoke box as described below.

An improvised hot smoke box

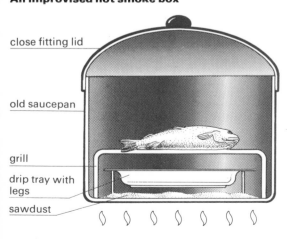

close fitting lid

old saucepan

grill

drip tray with legs

sawdust

4 Put in grid with food arranged so that there is room round it for smoke circulation.
5 Close lid and mount smoke box on heat source.
6 Heat source can be any type of heater. If it is to be a spirit stove or any other form of camp cooker a firm stand for the box must be used. Commercial smoke boxes usually supply a combined windbreak and stand.
7 Adjust heat so the sawdust smoulders gently.
8 Open box half way through cooking time, turn food over and continue smoking.
9 Smoke boxes are difficult to clean, but do your best with detergents, abrasives, and elbow grease. The drip tray can be covered with aluminium foil which catches the drippings and is afterwards thrown away.

What can go wrong

Sawdust not smouldering. This will happen if there is too little heat.
Food burning. Too much heat will burn food.
Food over- or under-cooked. Timing of recipes must be carefully followed.

Recipes for hot smoking

Hot Smoked Herrings Finnish Style

4 herrings
Pepper and salt

Serves 4

Scale, gut and clean the fish. Rub them all over with salt and pepper. Leave in a cool place for 2 hours. Wrap in greased, greaseproof paper and then wrap them round with several layers of damp newspaper.

Put this 'parcel' on the embers of a smoking camp fire and let the newspaper smoulder. When all the newspaper has burnt down, remove it from the embers and open it up. Serve hot from the fire. Small fish like herrings should be ready to eat in about 10 minutes. One or two experiments will show you how much newspaper you need. This can be successful with larger fish, if you wrap them up enough.

Hot Smoked Trout or Mackerel

Clean, gut and remove heads from fish. Make 2 diagonal cuts on each side. Spread 50ml (3 tablespoons) of sawdust to cover the bottom of the box. Smoke for 20 minutes for small to medium size fish up to 250g (8oz). Turn after 10 minutes. For larger fish allow proportionately longer time.

Hot Smoked Salmon

This bears no resemblance to the usual smoked salmon. Cutlets or fillets are best for cooking this way. Proceed as for smoked trout or mackerel.

Hot Smoked Sausages

Cooked like this even the most mediocre sausages taste and look attractive with shiny dark brown skins.

8 sausages
1 bay leaf, torn up

Serves 4

Spread 15ml (1 tablespoon) sawdust and the bay leaf evenly in the smoke box. Put in the drip tray and grid. Arrange the sausages so that they do not touch one another. Close box and put on heat source. Keep at high heat until sawdust is smouldering and a little smoke comes out of the box.

After $7\frac{1}{2}$ minutes, open box, turn sausages over. Close box and continue smoking for a further $7\frac{1}{2}$ minutes. Chipolatas will take less time. Eat hot or cold.

As an interesting alternative, spread a thin layer of curry paste over the sausages before smoking.

Warning. As sausages are greasy there may be quite a lot of burnt fat on the drip tray, so clean it off immediately.

Hot Smoked Chicken Drumsticks, Pork or Lamb Chops

4 drumsticks or 4 chops

Serves 4

Spread 30–50ml (2–3 tablespoons) sawdust in the box. Proceed in the same way as for sausages, allowing extra cooking time – about 15 minutes a side depending on size and thickness of food.

A Smoke'n Pit hot moist smoke box

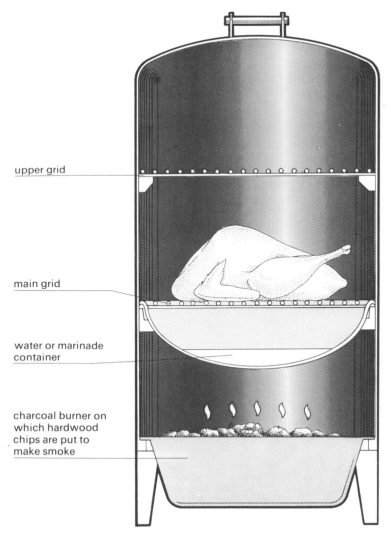

upper grid

main grid

water or marinade container

charcoal burner on which hardwood chips are put to make smoke

Cold smoking

All food to be smoked must be absolutely fresh and of good quality. It should not have been frozen, but chilled meat can be used. It is essential that all food to be smoked is kept refrigerated before being smoked. In the old days smoke curing was usually done in the cool days of autumn and early winter.

Fish **must** come straight from the water, and not from an inland fishmonger. In fact, fish smoking is only for you if your smoker is near a fishing port or if fishing is your successful hobby. (I know two Sydney surgeons who own a shack on the coast and have a smoke house up wind from them. They smoke their holiday's catch and transport it in triumph back to town.)

Examine your viands carefully, wash and wipe them and then dry salt or brine them (or both) according to instructions. Fish is always brined and dry salted, meat one or the other. Use the techniques outlined in the last chapter (see also page 216). After the specified salt-curing time, take the food from the brine, wash, wipe or brush off as much surface salt as possible. Hang in a cool, airy place, and let it dry. Use an electric fan if there is no natural draught. Fish takes from 1–3 hours, meat up to 24, depending on weight, to dry.

The smoker (see page 217) should be made operational, the fire started and smoke flowing. Make sure the smoke is untainted by any

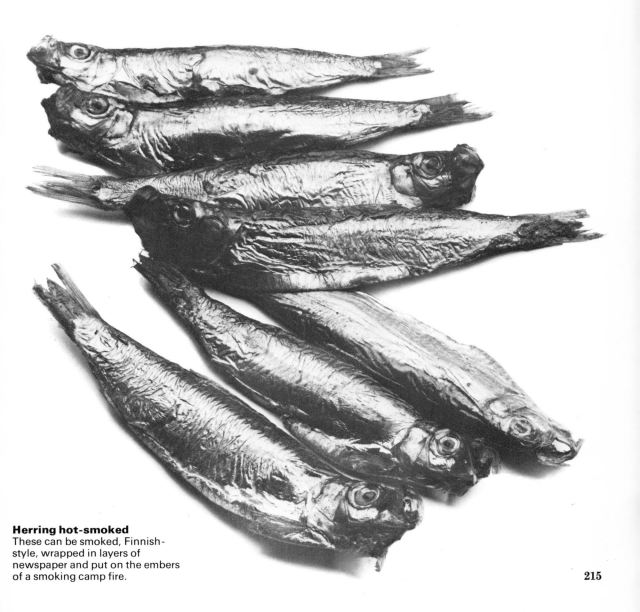

Herring hot-smoked
These can be smoked, Finnish-style, wrapped in layers of newspaper and put on the embers of a smoking camp fire.

215

Cold smoking

substance used to light it. The food should have a string tied round, or threaded through the end or shank, or it can be put on a sterile hook. The holes you see in a smoked haddock show how they have been hung by a string or rod through them. Everything should be hung in the smoker so that it is clear of the sides and other foods, for the smoke must circulate freely.

The temperature in the smoker should be between 21 and 33°C (70–90°F). Fish must be kept at the lower heat because it is so perishable. A really dense smoke with little heat is needed. Meat should be smoked near to the higher temperature. If the temperature is too high the heat melts the fat and forms a firm, smoky skin which prevents smoke penetrating and moisture escaping. If the fat of meat is melted it may become rancid.

For fish, smoke must be kept going continuously. For meat, it can be let out at night, and relighted in the morning, but the full number of hours in smoke must be adhered to.

After trying out our recipes (beginning on page 218), you may want to smoke other things so here are some possibilities with approximate smoking times. The method of salting, drying and then smoking must be carefully followed and you will need to experiment a little before you reach perfection.

Approximate smoking times for fish, depending on size and thickness, are:
Haddocks: 12 hours for a fair-sized one
Herrings: 6–8 hours
Plaice: 8 hours
Trout and mackerel: 12–14 hours

Meat needs a longer smoking time. Pork, beef, lamb and venison need about the same time as the ham and mutton given in the recipes, depending on the size and thickness of the joint, ie about three days.

The length of time of smoking depends to some extent on personal taste. After about three-quarters of the smoking time, you can test for texture and flavour by cutting off a small sample – if it is not to your liking, smoke longer. It is a good idea for beginners to experiment by smoking small items only.

At the end of the smoking time, remove fish from the smoker and let it air dry, then pack fish separately and store in the refrigerator for not longer than three months. Freezing is not recommended for home-smoked fish. Wrap meat in mutton- or cheesecloth and hang in a cool, airy, place for up to one year, or pack for refrigeration, (for short-term keeping).

Fish and meat suitable for cold smoking
Salmon, trout, mackerel, eels, herrings, haddocks, whiting and plaice.

Pork, beef, venison, lamb, mutton, breasts of geese.

All produce for smoking must be good quality and very fresh.

In other days and in other places every edible animal from elk and reindeer to ptarmigan and buffalo have been smoked. Dreadful to recount

smoked horse is popular in Belgium. In Scotland and Iceland smoked leg of mutton or lamb are treated like hams.

Preparation of fish
Scale, clean, and if necessary split and remove backbone, or fillet the fish. Small fish like sprats or young herrings can be smoked whole.

Brining and dry salting
It is most important to keep fish in a refrigerator. The brine should be ice cold before using. Spices, such as bay leaves, juniper berries, peppercorns, allspice, can be added to the brine according to taste.

Dissolve 1kg (2lb) common salt in 5 litres (8 pints) of cold water. Chill. Soak the fish in this for 3–4 hours according to size. This draws out the blood and firms the flesh.

Drain, wash and wipe the fish. It is now ready to be dry salted. Allow $1\frac{3}{4}$kg ($3\frac{1}{2}$lb) salt to every 5kg (10lb) fish. Spices can be added with the salt.

Put a layer of salt in a sterilised earthenware container. Rub the fish with salt, and put in layers with salt in between. Always put salt on top. Leave in a cool place for 3–4 hours.

Remove fish, wash thoroughly in cold water, pat dry and hang in a cool, airy place. An electric fan is useful. After 1–3 hours, depending on weight, the fish is ready for smoking. It should look smooth and shiny.

Cold smoking equipment
Smoker unit complete with firebox linked to it by piping, and chimney.
Hooks, rings or bars on which to hang foods in smoker.
String or hooks to suspend food.
Oven thermometer.
Sharp knives and saw for 'butchering'.
Poker and rake for firebox.
Fuel container.
Fuel for kindling fire. There are odourless barbecue lighters, solid and liquid, which are useful if you are using solid fuel. Do not use dangerous or smelly lighters, like petrol.
Smoke generating material and other fuels. Hardwood sawdust, chips, or green twigs, preferably hickory, apple, oak or hornbeam, but not resinous wood like pine. Aromatic woods, like bay or juniper twigs, or fennel stalks, give special flavours.
A heat source is needed to keep sawdust smouldering. A metal tray to hold the sawdust goes over a heat source in the firebox. The heat can be charcoal, camp stove of any sort, gas or electricity.
A stand for smoker to raise it above the firebox, or the firebox can be sunken.
Space in the open air to manoeuvre. This should be sufficiently isolated so that the smells are not a nuisance to yourself and others.
Packaging material for hanging, storing, re-frigerating smoked goods.
Materials for cleaning smoker and its accessories.

Guidelines for cold smoking

1 Meats and especially fish must be impeccably fresh.

2 They should be pre-salted or brined, or both, according to instructions, and air dried.

3 Prepare food for hanging with string or hooks.

4 Light fire, caring for it until it is smouldering and producing enough smoke. Make sure the smoke is untainted by substance used to light it.

5 Check temperature in smoker. You should have a thermometer.

6 Hang the food in the smoker so it does not touch any other food, or the sides of the smoker.

7 Close the door, or put on lid. Tend fire periodically, adjust air inlet if necessary, and stoke.

8 Fish smoking should be continuous for recommended period (see page 216 and recipes). When smoking meat, the fire can be let out and rekindled in the morning, but the full number of hours in smoke must be given (see page 216 and recipes).

9 It does not matter where the smoke goes if it does not annoy your neighbours.

10 Have packaging material ready for storage. Pack fish for the refrigerator. If you are going to hang hams or joints after smoking envelop them in mutton-or cheesecloth.

11 There are cold smokers available commercially now. If you buy one, follow the maker's instructions.

What can go wrong

Failure to keep well. Use of inferior food or insufficient salting will reduce keeping time and impair quality.

Melting fat. Too great heat in smoker tends to seal the surface of the food, so it cooks and the fat may run.

Unpleasant odours. Use of firelighters, petrol or other highly flammable fluids may create unpleasant and lingering odours which can spoil the product. This is also dangerous.

Failure of smoke to penetrate food. Too low a temperature in smoker.

Uneven curing. Foods touching one another may prevent even curing.

Too much flame without smoke. Bad control of firebox.

Erratic smoke flow. Inefficient stoking; or wood burning with flame.

Nauseous stink. Drippings or bits of food left in smoker, and allowed to decay.

To make a cold smoker

The core of your smoker is an enclosed area large enough to hold the food you wish to cure, with enough space for smoke to circulate freely round the hanging food.

To make a smoker you can use any available, or obtainable, metal, brick, or clay 'box'. The method is the same whether you use the oven of an old cooking stove, or an outbuilding. Basically there are two types of cold smoker, one with a door, the other with a lid.

Whatever you convert, the first step is to strip it of everything not needed for its new job. Take out the burners from a cooker, the freezer box from a fridge, or the shelves from a metal cupboard. If you use a metal drum, take off the top and thoroughly remove any trace of its original contents, ie burn out an oil drum. It should smell and look perfectly clean.

At this stage the services of a handyman are required. Two holes in which you can fix the piping must be cut in the smoker. One should be very near the bottom to take the pipe from the firebox, and the other at, or near, the top to take the chimney.

Hooks or rings should be screwed into the top of the smoker, or bars put across on which to hang the food. It may be possible to use the supports of the original shelves.

A clip can be put on the door or lid to hold a thermometer which can be seen quickly when the smoker is opened. Sophisticated smokers have an internal thermometer which can be read from the outside.

The firebox should be a nearly closed grate whose flue carries all the smoke generated through a pipe to the smoker. There must be a heat source within the firebox – this can be a brazier made from an old metal bucket with holes punched in it, a charcoal pan like that of a barbecue, or a gas ring or electric element.

If you are burning hardwood chips they will burn on their own, but if you use sawdust it must be put in a tray mounted above the primary heat source which keeps it smouldering. The top of the box, which can be cone-shaped, should be linked by piping to the bottom of the smoker. It is part of the flue. The fire should be at least 30cm (12in) from the smoker so that the smoke can cool before reaching the food.

The opening through which the fire is stoked should be adjustable so that the air intake can be controlled, as combustion must be slow. This only applies to solid fuel. Gas, oil or electricity are easy to regulate.

The chimney for the smoker need not be long, it completes the draught for the firebox. It can be in the top of the box, in the lid of a drum or the roof of a shed. I have even heard of smokers made of wattle and daub, but the system remains the same.

217

Cold smoking

Converting a refrigerator into a smoke-box

First, strip it of everything not necessary to its new role. Remove the ice-box and probably the shelves too, to give a freer circulation of smoke. Holes should then be cut, one for the intake pipe near the bottom of the refrigerator and one for the chimney near, or at the top. Hooks or rings for hanging the food should be screwed into the roof, and a thermometer clipped to the inside of the door. The firebox containing the heat source should be far enough from the smoker — at least 30cm (12in) — to allow smoke to cool before it reaches the food. (More details on page 217).

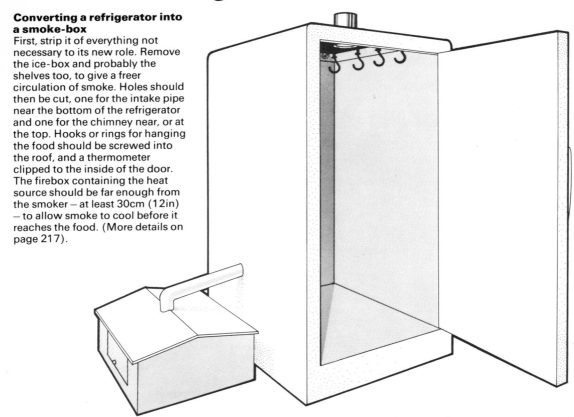

Recipes for cold smoking

Smoked Eels

I visited Steinhuder Meer, in north Germany, to find out how to smoke eels. The whole village lives by catching and smoking them.

Eels are usually wriggling round alive in a tank so you can be certain they are fresh.

Smoked eels to be enjoyed at their best should be eaten within a week. Then they are lusciously oily. Eels can be refrigerated or frozen, but they lose subtlety and flavour.

Split the eels, gut and remove the bones, leave the skin on. If you can get your fishmonger to do this for you, so much the better.

Follow the instructions for dry salting, brining and air-drying fish. Smoke for 24 hours continuously. The curing should not be too strong or it may drown the real, delicate flavour of the eels.

Keep in the refrigerator for up to 3 months if you must!

Mutton Ham

This is popular from Scotland through to Iceland, where they use lamb and eat it raw like Westphalian ham.

3–4kg (6–8lb) leg of mutton or lamb

For the brine
**1kg (2lb) common salt
3 litres (5 pints) water
2 bay leaves
12 crushed juniper berries
15g (½oz) coriander seeds
60g (2oz) peppercorns**

Add all the ingredients to the water, bring to the boil, skim thoroughly. Let it cool completely. Put the meat in an earthenware container, pour the brine over, cover and weigh down. Leave for 3 weeks in a cold place. Turn the meat over once a week during this time. Remove, wipe and hang up in an airy place to dry for 24 hours. Cold smoke for 72 hours (3 days). Store as Smoke-cured Ham.

Smoke-cured Ham

5–6kg (10–12lb) leg of pork

For the brine
**1½kg (3lb) common salt
500g (1lb) molasses
500g (1lb) brown sugar
9 litres (2 gallons) water**

Put the salt, molasses, sugar and water in a large pan, bring to the boil, then let it get cold. Lay the meat in a large earthenware crock, pour in brine, cover and weigh it down. Keep in a cool place or the refrigerator for 3 weeks. Turn the meat over once a week during this time. Remove from the brine, pat to get rid of

Improvised cold smoker
In this home-made cold smoker the length of the smoke duct is designed to allow the smoke to cool before reaching the food, and the chimney is set as far as possible from the intake so as to draw the smoke across the smoker before it makes its exit.

In practice it is better to hang food from hooks than to put it on shelves as the bars obstruct the smoke from enveloping the food completely. When hanging the food to be smoked, fish and meat should not be mixed as fish is smoked at a lower temperature (21 °C).

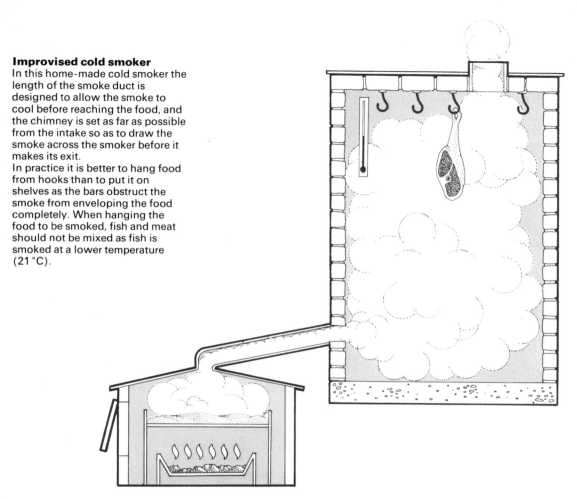

moisture then hang it up to dry for 24 hours. Smoke for 3 days (72 hours). Wrap in cheesecloth and hang in cool, dry, airy place until required (up to one year), or pack for refrigerator (for short-term keeping). To cook, soak overnight, put it into unsalted cold water, bring to the boil and simmer for about 4 hours until cooked. Remove rind and serve hot; or cool in liquor, drain, remove rind, serve cold.

Smoked Salmon

1 fresh salmon
Brine
Salt

Behead the fish, split in half and bone. Put it in brine (see page 216), leave for 2–3 hours according to thickness of fish. Dry salt for about 3 hours.

Remove fish, wash to remove salt. Air dry away from any heat for up to 4 hours. When it glistens and there is no visible sign of moisture it can be smoked.

This can take up to 4–5 days, so you must build up a long, slow-burning fire and keep it in all the time. This must be a slow process. Don't let it get over smoked so it loses its succulence and oiliness.

Even when smoked, fish spoils quickly, so eat at once, or pack and refrigerate. Do not keep longer than 28 days.

Smoked Goose Breast

This is a typical German Christmas dish. You only need the breast, so cook the rest in some other way.

Goose breast divided into 2 fillets
150g (6oz) common salt
5ml (1 teaspoon) saltpetre (optional)

Rub the breast fillets thoroughly with salt and the saltpetre if you decide to use it.

Put the goose in a dish, put in any leftover salt. Weigh down and keep in the refrigerator or a cold place for 5–6 days. Remove and pat dry. Cold smoke for at least 12 hours until it looks completely dry. Store as meat (see page 216), but do not keep longer than 6 months. When cut, it should look brown and not at all raw.

Serve cut in wafer-thin slices with rye bread, and if you have it, clarified goose fat.

How many people it serves will depend on how thick you carve it and whether it is an hors d'oeuvre or an entrée.

Duck, turkey and chicken breasts can be smoked in the same way.

Having removed the breasts for this recipe, save the drumsticks for recipe on page 214.

219

Making your own wine

Winemaking is no longer the obscure art it used to be. Today, in this country alone, there are thousands of amateur winemakers producing millions of gallons a year. This is the result of equipment and ingredients becoming available over the last 25 years on the open market – Campden tablets, wine yeast and nutrients to feed them, hydrometers, funnels – all can be bought in specialist shops distributed all over the country. Rising prices of imported wines have also encouraged the amateur to have a go. And how good is the wine that he makes? Obviously it varies enormously but the overall standard of home winemaking is said to have risen considerably since the Amateur Winemakers Guild of Judges was formed in 1963. And homemade wines are no longer the media's favourite joke. In this chapter Ben Turner gives a very clear explanation of how to make wine and beer, based on his own wide experience. He points out the snags and how to set about getting the best results. For the beginner at least it is important to read the how-to-do-it instructions before launching into the recipes, alluring as they are. To make good wine you have to know exactly what you are doing and why, and you will find it all clearly set out in the following chapter.

Making your own wine

There are three distinct types of winemakers, though they sometimes overlap.

The 'kit makers', the majority, buy a tin of grape juice concentrate, add water and the yeast that is provided and some weeks later have a drinkable wine.

The 'country winemakers' use some single ingredient – elderberries, perhaps, or rhubarb – plus sugar, water and yeast, and some of their products are quite delicious and 'civilised', while others should be sipped with caution. . . .

The 'amateur' winemakers are skilled enthusiasts who artfully blend and control their ingredients to produce table wines, dessert wines, apéritifs and liqueurs that are comparable with imported vintages.

To make wine at home is not difficult nor even very messy. Nor need it take up much room. Some kit winemakers produce $4\frac{1}{2}$ litres (1 gallon) every six weeks, which gives them a weekly bottle of wine with minimal trouble and equipment. Even someone living in a small flat can do that.

Basic principles

The winemaking process itself is quite simple. First step is to make the 'must', the basic fruit-pulp-and-water or other mixture of ingredients from which the wine is to be fermented. How the must is prepared will vary according to the ingredients being used – and sometimes according to the quirks of a particular recipe.

When the must (basic pulp) is ready, including the addition of sugar, it is transferred to a fermenting jar and yeast is added so that fermentation starts. This is simply the active yeast converting the sugar into alcohol and carbon dioxide. The jar is sealed with a simple airlock, which allows the gas to escape while protecting the wine-in-the-making from the outer air and possible airborne infection.

When fermentation is over the wine is carefully siphoned off the 'lees', the silt that forms at the bottom of the jar during fermentation, into storage jars and is left to clear and stabilise before final bottling.

This is a very basic account of winemaking, of course, and many variations, subtleties and skills can be brought into play, depending on the wine you set out to make.

The keys to successful winemaking are cleanliness and an understanding of what you are doing, so that when you come to the recipes they will make sense to you, even to the extent where you can vary them and invent your own.

Equipment

Winemaking is a very inexpensive hobby. Your outlay on equipment – and it can be used for many years – need be no more than £5 or £6, while the wine itself will cost you from 10p to 30p a bottle and will be equal to commercial vintages costing up to £2 a bottle or more.

How much equipment you need depends on how much wine you plan to make. For the occasional gallon or two you need only the basics:

The basics:
A colourless **polythene bin** with fitting lid.
A couple of **fermentation jars with airlocks**.
A lenght of **polythene tubing**.
A **polythene funnel**.
A **long-handled spoon** of wood or polypropylene.
A **nylon bag** for straining.
Some **wine bottles and corks**.
Less basic but very useful are:
A **kitchen thermometer**.
A **hydrometer**.
Extra **funnels** of different sizes.
A **nylon sieve**.
A **polythene measuring jug**.
A **preserving pan type of vessel**.
NB Don't use containers made of iron, copper, lead, zinc or cadmium, or plastic containers which have been used for non-food substances (eg, weed-killer!) for fermentation or storage.

Of course, you may already have some of these items for ordinary kitchen use. The rest may be bought at one of the 'home brew' shops which are now to be found in most towns, or in the excellent brewing and winemaking departments of Boots, the chemists. (See also Where to buy equipment).

You can add to your winemaking resources as you become more confident and ambitious. For more advanced and bigger-scale wine-production you will need a bigger bin and more fermentation jars with airlocks.

A hydrometer is not essential for making wine, but it is valuable for producing particular wines, especially dry ones, for it indicates the natural sugar content of the must and therefore how much more sugar should be added to get a particular result. Sugar content varies considerably between different fruits, and even between varieties of the same fruit. So it is useful to know the natural sugar content of the must before adding to it in order to produce a wine containing the right amount of alcohol for its type. A port type wine, for instance, should contain more alcohol than a light table wine.

Some winemakers also check on the amount of acid in a must, so that the acid content appropriate to a given wine can be made up. There are small acid testing kits to be had for this, and acid testing papers that give a general guide – low, average or high.

The plastic bin is for preparing the must. In it the fruit is mashed or left to steep, or other ingredients are mixed. The bins are light, strong, easy to clean and resistant to acids and alkalis. They come in several sizes – 10, 15 and 25 litre (2, 3 and 5 gallon). A 10 or 15 litre bin is adequate for the beginner.

Fermentation takes place in the fermentation jar, a narrow-necked glass 'demijohn' or 'gallon jar' which actually holds 4·8 litres ($8\frac{1}{2}$ pints), thus allowing air space on top of a fermenting gallon of wine for the 'action' to take place. Special corks, with holes through them, are sold for the jars. The vital airlock, which must be in place throughout fermentation, fits into the hole in the cork. The airlock U-bend is filled with Campden solution

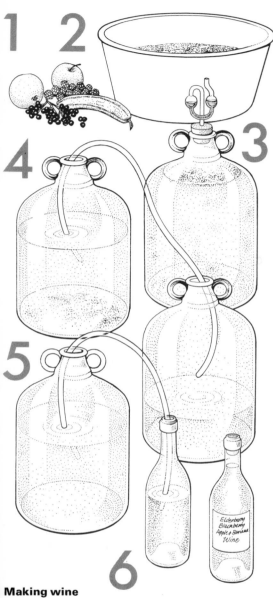

Making wine

1 Prepare the must by steeping, boiling, mashing the ingredients or by following whatever process the recipe requires. 2 Strain the liquor from the pulp, stir in the sugar and pour into the fermentation jar. 3 Fit the airlock to the jar, and then leave the contents to ferment to a finish. 4 Rack or siphon the clearing wine into a sterilised jar and discard the sediment. When this has cleared, rack off any further sediment and then add one Campden tablet. 5 After some months have passed, siphon the wine into bottles. 6 Keep for a while longer before serving.

which acts as a sterile trap.

Broadly speaking, once fermentation is under way the developing wine will look after itself until the process is over and it is time to 'rack' the wine – that is, siphon it off the lees.

Fermentation jars may also be used for storing wine while it clears and stabilises, though experts prefer glazed earthenware, which has good insulating properties and protects the wine from temperature changes. Being opaque, it also keeps out the light, which might cause the wine's colour to fade. Of course, wine in glass jars can simply be stored in a dark place. Also on this point, you can now get fermentation and storage jars in dark glass as well as clear.

Polythene containers are not recommended for storing wine. The material is not vapour-proof, it picks up certain flavour taints and there is some doubt about its total resistance to alcohol.

Bottle your wine only in orthodox wine bottles. Old labels should be soaked off and the bottles washed thoroughly and sterilised (a note on this later on) before filling. It is a good idea to use some half-bottles. These can be drunk first, leaving the wine in the whole bottles a little longer to mature.

For sparkling wines champagne bottles **must** be used. Ordinary ones are not strong enough, and may burst under the pressure of gases produced by the 'secondary fermentation' which goes on after bottling these wines.

Use new cylindrical corks for table and dessert wines, hollow-domed plastic stoppers for sparkling wines. The latter must have little wire cages to keep them on.

Labelling is important, however simply it is done. Labels should indicate the type of wine and the date of bottling. It is essential to be able to identify different wines if you have made and stored several types, while dating will help you to judge bottles of the same wine which have been left to mature for varying periods.

During fermentation temperature is important. For continuing and steady activity a temperature of about 20°C (70°F) is needed. Winemakers fermenting their musts in centrally heated homes need no aids. Others, making wine between September and May, will perhaps have to resort to a warm cupboard or an insulated box fitted with a low-powered electric light bulb and a thermostat. You can also buy electrically heated pads for placing under fermentation jars.

Some basic items that the winemaker keeps on hand are:

Campden tablets, which are dissolved in water to produce the winemaker's sterilising agent.

Dried yeast.

Yeast nutrient, to improve fermentation in musts that lack natural nutrients.

Grape tannin, which gives many wines a zestful 'bite' that they would not otherwise have.

Citric acid, to help fermentation and improve flavour.

Pectic enzyme in powder form, to hasten the breakdown of fruit musts and also ensure clear, haze-free wines.

223

Making your own wine

It is sometimes said that wine can be made from anything, and in fact excellent wines can certainly be produced from a great number of fruits – fresh, frozen, dried and canned – as well as from juices and jams, many vegetables, some flowers and herbs, leaves, saps, cereals and spices.

Grapes

Of them all certain varieties of grape, when grown in the right soil and climate, make the best wine. But other fruits – apples, apricots and gooseberries for white wines and bilberries, blackberries and damsons for reds – will produce good wines, sometimes better than those from some grapes.

But the juice of wine grapes contains all the nutrients that yeast requires and is the ideal medium for fermentation. For this reason it is sensible to include some grape in every wine. These can be fresh grapes, sultanas, raisins or concentrated grape juice, depending on the wine and the winemaker. What is important is to include **some** grape in one form or another. As little as 150g (5oz) per 4½ litres (1 gallon) is enough for light wines; 500g (18oz) is preferable for dessert wines.

For the best results you should first decide the purpose of the wine, then choose appropriate ingredients. Those that make, for instance, the best sparkling or light table wines are not usually right for the richer and fuller dessert wines.

Vegetables, fruits, flowers . . .

Vegetables – notably beetroot, carrot and parsnip – tend to be best for dessert wines, along with the more heavily flavoured fruits like blackberry, black currant, elderberry, loganberry, mulberry and raspberry.

Flowers, leaves, saps, herbs, spices and cereals make the best social wines – wines drunk on their own and not with a meal.

Fruits like apple, gooseberry, pear and rhubarb make excellent sparkling wines, while dried dates, figs, prunes, rose hips and citrus fruits produce delicious apéritif-type wines.

Bananas, dried apricots, raisins, rice and sultanas add extra flavour and body to any wine.

Frozen fruits may be used successfully just as if they were fresh ones so long as they have been treated before freezing to prevent them browning when they thaw. Any fruits that brown quickly, such as pears, apples and plums, should be dropped into cold water containing one Campden tablet and 2·5ml (½ teaspoon) of citric acid per 5 litres (1 gallon) as soon as they are cut or crushed. This will completely prevent the browning which would otherwise taint the wine.

Preparation

Fresh fruit should be stalked, washed and crushed after damaged portions have been removed. The pips of fruits like apples, grapes and raisins may be left in as long as they are not crushed or cut, which releases their bitter flavour. Citrus fruits should be peeled very thinly so that no white pith is removed. Only the parings and the pressed-out juice are used in the wine. The pithy hulk, which would make the wine bitter, is thrown away.

Dried fruits should be washed, then soaked overnight and boiled in the same water until just cooked. Both fruit and liquor are used for the wine. Canned fruits should be strained from their syrup (which should be saved) and mashed.

Grapes are important
Some grapes, whether fresh or sultanas or raisins, should be used in every wine since the juice of wine grapes contains all the nutrients that yeast needs and is the ideal medium for fermentation.

All fruits, whether fresh, frozen, canned or dried, should be steeped for 24 hours in a solution containing a pectic enzyme, a Campden tablet and a little citric acid. The enzyme breaks down the pectin in the fruit, allowing better extraction of juice and flavour, and ensures a haze-free wine. The Campden tablet and acid will protect the fruit from browning and from infection from the air.

Vegetables must be topped and tailed, scrubbed absolutely clean, diced and boiled until they are just tender. Only the liquor is used for winemaking, the cooked vegetables can be eaten.

Fruit juices containing saccharin are not suitable for winemaking; nor are jams that contain colouring, pectin and preservative. Only unsweetened juices should be used, and only natural jams made of fruit, sugar and water. Even so, use a double quantity of the enzyme when making wine from jam because the fruit pectin in jams is preserved to help setting.

Flowers for winemaking should be picked on a warm, dry, sunny day when flower heads are fully open. Collect them in a paper bag – not polythene, which causes sweating and loss of flavour. Pick off and use only the flower heads, the leaves and stems cause bitterness.

But leaves from the summer pruning of brambles and vines make a pleasant wine, and so do young oak and walnut leaves and the sap from silver birch and sycamore trees. The bracts and flowers of the lime tree are also suitable, but not the fruit, being too acid.

Leaves and flowers for wine should be mashed in hot water by being rubbed against the side of a bowl with the back of a wooden spoon to extract their essence. These wines need adequate sultanas or white grape juice added to them to provide 'vinosity' and balance; flowers and leaves can give only bouquet and flavour.

Herbs, including parsley, mint and thyme, are sometimes used to make attractive wines. They must be treated as leaves and flowers.

Other base ingredients
Coffee, tea, ginger, rice and wheat are also used as base ingredients for wines, but these too need added grape juice.

Sugar
Sugar is best in its ordinary white granulated form except for Madeira-type wines. In these, brown sugar contributes to the distinctive caramel flavour. Fructose or glucose may be used, but they are expensive. The special invert sugar, which speeds fermentation, is not worth buying as it can be made at home at no extra cost by simply boiling ordinary white sugar for 20 minutes with a little citric acid. The formula for this is: 5g of citric acid, 600ml of water and 1kg of sugar (1 teaspoon of citric acid, 1 pint of water and 2lb of sugar). It should be said that none of this is essential. Most winemakers use just ordinary sugar throughout.

Golden syrup may also be used, but not molasses, which taints the wine. Honey is not recommended as it, too, affects the flavour of wine, but it is used for making mead flavoured with fruit, herbs or spices. Orange blossom honey makes an excellent dry mead and clover honey a sweet one. Use the creamy, white honeys for light meads and the brown honeys for sweet and flavoured ones.

Acid
The key to flavour and bouquet is acid. Without enough acid, fermentation will not go well and the wine will taste 'medicinal'. A dry wine needs 4–5g per litre ($\frac{1}{2}$ teaspoon per pint) of citric acid, a sweet wine 5–6g per litre ($\frac{3}{4}$ teaspoon per pint) and a dessert wine 7–8g per litre (level teaspoon per pint). A little grape tannin also improves the character of a wine.

Yeast and Nutrient
Alcohol is formed from the sugar in the must by the action of the yeast, which is why you should always use a good wine yeast. The winemakers' shops now offer a good range of yeasts cultured from the well-known commercial ones for the various types of wines.

The yeasts are available in dried and liquid form. The dried ones are in putty-coloured pellets, sometimes compressed into tablets wrapped in foil, and usually mixed with a little nutrient to help fermentation. You can buy a sealed sachet of such yeast containing enough to ferment from 5 to 30 litres (1 to 6 gallons) of wine.

Liquid yeasts are supplied in a tiny phial or sealed sachet. They are mixed with distilled water but their shelf life is shorter.

Bakers' and brewers' yeasts are not suitable for winemaking as they impart a doughy or beery flavour to the wine.

To ferment well, yeast must be activated **before** being added to the must. This is done in a 'starter bottle' and is easiest with the compounds of dried yeast and nutrients. The compound is shaken up with tepid water in a small bottle and left to ferment for six to ten hours before it is needed for adding to the must.

Making your own wine

Wines are not classified merely as sweet and dry, but as apéritif, table wines (red, rosé and white), dessert, sparkling and social. You will find a full explanation of these on page 229.

You should make each wine for a purpose and select ingredients likely to give the best results along the lines suggested in the recipes. (How to prepare the must or basic pulp, is described in each recipe.)

Acid and sugar content

It is very important to get acid and sugar content right in relation to ingredients and purpose. Very acid fruit will need no additional acid, while bland fruit will call for a full quota of some 20g per $4\frac{1}{2}$ litres ($\frac{3}{4}$oz per gallon). How much acid to add is no problem if you think about the ingredients you are using and the purpose of the wine.

Sugar is a little harder to estimate but can be worked out with the aid of a hydrometer. After preparing the must, but before sugar and yeast are added, pour some of the must into a sterilised jar containing a hydrometer, filling until the hydrometer floats and stays steady. Note the figure on the scale where it is cut by the surface of the liquid. Let us say it is 1·030. Refer to the table given opposite and note the specific gravity (SG) equalling the alcohol content you want in your finished wine. Suppose it is 1·090, equalling 12 per cent alcohol. Deduct the original reading from this figure – 1·030 from 1·090. The remainder is 60, so now you know that you must add sugar equal to a reading of 1·060. The tables show that this is 680g to every $4\frac{1}{2}$ litres ($1\frac{1}{2}$lb to the gallon).

Though this method is fairly accurate one need not be absolutely precise and minor variations are acceptable. Even without a hydrometer you can perhaps guess nearly enough how much sugar to add by deciding whether your base ingredients have much sugar, if any. (Remember: about two thirds of the weight of dried grapes and concentrates is fermentable sugar.) What is important is not to add too much sugar at once, nor to add more than is needed for the purpose of the wine being made.

Adding the sugar

Experience shows that the sugar is best added to the must in several small doses rather than all at once, especially for making very strong wines, so that fermentation is not slowed by the weight of sugar.

Fermentation will stop when all the sugar has been converted or, prematurely, if the temperature gets too high or low or if there is too little acid or nutrient (see What can go wrong, opposite).

Racking

When fermentation is complete the bubbles of gas will stop rising through the airlock and the wine will begin to clear from the top downwards. A deposit of dead yeast cells and other matter will have collected at the bottom of the jar and the wine must be siphoned off without disturbing it. The siphon is just a length of polythene tubing. By placing one end in the wine, sucking on the other end until the tube is full, then placing that end in an empty jar standing below the level of the full one gravity will cause the wine to flow into the empty jar. If the end of the tube in the full jar is kept away from the silt and the jar is gently tilted when it is nearly empty all the wine can be transferred cleanly. This is called 'racking'.

There is more sophisticated siphoning equipment to be had, but the length of tube is very efficient once you have got the knack. Try it with two jars of water first.

When the wine is racked off into the storage jar a Campden tablet should be added to it to inhibit infection from unwanted micro-organisms and prevent oxidation, then it should be bunged tight with a sterilised cork and labelled. There should be no space between the wine and the cork. If the jar is a little less than full the space can be made up with a little cold boiled water, or even some glass marbles which have been first sterilised in Campden solution.

An airlock

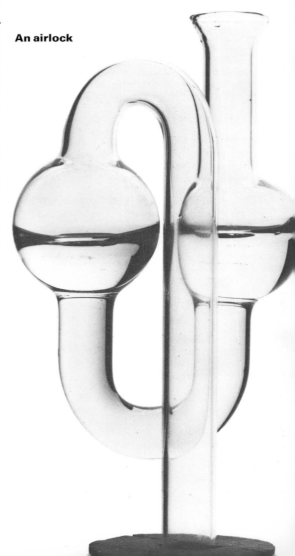

Storing

The wine should now be stored in a cool place for a few weeks until it is 'star bright'. There will now be a further small sediment, and the wine should be siphoned off this and stored again.

Some very light white wines may be ready for drinking about three months after starting. Others – some of the strong and heavy wines – may need as long as four years of maturation before they are drunk. Each type of wine has its own maturation time, so little guidance can be given. Your palate will tell you if a wine is ready or not. If in doubt – wait. Experience has shown that many white wines and nearly all red ones need to be kept for at least a year.

After six months' bulk storage white wines may be bottled, and after 12 months most of the red wines will be ready in their turn.

Bottling

Always sterilise everything before use. Make a sterilising solution with one Campden tablet and a pinch of citric acid to half a wine bottle of cold water (or larger amounts in proportion) and this can be used to rinse all your equipment before use.

When bottling your wine you should sterilise the bottles, drain them and fill them at once with wine. The corks should be softened beforehand by being soaked overnight in sterilising solution. Push the corks home flush with the rim of the bottle, using a corking tool, label the bottles and store them on their sides to keep the corks moist and swollen for a tight fit.

Guidelines for making wine

1 Prepare the must by steeping, boiling, mashing, etc, according to ingredients and type of wine.
2 Start the yeast fermenting separately a few hours before it will be needed.
3 Strain the liquor from the pulp and pour it into a fermentation jar.
4 Dissolve the sugar in hot water, making a syrup.
5 When the syrup is cool add it and the active yeast to the liquor.
6 Fit an airlock to the jar and leave the contents to ferment to a finish.
7 Rack the wine off the lees and leave it to clear and stabilise in a clean fermentation jar.
8 When the wine has cleared rack it off any further sediment, bottle it and leave it to mature.

What can go wrong

Most wine-making problems can be avoided by attention to hygiene, careful racking and the regular use of Campden tablets. Perhaps the most serious of these is:

Acetification. This is when your wine starts turning to vinegar! It is always caused by air being in contact with the wine or must and is the reason why the mixing bins have fitting lids and airlocks are used on fermenting jars. The airlocks are specially important because the smell of fermentation attracts the vinegar fly carrying bacteria that cause acetification.

Over-sweetness. This is the bane of the beginner. Use a hydrometer before adding the sugar to the must.

A medicinal flavour. Too little acid in the must can cause this. If it is slight it may be countered by adding a little citric acid to the finished wine. If it is pronounced there is little to be done.

A musty flavour. Caused by the wine standing for too long on the sediment of dead yeast. This can be prevented by racking the wine promptly as soon as fermentation is finished.

A metallic flavour. Produced by the use of metal utensils. Never let your wine, at any stage, come in contact with any metal except high-quality stainless steel.

Haze. Caused by the pectin in fruit musts or by insufficient care with initial straining when this has to be done. Always use a pectic enzyme when making fruit wines so that they will clear quickly. If haziness persists in a wine you can 'fine' it with isinglass, bentonite, beaten egg white or a proprietary fining. After adding a fining, stand the wine in a cool place for a few days, then rack the wine from the sediment.

A 'stuck fermentation'. This is one that has stopped fermenting before its time. It can happen if the temperature gets too low or too high or if there is too little acid or nutrient in the must. Moving the jars to a warmer or cooler place or adding a little more acid or nutrient may restart the fermentation. Occasionally a weak yeast culture will just die off and it will be necessary to activate another yeast. When this is fermenting strongly add the 'stuck' must to it a little at a time over several days, each time making sure that fermentation is continuing before adding more.

Specific Gravity, Sugar and Potential Alcohol Content

Specific gravity	Sugar in 1 gal.		Sugar in 4½ litres	Potential alcohol
1·005		2oz	0·057kg	0·07
1·010		4	0·113	1·39
1·015		6	0·170	2·05
1·020		8	0·227	2·71
1·025		10	0·284	3·42
1·030		12	0·340	4·08
1·035		14	0·397	4·75
1·040	1lb	0	0·453	5·44
1·045	1	2	0·510	6·13
1·050	1	4	0·568	6·79
1·055	1	6	0·624	7·47
1·060	1	8	0·681	8·18
1·065	1	9½	0·724	8·84
1·070	1	11	0·780	9·53
1·075	1	13	0·823	10·19
1·080	1	15	0·880	10·89
1·085	2	1	0·936	11·61
1·090	2	3	0·993	12·31
1·095	2	4½	1·036	12·92
1·100	2	6	1·070	13·54
1·105	2	8	1·135	14·24
1·110	2	10	1·192	14·98
1·115	2	11½	1·234	15·62
1·120	2	13	1·277	16·32
1·125	2	15	1·334	17·01

Note. 2lb sugar dissolved in a must occupies 1 pint
1kg sugar dissolved in a must occupies 0·62 litres

Making your own wine

Even when all techniques have been carried out properly the taste of the wine may not be quite what you want. The remedy is to blend such wines together. The results can be remarkable. A dull and insipid wine can take on a new character. Blending is constantly practised by commercial winemakers, and amateurs have a lot to learn in this respect. In general terms, you should blend opposites – even red with white. As long as wines are sound and free from infection they can be blended. Leave them for a few weeks to blend thoroughly and think up fancy names for them!

Always keep your wines in as even a temperature as possible, ideally between 10 and 15°C (50 and 60°F). Try also to put a few bottles aside for extra-long maturation. Quite often the last bottle turns out to have been the best, and one wishes one had not drunk the rest so quickly.

Serve your wines to their best advantage. Red wines, because of their higher tannin content, need to be served free from chill – about 20°C (70°F). They taste smoother and softer than when cold. On the other hand white wines, sparkling wines, rosés and apéritifs are all enhanced by being served at about 10°C (50°F) or even colder.

Wine, red wine in particular, benefits from being poured carefully into a decanter, so that any new sediment is left behind in the bottle, and being left to stand for a while. Even half an hour will make an improvement in the flavour.

All wines, except the sparkling ones, benefit from being decanted, not only because of the aeration but because wine looks so much better in

Racking
Siphoning off the wine from the fermentation jar into an empty storage jar is called 'racking' and can be done quite simply with a length of polythene tubing.

a decanter than in a bottle. Wine should also be served in appropriate glasses – copita types for apéritifs, goblets for table wines, flutes for sparkling wines and small goblets for dessert wines. Avoid coloured or decorated glasses and be sure that each has an incurved bowl to reduce the escape of the bouquet. Fill the glass to between half and two-thirds of its capacity, leaving room for the bouquet to collect. Pick it up by the stem and hold it by the base so that your hand does not hide the wine nor affect its temperature.

No wine will last long once the bottle is opened, but red and white will stay in good condition for a day or two if recorked and kept in the refrigerator. Remove the red an hour or so before serving so that it can warm up. Strong apéritifs and dessert wines will not keep in peak condition for longer than a week after being opened. Keep these, too, in a very cool place, even the refrigerator, to slow down deterioration. Having been so patient in making and maturing your wine, you are entitled to enjoy it at its best.

What type of wine?

Instead of making just any wine, the thoughtful winemaker considers the needs of the family and makes his wines in the quantities needed and for specific purposes:

Apéritifs are appetite-stimulators, often stronger than table wines but less so than dessert wines. They are usually fairly dry. Vermouth-type, sherry-type and dry citrus wines are the most popular.

Table wines are usually dry to accompany fish and meat courses, sweet to go with desserts. The alcohol content of table wines should not be less than 9 per cent nor more than 12 per cent.

Dessert wines are full, rich, sweet and as strong as they can be fermented. They need plenty of base ingredients, sugar, acid and tannin.

Sparkling wines must be light in body, flavour and alcohol. Ten per cent alcohol is about right at first; this is low enough to permit the secondary fermentation in the bottle which makes the wine sparkle.

Social wines are drunk with no more than a biscuit. Normally they are not sweeter than medium-dry nor stronger than 13 per cent alcohol.

Liqueurs round off a meal.

Light white or rosé wines are ideal for summer drinking, while heavier and stronger wines are better in winter.

Apéritifs of the vermouth type are made by 'fermenting on' with extra sugar an otherwise nondescript wine, flavouring it with a sachet of herbs containing wormwood and sweetening it to taste. Another way is to add a vermouth-style grape concentrate to a fruit or vegetable must.

'Fermenting on' is used in the making of all strong wines. You start fermentation in the usual way, with enough sugar to produce about 10 per cent alcohol. After a week or 10 days remove some of the wine, stir some more sugar into it and return it to the jar. Repeat this process several times so that the alcohol concentration is built up steadily.

A little extra yeast nutrient should also be added, together with some vitamin B. One 3mg Benerva tablet in $4\frac{1}{2}$ litres (1 gallon) is enough. This procedure will encourage the yeast to ferment up to 17 or 18 per cent alcohol.

Sherry-type wines are made in this way but with an additional technique to develop the distinctive flavour. Use a sherry wine yeast and ferment in a vessel not quite full and protected not with an airlock but with a plug of cotton wool, which permits a certain amount of oxidation. The wine must be matured in the same way.

Suitable ingredients for *fino* 'sherries' include Seville oranges, prunes, Victoria plums and dried rose hips with figs. Cream style 'sherries' can be made from a mix of rhubarb, dates, bananas and grape concentrate. In both types it is important to use a good-quality sherry yeast. Some winemakers also include 30g (1oz) of gypsum and 15g ($\frac{1}{2}$oz) of cream of tartar to each $4\frac{1}{2}$ litres (1 gallon) to heighten the sherry character of the wine.

Table wines should not be overwhelming in flavour or strength. The ideal is a nice balance of flavour, body, acid, tannin and alcohol. With the exception of the Sauternes-style ones, table wines should be dry – that is **all** of the sugar should be fermented out.

The fruit content of red table wines should be about 2kg per $4\frac{1}{2}$ litres ($4\frac{1}{2}$lb per gallon). Black currants and elderberries, with their strong flavours, should be used in moderation and the body of the wine made up with other fruit. The tannin content should be noticeable. Rosé table wines need a little less body and noticeably less tannin. They also seem to taste better when they are not absolutely dry; a specific gravity of 1·000 is about right. Dry white table wines should contain enough acid to taste fresh, clean and not too full. Sweet whites should be fuller, to match the residual sweetness; an SG of 1·010 is often adequate. It is usually easier to make such wines dry, then sweeten them shortly before serving them.

Dessert wines, such as the port-style ones, must be made with suitably coloured base ingredients – beetroot, blackberries, black currants, bilberries, damsons, elderberries and so on. The best results are often achieved with a multiple blend of ingredients. Such a blend would include grape in some form, with perhaps bananas for extra body and some dried apricots to enhance the flavour. For wines like this a fruit content of about 3kg per $4\frac{1}{2}$ litres ($6\frac{1}{2}$lb per gallon) is necessary, with adequate acid, tannin and alcohol from fermenting on to the maximum tolerance of the yeast. These wines must mature for several years and may then be sweetened to taste when they are bottled.

Madeira-style dessert wine needs brown sugar and Madeira yeast as well as appropriate base ingredients. It is fermented on until it is quite strong, and then, after racking and clearing, is stored in a very warm place – 50°C (120°F) – for up to six months while it acquires the caramel flavour of a good Madeira.

Sparkling wines

Sparkling wines are best made from green gooseberries, rhubarb, white currants, apples, pears and white grapes. Use a champagne yeast and only enough sugar to produce 10 per cent alcohol. When the wine is six months old, absolutely dry and star bright, reactivate it with 70g of caster sugar per $4\frac{1}{2}$ litres ($2\frac{1}{2}$oz to 1 gallon) plus champagne yeast and nutrient. Fit airlocks and as soon as the wine is fermenting again pour it into sterilised champagne bottles. Fill the bottles up to 5cm (2in) from the top, fit sterilised, hollow-domed, plastic stoppers and wire them down.

Store the bottles on their sides in a warm place until fermentation is complete (about seven days), then place them in a cool store, still on their sides, for at least six months.

The next job is to remove the sediment. Stand the bottles upside down for two or three weeks, giving them a daily twist and shake until all the sediment has moved down into the hollow stoppers. Now dip the bottle necks in a mixture of crushed ice and cooking salt for about 10 minutes until the wine in the stoppers is frozen. Stand the bottles upright, remove the wire cages and stoppers, sweeten the wine to taste with one or two saccharin tablets and fit new sterilised stoppers and cages. After that serve the wine as required. Always handle bottles of sparkling wine slowly and carefully to avoid shaking up the gas.

Liqueurs can be made at home simply by steeping washed and cut fruit in a sweetened spirit for three or four months (see end of bottling chapter). Examples are sloes in gin, morello cherries, apricots or peaches in *eau de vie*. Ordinary brandy is not suitable as it is already flavoured and coloured.

The French Noirot Liqueur Essences (obtainable from 'home brew' shops), added to vodka, sweet white wine and sugar make excellent imitation liqueurs, especially enriched with glycerine and with some oil of capsicum added to increase warmth. Here is the basic recipe:

15ml (1 tablespoon) Noirot liqueur essence of
    your choice
250ml ($\frac{1}{2}$ pint) vodka, 40 per cent alcohol
350ml (12floz) sweet white wine
150–200g (5–7oz) white caster sugar
15ml (1 tablespoon) glycerine and 12–15 drops
    oil of capsicum

Mix all ingredients together, stir slowly until the sugar is dissolved, taste and adjust with added extract or sugar as necessary. Bottle and keep for one week for liqueur to blend.

Wine and beer glossary

Acetification The process of wine turning into vinegar. Caused by Vinegar Bacteria (*mycoderma acetii*), which are airborne or carried by the vinegar fly.

Adjuncts Substances used for improving the body and flavour of beer.

Airlock A device to protect wine from airborne contamination during fermentation. Fitted to the fermentation jar, it excludes air while allowing carbon dioxide to escape. Also called Fermentation Lock or Fermentation Trap.

Body The fullness of a wine or beer.

Bouquet The aroma of a wine.

Campden tablets Tablets containing sulphur dioxide. They are dissolved in water to make a general sterilising fluid or added to musts and wines to protect them from bacterial infection and oxidation.

Carbon dioxide The gas produced by fermentation.

Demijohn Narrow-necked jar, holding 4·8 litre (8½ pints) in which wine is fermented. Also called Fermentation Jar or Gallon Jar.

Dry Term used to describe a wine from which all the sugar has been fermented out, ie, converted into alcohol.

End point In brewing, the point at which extraction from the mash is complete.

Fermentation The process by which the action of yeast converts sugar into alcohol and carbon dioxide.

Fermentation jar See **Demijohn**

Fermenting on The method of boosting fermentation, by periodic additions of sugar, to produce strong wines.

For special occasions
Sparkling wines should be light in body, flavour and alcohol, and when serving, bottles should be handled with care to avoid shaking up the gas.

Fining Clearing a cloudy wine or beer by filtering or adding 'finings'.

Finings Substances added to wine or beer to clear it.

Gallon jar See **Demijohn**

Hydrometer Instrument for measuring sugar content of a liquid and calculating the quantity of additional sugar needed to produce a given alcohol content.

Inverted sugar or **Invert sugar** Sugar whose two components, glucose and fructose, have been split chemically so that in fermentation the yeast does not have to do this. Its use can speed fermentation.

Lees Deposit of dead yeast cells and other solids which forms at the bottom of a vessel during fermentation.

Malt Barley specially prepared for brewing.

Mash Mixture of malt and hot water from which the wort is made for brewing beer.

Must Basic fruit pulp or mixture of other ingredients from which wine is fermented.

Nutrient Nitrogenous substance used in brewing and fermentation to improve the action of yeast.

Oxidation An effect of air on fruit after it has been cut or crushed, as illustrated by peeled apples turning brown. It can affect the flavour of wines and ciders.

Pectic enzyme A pectin-destroying enzyme added to musts to improve juice-extraction and the eventual clarity of the wine.

Priming The addition of extra sugar to beer before bottling to cause a second fermentation in the bottle.

Racking Removing wine or beer from the lees prior to letting it stand to clear and stabilise.

Specific gravity Density of a fluid as measured by a hydrometer, especially (in wine-making) the density caused by sugar content.

Stable A wine is stable when there can be no further fermentation.

Vinegar bacteria See **Acetification**

Vinegar fly See **Acetification**

Wort The liquor or infusion made from malt and fermented into beer.

Recipes for apéritif, sparkling

Yield: As all the recipes are made in a $4\frac{1}{2}$ litre (1-gallon) fermentation jar, you are basically making a gallon of wine each time, but the actual yield may vary according to the ingredients used. Don't mix them.

Seville Orange Sherry

5 Seville oranges
5 sweet oranges
500g (1lb) sultanas
Approx. 1kg (2lb) white sugar
25g (1oz) gypsum
15g ($\frac{1}{2}$oz) cream of tartar

$\frac{1}{2}$ teaspoon grape tannin
Campden tablets
Sherry yeast and nutrient
4 litres (7 pints) water

Peel the oranges very thinly, excluding all white pith, and leave peelings in a cool oven for about 10 minutes.

Wash and chop the sultanas, place them in a polythene bin with the orange peel, pour hot water on them, stir gently and leave to cool.

Add the juice of the oranges and discard the hulks. Stir in all the other ingredients except the sugar and Campden tablets. Cover and leave to ferment for five days, stirring daily.

Strain out and press the fruit, stir in half the sugar, pour into a fermentation jar, plug with cotton wool and leave for seven days. Stir in half the remaining sugar and, seven days later, the rest. Ferment out dry.

Rack into a sterilised jar, add one crushed Campden tablet, plug the jar with cotton wool and store in a cool place for 18 months before bottling.

Victoria Plum Sherry

$2\frac{1}{2}$kg (5lb) ripe Victoria plums
500g (1lb) concentrated grape juice
Approx. 1kg (2lb) white sugar
25g (1oz) gypsum
15g ($\frac{1}{2}$oz) cream of tartar
10g (2 teaspoons) citric acid
3g (1 teaspoon) grape tannin
Pectic enzyme
Campden tablets
Sherry yeast and nutrient
4 litres (7 pints) water

Wash and stone the plums and drop them into a bin containing the water, acid, pectic enzyme and one crushed Campden tablet. Cover and leave for 24 hours.

Stir in the grape concentrate, gypsum, cream of tartar, grape tannin and previously activated yeast and nutrient.

Ferment for four days, stirring daily, then press the fruit dry and continue as for Seville Orange Sherry.

Prune Sherry

1kg (2lb) large prunes
500g (1lb) sultanas
1kg (2lb) white sugar
10g (2 teaspoons) citric acid
3g (1 teaspoon) grape tannin
Pectic enzyme
Campden tablets
Sherry yeast and nutrient
4 litres (7 pints) water

Soak the prunes overnight in cold water, then boil until cooked, stone them and add the fruit and juice to a bin containing the rest of the water, washed and chopped sultanas, the acid, tannin, pectic enzyme and one crushed Campden tablet. Cover and leave overnight in a warm place.

Add the previously activated yeast and nutrient and continue as for sherry recipes above.

Gooseberry Sparkling Wine

$1\frac{1}{2}$kg (3lb) green gooseberries
250g (8oz) sultanas
850g ($1\frac{3}{4}$lb) white sugar
5g (1 teaspoon) citric acid
1·5g ($\frac{1}{2}$ teaspoon) grape tannin
Pectic enzyme
Campden tablets
Champagne yeast and nutrient
4 litres (7 pints) water

Wash, top and tail the gooseberries, place them in a bin with the washed and chopped sultanas and pour boiling water on them. When the berries are cool, crush them with your hands and add the acid, pectic enzyme, grape tannin and one crushed Campden tablet. Cover and

and rosé wines

leave for 24 hours.

Add the activated yeast and nutrient and ferment on the pulp for three days, keeping fruit submerged with a china plate.

Strain out and press the fruit, stir in the sugar, pour wine into a fermentation jar, fit an airlock and ferment to dryness.

Rack into a sterilised jar, add one Campden tablet and, when clear, rack again and store for six months.

Stir in 70g (2½oz) of caster sugar and an activated champagne yeast and nutrient. When wine is fermenting well again pour it into sterilised champagne bottles, fit hollow-dome plastic stoppers with wire cages and continue as on page 230.

Apple and Pear Sparkling Wine

1½kg (3lb) cooking apples
500g (1lb) dessert apples
1kg (2lb) cooking pears
250g (8oz) sultanas
500g (1lb) white sugar
5g (1 teaspoon) citric acid (no tannin)
Pectic enzyme
Campden tablets
Champagne yeast and nutrient
3 litres (5½ pints) water

Wash and crush the apples and pears and drop them into a bin containing the water, washed and chopped sultanas, acid and pectic enzyme. Cover and leave for 24 hours.

Add the activated yeast and nutrient and ferment on the pulp for five days, keeping the pulp submerged. Strain out and press the fruit dry, stir in the sugar; continue as for gooseberry sparkling wine above.

Grape Sparkling Wine

8kg (18lb) fresh grapes, black or white, preferably English
Pectic enzyme
Campden tablets
Champagne yeast

Stalk, wash and crush the grapes, then press the pulp dry. Add to the juice 5ml (1 teaspoon) pectic enzyme and one crushed Campden tablet. Cover and leave for 24 hours.

Stir in activated yeast, pour into a fermentation jar, fit airlock and continue as for the other sparkling wines above. If grapes are very sharp and low in sugar add enough sugar, dissolved in a little warm water, to achieve SG 1·075 in the must.

Soft Fruit Rosé

1½kg (3lb) mixed soft fruit
1kg (2lb) fresh white grapes
850g (1¾lb) white sugar
5g (1 teaspoon) citric acid
1·5g (½ teaspoon) grape tannin
Pectic enzyme
Campden tablets
Sauternes yeast and nutrient
3½ litres (6 pints) water

NB The soft fruit may include cherries, black/red/white currants, raspberries, strawberries, gooseberries, loganberries and early plums etc. Use ripe fruit with no one kind predominating. Failing fresh grapes use 250g (8oz) sultanas.

Stalk, wash, stone and crush or liquidise the fruit and add it to a bin containing the water, acid, pectic enzyme, and one crushed Campden tablet. Cover and leave for 24 hours in a warm place.

Add the tannin, activated yeast and nutrient and ferment for four days, keeping pulp submerged. Strain out the fruit with a nylon sieve, stir in the sugar, pour into a fermentation jar, fit an airlock and ferment out.

Rack into a sterilised jar, add one Campden tablet and store for one year, then bottle, adding one saccharin tablet to each bottle.

To stimulate the appetite
Apéritifs are stronger than table wines and usually fairly dry. Sherry and vermouth types are the best liked.

Recipes for table wines

Apricot, Gooseberry and Golden Plum Wine

453g (1lb) tin of each fruit
250g (8oz) concentrated grape
  juice
850g (1¾lb) white sugar
15g (½oz) citric acid
1·5g (¼ teaspoon) grape
  tannin
Pectic enzyme
Campden tablets
Hock wine yeast and
  nutrient
3½ litres (6 pints) water

Open the tins, strain out the fruit and save the syrup. Mash the fruit, discarding stones, add the water, enzyme, acid and one crushed Campden tablet. Cover and leave for 24 hours.

Stir in the grape juice concentrate, fruit syrup, tannin, activated yeast and nutrient. Ferment on the pulp for three days, keeping the pulp submerged, then strain out the pulp through a nylon sieve. Stir in the sugar, pour into fermentation jar, fit an airlock and ferment to a finish.

Rack into a sterilised jar, add one Campden tablet and store in a cool place until clear, then bottle.

This wine is usually ready for drinking about four months after starting.

NB Instead of the mixed fruit 1kg (2lb) of apricot pulp or pieces and four very ripe, skinned bananas may be used.

Rhubarb Wine

2kg (4½lb) cherry red rhubarb
250g (8oz) sultanas
1kg (2lb) white sugar
Lemon rind
Pectic enzyme
Campden tablets
Chablis yeast and nutrient
3½ litres (6 pints) water

Top, tail and wipe the rhubarb. Crush or chop finely and add to a bin containing the water, the washed and chopped sultanas, thinly pared lemon rind, pectic enzyme and one crushed Campden tablet.

Next day stir in the activated yeast and nutrient. Ferment on the pulp for four days, strain out and press the fruit. Stir in the sugar and continue as for apricot, gooseberry and golden plum wine above.

Greengage Wine

2kg (4½lb) fresh greengages
250g (8oz) concentrated grape
  juice
1kg (2lb) white sugar
10g (2 teaspoons) citric acid
1·5g (¼ teaspoon) grape
  tannin
Pectic enzyme
Campden tablets
Chablis yeast and nutrient
3½ litres (6 pints) water

Stalk, wash, stone and crush the fruit and continue as for the other table wines, above.

NB Golden plums, fresh apricots and peaches may all be used in the same way. A Sauternes yeast should be used with peaches, which should be skinned. Finish peach wine medium sweet to serve with the dessert course of a meal.

Apple Wine

4kg (9lb) assorted apples etc
  (see recipe)
250g (8oz) concentrated white
  grape juice
850g (1¾lb) white sugar
5g (1 teaspoon) citric acid
Pectic enzyme
Campden tablets
Sauternes yeast and nutrient
3 litres (5½ pints) water

Use a mixture of cooking, dessert and crab apples, hard pears and quince (Cydonia japonica). Windfalls will do, but cut out any damaged parts and maggot caves.

Dissolve the acid, pectic enzyme and one Campden tablet in the water and drop the washed and crushed fruit into it. Cover and leave for 24 hours.

Add the concentrated grape juice, activated yeast and nutrient and ferment on the pulp for seven days, keeping the fruit submerged. Then strain out and press the fruit dry, stir in the sugar and continue as for other table wines, above.

NB This wine is well worth making in large quantities. A temporary fermentation bin can be fashioned from a large polythene bag in a cardboard carton. Secure the neck with a rubber band close to the surface of the must.

Blackberry Wine

2kg (4½lb) cultivated
  blackberries
250g (8oz) concentrated red
  grape juice
1kg (2lb) white sugar
10g (2 teaspoons) citric acid
3g (1 teaspoon) grape tannin
Pectic enzyme
Campden tablets
Burgundy yeast and nutrient
3½ litres (6 pints) water

Stalk, wash and crush the blackberries and make the wine as for the other fruit wines, above. Ferment on the pulp for four days. Mature for at least one year and preferably two.

Damson Wine

2kg (4½lb) ripe damsons
Other ingredients as for
  blackberry wine above

Stalk, wash and stone the fruit before crushing and continuing as for the other fruit wines, above.

NB Black cooking plums may be used instead of damsons. There is less colour in the skins and the result is a light red wine. Morello cherries, when black ripe, also make excellent wine. Dessert plums are not so suitable for making wine.

Mead

1½kg (3lb) orange blossom
  honey
25g (¾oz) citric acid
3g (1 teaspoon) grape tannin
Maury yeast
5g (1 teaspoon) yeast
  nutrient
3½ litres (6 pints) water

Dissolve the honey in warm water and when cool add all the other ingredients. Pour into a fermentation jar, fit an airlock and ferment to dryness. Continue as for any other wine and keep for at least one year.

Elderberry wines

The flavour of elderberries is so strong that they are best used in conjunction with other fruits. For example:

500g (1lb) ripe elderberries
500g (1lb) hedgerow
 blackberries
1kg (2lb) cooking apples
4 ripe bananas
250g (8oz) concentrated red
 grape juice
10g (2 teaspoons) citric acid
1kg (2lb) white sugar
Pectic enzyme
Campden tablets
Bordeaux yeast and nutrient
3½ litres (6 pints) water

Stalk and wash the elderberries, peel and slice the bananas and boil them with half the water for 20 minutes. Leave to cool, then strain and press.

Pour this liquid into a bin containing the rest of the water, the acid, pectic enzyme, one crushed Campden tablet and the washed and crushed apples and blackberries. Cover and leave for 24 hours.

Stir in the concentrated grape juice and an activated yeast and nutrient. Ferment for five days, keeping the fruit submerged, then strain and press.

Stir in the sugar, pour into a fermentation jar, fit an airlock and continue the fermentation to dryness. Mature for at least one year.

NB 250g (8oz) dried apricots, rose hip shells or runner beans may be used instead of the bananas. 500g (1lb) black cherries, black currants or damsons may be used instead of the blackberries. 250g (8oz) washed and chopped raisins may be used instead of the grape juice. The variations are almost endless.

Wines for the table
The ideal table wine is a nice balance of flavour, body, acid, tannin and alcohol.

Recipes for port and brandy

Parsnip 'Madeira'

2kg (4½lb) parsnips (freshly dug)
500g (1lb) raisins
Approx. 1kg (2lb) brown sugar
25g (¾oz) citric acid
3g (1 teaspoon) grape tannin
Madeira wine yeast and nutrient
4 litres (7 pints) water

Rich in flavour
Dessert wines are full and sweet, with a rich bouquet and a high alcohol content.

Thoroughly scrub the parsnips to free them of soil, cut into small, dice-sized pieces and boil in the water until cooked.

Strain the liquor on to the washed and chopped raisins, acid and tannin and when cool stir in an activated yeast and nutrient. Cover the bin and ferment for four days, keeping the fruit submerged, then start adding the sugar at the rate of 250g (8oz) every five days, making sure that it is thoroughly dissolved.

Just before the last addition, strain out the raisin pulp and press it dry. After the sugar has been added pour the must into a fermentation jar, fit an airlock and ferment out.

Finish the wine sweet – around SG1·020 – if need be by adding more sugar when fermentation has finished.

Rack, clear and store in a very warm place, 50°C (120°F), for about six months. Keep in cool store for a further year before bottling. This is a full-bodied wine with the characteristic flavour of Madeira. Serve it cool with plain cake.

Bilberry 'Port'

500g (1lb) bottled bilberries
500g (1lb) ripe elderberries
500g (1lb) ripe wild
   blackberries
250g (8oz) black currants
250g (8oz) dried apricots
2 very ripe bananas
250g (8oz) concentrated red
   grape juice
15g (½oz) tartaric acid
1kg (2lb) white sugar
Pectic enzyme
Campden tablets
Port wine yeast and nutrient
3½ litres (6 pints) water

Wash the apricots, cut into small pieces and soak overnight in some of the water.

Stalk and wash the elderberries, peel and slice the bananas and boil them both with the apricots for 20 minutes. Leave to cool.

Stalk and wash the blackberries and black currants, crush them and place in a bin containing the rest of the water, the acid, pectic enzyme and one crushed Campden tablet. Open the bottle of bilberries, mash the fruit and pour it with the syrup into the bin.

Strain out dried apricots, bananas and elderberries, pressing gently before discarding, and pour only the liquor into the bin. Cover, leave for 24 hours.

Stir in the concentrated grape juice and an activated port wine yeast and nutrient. Ferment on the pulp for five days, keeping fruit submerged.

Strain out and gently press the fruit, and stir in the sugar at the rate of 250g (8oz) every five days. Finish the wine sweet – SG 1·020 – rack and store (as for the other fruit wines) for at least two years before bottling.

Morello Cherry 'Brandy'

1kg (2lb) black ripe morello
   cherries
2½ litres (4 pints) strong ale
500g (1lb) soft light brown
   sugar
7g (¼oz) citric acid
Tokay yeast and nutrient

Stalk, wash and stone the cherries. Pour on the strong ale, making the minimum of froth, stir in the sugar, acid, yeast and nutrient. Use a vessel just large enough for the purpose and cover it with a sheet of polythene secured with a rubber band, but not gas tight. Leave it in a warm place until fermentation has finished.

Strain out and shake the cherries in a nylon sieve (you can use them in an open tart). Leave the 'brandy' in a cool place for a few days and as soon as it is clear siphon it into small bottles and keep it for one year. It is strong, smooth and delicious; very popular with the country folk of Kent.

Flower wines

Scented rose petals, elderflowers, May blossom and dandelions are the most widely used flowers.

Elderflower Wine

1 litre (1 quart) elderflowers
1kg (2lb) concentrated white
   grape juice
150g (5½oz) white sugar
5g (1 teaspoon) citric acid
Campden tablets
Sauternes yeast and nutrient
4 litres (7 pints) water

Pick the florets free from stalk and leaf; place them in a measuring jug and shake down but do not press. Empty them into a large bowl and pour hot water over them. Rub the florets against the side of the bowl with the back of a wooden spoon to extract the essences. Add the acid and one crushed Campden tablet and cover. Repeat the rubbing process for three days, then strain and press the flowers.

Stir the concentrated grape juice into the flower water, add

an activated yeast and nutrient and pour the must into a fermentation jar. Fit an airlock and ferment out.

Siphon the clearing wine into a sterilised storage jar, add one Campden tablet and store until the wine is bright. Sweeten to taste, bottle and serve quite cold.

NB Instead of elderflowers you may use 2 litres (2 quarts) of dandelion heads, May blossom or scented red roses. The last makes a particularly attractive rosé wine.

Sweet Mead

2kg (4lb) clover or similar
   honey
30g (1oz) citric acid
3g (1 teaspoon) grape tannin
Campden tablets
Sauternes yeast and nutrient
3½ litres (6 pints) water

Make the sweet mead in the same way as for the dry mead (see page 234). Finish it sweet by stopping the fermentation at SG 1·020 with two crushed Campden tablets, racking, fining and filtering. Store for two years before bottling.

Mulled Wine

1 bottle strong red wine
Rind and juice of 1 lemon
70g (2½oz) sugar
6 cloves
1 piece of bruised ginger root
Small piece of cinnamon

Very thinly pare the lemon, chop the peel and place it in a saucepan with the spices, sugar and wine. Set the pan on a low heat and stir slowly to dissolve the sugar. Check the temperature from time to time and remove the pan from the heat when the temperature reaches 60°C (140°F). Stir in the juice of the lemon and serve at once in heated glasses.

NB It is most important not to allow the wine to get any hotter than 60°C (140°F). Above this temperature the alcohol is driven off and leaves only flavoured water. Elderberry wine is particularly suitable for mulling.

Brewing your own beer

Beers and ales – in modern usage they are synonymous – are fermented from malt, which is barley after it has been specially prepared for brewing, together with hops and other flavourings added to help determine the type of beer: bitter, stout, brown, mild and so on.

Malt extract, rather than the actual malt, is widely used by home brewers as their base ingredient, and the very easiest way to make beer at home is with a kit containing the extract, hop oils and appropriate flavouring. Only sugar, water and yeast need be added (some kits include the yeast too), so that the job could scarcely be made easier.

Equipment

To make your own beer you will need some basic equipment:

A **polythene bin** with close-fitting lid for the actual brewing. They come in 10 to 25 litre (2 to 5 gallon) sizes.

Beer bottles for maturing the beer. Suitable sizes are 250ml, 500ml and 1 litre; imperial ones are $\frac{1}{2}$ pint, pint and quart. Metal crown caps are mainly used for sealing the bottles and a simple **capping tool** can be bought for this. **NB:** Do **not** use other than proper beer bottles, which are made to withstand the pressure of gases in the beer.

Plastic storage kegs are available for lovers of draught beer, usually with carbon dioxide injectors to keep the beer in good condition.

A **boiling pan** for some brewing methods.

A **polythene funnel**.

Polythene tubing for siphoning.

A **polypropylene spoon or paddle** for stirring.

A **hydrometer** and a **thermometer** will also prove useful.

Brewing up

As in winemaking, one key to successful home brewing is attention to hygiene. All equipment, bottles and caps should be carefully washed and sterilised before use.

It also pays to use the best ingredients. You can afford to when you compare the low cost of brewing-your-own with the prices of commercial beers. So never buy cheap hops that are stale.

Having sterilised the vessels to be used you must first dissolve the malt extract and sugar. It is best done in warm water with gentle stirring until no solids are left. This is done in the bin.

The hops must now be boiled to extract their essential oils and resins. The quantity depends on the type of beer being brewed and varies from 15g to 45g per 5 litres ($\frac{1}{2}$oz to 1$\frac{1}{2}$oz per gallon). Boil the hops vigorously for 45 minutes, strain off the liquor into the 'wort', the malt-and-water mixture, then wash the hops in a little hot water and add this to the bin. Add the rest of the water, cold, according to recipe, cover and leave to cool. Meanwhile activate a beer yeast in half a cupful of a weak solution of malt, and when the temperature of the wort has fallen to below 20°C (70°F) stir in the yeast and replace the cover.

If your malt extract is from a kit and already contains hop oils and resins simply dissolve it in warm water, then add the rest of the water, cold, according to recipe, and add the activated yeast. From this point all brewing follows a pattern.

Next day there will be a frothy head on the wort and it will increase rapidly and become flecked with particles of hop pollen and the like. On the second day skim off all the froth and discard it, give the wort a gentle stir with the paddle and replace the lid. Repeat the skimming and stirring on the third day, then leave the wort to finish fermenting after making sure there is no scum mark on the bin at the surface level of the wort. The bubbles will gradually diminish, then disappear. The beer will now begin to clear and should be siphoned into a sterilised container, leaving a thick paste behind to be discarded.

If finings are to be used they may be added now, following the maker's instructions. Move the beer to a cool place for a couple of days to encourage it to clear, and prepare to bottle it.

Bottling

Collect enough beer bottles and wash and sterilise them. Dissolve 45g (1½oz) of sugar in a little of the beer and distribute this proportionately between the bottles, ie, twice as much in a 500ml bottle as in a 250ml one, twice as much in a pint as in a half pint. Now siphon the cleared beer into the bottles, taking care to leave a 'headspace' of between 3 and 5cm (1 and 2in).

The extra sugar is called 'priming' and its purpose is to cause fermentation in the bottle and so provide life and condition for the beer when the bottle is opened. During the few days after bottling the sugar will ferment and the gas produced will remain in the beer until it is poured out, when a good head will form.

The bottles must be sealed with crown caps or screw stoppers according to the bottles you have. Whichever you use, sterilise them first and fasten them securely so that they will be gas-tight under

Simple ingredients
Beer is made from malt extract, sugar, hops, water and yeast. Buy only enough malt extract and hops for immediate use as they deteriorate with lengthy storage.

Brewing your own beer

pressure. Label the bottles with a note of contents and date and leave them in a warm place for a week. Next move them to a cool store for at least two weeks, preferably two months. Though the beer will be drinkable within a week it improves greatly if it is allowed more time to mature.

Bottles of beer are best stored upright so that the sediment from the bottle fermentation settles at the bottom. Take care, when you eventually pour the beer, not to disturb this silt. The bottle should be held horizontally until all the beer is poured. If it is returned to the upright before it is emptied the sediment will lift off the bottom with the movement of the beer.

The temperature at which beer is served is a matter of preference. Lagers and light ales are often best when chilled. Brown ale and stout seem to have more flavour when served at room temperature or just below.

Draught beer is made in the same way as bottled beer, but instead of being bottled it is poured into a pressure keg, primed with the extra sugar in the right proportions and left for a week. Quantity is a problem here. The $22\frac{1}{2}$ litres (5 gallons) usually needed to fill such a keg will not keep in prime condition for more than a month and is worth making only if you know it will be consumed before it goes off. If you are only a modest drinker it is better to brew and bottle 5 to 10 litres (1 to 2 gallons) of several different varieties than $22\frac{1}{2}$ litres (5 gallons) of one.

Brewing directly from the malt

Some enthusiasts prefer brewing their beers not from malt extract but direct from the malt, that is 'malted' barley grains, and you may wish to try it. Buy the best crushed grains that you can and keep them in an absolutely dry condition before use. Pale malt is the basis of every brew but others are added for colour and flavour. There are also adjuncts (eg flaked maize, rice, additional different malts) for improving body and flavour.

The malt and adjuncts should be mashed together in hot water – hard or soft, depending on the type of beer being brewed – so that their goodness is extracted. An even temperature of 66°C (152°F) should be maintained for two to six hours. Home brewers manage this with an insulated polythene bin fitted with an immersion heater controlled by a thermostat. The grains must be 'roused' with a paddle at half-hour intervals to prevent a 'set mash' – one that looks like porridge.

After about two hours take out a tablespoonful of the wort and drop into it a few drops of tincture of iodine. If the wort's colour darkens extraction is not complete, so mashing must continue and the test must be repeated every half hour until there is no colour change. This is the 'end point'. The heating is now switched off and the wort drained from the mash. The grains are washed in hot water to retrieve the last traces of malt and this water is added to the rest of the wort. The used grains are discarded.

Now the hops are added to the wort and it is boiled vigorously for 45 minutes. The hops are strained out and washed in the same way as the barley grains, and this water is then added to the wort. Then the rest of the water is added, cold, according to recipe, and the specific gravity is adjusted to the style of beer being made. The SG varies from 1·030 for a light ale to 1·055 for an export ale and 1·090 for barley wine.

The beauty of brewing your own beer is that you can adjust and vary the ingredients to suit your own palate. The alcoholic strength of a beer depends on how much malt and sugar are used. If there is too much sugar the beer will be strong but thin, and good beer contains not less than two-thirds malt to one-third sugar; even better is three-quarters malt to one-quarter sugar. Adjuncts ought not to exceed 10 per cent of the malt, ie, 100g of adjuncts to 1kg of malt (3oz adjuncts to 2lb malt).

After mashing and boiling the wort is fermented exactly as described above for malt extract beers. Again the equipment and bottles are sterilised before use, the yeast head is skimmed off, the beer is kept covered, then primed with extra sugar and the filled bottles are sealed. The important factors are good ingredients and attention to hygiene.

A note on ingredients

Malt extract can be bought in one form like toffee and another like flour. Buy only enough for immediate needs, for both kinds deteriorate in lengthy storage.

This is even truer of hops, which soon go stale. Buy the hop called Fuggles for brown ales and stouts and the one called Goldings for light ales and bitters. Lager needs a different malt from other beers, also a special hop, such as the Continental seedless one called Hallertau.

Malt grains may be had in a range of different roastings from pale through crystal and chocolate to black. The last two are often used by home brewers in conjunction with malt extract to give colour and flavour to brown ales and stouts. The grains must be crushed before mashing, and for this a domestic mincer is handy. Ready-crushed malt grains can be bought from the 'home brew' shops. Though the enthusiast will want to try brewing direct from grains, beer made from a good malt extract is just as good by most people's standards. On the other hand grain is cheaper than extract and lends itself to varying the character of the beer. Such beers are often quite superb.

Commercial brewers use invert sugar to speed fermentation and increase output, but there is no need for this at home. Ordinary granulated white sugar is quite adequate. Honey, golden syrup or brown sugar may be used, but these will affect the flavour.

You may find invert sugar useful for priming, and there is a note on this sugar on page 225. Ordinary sugar actually consists of two sugars, fructose and glucose, in combination. It is unfermentable in its combined state but the yeast cells secrete enzymes which break the combination as a step towards fermentation. Priming with invert sugar, in which the two component sugars are already separated, helps fermentation to start at once.

Lactose, a non-fermentable sugar, is usually added for sweetening, especially to those stouts once known as milk stouts.

Bitter beers need hard water, and hardening salts, may be bought for use in soft water areas. Brown ales and stouts need soft water, and a small quantity of common salt should be used in hard water regions.

Finings of isinglass or gelatine are sometimes added to speed up the clearing process in beer, but most beers clear naturally if left for a week or so in a cool place. However, if finings are used the maker's instructions should be followed carefully.

Guidelines for making beer (from malt extract)
1 Make the wort by dissolving the malt extract and sugar in warm water.
2 Start the yeast working in a small quantity of wort.
3 Boil the hops and add their liquor to the wort, then wash them and add that water too.
4 Make up the wort with the rest of the water, cold, according to recipe.
5 When the wort is cool enough add the active yeast, fit the lid and leave the wort to ferment.
6 On the second and third days skim off the froth and gently stir the wort, then leave the beer to ferment out.
7 Rack the beer off the lees into a sterilised container, cover it and leave it to clear in a cool place.
8 Dissolve some sugar in a small amount of beer and put a little in each bottle, then fill and seal the bottles.
9 Store the bottled beer in a warm place for one week, then in a cool place for two weeks.
10 NB For draught beer add the sugar-beer solution to the pressure keg, then seal and store in the same way as the bottles.

Guidelines for making beer (from malt)
1 'Mash' the malt and adjuncts in water at a steady 66°C (152°F), stirring gently every half hour and testing samples with tincture of iodine until extraction is complete.
2 Activate the yeast a few hours before it will be needed in a small amount of the cooled wort.
3 Drain the wort from the mash, wash the grains and add this water to the wort.
4 Add the hops to the wort and boil it vigorously for 45 minutes.
5 Strain out the hops, wash them and add this water to the wort.
6 Make up the wort with cold water according to recipe.
7 Test the specific gravity of the wort with a hydrometer, and by adding sugar adjust the SG to the style of beer being made.
8 When the wort is cool enough add the active yeast, fit the lid and leave the wort to ferment.

From this point on the procedure is the same as for making beer from malt extract.

What can go wrong?
Beer flat and lifeless when poured. Three possible causes: (a) Priming sugar was omitted or insufficient. Add one level teaspoonful of white sugar per pint and re-seal. Wait two weeks before trying again. (b) Imperfect seal due to poor crimping of crown cap or a perished rubber on the stopper. Re-prime and re-seal – perfectly. (c) Beer was poured into an oily or greasy glass or one that had been washed in detergent and not rinsed. Use clean, well polished glasses.
Lack of head retention. Caused by poor quality ingredients, fermentation at too high a temperature, use of unsterilised equipment or serving the beer before it is sufficiently mature. No remedy. Take more care next time and try adding a 'head retention additive' to the wort. This is available from home brew centres, but is not always successful unless good quality ingredients are used and fermented correctly in sterilised equipment.
Beer gushes uncontrollably when opened. Caused by bottling the beer before fermentation was completed, or with too much sediment, or with too much priming sugar or a combination of all three. Beer will also gush if it is served when it is warm, or if the bottle is shaken before it is opened. You can rescue the beer: first, wipe the outside of the bottles with a cloth sterilised in Campden solution to prevent contamination; then cool the beer in the refrigerator to as low a temperature as possible. Place the bottles in a sterile polythene bin and gently ease off the caps. When the froth subsides, re-bottle the beer and re-seal it. Keep it for a further week before serving. Next time, make sure that fermentation has finished by giving the beer a good rousing, leave it to clear before bottling and prime it carefully.
Beer too bitter. Caused by using too many hops. Blend with one not containing enough or use fewer next time.
Yeast 'bite'. Caused by inadequate skimming of dirty froth during fermentation and failure to remove yeast ring around the bin. There is no remedy. Take more care next time.
Off flavours. Caused by using stale hops and/or malt, unsterilised equipment, imperfect skimming, failure to keep beer covered, failure to remove beer from yeast sediment, storage in a warm place. No remedy. Take proper care next time.

Recipes for beer

Yield: As all the recipes are based on 9 litres/2 gallons, you should make about 16 × 1 pint bottles each time, but the actual yield may vary according to ingredients used.

Mild Ale

1kg (2lb) malt extract
45g (1½oz) Fuggle hops
8½ litres (15 pints) water
Beer yeast

No sugar is required. Follow our brewing instructions starting on page 238, and the result is a malty beer with a subtle rather than a distinctive hop flavour. Don't keep this one too long.

Basic Bitter Beer

1kg (2lb) malt extract
60g (2oz) Golding hops
500g (1lb) white sugar
8½ litres (15 pints) hard water
Beer yeast

Brew as instructions to make 9 litres (16 pints) of an excellent beer.

Best Bitter Beer

500g (1lb) malt extract
500g (1lb) crushed crystal malt
500g (1lb) Golden syrup
100g (3oz) Golding hops
10 litres (15 pints) water
Hardening salts if required
Beer yeast
5g (1 teaspoon) citric acid

Dissolve the malt extract, Golden syrup, acid and hardening salts, if needed, in half the hot water. Boil the crushed crystal malt with 85g (2½oz) of the hops in the rest of the water. Then follow the brewing instructions starting on page 238. Place the remaining 15g (½oz) hops in a loose muslin bag and suspend them, weighted down with a glass marble or washed pebble, in the fermentation bin. This is known as dry hopping, and sharpens the hop flavour in the finished beer. The hardening salts are only necessary in soft water districts.

This is a malty beer, worth maturing for at least four weeks.

Old Ale

1kg (2lb) malt extract
500g (1lb) light brown sugar
250g (8oz) crushed pale malt grains
250g (8oz) crushed crystal malt
9 litres (14 pints) water
100g (3oz) Fuggle hops
1 pinch table salt
5g (1 teaspoon) citric acid
5g (1 teaspoon) yeast nutrient

Boil the crushed pale malt and the crystal malt with the hops for one hour to produce a well-bodied beer with a little residual sweetness. Wash them thoroughly in hot water so as not to waste any goodness. Dissolve the malt extract with the sugar in warm water and mix the two worts together. Then follow the brewing instructions starting on page 238. The salt is not necessary in soft water areas, but the acid and yeast nutrient help to ensure a strong fermentation.

This is a very strong beer that needs to be matured for around three months. It makes an ideal base for the Morello Cherry 'Brandy' recipe.
NB The metric version makes 10 litres, the imperial makes 2 gallons.

Brown Ale

1kg (2lb) malt extract
125g (4oz) chocolate malt grains
250g (8oz) soft brown sugar
45g (1½oz) Fuggle hops
8½ litres (15 pints) water
Beer yeast

In hard water areas include a large pinch of salt. Boil the chocolate malt grains with the hops to extract the colour and flavour. Brew in the usual way and mature for about three weeks.

Irish Stout

1kg (2lb) malt extract
200g (6oz) black malt grains
500g (1lb) brown sugar
60g (2oz) Fuggle hops
8½ litres (15 pints) water
5g (1 teaspoon) citric acid
5g (1 teaspoon) yeast nutrient
Stout yeast

Follow brewing instructions (page 238). In hard water areas a quarter teaspoonful of table salt should be dissolved in the water. The beer should taste quite dry when finished, so use a malt extract with a low-dextrin content. The acid and nutrient will help the yeast to ferment all the sugar.

Milk Stout

Vary the last recipe by using a high-dextrin malt extract, including 250g (8oz) lactose and omitting the yeast nutrient. The result is a smooth, sweetish stout that needs a month or more to mature.

A basic grain mashed bitter

1½kg (3½lb) crushed pale-malted barley
100g (4oz) flaked maize
200g (8oz) white sugar
50g (2oz) Golding hops
9 litres (2 gallons) water
Beer yeast and nutrient

In soft water areas a sachet of hardening salts will be needed.

Heat 8 litres of water to 70°C (160°F) and stir in the hardening salts, if required, the crushed barley, flaked maize and sugar. Maintain the temperature at 66°C (152°F) for at least two hours, stirring the grains every half hour to stimulate the extraction.

After two hours check for the 'end point' (see page 240). When this is reached strain off the liquor, wash the grains, and add the water.

Add the hops, wetting them thoroughly until they sink, then boil the wort vigorously for 45 minutes. Strain out the hops and wash them and add the water.

Cover the vessel containing the wort and leave to cool. When the temperature reaches 15°C (60°F) adjust the quantity to 9¼ litres (16½ pints), and the specific gravity to 1·040, adding more sugar to do so if necessary.

It is important to follow either the imperial or the metric weights and measures in any one recipe. Do not mix them.

Add an activated yeast and continue the fermentation, skimming, racking, fining, priming and bottling (see page 239). Mature for a minimum of three weeks.

NB Vary the ingredients with crushed crystal-malted barley instead of maize, or add chocolate-malted barley to make a brown beer, or black-malted barley to make a stout. You can add 125g (4oz) flaked rice to give additional body, or use different, more or fewer hops to vary the bitterness to suit your palate. The original gravity can go up to 1·050 or down to 1·030 or anywhere in between. The combinations and variations are infinite.

Barley Wine

1kg (2lb) malt extract
250g (8oz) brown sugar
60g (2oz) wheat syrup
15g ($\frac{1}{2}$oz) diastatic malt
    extract
4$\frac{1}{2}$ litres (8 pints) water
25g (1oz) Golding hops
1 pinch table salt
1 pinch yeast nutrient
Brewers' yeast
2·5g ($\frac{1}{2}$ teaspoon) citric acid
Champagne wine yeast
45g (1$\frac{1}{2}$oz) caster sugar

Dissolve the malts, syrup and sugar in 1 litre (1 quart) warm water. Boil the hops in 2 litres (2 quarts) water for 45 minutes. Strain on to the wort, adjust with cold water. When cool, stir in the acid, salt, nutrient and an activated brewers' yeast. Ferment and skim as usual.

Rack off the lees when fermentation is finished, fine and when clear stir in 45g (1$\frac{1}{2}$oz) caster sugar and an activated champagne wine yeast. Bottle in 250ml ($\frac{1}{2}$ pint) bottles and store for at least one year.

Best bitter
The beauty of brewing your own beer is that you can adjust and vary the ingredients to suit your own palate. This recipe yields a tangy, malty beer worth maturing for at least four weeks.

Cider and perry

It should be said right away that cider and perry are rather more difficult for the amateur to make than wines and beers. The appropriate apples and pears are hard to get, the necessary equipment – notably the fruit press – is rather expensive and a successful technique comes only with some practice. All this means a greater possibility of disappointment for the beginner.

Cider apples, quite different from those used for cooking and eating, are very hard and must be well mellowed before being crushed. For best results three or more varieties are mixed together. Some are mainly bitter, to give tannin and character, some mainly sharp for acid and freshness and some mainly sweet to provide alcohol. Some varieties have dual qualities. 'Bulmer's Norman' and 'Yarlington Mill' are both bitter and sweet, while 'Kingston Black' is bitter and sharp. Among other varieties are 'Sweet Coppin', a sweet one, and 'Crimson King', which is sharp. The art in cider-making is to blend the different apples together in the right proportions, depending on their different characteristics, to produce a 'harmonious' cider.

The fruit to use
Few of us have access to these special cider apples, but a palatable cider may be made by blending at least 7kg (15½lb) – preferably more – of cooking, eating and crab apples. A few pears also improve the character of the cider.

Similarly, two or three kinds of pears may be blended to produce a drinkable perry. Perry pears are very hard to come by, and you may have to use whatever you can get, bearing in mind the need to blend sugar, acid and tannin.

A basic cider blend could be 3kg (6lb) cooking apples, 4kg (8lb) eating apples and 1kg (2lb) pears or crab apples.

Try to use only perfectly sound fruit so that it can be left to mellow without danger of its going bad. If you grow your own fruit leave it on the tree as long as possible. In any case bruised or damaged portions must be cut away to prevent an off flavour in the finished cider. When the fruit is ready for crushing wash it – to remove dust, mites and fungi spores – in cold water containing 50ppm (parts per million) of sulphite: ie, one Campden tablet per 4½ litres (1 gallon).

Crushing and pressing
The tricky part of crushing is to prevent oxidation of the fruit, so this should be done by using one Campden tablet for every 5kg (1lb) of fruit from the outset.

As soon as the fruit is crushed it should be pressed – almost impossible without a basket press of some kind. Before pressing wash the press with Campden solution and rinse the hessian or nylon bag in it. Pour the crushed fruit and juice into the bag in the press and collect the pressed-out juice in a jar containing one Campden tablet and one tablespoon of pectic enzyme for every 4½ litres (1 gallon) of juice.

Fill the jar, cork it and leave it in a warm place for 24 hours while the enzyme destroys the pectin. A new and developing practice is to add 'fining' at the same time, that is a preparation which clears the must by removing the solids suspended in the fluid. For the beginner a proprietary brand is best, used according to the maker's instructions. Finings cause a deposit, and the must should be racked off this before the yeast is added.

Since you may not have managed a perfect blend of fruit it is as well to check the specific gravity of the must before adding the yeast. Any hydrometer reading between 1·045 and 1·060 will provide an alcohol content of 6 to 8 per cent. Cider is usually drunk by the tumbler, so it should not be too strong and you may prefer the lower figure. In any case, if the natural sugar content is below 1·040 you should stir in some white sugar to increase the SG to the required figure. Adding 50g (2oz) of sugar to 4½ litres (1 gallon) will raise the reading about four points. Acidity, too should be checked, though if the cooking apples are sour enough the acid content should be adequate.

There is no specific yeast for cider but a champagne wine yeast will give good results. Activate it beforehand so that it is fully active when it is needed and continue as for wine. When the fermentation is finished rack the cider from its sediment, sulphite it at 50ppm (one Campden tablet per 4½ litres 1 gallon) and store it for three months to mature.

The procedure given here produces a dry cider. It may be sweetened to taste with lactose at the rate of 100g per 4½ litre (4oz per gallon). Alternatively a cider with a high original specific gravity may be finished sweet by racking it at, say, 1·010, then filtering and adding two Campden tablets per 4½ litres (1 gallon) to stop further fermentation.

Sparkling cider may be made in the same way as sparkling wine. Alternatively the cider can be poured into a plastic beer keg fitted with a CO_2 bulb and used in the same way as a draught beer. A low alcohol cider is best for this bulk method and a slightly higher one of superior quality for the bottled fermentation method.

Perry is made exactly as cider and with the same precautions. It is a lighter and more elegant beverage provided you use the right blend of different pears.

A second run wine
When all the juice has been pressed from the apples much goodness remains and they may be used again. An excellent second run wine may be made by adding a small tin of concentrated elderberry and rose hip juice, 500g (1 pint) of concentrated white grape juice and 9 litres (2 gallons) of water to 10kg (20lb) fruit pulp. Add an active yeast, ferment on the pulp four days, strain and press the fruit as dry as possible. Stir in 1½kg (3lb) white sugar and continue fermentation in the usual way. After pressing the fruit pulp may be thrown on the compost heap. The excellent rosé wine produced from this second run may be enjoyed within the year.

Storing garden produce

Some fruit and vegetables may be stored in their fresh state and will keep very satisfactorily for 4–6 months in the correct conditions. This saves space, most especially in the freezer, which may be more profitably put to use for crops that do not store well. The best produce for fresh storage are the keeping varieties of apples and pears, marrows, onions and root vegetables. Use maincrop varieties and start storing them away from October onwards.

Some vegetables, such as parsnips, can be left in the ground and dug as required for table use as winter conditions do not adversely affect them. When warmer weather approaches it is necessary to stop them growing on again and they may then be lifted for storage.

General rules

Store only perfect vegetables and fruit and handle gently to avoid bruising. Even potatoes should be moved carefully and not just tossed down on to the ground. Bruising may spread and cause rot during storage. Pest and insect bitten crops must be used as quickly as possible.

Rub off as much soil as possible from vegetables so they are clean, wipe apples and pears gently if necessary.

Add to your store as the season progresses but always keep the vegetables covered so they do not dry out. This also applies as you begin to take away from the store for use. Straw or a piece of sacking is an easily removed protection against frost for vegetable clamps that have been opened. Potatoes turn green if not kept in the dark and should not be used in this condition. Do not store different vegetables in the same box.

Beetroot

Lift carefully from the ground taking great care not to damage the skins. Twist off the leaves about 5cm (2in) from the root and discard them. Store roots in boxes or heaps against an inside wall of a frost-free shed in layers covered with damp sand.

Carrots

Twist or cut off leaves and discard. Store roots in boxes or heaps against an inside wall of a frost-free well-ventilated shed in layers of slightly damp sand.

Alternatively store in a clamp in the open. Choose a fairly dry and sheltered position so that damp does not penetrate from underneath. Make a neat mound of the carrots with the stalk ends outwards and cover completely with a thick layer of clean straw. This is best done on a windless day so it does not blow about. Press on a 5cm (2in) layer of slightly damp soil to cover all the straw and pat down firmly to prevent rain washing it away. Check occasionally and re-cover with more soil if necessary.

Marrows

Cut before the frosts start and leave on a 5cm (2in) stalk. Hang in nets so air can easily circulate round about. Old string vests sewn up across the bottom are useful as they can be hung up by the shoulder straps. Store in a well sheltered shed or very cool kitchen larder.

Onions

When ripe, lift from the soil and leave on the surface to dry. In wet weather spread them out on sacks or fine netting and keep under cover except on sunny days. They may go mouldy and rot if stored before they have dried off enough. Remove loose skins and stalks, arrange on slatted shelves, in net bags, or in nylon tights, with a knot between each onion so one can be removed from the base without disturbing the others. Alternatively make onion plaits. Do not remove the stalks (or tops) of the onions but tie them with thin string to a length of rope starting at the bottom. Bind the stalks close together so that the onions hang one on top of the other. Trim surplus leaves afterwards. Work up until the rope is nearly full (it will weigh quite heavy) and hang in a cool, airy place.

Shallots and garlic

Store as for onions. Dry off, tie in bunches or place in fine meshed net bags and hang in a cool place.

Parsnips

Twist or cut off the leaves and discard. Store roots in boxes or heaps against an inside wall of a frost-free shed in layers of slightly damp sand.

Potatoes

Spread out on the floor of a shed or garage for the skins to dry off. Then pack carefully into wooden boxes or barrels and cover so no light penetrates. Keep in a frost-free shed. Alternatively store in a clamp. Make a base with a thick layer of straw and heap on the potatoes. Cover as for carrots but more thickly to give greater protection. Leave the top open for a week to ventilate the clamp (but cover temporarily if there is danger of rain). Then cover the top thickly with soil and press down well. Check occasionally to see the soil has not been washed down, add more if necessary.

Turnips and Swedes

Twist off the leaves and discard. Store in layers in dry sand in a box or against the inside wall of a frost-free shed. Or store in a clamp as for carrots.

Apples

Wrap loosely in squares of newspaper to prevent moisture loss. This is not essential but it helps to stop any rot spreading. Apples need dark, cool and humid conditions – dryness will cause them to shrivel. They may be stored unwrapped on slatted shelves but they should not touch each other, in strong polythene bags with small air holes or with the tops unsealed, in specially formed cardboard trays (like egg trays). Inspect regularly and remove any that are starting to rot.

Pears

Store as for apples, but they do not need such humid conditions.

The preserving year 1

	Jan/Feb	March/April	May/June	July
Jams, Jellies and Marmalades	Seville oranges Tangerines		Elderflower Gooseberries	

Rhubarb ▬▬▬▬▬▬▬▬▬

Most foods are available all year round because they are imported from different countries to cover the seasons when our home grown varieties are not ready for market. We also import exotic foods which do not grow in our climate. Preserving is most usefully and economically carried out in each season's abundance when produce can be picked straight from the garden or bought at its most plentiful. This guide indicates the best months for availability but these will vary from year to year, according to area and weather.

Rose petals ▬▬▬▬▬▬▬
Strawberries ▬▬▬▬▬▬

Apricots ▬▬▬
Bilberries ▬▬▬
Currants ▬▬▬
Loganberries ▬▬▬
Raspberries ▬▬▬

Fruit Cheeses, Butters and Curds

Apricots ▬▬▬
Currants ▬▬▬
Raspberries ▬▬▬

Candied, Crystallised and Glacé Fruits

Angelica
Cherries ▬▬▬▬▬▬▬▬▬

Rose and flower petals
Apricots ▬▬▬
Peaches ▬▬▬

| **Bottled Fruits, Syrups and Squashes** | Seville oranges | Rhubarb ▬▬▬▬ | | Apricots ▬▬▬ |

Cherries ▬▬▬▬▬▬
Gooseberries
Strawberries ▬▬▬

Bilberries ▬▬▬
(Whortleberries)
Currants ▬▬▬
Loganberries ▬▬▬
Peaches ▬▬▬
Raspberries ▬▬▬

246

The coloured lines indicate only roughly the span of
each item which depends on variations in area and
weather conditions.

August	Sept/Oct	Nov/Dec	All Year
Barberries	Apples	Tangerines	Citrus fruits
Blackberries			Dried fruits
Greengages	Chestnuts		Melons
Marrows			Pineapples
Morello cherries	Cranberries		
Mulberries			
Plums			
	Damsons		
	Elderberries		
	Herbs		
	Japonica fruit		
	Medlars		
	Quince		
	Rowan berries		
	Sloes		

	Apples		Citrus fruits
	Cranberries		Dried fruits
	Damsons		
	Medlars		
	Pears		
	Quince		
Marrows			
Plums			

Greengages			Citrus fruits
Plums			Grapes
Tomatoes			Pineaples
	Chestnuts		Tinned fruits
	Pears		

	Apples		Citrus fruits
Blackberries			Grapes
Figs			Pineapples
Greengages	Damsons		
Morello cherries	Pears		
Mulberries	Quince		
Plums			
Tomatoes			
	Rose hips		
	Sloes		

247

The preserving year 2

	Jan/Feb	March/April	May/June	July
Drying			Apricots ▬▬▬
			Herbs ▬▬▬▬
			Rose and flower petals ▬▬
			Peas
			Pimientos ▬▬
			Beans ▬▬▬
			Peaches ▬▬
Salting		Broccoli ▬▬▬▬▬	
			Salmon ▬▬▬▬▬
			Vine Leaves ▬▬▬
			Beans ▬▬
			Kohl rabi ▬
Smoking	Geese		
	Haddock		Salmon ▬▬▬▬
	Mackerel ▬▬▬▬▬▬▬		
	Plaice ▬▬▬▬▬		
	Whiting		
Pickles, Chutneys and Sauces		Rhubarb ▬▬▬▬▬▬▬	Apricots ▬▬
			Beans ▬▬▬
			Cherries ▬▬
			Gooseberries
			Beetroot ▬
			Green peppers
			Cucumbers ▬
			Currants ▬
			Peaches ▬
			Raspberries ▬
			Walnuts
Wines	Seville oranges		Cherries ▬▬▬
	Parsnips		Elderflowers ▬▬▬
		Rhubarb ▬▬▬▬▬▬	Apricots ▬▬
			Currants ▬▬
			Loganberries ▬▬
			Peaches ▬
			Gooseberries
			Rose petals ▬▬
			Strawberries ▬▬
			Raspberries

The coloured lines indicate only roughly the span of each item which depends on variations in area and weather conditions.

August	Sept/Oct	Nov/Dec	All Year

Apples — Grapes

Garlic — Mushrooms
Onions
Plums

Nuts
Pears

Chinese cabbage — Beef, ox tongue
Onions — Cabbages
Turnips — Herrings
Pork

Pimientos

Eels — Most meat, poultry, fish —
Geese — some at best in
Haddock — certain months
Whiting

Apples — Bananas
Mint — Cranberries — Cauliflowers
Damsons — Citrus fruits
Elderberries — Dried fruits
Figs — Eggs
Pears — Grapes
Red Cabbage — Mushrooms
Pineapples

Blackberries
Marrows
Onions
Plums
Tomatoes

Greengages — Apples — Parsnips — Grapes
Damsons
Elderberries

Pears
Morello cherries — Quince
Plums
Blackberries

Index

Index

Index

Where to buy equipment

Jams, jellies and marmalades, fruit cheeses, butters and curds

Packets of jam covers, including waxed discs and labels, are obtainable from stationers in Great Britain. In Australia, try kitchen departments of major department stores and kitchenware specialists shops. Some hardware shops in New Zealand stock them or try supermarkets. These are suitable for jams, jellies, marmalades, fruit cheeses and fruit curds. They are **not** suitable for fruit butters, in which the sugar content is lower. **Twist-top covers** are not generally obtainable, though some people may be able to get them. The twist-tops on commercial jam jars can be reused once. These are suitable for jams, jellies, marmalades, fruit cheeses and fruit butters. They are **not** suitable for fruit curds, as the curds are not brought to a high enough temperature to make a seal.

Home freezing
Cooking for the freezer

Freezer packaging material, including freezer film, polythene bags, foil containers, plastic containers, labels, etc, can be obtained from kitchen equipment stores, electricity board showrooms and stationers in Great Britain. In Australia or New Zealand, try kitchenware equipment shops but in Australia you can also try freezing packaging specialists and in New Zealand supermarkets or hardware stores. **Freezer/Cooking (or 'boil-in-bag') bags** are obtainable from Porosan (D.I.Y.) Ltd, P.O. Box 4, 57 Oving Road, Chichester, Sussex PO19 4EN, and other freezer packaging specialists. In Australia freezing/cooking bags (such as Glad Ovenbags, made by Union Carbide Australia Ltd) are widely available from supermarkets stores and other freezing packaging specialists. In New Zealand also they are readily available from supermarkets.

Pickles, chutney and sauces

No special equipment is sold for this. For **Twist-tops**, see Jams, jellies, etc. For **preserving jars**, **Porosan Preserving Caps and Rings and Porosan Preserving Skin**, and **corks**, see Bottling.
In Australia and New Zealand no specialist equipment is sold, apart from **Agee Preserving caps and rings**, see Bottling.
Commercial pickle and chutney jars and sauce bottles can be re-used, providing their covers are in good condition. Disposable mineral-water bottles can also be used for sauces, syrups and vinegars.

Bottling

Kilner jars (with covers and rings) and **Le Parfait jars** (with clips) can be got from many hardware shops, some kitchen departments of stores and some supermarkets.

Le Parfait jars are also obtainable from Houseware Departments of Boots.
New covers, rings, etc, to fit many different kinds of preserving jars, including older types no longer made, and Nescafé jars (but not 'Gold Blend' jars) are obtainable from Geo. Fowler Lee & Co, 82 London Street, Reading. Write to them for their mail order list, enclosing sae – it also includes jam jar covers, jelly bags, etc.
Porosan Preserving Caps and Rings (to fit standard 1lb and 2lb jam jars, both old and new types) and replacement rings, and **Porosan Preserving Skin** (to use on any jar or bottle, including screwtops – size 22in by 36in covers about 25 jars) is obtainable from the manufacturers, Porosan (D.I.Y. Ltd, P.O. Box 4, 57 Oving Road, Chichester, Sussex PO19 4EN – write for price list), and from Houseware Departments of Boots.
Juice extractors (for fruit syrups and squashes) are obtainable from kitchen equipment stores and electrical goods shops.
Corks are obtainable from Home Brew shops and large branches of Boots.
In Australia, **Fowlers Vacola jars**, (with covers, rings and clips) and **Le Parfait jars** (with clips) can be got from many hardware shops, some kitchen shops, departments of stores or supermarkets and from kitchenware specialists.
In New Zealand **Agee Preserving Caps and Rings** (to fit standard 1lb and 2lb jars, both new and old types) and **replacement rings**, and **wax** (to use on any jar or bottle) are obtainable from supermarkets.

Smoking

Hot smoke boxes, from £8·50–£11·50, and the **British Salmon King cold smoker**, price about £52, are obtainable from various stores. If you have difficulty in finding them, write to the manufacturers, Brook's Original Home Smokers, 88 Windsor Road, Southport, Merseyside, who can also supply **wood chips and smoking powder** for hot and cold smoking.
Charcoal can be bought from barbecue suppliers.
The Smoke 'N' Pit charcoal/water smoker (for hot moist smoking), price about £50, is obtainable from various stores. If you have difficulty in finding it, write to: Frank Odell & Co, Ltd, 43–45 Broad Street, Teddington, Middlesex TW11 8QZ.
Smoke boxes, in Australia and New Zealand, are available from sports equipment shops. Charcoal can be bought from barbecue suppliers.

Wine and beer

All equipment is obtainable from Home Brew shops throughout the country, and larger branches of Boots, and available by mail order from W. R. Loftus (Retail) Ltd, 1–3 Charlotte Street, London W1P 1HD – write to them for a price list.
In Australia equipment is obtainable from home brew shops throughout the country and in New Zealand equipment is available from branches of Boots.

EPSOM LIBRARY
Tel. EPSOM 21707

-6. OCT. 1981

23 SEP 1982

30. JUN 1983

26. JUL 1983

25 AUG. 1983

14. SEP. 1984

24. OCT. 1984

PLEASE SEE
FRONT
LABEL

SURREY COUNTY LIBRARY
(Headquarters, 140 High Street, Esher)

| 6 | 78.200451 |

This book must be returned to the Branch or
Travelling Library from which is was borrowed, by the
latest date entered above.

Charges will be payable on books kept overdue.

L22